# UNDERSTANDING
# THE COUNTRYSIDE

# UNDERSTANDING
# THE Countryside

## Ron Scholes

MOORLAND PUBLISHING

British Library Cataloguing in Publication Data

Scholes, R.
  Understanding The Countryside.
  1. Human Settlements — Great Britain
  2. Archaeology — Great Britain
  3. Great Britain — Antiquities
  I. Title
  936.1   DA90

ISBN 0 86190 077 4

Printed in the UK by
Billings & Sons Ltd,
Worcester.
Published by
Moorland Publishing Co Ltd,
Station Street,
Ashbourne, Derbyshire,
DE6 1DE England.

**Acknowledgements**

I would like to acknowledge the kindness and
assistance from many libraries and museums throughout the country. I wish to record with appreciation the
help and co-operation given by farmers, landowners and
people with local knowledge.

For specific assistance I am indebted to Nigel
Scholes who drew the sketch maps; Richard Scholes
who helped me on my journeyings; the County
Record Office at Stafford, the Staffordshire County
Planning Department and the Borough Surveyor's
Department, Stafford. I am grateful to Cecil Hughson
of Lerwick, Angus Smith of Stornoway and the late
Edgar Hinchcliffe of Hilton, Cumbria.

Acknowledgements and thanks for permission to
reproduce the photographs of stone axes from
Graiglwyd and Mynydd Rhiw are due to Dr H.S.
Green, Archaeology Department, National Museum
of Wales, Cardiff. I am grateful to Miss A.R. Plint of
Kendal who allowed me to photograph her specimen
of a Langdale stone axe.

Finally, my special thanks go to Betty and Alfred
Wainwright for their hospitality, interest and constant
encouragement.

All the remaining black-and-white illustrations
were taken by the author and the colour illustrations,
except Arthur's Stone, Portchester and Grassington
Moor which were provided by J.A. Robey.

For Jeanie

# Contents

# Introduction

For thousands of years men and women, both natives and invaders, have fashioned the landscape according to their needs by the processes of farming and industrial development. The geology of an area, and the effects of climatic variations have had a great influence on where people choose to settle, For example, in the Bronze Age, a warm dry climate meant the colonisation of some of the upland regions. A change to cooler, wetter conditions forced people to move into the valleys at the beginning of the Iron Age. Settlement patterns with their hut circles, burial mounds, defensive sites, trackways, field systems, boundary marks, buildings and rural industries are the heritage left by countless generations of humans from the Stone Age to the dawn of the Industrial Revolution.

In my youthful days a walking tour in the Yorkshire Dales implanted in me a love and appreciation of the countryside that has always been a source of delight, stimulation and fellowship. It led me to a desire to understand not only the geography and geology of the landscape, but to a gradual understanding of ancient objects and landmarks. On the other hand, a combination of exploration and understanding was the ultimate joy, amidst scenery that has no equal in its variety throughout the world. Our land displays a marvellous pattern of changing skylines; a countryside seasoned by settlements with the splash of red brick and stone against an emerald background.

In many parts of Britain, the influence of mankind can be seen on many small tracts of land, an influence which can on occasion date back some five thousand years. For example, in the brown moorland solitude of Caithness lie the Neolithic burial chambers attractively called 'the Grey Cairns of Camster'. In south-west Wales the extensive remains of a fortified Iron Age village complete with defensive wall, pounds and hut circles crown the summit of Mynydd Carningli overlooking the sands of Newport Bay. The Welsh border country contains the impressive earthwork of Offa's Dyke, built about AD780 as a boundary between the Kingdom of Mercia and the various principalities of Wales. One is able to admire the engineering skill employed in its construction on the section between Llanfair Hill and Spoad Hill in Shropshire. Here the Dyke, massive and magnificent, utilises every natural feature of the terrain. The lost villages on the Wolds of Lincolnshire tell the story of their abandonment after many struggles trying to farm the thin soils, and their final elimination by the Black Death. In Cumbria, a seldom-visited packhorse bridge crosses little Swindale Beck, a tributary of the River Lowther, close by the ruins of Shap Abbey. From Roman times up to the end of the nineteenth century, thousands of miners gouged out profitable quantities of galena from the workings in Swinnergill and Gunnerside Gill. Today, the moorland fringe of Swaledale exhibits its monuments of spoil heaps, adits, hushes and the skeletons of abandoned derelict buildings. At the bottom of a surburban garden in Stoke-on-Trent lies an ice-house that once belonged to the Minton pottery family. It was erected more than one hundred years ago to meet storage problems before the refrigerator was invented.

My purpose in writing this book is to stimulate interest in man's involvement in the landscape, to enable the countryside traveller to understand existing features, and to look about him with greater knowledge and perception. It is of course an experience to explore the incomparable British scenery, where at certain sites, and in any setting, the mind may be allowed to wander back into the mists of time.

To help the reader understand these man-made features of the countryside, numerous examples of the most outstanding or most typical sites have been described and illustrated. The sites are many and varied and are located in widely different regions of the British Isles. Whether travelling on foot or by car it is advisable to use the excellent Ordnance Survey maps. Therefore, to assist in the location of the site, I have included details of all 1:50,000, 1 in to 1 mile, and 1:25,000 sheets, together with National Grid References, and access details. A selection of scenically attractive walking routes, with cycling and motoring approach roads, covering interesting areas and objects, is also included.

Perhaps it should be added that observation of the features still to be seen on the ground is often not sufficient for a positive identification, or the period, to be obtained. Fieldwork has to be supplemented by scientific excavation, which **must always** be done by experts, as valuable information can be destroyed inadvertently. If this book encourages the reader to examine the landscape with an enquiring mind and leads him or her to delve deeper into the subject it will have succeeded in its task.

This book will not enable the reader to establish the identity of those mysterious mounds or other features in the landscape whose origin is not always obvious; no book alone can be expected to achieve this. But given a good clue — 'Hillfort', 'Tumuli', or 'Roman Villa' for instance on Ordnance Survey maps — then this book will enable the site to be more easily understood and compared with other similar sites in Britain.

CHAPTER ONE

# Geology-The Foundation
# of the Landscape

The physical character of the landscape of the British Isles bears a close relationship to what lies in layers beneath the surface. Like the colours and tints on an artist's canvas, the geology of the rocks has shaped the foundations of the landscape's scenic picture. From Pre-Cambrian times, a geological period which may have lasted some 4,000 million years, sediments were laid down under marine, deltaic and freshwater conditions. Throughout their long history, the deposits of sandstones, conglomerates, grits, shales, limestones, clays, coal seams, chalk and sands have been affected by earth movements as the strata were uplifted, squeezed, folded and faulted. At various intervals there were variations of sea level, accompanied by the continual process of erosion and deposition. During periods of volcanic activity, there were extensive lava flows, mineralisation, metamorphism and igneous intrusion over many areas of the land mass. These events have been partnered through time by climatic changes from tropical to arid, temperate to glacial.

The scale of geological time is marked in millions of years, an evolution divided by geologists into great eras each containing a number of periods which seemingly follow each other in quick succession. In the British Isles it is possible to trace examples of rocks that are representative of all the major periods in the earth's geological history.

The periods of the Ice Ages and of prehistory are seen on a scale which is divided by centuries totalling almost a million years. Although climatic changes appeared in quick succession during the build-up and retreat of several ice-sheets, the evolution of the land surface continued at a much slower rate. It is a fact that, during the last million years, some parts of the physical landscape have been altered, but there have been few modifications to the landforms.

Britain contains a tremendous variety of scenery, unequalled anywhere in the world: a priceless heritage of rugged mountains, high smooth hills, expansive moorlands, rolling pasture land, wide fertile plains, narrow dales and rocky coastlines; unifying elements of a landscape intimately marked and patterned by the work of man.

Unquestionably, the single most important factor determining why land was settled by man, and consequently how the landscape was influenced by them, was the geological development underlying the formation of the landscape. Britain is fortunate enough to contain evidence of the passing of many geological periods, and various areas of the country provide splendid examples of different formations. The rest of this chapter is devoted to these examples, showing how the underlying rocks have influenced man's involvement with the landscape.

In the North-West Highlands of Scotland beds of Lewisian gneiss, one of the oldest rocks in Britain dating back some 2,600 million years, form the platform for layers of Torridonian sandstone laid down almost 2,000 million years later.

Lovers of spectacular mountain scenery will appreciate the stark outlines of Suilven, 2,399ft (731m), and be impressed by its long narrow triple-peaked ridge, and the great rock walls of Caisteal Liath. A short distance away to the west, noble Stac Pollaidh, 2,009ft (613m) stands amongst lochan-dotted wild moorland, a region gouged and scraped bare by the ice sheets of long ago.

In Shropshire, Pre-Cambrian sediments formed the Long Mynd, 1,695ft (517m), and at the same time volcanic activity formed the masses of Caer Caradoc, 1,506ft (459m) and the Wrekin, 1,334ft (407m).

Long before the volcanic upheavals of Central Lakeland the Skiddaw Slates were formed from muds and clays laid down in a shallow sea in the late Cambrian/Ordovician Age. These sedimentary shales which break down into thin flakes give Skiddaw, 3,053ft (931m), a smooth angular appearance, compared with the craggy shattered outlines of the volcanic peaks of Central Lakeland. Here among the volcanic rocks of Great Langdale, Neolithic man discovered and used a fine-grained tuff, a very hard stone, which he skilfully worked like flint to achieve a very sharp edge. The vein of rock was found along a high-level contour around the head of the valley, and in recent years many specimens have been collected from the south scree gully of Pike o' Stickle (NY273073).

Some 570 million years ago, in the Grampians and Highlands of Scotland, vast deposits of sands, shales, grits, mudstone, clays and limestone filled a basin in the earth's crust, only to be altered by heat and pressure (metamorphosed), into foliated crystalline rocks. The Grampians are composed in the main of these metamorphic rocks belonging to the Moinian and Dalradian Series. During the Caledonian mountain-building period the micaschists, gneisses and quartzites were uplifted, faulted and severely overfolded. In the Cairngorms, a large body of igneous rock was intruded, and the whole mass worn down by erosion and denudation into a complex geological structure. The monotonous rolling peat uplands of the Monadhliath (Gaelic for 'Grey Mountains'), south-west of Inverness, are in extreme contrast to the granite Cairngorms. The high peaks of Ben Macdhui, 4,296ft (1,310m), Braeriach, 4,248ft (1,295m), Cairn Toul, 4,241ft (1,293m) and Cairn Gorm, 4,084ft (1,245m), are the smootheddown tops of this igneous mass, with rolling summits of rose-coloured granitic boulders, rock tors and glacial corries.

Below this well-worn-down highland mass the glens are clothed with trees, newly planted stands of spruce as well as pine. Although there are remnants of the indigenous Scots Pine forest, the original natural tree cover was severely exploited by man, particularly with the coming of the sheep and the subsequent Highland Clearances after Culloden.

Off the north-west coast of Wales, the Isle of Anglesey consists of an ancient platform of folded crystalline Pre-Cambrian rocks. Continual erosion wore down the land to a low, undulating surface almost at sea level. In time, a pleasant green fertile landscape evolved, which attracted the early Neolithic farmers. They established settlements in parts of the island that were more favourable to simple farming methods. Today, remarkable evidence of their culture may be examined in the passage graves thought to have been erected by the second phase of immigrants from Ireland between 2,400BC and 1,600BC. The most famous of these is Bryn Celli Ddu, 'The Mound in the Dark Grove', (SH508702); a burial chamber which was built on the foundations of a stone circle about 1,600BC. In North Wales, the Cambrian sediments of sands, shales, grits and muds were deposited some 570 million years ago, accumulating into a great thickness on the ocean bed. The sedimentary rocks were raised forming some prominent ridges such as Elidir Fawr, 3,030ft (924m), and Carnedd y Filiast, 2,695ft (821m). From the rocky shattered ridge of the Elidir, one is able to look down into the compensation reservoir of Marchlyn Mawr, an essential part of the huge Dinorwic hydroelectricity scheme. The bands of fine-grained mudstones were metamorphosed into the famous purple slate deposits which have been extracted since the latter part of the eighteenth century from the great Penrhyn, Dinorwic and Nantlle quarries.

To the south the Rhinog range climbs and dips over fifteen miles of the roughest terrain in Britain. Geologically speaking, the rocks are composed of thickly bedded, hard and massive gritstones forming the largest area of Cambrian rock in Wales. Early man, from Neolithic times to the Iron Age, found the lower western slopes of the Rhinogs an agreeable area in which to settle. From Cors-y-Gedol, the track south east to the Bwlch y Rhiwgyr passes close to the burial cairns of Carneddau Hengwm ('Cairns of the Valley of

*Carneddau Hengwm Burial Cairns*

the Old People') dating from about 2,400BC. In fact few routes traverse this rugged countryside. The old road from Bontddu to Tal-y-bont crosses the Afon Ysgethin by a pack-horse bridge called Pont Scethin, remarkable for its setting amongst wild surroundings.

Volcanic upheavals in the Ordovician Period meant that the igneous rock was responsible for many of the chief mountains of North Wales. In Snowdonia, the jumbled rock-strewn summits of the Glyders, Glyder Fawr, 3,279ft (999m), and Glyder Fach, 3,262ft (994m), were formed of resistant lavas. Snowdon, 3,560ft (1,085m), too, has been shaped out of volcanic tuffs ejected from undersea eruptions in a series of violent explosions.

South-west of Snowdon the beautiful lonely valley of Cwm Pennant is flanked by the rounded lava tops of Moel Hebog, 2,566ft (782m), and Moel Lefn, 2,094ft (638m), and by the crests and corries of the Nantlle Ridges. In the mid-nineteenth century the valley was the scene of several mining and quarrying ventures, some, alas, doomed to failure from the start. From Portmadoc, the Gorseddau Tramway travelled into Cwmystradllyn to serve the Gorseddau Quarries high on the southern slopes of Moel Hebog. An extension of this railway contoured the slopes of the Pennant valley to the Cwm Dwyfor Copper and Silver-lead Mine. Unfortunately, no sooner had the rail connection been made than the mine got into difficulties. When the nearby Prince of Wales Quarry failed, the railway finances declined rapidly as traffic dwindled to zero. The line of the railway may be followed up Cwm Pennant, and there are many signs of man's involvement in quarrying and mining activities. At Ynys-y-pandy, the elegant impressive ruin of the slate mill stands roofless against the elements, a structure of some beauty set against the harsh surroundings.

Silurian times followed Ordovician with the old sea basin slowly being filled in with sands, muds and silts, forming reefs of limestone rock alternating with bands of shales in the shallower water conditions. In south-west Shropshire the long ridge of Wenlock Edge, and the hills of the Leinthall and Bringewood areas, are splendid examples of well-wooded scarp and dip slope scenery. In southern Scotland the complex folding of Ordovician and Silurian sedimentary rocks form the massif of the Southern Uplands. The Galloway coast, and the hills of Nithsdale, Lowther and Tweedsmuir, especially overlooking important valley routes, became ideal sites for Iron Age and Dark Age forts. On the western side of the Fleet estuary a vitrified fort was erected on Trusty's Hill (NX588560) with further extensions made to the fortifications some time at a later date.

Between the Silurian and Devonian periods, Caledonian earth movements squeezed and faulted the rocks, thereby creating fold mountains and intervening valleys. Rivers flowing away from the highland mass carried down vast quantities of sands, grits and muds to be deposited in the valleys. Volcanic activity injected lava flows into the sedimentary bedding, helping to form the Ochil and Sidlaw Hills. The Old Red Sandstone rocks have endowed the vales of Strathearn and Strathmore with fine rich soils creating the best in Scottish lowland scenery. Glacial erosion shaped the landscape of Strathearn by eroding its surface and leaving behind deposits of morainic material.

The extent of Roman occupation of Northern Britain was a line of marching camps, forts and signal stations guarding the valleys leading to the Highlands of Scotland. In Strathearn, some fifteen miles to the west of Perth, the Romans established a line of signal-stations on the prominent Gask Ridge, itself formed to some extent from a sheet of hard igneous dolerite. Although many Roman signal-towers have been destroyed by extensive cultivation, the best example is to be found in a woodland clearing just two miles north of Kinkell Bridge. The site consists of a circular platform of earth and stones encircled by a ditch and raised bank. The centre of the raised mound would have supported a wooden tower served by a single access pathway.

In the Devonian period Exmoor lay under the sea. The great Caledonian land mass to the north was heavily eroded, and the resulting detritus was carried off by the rivers and deposited on the ocean bed. After millions of years of deposition, the sea bed was raised and folded by violent earth movements to form Exmoor, essentially as it is today. Here, high windswept moors, peaty and wet, sweep down to more freely-draining lower hill slopes, and narrow wooded valleys carry their frantic dashing streams to the sea.

From medieval times to the beginning of the nineteenth century, the area of upland known as Exmoor Forest alternately belonged to the Crown, to Wardens who were granted the office for a lifetime, and to Wardens who leased the forest itself as well as its care, from the Monarch. The title 'forest' is a misnomer, for apart from the outlying river valleys, Exmoor today is a windswept treeless moorland, due in most parts to woodland clearances in the reign of Edward I.

Strong walkers with a sense of adventure may set out to tramp the complete route of the ancient forest boundary, and in so doing explore the lonelier parts of Exmoor. For example, from Alderman's Barrow (SS837423) north to Black Barrow (SS832442) several boundary stones or merestones follow this old boundary line. One continues cross-country, climbing hills, negotiating steep combes, locating further merestones, and heading for the prominent landmarks of the Bronze Age barrows beyond Mole's Chamber (SS718394). In all, the complete circumambulation of the ancient forest boundary is a distance of some twenty-eight hard miles. But whether by short walk or long expedition, the brooding loneliness of Exmoor will long impinge upon the memorary as a true microcosm of scenic beauty.

In the North of England the Pennine uplands are formed almost entirely from rocks classified by geologists as belonging to the Carboniferous period. Older rocks were squeezed and folded into mountain ranges, only to be worn down as part of a continuous cycle of compression, folding erosion and sinking. Rivers and streams flowing off the northern mountains brought down great quantities of sediment which accumulated in the deeper hollows of the sea bed. Further south the sediments were deposited in clearer waters which gave rise to the information of the Great Scar limestone such as in the Craven area of Yorkshire. Deposits of muds and sands also collected in the shallow lagoon-type waters and river estuaries to play an important role in the physical character of the Dales. In Wensleydale and Wharfedale bands of sandstone, limestone and shale alternate up the valley slopes, with the massive limestone crags, or scars, as the outstanding features. Most of the high ridges and hill summits above the dales are composed of thick coarse gritstones, the remnants of vast dumpings of sands and muds in the former river deltas and estuaries. This Millstone Grit forms the crags of Wild Boar Fell, 2,324ft (708m), overlooking Mallerstang, and the resistant tops of those noble hills, Penyghent 2,273ft (694m) and Ingleborough 2,373ft (723m).

From the sixth century, Anglian invaders from Northern Germany settled in the eastern part of Northern England, and gradually moved inland up the river valleys where they cleared the native oakwoods on the gritstone soils. Their simple farming settlements are now known from the suffix ley derived from the old English element *leah*, 'wood' or 'glade'. Places like Weardley, Castley, Leathley, Otley, Burley, Ilkley, Beamsley and Drebley indicate their exploitation of the wooded Wharfe valley.

Later on, in the early tenth century, Norse invaders penetrated into upper Wensleydale from the west and continued to follow their traditional pastoral farming methods. Cattle were grazed in the valleys during the autumn and spring months, and then taken up on the hill slopes during the summer months. The spring shieling was a pasture and homestead called a *saetr*. This name appears in the Yorkshire Dales together with its variations of -satter, -seat, -sett and -side. In Upper Wensleydale and Raydale there are settlements called Appersett, Burtersett, Countersett and Marsett. The latter two lie close to Semer Water in an area noted for its associations with Bronze Age and Iron Age peoples, and the ancient legend that a town lies drowned beneath the dark waters of the lake.

In the Permo-Triassic period the area of what is now the Midland Basin experienced the full rigours of Sahara-like desert conditions. Bounded on three sides by highland blocks the basin was subsequently filled by sediments of red sandstone and breccias carried along by violent storm torrents and desert winds. Salt deposits formed in pockets due to solar evaporation, and flash floods carried vast quantities of rounded pebbles down gullies to create great thicknesses of Bunter Pebble Beds. For millions of years strong winds carried slightly calcareous dust to dry ground or into standing water, eventually to become consolidated into the heavy Keuper Marl which provides the surface soil over much of the region today. Essentially unchanged since its original colonisation in the late Saxon or early medieval period, it is a landscape of plains and wide vales occasionally overlooked by outcrops of harder rock; a gently undulating countryside of red soils and hawthorn-hedged fields bounded by the rivers Avon, Severn and Trent.

In the heartland of Staffordshire lies the dome-like upland of heath and woodland with its quick-draining Bunter Pebble subsoil. Formerly a royal hunting forest, Cannock Chase has been much reduced by the ravages of charcoal burners, coal mining and gravel extraction. The Chase provides a lung for over three million people who live within twenty miles of it. Cank Thorn (SJ983153) is the destination of the second stage of the Staffordshire Way, a long-distance footpath for 90 miles, created by the

*View from Bainbridge Roman Fort, Wensleydale*

Staffordshire County Council between Mow Cop in the north and Kinver Edge in the south. A thorn-bush has existed here for centuries as the meeting place of the three ancient manors of Penkridge, Rugeley and Cannock. In an area west of Stafford are to be found examples of moated sites, part of a complement of 109 proven and 36 possible sites of this kind that have so far been identified in Staffordshire. At Norbury Manor (SJ797233) the site still survives as a rectangular wet moat with a further wet area to the south. There is evidence of stone walling rising from the moat at the edge of the internal platform. The site is recorded in Plot's *The Natural History of Staffordshire* (1686), which contains an engraving of the fortified manor house that stood there. It has been suggested that the building was possibly constructed in the late thirteenth century, and re-designed in the sixteenth century. It appears to have been demolished in the nineteenth century.

In Jurassic times, during a warm and humid climatic period, sediments of muds, sands, broken shells, bones and pebbles were laid down in comparatively shallow warm waters. The Cotswold Hills were formed from a number of these beds in a complex manner, with each fine layer taking millions of years to accumulate. The clays of the Lower Lias deposits are very fossiliferous, containing great quantities of ammonites and the bones of other marine and amphibian creatures. Some of the clearer waters, when allied with strong currents, allowed the chemical deposition of calcium carbonate to envelop minute grains of sand forming rounded spheres of calcareous material known as oolite, from the Greek *oon:* egg, and *lithos:* stone.

After the last of the Great Oolite series had been laid down, the retreating sea and the slowly rising land began to expose the beds to erosion and denudation. Movements of the earth's crust gently tilted the limestone beds towards the south-east, leaving the steep scarp slope on the north-west, and the long, gentle dip slope down to the clay vales on the south-east. The original deposited limestone beds were probably submerged and uplifted again with the weaker parts of the scarp widened into valleys by the immense volumes of water released as the ice sheets

gradually melted. The cliff-like north-west scarp of the Cotswolds escaped the ice, but was eroded by the waters of the huge glacial Midland lake.

The history and growth of the Cotswold wool industry is a subject which there is not enough space in this book to examine fully. Suffice it to say that it provided Britain's main export from about 1400 to the seventeenth century. Settlement names illustrate their association with the prosperous wool industry listed in the Domesday Book, and were probably founded during Anglo-Saxon times. Three Shiptons (sheep-tons) are recorded, a Sheepscombe (SO892103) and a Sherborne (SP170147) the 'clear stream' used for washing the sheep. The name Cotswold is derived from the Old English *Cod's weald*, meaning Cod's (a personal name) forest. Villages with strings of weavers' cottages, fulling mills and dyeing sheds became a feature of many a Cotswold valley. Newington Bagpath (ST818-948) had a mill as well as the weavers' cottages which still stand there today. Fulling mills were built by the monastic owners of these incomparable sheep pastures, taking advantage of the clear Cotswold streams such as the Churn, the Coln and the Windrush. The first recorded fulling mill in England (1185) was at Barton in Temple Guiting (SP100254), where all that remains is a weed-clogged mill pond.

The availability of superb building stone was the key that locked all the Cotswold pieces together. Readily available and easily worked, the stone exhibits its wonderful tints in great manor houses, churches and cottages, down to present-day bus shelters and public conveniences. From the crest of the steep northern scarps, low stone walls divide the fields that sweep and curve in graceful lines, down to villages nestling alongside crystal-clear streams that yield plentiful supplies of trout. Many ancient routes such as salt ways and drover's roads cross the area, all visible reminders of bygone days when salt was carried from Droitwich by pack pony, and cattle were driven from Wales.

Following the gradual disappearance of the Jurassic sea in the part of Britain we now know as Kent and Sussex, rivers flowed from the highlands in the west and south-west carrying coarse-grained sediments. These rivers at the beginning of the Cretaceous period emptied into a huge freshwater lake which accumulated thick deposits of sand and clay, now known geologically as the Wealden series. The land then slowly sank, and the area was covered by the inrushing sea depositing more sands and clays. These newer deposits are known as the Upper and Lower Greensand and the Gault Clay. Probably due to a change in temperature, chalk sediments began to be deposited, increasing in purity throughout the passing of millions of years. The chalk sea covered much of what is now England and possibly also Wales. Laid down in nearly level sheets the chalk is a pure fine-grained white limestone composed of shells of countless minute sea creatures called Foraminifera. Their calcareous skeletons, together with the fragments of larger shells, sank to the bottom of the sea forming layers of almost pure calcium carbonate. At the end of the Cretaceous period further deposits of sands and clay were laid down, covering the beds of chalk. In south-east England violent earth movements uplifted the Wealden rocks and pushed the sedimentary deposits into a dome formation. Erosion from rivers and weathering from rain, wind and frost removed the chalk from the centre of the dome, and attacked the clays and sands underneath, to leave a picture of our present landscape. The chalk North and South Downs are the remaining edges of the dome, with steep scarp slopes facing the central undulating area of sandy hills and clay vales — the Weald of Sussex and Kent.

The Sussex High Weald (Old English, *Wald:* a forest), stretching from Horsham to Hastings, is an upland area sharply cut by young valleys. The hills were for a long time covered by wide-ranging woodland dominated by hardwoods, particularly the oak. The Wealden Clay vales almost completely surround the High Weald, and their sticky clays give rise to heavy sodden soils — a featureless wooded landscape.

During the early Middle Ages each landowner had the right of pasturing pigs over certain parts of the woodland. Clearings were made in the forest and settlements were established, with names ending in *-ing:* belonging to a family or tribe, *-den:* a valley or clearing for grazing animals.

Rapid changes took place in the forest with the discovery of iron ore, which, allied with the abundant wood for making charcoal, gave rise to the Sussex iron industry. The iron was made by the simple bloomery process with the use of a crude hearth. The visible remains of the early iron industry on the ground are usually overgrown mounds of slag, cinders and traces of charcoal, burnt clay and partially roasted ironstone. Many copses of woodland, hill slopes and meadows are riddled with water-filled hollows. In south-east England, particularly in Sussex, an examination of the 1:25,000 Ordnance Survey maps will reveal countless small ponds, and names such as Minepit Shaw (TQ441408), Minepit Wood (TQ225253), Marlpit Shaw and Marlpit Wood; all evidence of former iron mining activity. There are innumerable sites tucked away in rural corners of the Weald that are not so obviously named, and which are attractively disguised, so that they do not readily reveal their industrial past. For example, Tugmore Shaw, Hartfield, (TQ458372), and Mount Noddy, Cowden, (TQ483419). There are many other sites that lie deeply embowered in remote Wealden woodland, difficult of access and lying on private ground.

Blast furnaces, developed in Tudor times, required a good head of water to operate the bellows. The early Sussex ironmasters, limited by the lack of swiftly running streams, constructed ponds or bays to maintain a powerful reservoir of water. The northern edge of Ashdown Forest became a complex of iron works, forge hammers and furnace ponds surrounded by the scattered cottages of the workers. There is a blast furnace site at Newbridge (TQ455324), and it is believed that towards the end of the fifteenth century it was one of three furnaces in blast in this part of the country. At the height of its operations, its furnaces and forges produced large quantities of cast iron for cannon shot and cannons. Acres of land were utilised, water was impounded, and today there are remains of the pond bay on either side of the road, and one of the hammer ponds partially reclaimed.

Although the tree cover was heavily depleted by the iron industry, historians believe that the

*Giant's Causeway*

greatest devastation was caused by the clearance of the forest, and cultivation of the land between the ninth and fourteenth centuries. Today, the lovely acres of Ashdown Forest retain a mixture of enclosed and open forest landscape; a pattern of cultivated cottage gardens, rich meadows, copses of trees and broad expanse of fern and heather. Elsewhere in the High Weald, estated avenues of tall beech trees exist with gnarled and twisted oaks — remnants of uncleared forest cover.

The Antrim plateau of Northern Ireland is based on basalt sheets of Tertiary Age some sixty-five million years ago. The outpourings of molten rock welled out of fissures to cover the existing chalk surfaces with great thicknesses of lava. The plateau collapsed in the middle to be covered by the shallow waters of Lough Neagh — the largest lake in the British Isles. During the volcanic activity, cones and craters were formed which were eventually eroded away, leaving the lava plugs of hard dolerite rock standing up above the rolling plateau landscape. Fine examples of these conspicuous steep-sided hills are to be found in Slemish 1,437ft (437m), D221054, and in Tievebulliagh 1,346ft (402m), D193268. The latter peak, rising from the edge of the Antrim plateau, is famous as a site of a Neolithic axe-factory. Its products, much in demand by early man, have been identified as far away as Northern Scotland and Southern England. Below the dolerite summit is a small exposure of bluestone (porcellanite) which occurs on the east face of the hill. The screes below contain many waste chippings, and other rejected material can be picked up in the surrounding peaty hollows.

Along the northern coast the slow cooling rate of the lava flows led to the formation of the Giant's Causeway. In this magnificent wilderness, surely one of the scenic wonders of the world, layer upon layer of basaltic lavas rise in steps up the cliffs. These fluted columns spread a hexagonal mosaic across the main causeway, with some features named, like the Organ and the Giant's Chair. The spectacle represents the most perfect record of volcanic activity in Ireland.

Northern Ireland is a land where the past is ever present. Lying on the mainstream of movement from the European mainland, the north-eastern area attracted many settlers. This part has the longest archaeological record, with impressive remains of Neolithic antiquity erected before any metal tools were known. Burial cairns, chambered graves and standing stones were raised on the hilltops, although many remains are now covered by peat bogs. One reason why the early colonists were attracted to the region we now call Antrim was the band of chalk preserved by the basalts which contained plentiful supplies of flint — that most precious of raw materials to early man. Great numbers of worked flints have been found along many parts of the Antrim coast, particularly on the Curran (D413016), a raised pebbly beach near to Larne. Not only did the settlers seek flint and other hard stones, but also suitable land to grow wheat and barley, and to raise cattle, sheep, pigs and goats.

Throughout Antrim there are many examples of circular or near circular rings called raths, consisting of one or more earthen banks and ditches. Although they are often called ring-forts, because of their impressive defensive appearance, excavations have shown that they were essentially domestic in purpose. Sometimes constructed with more than one bank and ditch, these raths were thought to be used as meeting places or for ceremonial occasions. The general findings of excavations show that the great majority of the single-ditch raths were the homes of farmers, and that the farmsteads date from the millenium preceding the Anglo-Norman invasion. On the mid-slope of the Antrim plateau there are two raths by the roadside at Budore (J234762). One of the features has one ditch which has been almost filled in; the other, with two ditches, has a well-preserved inner fosse and a raised interior platform. The clear outline and good condition of the second rath suggest that its period is medieval.

The isolated farmstead is a characteristic feature of the Irish landscape as it was adapted to a mainly pastoral economy. For example, a quick look at the area north and east of Ballymoney (C949259) on Sheet 5, 1:50,000 Ordnance Survey map of Northern Ireland will readily support this statement.

From the low-lying shores of Lough Neagh to the magnificent headland of Fair Head, the Antrim landscape is seamed with delightful contrasts. Great stretches of undulating heathery moorland, peaty in some parts, boulder-strewn in others, sweeps across to the east. Above the coast the plateau ends abruptly in many places, as the forbidding black basalt cliffs overlook the famous glens, notably Glenariff. Here the streams that rise on the plateau tumble over the edge as picturesque waterfalls, plunging down to the colourful strips of farmland on the valley floor. Also strikingly different are the areas where the chalk bedrock peeps through to form short springy turf, with grass similar to that found on the downlands of Southern England.

The landscape of Eastern Norfolk with its foundation of chalk deposited by the Cretaceous seas was drastically altered later on by the passage of several great ice sheets. During the Pliocene and Pleistocene epochs when England was still joined to Europe, the chalk deposits were followed by those of shelly red crag, coralline crag, estuarine gravels and shelly sands. The crag deposits, now at sea-level, show the amount of tilting that the land has undergone. Eastern Norfolk and Eastern Suffolk formerly lay on the shores of a great gulf which occupied much of the area of the North Sea. The Rhine, joined by the Thames, flowed into this gulf contributing to the formation of the red crag. The rivers also laid down beds of peat in north-east Norfolk where it can be seen in the cliffs amongst the shelly deposits. The glaciers were largely responsible for the nature and form of the soils, and for the great variety of scenery in this part of East Anglia. A great mixture of glacial detritus such as sands, gravels and loams were collected, formed and deposited when ice-sheets invaded the area. This produced a patchwork of diverse soils, and a wide range of natural vegetation and scenery. Much of the soil, clay, chalk lumps and flint came from near at hand, but the ice also brought 'erratics' from Northern England, from Scotland and from Scandinavia, and these lumps of basalt, granite, sandstone, limestone and quartzite can be seen in the fields. It seems certain that there were changes of climate between the periods of ice movement in East Anglia, and flint from the chalklands attracted prehistoric man from almost the beginning of human history.

The area of high land stretching westwards along the coast behind Cromer and Sheringham is a series of moraines left by glaciers which approached from the north and north-west. Some beautiful wooded country rises to Beacon Hill 327ft (100m), (TG186413), the highest point in Norfolk, and equally fine views can be obtained from two other glacial hillocks called

Muckleburgh and Telegraph. Other parts of the Cromer Ridge consists of sandy and gravelly heights showing obvious traces of prehistoric man. The windswept heathland, quite outstanding in a landscape of such low profile, is ablaze with colour at certain times of the year from the tracts of heather, bracken, rosebay and gorse. One looks seawards from a modest altitude of two hundred feet, to the cliff tops which lie exposed and covered only with thin top soil. This sparse covering supports birdsfoot trefoil, ribswort plantain and colourful masses of sea pink or thrift. The soft glacial sands and clays are no match for the incessant pounding of the sea. Cliff falls are frequent with huge masses of the glacial material cascading down to the beach below. The sands, clays, chalk lumps, knobbly flints and peat are swept up by the tides and deposited further down the coast. Attempts are being made by the local authorities to slow the speed of erosion, and if possible to prevent it, by protecting the seaward approach to the cliffs with stakes and steel piles.

In Anglo-Saxon times the landscape north and north-east of Norwich was covered by dense forest. The area was heavily settled as seen by the large number of place name elements ending in 'ham': a homestead linked to a family name; like Erpingham, Aylsham, Antingham and Stalham. Other homesteads of a later group of colonists are indicated by 'ton' in their placenames, such as Cawston, Buxton, Swanton and Knapton. The maze of small roads, the lack of many lengthy straight stretches of road, and the meandering nature of the roads, point to the fact that small enclosed pieces of arable or pasture land had been won by individuals from the virgin woodland. The road pattern also suggests that the abundance of small enclosed fields was an ancient and widespread development of the area.

Where fields have not been grubbed up by farmers wishing to create 'prairie-like' acres, the field boundaries and hedges are usually old. Between Paston (TG322345) and Knapton (TG307342), the lane that serves as the parish boundary has hedges that date from the fifteenth or sixteenth centuries, although the boundary itself is of much older duration. In fact, a tremendous number of small parishes all point to a dense settlement before the Norman Conquest. Many of the villages lack compactness, with houses dispersed and the churches sited some distance away, like Witton (TG331316) and Edinthorpe (TG323332). Some may have always been scattered settlements with dwellings constructed as portions of the forest were cleared. In some circumstances the local squire could have intervened, but in most events the inhabitants have moved out to settle on the edge of the common land, leaving the church standing alone, usually on higher ground, and acting as a splendid landmark for miles around.

This has brought us to the end of a geological journey that began with the ancient rocks of the north to the formation of East Anglia — the youngest area of Britain. The geological saga is not yet finished, for even now, eroded material from the hills is being carried down to the lowlands and thence to the sea.

Geology and topography are only part of the story concerning the examples of man's involvement in the landscape. The controlling effect of changing climatic conditions, the availability of a good reliable water supply, and the historical use of the land are also physical conditions by which men and women have influenced the landscape. Some groups like prehistoric man, the Romans, the monks and the early industrialists made a more powerful impression on the landscape, with many examples of their occupation as evidence. It is time to seek, explore and understand.

# CHAPTER TWO

# The Stone Age- Palaeolithic and Neolithic Man

During the Pleistocene geological era, four major Ice Ages were separated by periods of fluctuating climatic conditions. Primitive man existed as nomadic hunters, living in the open air and camping beside rivers or in the mouths of

TIME CHART

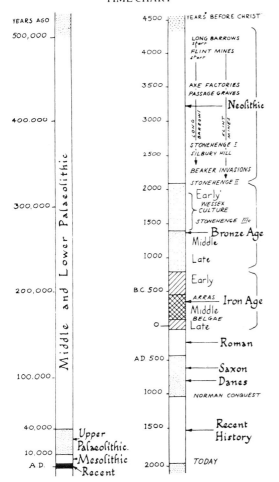

*The whole of the column on the right fits into the black area of the left-hand column.*

caves. They came across the land bridge from Europe following wild animals, such as mammoth and reindeer, slaying and preparing them using simple flint implements. Their tools have been found in the Thames gravels and consisted of flint flakes and crude stone hand axes. Upper Palaeolithic man developed skills in the manufacture of specialist tools from flint, bone, ivory and antler in the form of scrapers, knives and borers. They lived as cave dwellers, knew how to make fire and how to make clothes from skins to escape the bitter glacial cold. Many remains of implements and animal bones have been found in Kent's Cavern, Torquay; Gough's Cave, Cheddar and Wookey Hole, in Somerset; Creswell Caves, Derbyshire; Victoria and Kinsey Caves near Settle, Yorkshire.

From 11,000BC onwards, following the rise in temperature after the retreat of the final ice sheet, the tundra-like vegetation cover of sedge, grass and moss gave way to prairie-like grassland with patches of hazel and alder. A milder and damper climate induced the growth of woodland with forests of birch, pine, oak, lime and elm. The immense mass of water resulting from the melting ice gradually rose to cover the remaining land bridge, possibly about 6,500BC, and thus Britain became separated from the mainland of Europe. The people of the Mesolithic or Middle Stone Age period fashioned spearheads from antlers and arrows with tiny worked pieces of flint called microliths. The extensive forest cover attracted herds of red and roe deer, accompanied by boar, ox, wolf and brown bear. An early British Mesolithic site is at Star Carr near Scarborough, Yorkshire (TA028810), where the dwellings were situated on the marshy shore of a lake.

Although evidence of habitation from the Old Stone Age and Middle Stone Age has been found in many parts of Britain, these made little, if any, impact on the landscape. Some of the caves in which the early settlers lived may be visited, but there is little to indicate their former presence. It is not until the immigrant farmers of the New Stone Age arrived that they produced any features that are readily identifiable today, so this book concentrates on the more recent periods.

## CAUSEWAYED CAMPS

In the New Stone Age groups of farmer immigrants established themselves on the chalk Down country of Southern England soon after 4,500BC, and carried out the growing of grain and the rearing of stock. Small areas of ground were worked, and then abandoned when the fertility of the soil became exhausted. Evidence of their occupation has been left in the form of causewayed camps. These were marked by one or more concentric rings of banks and ditches around hill tops. A number of recognised sites have shown causeways across the ditches which correspond with openings in the banks. These clearly associated features distinguish these camps from the hillforts of the Iron Age, and were no doubt used as gathering areas for meetings, religious ceremonies and trade. Evidence has shown that the sites, particularly the pits and ditches, were used for the deposition of human remains, animal bones and discarded pottery. The ditches became silted up when the bank material was thrown in to cover ditch deposits.

---

**Identifying Features**

- Large circular area around hilltops.
- One or more concentric ditches or extended pits.
- Paths or causeways across the ditch correspond with openings in the banks.
- Internal banks may now only be slightly visible, or even obliterated.

---

**Outstanding Sites**

### Knap Hill Causewayed Camp
Alton Barnes, Vale of Pewsey, Wiltshire
OS173, (1in 167), SU121636
This magnificently situated causewayed camp is one of the many ancient remains that litter this area of the Wiltshire Downs. Its prominent scarpland viewpoint is shared by the nearby figure of a white horse cut into the chalk hillside. Both keep guard over the hazy Vale of Pewsey.

The camp is composed of a single ditch curving round the northern flanks of the hill forming a summit enclosure of 4 acres (1.6ha). The ditch, which varied in depth between 4ft (1.2m) and 9ft (2.7m) is crossed by a number of causeway paths. Little is to be seen of the inner bank to the ditch. Some Neolithic and Beaker pottery fragments have been found, respectively, in the lower and upper parts of the ditch.

**Access** Lying some 7 miles (11.2km) south-west of Marlborough on the minor road from Lockeridge to Alton Barnes. At SU116638, take the track south-west, and just before it descends steeply, bear left uphill along the edge of a field to reach the camp.

*Knap Hill Causewayed Camp*

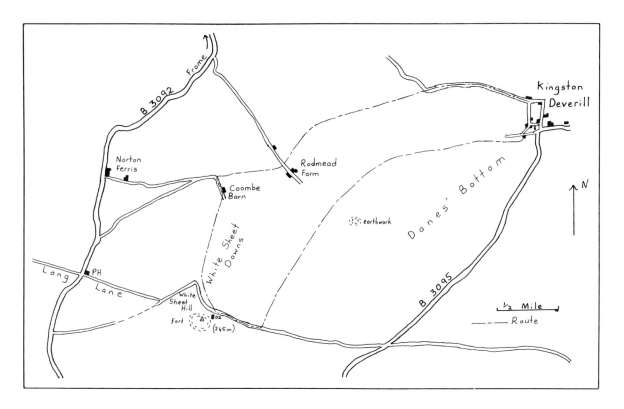

## White Sheet Mill Causewayed Camp

Stourton, Wiltshire
OS183, (1in 166), ST802352
MAP
The camp has a single bank, and the causewayed trench can still be seen at certain points. On excavation, it was found that the ditch was about 10ft (3km) wide and about 5ft (1.5m) at its deepest point. On the south-eastern side a Bronze Age bowl-barrow lies across the ditch of the camp.

**Access**  Situated on White Sheet Downs the site may be approached from the B3092 road at ST782344. There is a walk along a track and footpath to the foot of the hill, and a final stony track before it swings sharply to the right. Distance 1½ miles (2.4km).

Alternatively, a longer round walk on footpaths from Kingston Deverill over Rodmead Hill, White Sheet Downs, Coombe Barn, and east to the minor road below Dairy Farm. Return to Kingston Deverill. Distance 7 miles (11.2km).

## Hembury Causewayed Camp and Hillfort

Awliscombe, Honiton, Devon
OS192, (1in 176), ST113031
This fine hillfort occupying a commanding position lies on a north-south axis. Its history began in Neolithic times when eight sections of ditch were dug across the hill from east to west. The trenches, which stretch in a curved line, are 6-7ft (1.8m-2.1m) deep. There are distinct traces of a defensive bank on their southern side. In the north-west corner of the fort another short length of Neolithic ditch has been found with signs of postholes indicating a previous palisade.

On excavation, many examples of pottery, flint arrow heads, charred grain and Cornish greenstone axes have been found. The ramparts and ditches encircling the hill were constructed at various intervals throughout Iron Age times. Finds of pottery show that the fort was occupied after the Roman conquest.

**Access**  Situated 3½ miles (5.6km) north-west of Honiton, on the north side of the A373 Cullompton road. Access by footpath just off the junction of minor roads.

## Windmill Hill Causewayed Camp (NT)

Avebury, Wiltshire
OS173, (1in 157), SU087714
This is a prehistoric occupation site of the greatest importance, and is the largest enclosure of this type known in Britain. The earthwork consists of three concentric ditches roughly circling the hill. Commencing with the outer circle, the ditches have diameters of 1,200ft (365m), 665ft (210m) and 279ft (85m) respectively. They are irregular in construction, with the width and depth varying from section to section. It is possible that they were excavated at different times by different groups of labourers. Gradually the chalk rubble was removed by a combination of causes, such as covering over material thrown in the ditch, gradual erosion through time, or ploughing. There is now only a small section of the eastern outer circle bank visible. Excavations carried out over a number of years have yielded numerous and important finds of Neolithic pottery, antler picks, implements of stone and flint and human bone. Two Bronze Age barrows lie at the eastern side of the middle enclosure; the larger mound being a bell barrow.

**Access**   By footpath almost opposite East Farm on the A361, $\frac{3}{4}$ mile (1.2km) north of Avebury village. Walking distance 1 mile (1.6km). Alternatively, take the A361 south west of Avebury for $\frac{1}{2}$ mile (0.8km). Turn right, signposted, through Avebury Trusloe for just over a mile. Then a short walk to the causewayed camp.

---

# FLINT MINES

---

Flint was the essential equipment of the Neolithic period for hunting, fighting and general domestic use. The flint mines provided the Neolithic farmer with the flint axes he needed to clear the forest. The best raw material could only be obtained by mining, as the surface flints were usually unsuitable for quality tools and implements. The surface of the mining area is recognised by its dimpled appearance due to the depressions left by the filled-in shafts. Using wooden shovels, the Neolithic miner removed the sand and clay overburden, then cut through the hard chalk with antler picks. The shafts were laboriously sunk sometimes thirty or forty feet down to the floor-stone where the best flints lay. At the bottom of the shafts, galleries were worked which eventually linked up with the next pit. Working in very cramped conditions, by the aid of a tallow light burning in a chalk cup, the miners extracted the flint nodules with antler picks and scraped all the material back to the foot of the shaft. Here the flints and unwanted spoil would be rope-hauled to the surface in skin bags or woven baskets, where the flints were roughly shaped on the site.

---

### Flint Mines
### Identifying Features

- A pock-marked surface of shallow depressions or pits on chalky ground.
- The hollows are surrounded by low irregular mounds of chalky earth and flints.
- The circular depressions had been, the
- The circular depressions may be observed by changes in vegetation cover.

---

## Outstanding Sites

### Grimes Graves Flint Mines

(DoE)
Mundford, Norfolk
OS 144, (1in 136), TL817898
During Neolithic times the Breckland area of Norfolk was probably covered by a vast oak forest. As the forest was cleared, patches of land called 'brecks' or 'brakes' were cultivated, and then abandoned as the fertility of the light sandy soil became exhausted. The grazing of stock further compounded the process, and the area became a sandy heathland. Today the Breckland is extensively forested once more, not by oak, but by the dull blanket of conifer plantations.

For our Stone Age ancestors the ground was rich in flint deposits, and the Grimes Graves site was thoroughly mined over many acres of land. Excavations on this interesting prehistoric site have revealed, that on the northern side, the flint was quarried by opencast methods or by means of a simple bell-shaped pit. In other parts of the mining area, particularly where the seams dipped, hourglass shafts were dug up to 40ft (12m) deep. Each shaft would also have radiating galleries leading off the bottom. There would appear to be up to 380 depressions covering the site, each one representing a buried flint mine, and each separated by its own spoil heap. It would seem that as soon as one pit was worked out, it was filled in by newly excavated waste material from the next mine.

The area was held in great superstition by the Anglo-Saxon people, and the name 'Grim' or 'Grime' probably dates from these times.

At the present time, two of the mines have been capped, and it is possible to descend to the bottom of one of them by means

*Grimes Graves*

of a metal ladder. An interesting find in one of the pits was a crudely sculptured chalk figure, faced by a chalk phallus and globes of chalk overlooking a pile of flints, on which had been placed a number of deer antler picks. Obviously they were set out by miners, in hope of ensuring that the mine or the next

venture would be productive.

**Access**  2 miles (3.2km) south-south-east of Mundford on the A134 Thetford road, at its junction with the B1108. Turn right for 660yd (0.6km) to a signposted turning on the left. There are car parking facilities, and an information stall.

## Cissbury Rings Neolithic Flint Mines and Iron Age Hillfort (NT)

Findon, Worthing, Sussex
OS 198, (1 in 182) TQ139080
Prominently situated 600ft (183m) up on the South Downs, and overlooking the seaside town of Worthing, lies the Iron Age fort of Cissbury Rings. At this lovely spot on a clear and breezy day, commanding views are obtained along the coast towards Beachy Head in the east and the Solent in the south-west.

Over 200 flint mines are to be found both inside and outside the Iron Age defensive earthworks at the south-western end

of the fort. The pits and depressions left by the Neolithic flint mines are now covered by bushes. Using deer antler picks as tools, the shafts were excavated as deep as 40ft (12m). As at Grimes Graves site in Norfolk, galleries radiated out from the bottom of the shafts. At the foot of one of them, nineteenth-century excavators discovered the skeleton of a young woman who may have tumbled in at unknown date. Another mine contained the crouched skeleton of a young man, obviously buried with ceremony, as the remains were surrounded by a ring of chalk blocks. Other finds

have included Neolithic pottery and deer antler picks.

**Access**  Take the signposted minor road for 1½ miles (2.4km) east from the village of Findon, which is just outside the northern suburbs of Worthing. Then a short climb up to Cissbury Rings.

It can also be approached by a footpath from the A24 at TQ137054, and north across the golf course for 1½ miles (2.4km), or from point TQ162100 on the South Downs Way long distance footpath; walking distance 2 miles (3.2km).

### Harrow Hill Neolithic Flint Mines

Patching, Angmering, Sussex
OS 197and 198, (1in 182),
TQ081100

The dimpled nature of this hill top site indicates the presence of considerable flint mining activity in Neolithic times. The mines were thought to have been worked round about the same time as those at Cissbury, some 3¾ miles (6.0 km) to the east. Excavations in 1924-5 uncovered an oval-shaped shaft some 22ft (6.7m) deep, descending through three seams of flints, with a number of galleries leading off the bottom. Interesting and poignant discoveries were the smoke smudges made by the miners' lamps on the passage roofs. It is thought, as with other flint mining sites, that the precious material was traded at some considerable distance from the extraction points.

Harrow Hill also contains a small Iron Age enclosure, with ditch, bank and two entrances, constructed over a small number of comparatively shallow shafts. The enclosure was probably intended for the holding of cattle prior to slaughtering, as many ox skulls were found.

**Access   a**   Join the South Downs Way at the point on Highden Hill where it meets the A24 at TQ119120. Walk west

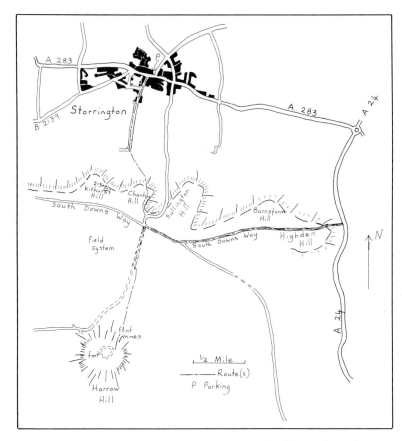

along the Way to a point just before the meeting of a minor road from Storrington. Bear left for Harrow Hill. Distance 3½ miles (5.6km).

**b**   From the centre of Storrington village, leave by the church on the minor road south. Take the footpath that climbs the west side of Chantry Hill, to reach the minor road from Storrington and the South

Downs Way. Route from then as above. Distance 2¾ miles (4.4km).

**c**   From Patching Village north of Angmering. Take the track east of the church and bear north-west across Patching Hill. At a junction of paths in woodland, head north passing Michelgrove Farm towards Harrow Hill. Distance 2½ miles (4km).

## STONE AGE FACTORIES

From Neolithic times and well into the Bronze Age, stone was of great significance in the production of tools and weapons, particularly before the working of copper, bronze and iron. During the Neolithic period flint was used as it had the necessary qualities of hardness and

durability. Initially, seams of flint exposed by the sea were worked, but it was not of high enough quality and so they had to mine for it. Grimes Graves near Thetford in East Anglia is one of the most important prehistoric sites which produced fine flint for axes capable of clearing woodland. Such was the output that this highly prized material was exported to other parts of Britain.

In areas where flint was not found it was likely that early man had been experimenting with other forms of rock, but very few rock types satisfied the requirements for making stone tools. It is perhaps a wistful thought that a chance find by some Neolithic traveller led to the initial discovery of a rock type that could be split to give fine cutting edges. A rock was needed that would have uniform texture, hardness and conchoidal fracture; all essential qualities for the production of stone axes by flaking. Good implements were of such value to Neolithic farmers for woodland clearance that the manufacture of axes for this purpose, for breaking ground and for the cutting of branches for fodder, became the most important industry in Neolithic and Bronze Age Britain; to such an extent that the establishment of an 'axe factory' may have controlled the siting of settlements, which in turn became part of an efficient trade network.

Examples of polished stone axes have been discovered hundreds of miles from their rock source, and although long distance travel was obviously undertaken, no one is sure of the exact routes used by the traders. For example, numbers of Cumbrian axes from Langdale have been found in the south-east of England and Hampshire, as well as in parts of the Isle of Man, Ireland and Scotland. Implements from Graiglwyd above Penmaenmawr have been recognised by geological examination in Somerset, Wessex, South Wales, Lands End, East Anglia, the Severn Valley, along the Solent and in the river valleys of North Wales. Axes and flakes of Mynydd Rhiw rock from the Lleyn Peninsular, have been found in South Wales, mid-Wales, Anglesey and North Wales. The axes from Tievebulliagh, County Antrim have been discovered in north-east Scotland and the Thames valley.

---

## Identifying Features

- Look for axes in various stages of manufacture, for broken or unfinished axes, for chippings and pieces of rock with signs of flaking.
- Very generally the implements measure 8½-11in (216-272mm) long, with a width of 3in (76mm) and a maximum thickness of 1½-2in (38-50mm).
- All tools are of a pointed oval section. Some tools are thin butted, or thin pointed, characteristic of late Neolithic times.
- Examine the specimen carefully to see if the longitudinal and lateral thinning flakes have the bulbs of percussion and striking platform charac- teristic of man-made flakes.
- It is probable that the tools were roughed out by resolved flaking against an anvil stone, and that a hammer stone was used for the final trimming.
- It is advisable to carry out some background study of stone axes. In particular, look at photographs and drawings of the smoothed and roughed out axes, and acquire some knowledge of the particular rock type in question.
- Note that the objects are not easy to identify amongst a mass of scree or other rock debris.

---

## Outstanding Sites

### Pike o'Stickle Stone Axe Factory
Mickleden Valley, Great Langdale, Cumbria
OS 89, (1in 82), NY 274072; 1:25,000, 'English Lakes' SW Sheet
The Neolithic inhabitants of Lakeland found a seam of fine grained, grey-green volcanic tuff that emerged on the surface along a high level contour around the head of the Langdale valley. To find this thin vein of stone amongst the mass of Borrowdale Volcanic rocks was a significant achievement, which gave rise to an important stone axe manufacturing industry. This extremely hard stone was particularly suitable, as it could be skilfully worked into a very sharp edge. The greatest activity was certainly centred on and about the wide gully which falls to the east of the summit of Pike o'Stickle, and extends to within a short distance of the Mickleden valley bottom. Abundant flakes and discarded

*Langdale Pikes from Tarn Hows*

*Stone axe from Langdale*

axes have also been discovered in the screes to the west of the south scree gully directly below the summit of Pike o'Stickle. At a point some 1,800ft (549m) above sea-level is a small, irregularly shaped but artificial cave, which may or may not have been connected with the stone axe manufacture. Another belief is that it was made during more recent times during the search for ores, especially haematite.

Further 'factory' sites have been discovered on the south and south-western slopes of Scafell Pike, on various sites between contours 2,750ft (839m) and 3,000ft (916m):

**a**   Ascending Scafell Pike on the Lingmell side at NY213075.
**b**   From Mickledore, left of the path to the summit of Scafell Pike, (NY211072, NY212073).
**c**   From Mickledore, right of the path to the summit of Scafell Pike, (NY213070).
**d**   Also on Mart Crag, Langdale (NY264078) and Loft Crag (NY278071).

Note that owing to the steepness of the terraces and looseness of the rock, the sites on the face of Pike o'Stickle and in the gullies lying between South Scree and Gimmer Crag should only be visited in the company of experienced climbers.

Completed axes have not been found in the screes or on the various chipping sites, and evidence indicates that the roughly shaped tools were transported to the coast to be polished with sandstone. From the coast the axes were taken by land or water to other parts of the British Isles.

**Access**   Take the B5343 from Ambleside for a distance of 7 miles (11.2km) to the Old Dungeon Ghyll Hotel. (Parking facilities close by). Take the footpath on the north side of Mickleden Beck. To the right, the south scree gully runs down from the summit of Pike o' Stickle.

Walkers may care to continue up the Mickleden path and ascend the zigzags of Stake Gill to the top of the Stake Pass. Bear right at the cairn, and climb leisurely across Martcrag Moor to the summit of Pike o' Stickle, 2,323ft (708m).

Note that great care should be taken if a decision is made to descend the steep open gully immediately east of the summit for a direct descent to Mickleden. Here, the constant passage of many feet has made the surface very smooth and slippery.

**Routes to Scafell Pike**

From Wasdale Head via Brown Tongue is 3,000ft (916m) of ascent, with magnificent rock scenery of beetling crags and tremendous buttresses. The route bears right at a cairn on Brown Tongue into Hollow Stones, and then a steep scree gully climb to the Mickledore gap. Bear left and ascend across stones to the summit. If you have searched long and hard, and time is short, descend to Ling-mell col, and follow the cairned path left down to Brown Tongue and Wasdale. Distance 6½ miles (10.4km).

Alternatively, if you have come for a mountain walk, and regard hunting for stone axes as being of secondary importance, then take the following route back to Wasdale Head. Descend to Lingmell col, or if there is mist continue from the summit to Broad Crag col and descend to meet the Corridor Route. This interesting and most scenic of footpaths slants down to meet a junction of routes at Sty Head. On the way, one is able to gain a striking view down the fearsome abyss of Piers Gill. Here, ignore the army of walkers clattering off down the main path to Wasdale, and take a slightly longer route that zigzags delightfully down the slopes alongside Spouthead Gill. You will probably have this path to yourself! Rejoin the main track further down Lingmell Beck. Total distance 8½ miles (13.6km).

Other approach routes:
**a**  Seatoller (Borrowdale), Seathwaite, Sty Head. Distance 6 miles (9.6km), 3,000ft (916m) of ascent.
**b**  Seatoller, Seathwaite, Esk House. Distance 5½ miles (8km), 3,200ft (975m) of ascent.
**c**  Dungeon Ghyll Old Hotel, Great Langdale, Mickleden, Rossett Gill, Angle Tarn, Esk House. Distance 5½ miles (8km), 3,400ft (1,037m) of ascent.
**d**  Eskdale (Whahouse Bridge), Samson's Stones, Cam Spout, Mickledore. Distance 6 miles (9.6km), 2,919ft (892m) of ascent.

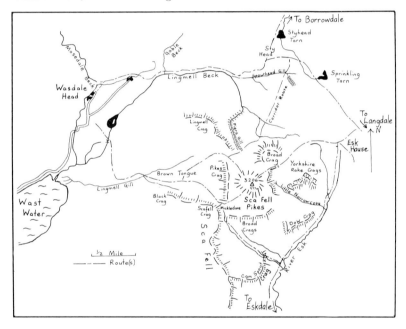

**Tievebulliagh Stone Axe Factory**

Cushendall, County Antrim, Northern Ireland
OS Northern Ireland, Sheet 5, (1 in 3), D193268
On the eastern edge of the Antrim Plateau a conspicuous peak rises to an altitude of 1,346ft (402m). The dark green-brown colour of the surrounding moorland contrasts sharply with the brighter chequer-board pattern of fields bordering Cushendall Bay. Beyond there is a distant headland; its rocky coastline is hugged by the scenic Antrim coast road.

Tievebulliagh is an old volcanic plug, and geological conditions formed a band of olivine dolerite rock that cut through the basalt bed, altering the igneous rock into an extremely hard speckled metamorphic rock termed porcellanite. It was here that early man discovered the small outcrops and realised their potential as a suitable rock for fashioning into axes and other implements. The exposures occur on the higher south-east slopes of the peak, and the scree beneath contains many waste flakes and much rejected material. Waste chippings can also be found in the surrounding peat hollows, although over the years the peat has gradually covered over the trimming sites. Many finished porcellanite axes have been found along the beach at Whitepark Bay on the north coast of Antrim. Most likely they were brought here from Tievebulliagh to be polished and washed with sand and water.

**Access** The site is situated some 3 miles (4.8km) west of Cushendall. From the village take the A2 road north for ³/₄ mile (1.2km), turn first left and then immediately right. The narrow lane climbs gradually for 1¼ miles (2km) before petering out into a track. The conspicuous hill is easily visible and may be approached by an easy walk of 1 mile (1.6km) across the hillside.

*Tievebulliagh*

### Mynydd Rhiw Stone Axe Factory

Bryncroes, Porth Neigwl Bay, Lleyn Peninsula, Gwynedd, North Wales
OS 123 (1in 115), SH234299
Situated near the tip of the Lleyn Peninsula, the oval-shaped hill Mynydd Rhiw forms the basis of the higher ground on the western side of Porth Neigwl Bay. The hill, some 999ft (305m) high, offers a splendid panoramic viewpoint overlooking this lovely western tip of Gwynedd.

On the north-eastern shoulder of the hill are a number of hollows surrounded by low banks. On excavation, the hollows turned out to be the quarrying areas, dug to a depth of 11ft (3.3m), and the ring banks contained the debris of chippings and rejected flakes. This was another example of site located by Neolithic and Bronze Age man in his search for a rock possessing conchoidal fracture, and a particular hardness for sharp cutting edges.

The rock at Mynydd Rhiw is a sedimentary shale altered by intense heat to a metamorphic rock of uniform texture. The porcellanite of Tievebulliagh was similarly formed. The rock had been worked for axes, adzes, knives and scapers, and although the heavy axes were exported, specimens of lighter weight axes and various cutting tools have been found on the site. The stone seems to have

been worked from Neolithic times into the Bronze Age.

**Access** 3¾ miles (6km) north-east of Aberdaron, on the B4413 road at its junction with the B4417. Turn right, and then first left and proceed for 1¼ miles (2km). Turn right, then left, and right again. After 550yd (0.5km) take a footpath on the right that climbs gently across the common land to the north-east shoulder of Mynydd Rhiw.

*Stone axe from Mynydd Rhiw*

## Graiglwyd Stone Axe Factory

Penmaenmawr, Gwynedd, North Wales
OS 115, 2½in OS sheets SH77/87
Llanfairfechan
OS 115, 2½in OS Sheets SH67, SH77/87

The volcanic outcrops behind Penmaenmawr provided an excellent very hard material, in the form of an augite granophyre rock, which could be shaped into tools and implements. The Graiglwyd Quarries have bitten deeply into Graiglwyd hill, and most probably the original Neolithic quarry site has been destroyed. However, many rough or broken axes, chisels, adzes, scrapers, boring tools and battered hammer stones have been found round the southern heights of Graiglwyd (SH717750), Dinas (SH700738), Garreg Fawr (SH690733), and on the surrounding moorland.

It was obviously a very difficult operation to chip the axes thin enough, as many chippings, flakes and rejects were scattered about. This was an important site with many ancient trackways crossing an area that would have been fairly populous in Bronze Age times. Signs of man's involvement are to be found in the form of hut circles, cairns, settlements, stone circles and standing stones. As the quarry sites were close to the coast it is possible that the axes and other tools were transported by sea. Products from the Graiglwyd sites have been found as far away as Lands End and along

*Stone axe from Graiglwyd*

the shores of the Solent.

**Access**   The area is lovely walking country, so of the many routes to choose from the following are suggested:

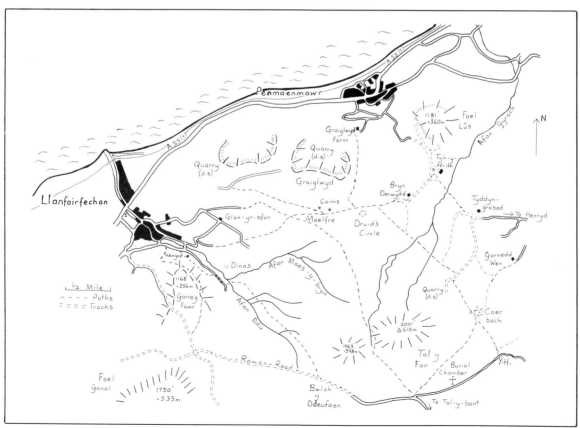

**a** Penmaenmawr, Pen-y-Coed. A path leaves the minor road at SH720759, via Graiglwyd Farm. Ascend to a trackway running east/west. Bear right for 550yd (0.5km) to boundary stones and cairns; the immediate area to the north is the location of the Graiglwyd outcrops. Take care of quarry workings. The Druids' Circle is close by at SH723746. Total walking distance 3-4 miles (5-6km).

**b** Follow minor roads from the Conwy valley towards Bwlch-y-Ddeufaen. A path leaves the road just west of a junction with a track at SH731715. Proceed across moorland for nearly $2\frac{1}{2}$ miles (3.8km) to meet a track running east/west. Turn right for boundary stones, as in **a**. To make a round trip, return via a footpath running south-east of Cefn Coch (SH725748), over the shoulder of Tal y Fan hill, passing the standing stone Maen-Henddu, to a junction of paths south of Caer Bach fort. Continue south-west returning to the starting point near Cae Coch. Total walking distance 7 miles (11.2km).

**c** Llanfairfechan, Nant-y-pandy. A footpath at SH685740, climbs uphill to the eastern shoulder of Garreg Fawr. Distance there and return, $2\frac{1}{2}$ miles (4km).

For a longer walk, continue on the footpath past Garreg Fawr to meet a path running east/west. Bear left and follow the electricity pylons along the line of a Roman road to Bwlch-y-Ddeufaen. Turn left and follow a moorland path north-west to descend to the Afon Ddu stream. Accompany the stream on left bank for 330yd (0.3km), and then bear left on a footpath to Hengae. Follow the road to the starting point. Total walking distance 6 miles (9.6km).

## EARTHEN LONG BARROWS

The first farmers of the Neolithic Age brought with them from what is now continental Europe not only a knowledge of simple farming methods, polished flint implements and simple pottery, but the practice of burying some of their dead under long earthen barrows. Perhaps some disaster such as failure to grow corn, or ill-success at hunting, induced the people to bury their dead in the earth. Most likely, important dead from ruling families were buried with accompanying rituals beneath the often broader easterly ends of the long barrows. It seems that the human remains were placed in an inner mausoleum with objects for the after-life, such as pottery bowls, broken sherds and flint implements.

However, excavations have shown that these earthworks covered successive structures of wood and turf, some lined with stone slabs. Often, cremated remains, as well as many dismembered skeletons, were discovered inside the tombs, having been pushed to one side to make room for other burials. The human remains may have been allowed to rest in the mortuary structures before the final enormous covering of earth and small stones.

In external appearance the long barrows vary somewhat in shape, and the searcher will ultimately detect their wedge, pear-shaped or parallel sided characteristics. Their length usually varies from 65ft (20m) to 350ft (106m). Longer versions, termed 'bank barrows' seem to have been constructed for the same purpose, and may also be a development of the thought behind the raising of the long parallel earthworks known as 'cursus'. One example sited at the western end of

---

**Identifying Features**

- Usually situated close to, or on, chalk or limestone strata.
- The mound is normally between 60ft (18.3m), and 350ft (106.7m) long, and from 30ft (9.4m) to 70ft (21.3m) broad.
- It may be wedge-shaped, pear-shaped or parallel-sided.
- The broader end tends to face the east.
- On the chalk downland, flanking ditches follow the sides of the long barrow. An earth platform may separate the mound from the ditches.
- The ditches may continue beyond the mound and turn inwards at the broader end.
- The ditches may have become obscured or obliterated due to silting or constant ploughing.
- It may be possible to identify the position of the ditches by lush growths of grass, nettles and other weeds.

Maiden Castle hillfort in Dorset (SY665886) is 1,790ft (546m) long.

Earthen long barrows are common features of the rolling chalk countryside of Sussex and Wessex. These first prehistoric structures, situated in conspicuous positions on the slopes or brows of hills, are now thought to have been centres of religious practices, and burials were not the only reason for these impressive mounds. Their siting on chalk downlands seems to assume a particular significance, with an obvious connection between them and the cursus monuments. The long earthen barrows and the cursus seem to point to a well organised use of manpower with the energy directed towards a common belief.

## Some Sites

### Thickthorn Long Barrows
Blandford Forum, Dorset
OS 195, (1in 179), ST971124
These two earthen mounds are situated at the south-western end of the Dorset Cursus. They lie in an area particularly noted for long barrows. There are fine examples to the north-east of Gussage Hill (ST994139, ST993131) and Bokerley Down (ST041191, ST041187) and south-west at Pimperne (ST917105).

The two Thickthorn long barrows vary in length from 150ft (45.7m) to 100ft (30.5m) with each one about 70ft (21.3m) wide and 7ft (2.1m) high. The north-western long barrow has a U-shaped ditch which is clearly visible on the side nearest the minor road. The eastern long barrow also has a U-shaped flanking ditch, and in both examples, the open ends of the U face the south-east.

The eastern long barrow appears to have been a cenotaph, as a thorough excavation in 1933 failed to locate the remains of a primary interment. Nearer the surface, remains were found of crouched secondary burials with beakers of the late Neolithic/ Early Bronze Age period. Two chalk phalluses were discovered in the lower silt deposits of the quarry ditch.
**Access**  From the main A354 road, Salisbury to Blandford Forum, take the minor road south-east of Thickthorn Down (ST965130) for ½ mile (800m).

### Bevis's Thumb Long Barrow
East Marden, West Sussex
OS 197, (1in 181), SU788155
This is the largest of the Sussex long barrows known by the alternative names of Solomon's or Baverse's Thumb. Lying on an east to west orientation it is 210ft (64m) long, 60ft (18.3m) wide and 7ft (2.1m) high at its highest end. There were flanking ditches at one time running along the north and south sides, but the northern ditch has been disturbed by the minor road. The long barrow has not yet been scientifically excavated.
**Access**  Approach along the Petersfield to West Marden road, B2146. Turn east at SU770155, along a minor road for just over 1 mile (1.6km) or approach from East or Up Marden.

### Willerby Wold Long Barrow
Staxton, North Yorkshire
OS 101, (1in 93), TA029761
Situated on the northern edge of the Yorkshire Wolds, the long barrow has a west to east orientation. Excavations have shown that the mound was a cremation long barrow with an inner mortuary enclosure towards the eastern end. Bodies placed in the structure on the original ground surface gradually decomposed, and the disarticulated skeletons were covered with chalk lumps and pieces of wood. A huge chalk mound was then raised over the burials and the remains fired using the available draught. Cremation was thus achieved by this simple flue method.

**Access**  About 10 miles (16km) south of Scarborough, leave the B1249 Staxton to Langtoft road at TA012763. Proceed east for 1¼ miles (2km). The long barrow is immediately south of a right-angled bend in road. The site may be approached from the village of Fordon (TA050751), a similar distance to the east.

# CURSUS

Long parallel earthworks consisting of ditches and banks with squared or curved ends are known as cursus. The significance of these monuments is not easy to understand, for they may have been used for astronomical, ceremonial (such as funeral ritual), or sporting purposes. The cursus may vary from 200yd long (183m), to the massive Dorset Cursus which runs for no less than 6 miles (9.7km) across the downland. In the Stonehenge Cursus the earthwork banks are over 330ft (100m) apart. Indeed, one can only imagine the ideas and inspiration behind these enclosures, for they must have posed considerable engineering problems for early man. It seems that there is a connection between the cursus and the communal burial mounds or barrows of the first farmers.

---

**Identifying Features**

- Long parallel banks with external ditches.
- Earthwork enclosure with squared or curved ends.
- Looks like a processional way.
- Often associated with communal burial sites such as long barrows.

---

## Outstanding Sites

### Dorset Cursus
OS 184 and 195, (1in 179)
The cursus begins near the mounds of a Neolithic long barrow ((SU040192), on the western side of the Bokerley Ditch, a huge fourth-century AD defensive dyke. Although only faintly represented on the ground due to ploughing, the cursus runs south-west, roughly parallel to the A354, Salisbury to Blandford Forum road. In the neighbourhood of Bottlebush Down and Gussage Hill more evidence of the cursus may be seen, together with burial mounds. On the crest of Gussage Hill (ST993138), a long barrow blocks the path of the cursus exactly at right angles. It is interesting to note that the western terminal of the earthwork ends close to the long barrows on Thickthorn Down (ST971124).

The Dorset Cursus may have been constructed for an astronomical purpose with solar and lunar alignments. A barrow could be sighted at some distance, through gaps in the banks.

### Access and Vantage Points
**a**   Footpath from the A354 at Woodyates (SU030193), east for ¾ mile (1.2km), or along the edge of Bokerley Ditch from the A354 at SU035200, south-east for ¾ mile (1.2km) and west for ¼ mile (0.4km).
**b**   Footpaths from the A354 at Oakley Down (SU021177) south-east, or for SU019174, east-south-east for ½ mile (0.8km). Both paths cross the Ackling Dyke Roman road, a few yards after leaving the main road.
**c**   Follow the minor road, B3081, from Handley Hill (SU011166) south-east for 1,100yd (1km). Note that the road crosses a fine stretch of the Ackling Dyke Roman road after 600yd (500m).
**d**   Track from the A354 at ST988145, south-east to Gussage Hill for 990yd (0.9km).
**e**   Take the minor road from the A354 at Thickthorn Down (ST965130) south-east for ½ mile (0.8km).

### Stonehenge Cursus
OS 184, (1in 167), Vantage point SU124430, see map p71. Looking very much like a processional way, this earthwork enclosure stretches for 1¾ miles (2.8km) from east to west. Over 110yd (100m) apart, the parallel twin banks and ditches cut in the chalk are now only faintly visible. Close by to the south are a group of Bronze Age barrows, and the eastern end of the cursus once terminated at a long barrow. However, no traces of this burial mound remain. The earthwork was explored in 1723 by William Stukeley, the famous antiquary, who called it a 'cursus' because of its resemblance to a racecourse. From Stonehenge the cursus is ½ mile (0.8km) due north.
**Access**   Follow the Larkhill track from the A344, Shrewton to Amesbury road, at SU120423 for ½ mile (0.8km).

## Thornborough Cursus and Henge Monuments

West Tanfield, North Yorkshire
OS 99, (1 in 91), SE283793,
SE285795, SE280800
The cursus was the primary religious monument before the construction of henge earthen circles in the vicinity of the River Ure. The central henge of the line of three, with its two parallel banks and adjoining ditches, was raised on top of the cursus, which ran for about 1½ miles (2.4km) from the south-west to the north-east. At the south-western end, a section of the cursus can be observed in the disused quarry workings. Gradually over a long period of time, the cursus ditches became filled from repeated ploughing. However, in drought, or even after three or four weeks of dry weather, it is possible to trace the line of the cursus monument. This is due to the fact that the depth of soil in the original ditches hold more moisture, and therefore the crops grow taller and greener in those sections.

Each of the three Thornborough circular henges has a diameter of almost 820ft (250m). Entrances are on the south-eastern and north-western sides. Originally, each monument was constructed with a considerable earthen bank and an inner and outer ditch. Excavations have revealed the presence of white gypsum chippings that may have been spread on the bank sides.

**Access** From the village of West Tanfield head east on the minor road alongside the River Ure. Take the second turn on the left, and continue for nearly ¾ mile (1.2km). Turn left and proceed for 220yd (0.2km) to be on the line of the cursus running south-west. The central henge monument may be observed from the minor road north-east of this point. To view the northerly henge, keep straight on from SE283793 for ½ mile (0.8km) past Camp House. The henge is situated on the right, planted with trees.

## CHAMBERED LONG BARROWS

The Neolithic (New Stone Age) practice of communal burial for members of the same clan or social group was established at an early date in parts of continental Europe. The burial custom began with the use of natural features, such as caves, and then progressed to earthen long barrows and megalithic chambered tombs. It is certain that both types were in use in southern England, but their relationship is not clear enough to establish which had priorities, except in different areas. However, it would seem to be an improvement to design a tomb for the purpose of successive burials, where the chamber could be opened and resealed after each interment. Taking into account the availability of suitable construction materials, the megalithic chambered tomb would act as a status symbol and a focal point for the surrounding area.

It may be that the shape of the mortuary enclosures in some of the earthen long barrows inspired the rectangular or polygonal burial chambers, and that in time the covering mounds assumed a similar, although much larger trapezoidal plan.

There are a number of distinct regional groups of Neolithic communal tombs in the British Isles which may reflect in varying degrees a number of continental influences. A large number of tombs in our islands differ from the continental ones in the way that the burial chambers are covered by oblong or wedge-shaped mounds or cairns. It is difficult to assess the part, if any, played by continental ideas, but it is possible that Britain had its own simple forms of chambered tombs. These monuments to the dead, requiring a tremendous amount of man-power, energy and organisation, were constructed with stone-lined vaults and entrances. Huge blocks and slabs of stone called megaliths (from the Greek *megas*, large, and *lithos*, stone) were raised forming sectional or chambered passages, where many remains were interred over a wide span of years. It is possible that ceremonies were enacted before and after the burials, to satisfy the spirits of the dead; or maybe fires were lit, and dancing and processions took place. The forecourt or entrance of the tomb was particularly holy, and was reserved for the important ritual of opening the vault and re-sealing it with stone.

Chambered tombs were first of all built on a modest scale, and like ancient parish churches and castles, were altered in design over a

*Silbury Hill*

and the earth mounds have weathered away or simply been ploughed out. In many cases, only the large upright stones of the funerary chamber, perhaps with a roofing stone or capstone, remain standing. These isolated upright stones known as dolmens, or quoits in Cornwall, or cromlechs in Wales, are poignant reminders of the power of Neolithic religion. The chambered tombs that are intact, many of which are preserved and restored, can actually be entered; here the spirit of their age may be experienced.

It is no wonder that this feeling of timelessness is heightened by the fact that many of these monuments are situated amidst scenery of great natural beauty.

The types of megalithic chambered tombs can generally be classified into two main groups; gallery graves and passage graves. The design of these monuments is subject to several variations, and the two main types have developed variants and hybrids that are widely distributed throughout the British Isles. In addition to the possible movement of ideas from northern Europe, it is thought that some stimuli in the design of chambered graves came from structures within our own shores. Tombs situated along the Bristol Channel, on the Mendip and Cotswold hills, on the rolling downlands of North Wiltshire and Berkshire are known as **gallery graves of the Severn-Cotswold Group.**

considerable number of years. At the height of their influence, these burial temples became the most imposing man-made features of Neolithic times. The practice of collective burial gradually petered out, but some chambered tombs were used well into the early Bronze Age.

These burial vaults are scattered mainly over the upland areas of Britain with some isolated examples in the lowlands. Most of the tombs have been affected by time and weather, and by the depredations of local inhabitants who found in the earth and stone a ready supply of raw material. The stone was incorporated into the building of houses, field walls and gate-posts,

*Wayland's Smithy*

*Cairn Holy Chambered Tomb*

On the chalk downs of southern England a row of sarsen (sandstone) stones, the largest 12ft (3.6m) high, block the entrance of the West Kennet chambered tomb, (SU104677). They stand at the eastern façade of a great wedge shaped mound 330ft (100m) high, on rolling Wiltshire farmland close to the huge mysterious earthwork of Silbury Hill. One can walk into the burial chamber, which is 40ft (12m) long and contains two pairs of side chambers and a terminal chamber.

High on the Oxfordshire Ridgeway with its fine views, the embowered chambered tomb called Wayland's Smithy (SU281854), reminds the traveller of the local legend of Wayland the Smith and his association with the nearby Uffington White Horse. On investigation it was found that the chambered tomb and its wedge shaped mound had been raised on top of an earlier long barrow with a wooden mortuary enclosure. This single burial chamber had a stone floor, enclosed by sarsen stones, and the whole structure was covered with an oval mound of chalk excavated from side ditches. Completely hiding this from view today is a wedge-shaped earthen barrow about 180ft (54m) long and 48ft (14.4m) wide at the imposing façade entrance. At one time six large sarsen stones flanked the original entrance to the tomb; four now remain standing. The burial chamber is a cruciform-shaped passage some 21ft (6.4m) long with a single chamber on either side. The chalk rubble used for covering the burial chamber was obtained from long flanking side ditches.

The Neolithic culture spread north along the western coasts of Britain and examples of **gallery graves of the Clyde-Carlingford Group** are to be found in Northern Ireland, in Galloway, the Isle of Man and the islands of Arran and Bute in the Clyde estuary. A few tombs in the southern Peak District may belong to this group.

On the southern slopes of Cairn Holy Hill overlooking Wigtown Bay in Galloway lie the Cairnholy chambered cairns I and II (NX517538). The southern cairn, Cairnholy I, measures about 170ft (51.8m) by 50ft (15.2m) with a crescent-shaped façade of tall stones embracing a forecourt. The burial chamber, now ruined, was divided into two parts. Cremation burials were placed in the chamber and the entrance was blocked. Bereft of their covering mound, the tall façade stones and burial chamber are starkly exposed.

Simple forms of gallery graves, called **portal tombs** (also known as cromlechs or dolmens), are distributed throughout Northern Ireland. They are particularly in evidence in central and western Ulster and in County Down around Carlingford Loch. Tombs with similar features are found in Wales and in Cornwall, where the burial chambers are known as quoits. In many cases the covering mound has been eroded by natural forces, or robbed of its material by later generations, leaving the dramatic outlines of the stone burial chamber resembling a sculptured stone tripod. It is indeed thought-provoking to stand close by one of these megalithic structures and wonder how the enormous horizontal capstone was raised on to its supporting stone pillars.

In County Down, the rocky slopes of Cratlieve, an outlier of Slieve Croob, bear the Legananny tripod dolmen (J289434). This spectacular and graceful chambered tomb with a capstone nearly 10ft (3m) long and 6ft (1.8m) from the ground is raised in front by two portal stones and supported by a shorter third stone at the back. It takes a little careful map reading to locate its position, hidden as it is by a maze of country lanes. Approaching the monument on a misty day, a certain degree of apprehension is evoked as the dolmen suddenly appears like some prehistoric creature. On a fine day a splendid view may be obtained of the surrounding Mourne Mountains.

Some of the earliest chambered tombs in Ireland appear to have evolved from the idea of gallery tombs. These are called **court tombs** because the tombs have an open space or court flanked by stones leading into the gallery. In time they developed elaborate variations such as double, back to back, full and centre court tombs. Certain characteristics point to a close association with tombs of south-west Scotland.

North of Lough Neagh in County Antrim and lying to the east of the lush valley of the sluggish River Bann, is a long parcel of higher land called, somewhat optimistically, Long Mountain. The court tomb at Ballymacaldrack (023183), marked on the map as Dooey's Cairn, is situated in a field at the foot of the gentle eastern slopes close to the Ballymoney to Cullybackey road. The tomb is an egg-shaped mound bounded by a kerb of small boulders, with a single burial chamber and passage; the latter was probably used for cremations. The forecourt is marked by a fine line of upright stones with small stones filling in the gaps. Examinations have revealed that the forecourt was constructed at least 500 years after the cairn, which may be a vital clue to the gradual development of court tombs in Ireland.

The megalithic chambered tombs attained their most impressive characteristics at the end of the Neolithic Period. These magnificent prehistoric structures are known as **passage graves**. As with the gallery graves, we are not certain as to the importance of local ideas; but the design of these impressive monuments may well have originated in the Iberian peninsula, before spreading northwards to Brittany, Anglesey, eastern Ireland, Scotland and the northern Isles. The main plan is a large round or elongated cairn leading to a central stone chamber, often with side chambers. In Scotland, variations occur on the same theme such as the passage entering from the side of the mound, or the chamber divided into many stalls or sections. In Scotland the various tomb groups are scattered over a wide area such as the Hebrides, the Orkney and Shetland Isles, the Highland Region (districts of Cromarty, Caithness and Sutherland) and around the Moray Firth; all of these are passage graves, even though gallery grave characteristics occur in some of them. There is a very fine example at New Grange, County Meath, Republic of Ireland, and there are tombs with similar features on the Isle of Anglesey.

One of Anglesey's most famous tombs is Bryn Celli Ddu (SH508702); translated it means 'the mound in the dark grove'. Excavations have shown that the chambered grave and its covering mound was raised above an earlier henge monument. (This is the name given to a type of ritual monument, comprising a circular area enclosed by a ditch and a bank.) After restoration, the circular mound which is 85ft (25.9m) in diameter, and held in position by a border of large stones, covers a polygonal chamber 8ft (2.4m) across. From an entrance on the eastern side a roofed passage 26ft (7.9m) long leads to the burial chamber. A stone pillar stands in the interior and one of the chamber wallstones has a decorated spiral marking. The north side of the passage contains a low stone bench. An interesting discovery at the centre of the original stone circle was a small pit. Close by was a large stone slab decorated with incised continuous zigzags — a cast of the original now remains at the rear of the chamber. The designs on this magic stone are

*Bryn Celli Ddu Chambered Tomb*

related to patterns found in megalithic tombs in the Iberian peninsula. This tomb may well have been a temple.

Other regional groupings of megalithic chambered tombs, called **entance graves,** may be found in Cornwall, the Isles of Scilly and in West Wales. They consist of a short rectangular passage under a round mound. In the extreme western tip of Cornwall, investigations have shown that the Penwith entrance graves were probably constructed about the time of the other Neolithic tombs, and similarly were also in use well into the Bronze Age. It is possible that the entrance graves on the Isles of Scilly were constructed at a later date than those entrance graves on the mainland.

Astride the northern edge of Helvear Down on St Mary's, Isle of Scilly, (SV921127), the Innisidgen

*Innisidgen Entrance Grave*

entrance graves look across Crow Sound to St Martin's and the eastern isles. The upper site is a grass covered mound stone 26ft (7.9m) in diameter. The entrance passage, which is in line with the outside retaining wall of the mound, leads into a 15ft (4.6m) long burial chamber built of irregular side stones and roofed by five large capstones. At a lower level, and nearer to the sea, is the other Innisidgen entrance grave. A covering mound some 20ft (6.1m) contains a burial chamber which is now open at both ends. Both entrance graves are probably of Late Neolithic or Bronze Age date.

The **Medway chambered tombs** in Kent show affinities to the megaliths of the Cotswolds and the west of Britain. Here tombs are made from enormous sarsens, slabs of crystalline sandstone, found around the Medway Valley. Bearing in mind the nearness of the sea and the navigability of the River Medway, it is possible that these burial chambers may be related to Northern European and Scandinavian tombs.

In Kent, to the north-west of Aylesford (TQ745608), is a megalithic tomb protected by unsightly iron railings called Kits Coty House. The enormous sarsen stones, which may have been a false entrance or part of a burial chamber, are roofed by a giant capstone measuring almost 13ft (3.9m) by 9ft 3in (2.8m). The supporting uprights stand about 8ft (2.4m) high. In the early eighteenth century Stukeley records a sketch which shows a long mound some 180ft (54.9m) in length.

---

### Gallery Graves of the Cotswolds and Severn Group
### Identifying Features

- A large oblong or wedge shaped covering mound of earth and stone rubble.
- There may be traces of long flanking ditches from which the mound material was obtained
- A kerb of stones may be observed defining the limits of the mound.
- The mound contains a gallery passage with side chambers, usually lined with stone slabs.
- The entrance passage is usually situated at the wider end of the mound.
- Before the entrance there may be evidence of a shallow forecourt defined by boundary stones.
- Large slabs of stone called sarsens may block the entrance to the gallery passage.
- The covering mound was considerably larger than the interior structures.

---

## Outstanding Sites

**Stoney Littleton Chambered Tomb** (DoE)
Wellow, Avon
OS 172 (1in 166), ST735572
This is a splendid example of a Neolithic chambered tomb with a wedge shaped mound 107ft (32.6m) long and 54ft (16.5m) wide, lying in a south-east/north-west position. The grass covered mound is contained by a dry stone wall which curves in at the south-eastern end to form a horned entrance. Beyond the initial chamber, the narrow passage 48ft (14.6m) long and built of stone slabs and walling stone, has three pairs of burial chambers leading off it.
**Access** Proceed to Stoney Littleton Farm via the minor road from the A366. A key may be borrowed from the farm for a small fee. There is then a walk of ½ mile (0.8km) to the monument which is situated on the hillside overlooking Wellow Brook and the village of Wellow.

Alternatively, approach the Wellow Brook and Stoney Littleton Farm from the A367 and the village of Peasedown St John.

**Belas Knap Chambered Tomb** (DoE)
Winchcombe, Gloucestershire
OS 163, (1in 144), SP021254
This long barrow stands high on the edge of the Cotswolds above Winchcombe. The strange name, meaning a hilltop beacon, tells of the mound's use by the Anglo-Saxons. Carefully, although not altogether accurately restored, the wedge shaped mound over 170ft (52m) long and roughly 60ft (18m) wide is aligned along an almost north to south axis. The covering mound, contained with dry-stone walling (almost modern), leads to a horned entrance of tall slabs, which on excavation proved to be a false

one. The burial chambers constructed of stone slabs and an infilling of dry-stone walling are to be found along the flanks of the cairn. There are two along the eastern side, one on the opposite western side and one at the southern end. The chambers may have had corbelled roofs, but there is some doubt about this.

**Access**   Situated some 2 miles (3.2km) south of Winchcombe, on an upland site overlooking Humblebee Wood. A signposted footpath climbs steeply uphill from the country lane to Charlton Abbots.

### Capel Garmon Chambered Tomb (DoE)

Capel Garmon, Llanrwst, Gwynedd
OS 116, (1in 107), SH818542
The wedge shaped covering mound of the inner cairn was originally 93ft (28m) long and 42ft (13m) wide at the broad eastern end. The cairn was contained by a kerb of stones leading to a horned entrance of two tall slabs at the eastern end, which on excavation proved to be a false one. The true entrance is on the south side. Here, a passage which was roofed by corbelling leads to a long tri-partite dumb-bell shaped chamber. This is constructed of stone slabs with the gaps infilled with dry-stone walling. The western part of the burial chamber still has a large cap-stone in position.

**Access**   Proceed west from

*Capel Garmon Chambered Tomb*

Pentrefoelas on the A5 for 3½ miles (5.2km). Turn right on the minor road to Capel Garmon for just over 1 mile (1.6km). The track signposted at the road passes the farm en route to the site.

Alternatively, take the A470 south of Llanrwst for 2 miles (3.2km) and thence the minor road to Capel Garmon. The track entrance is ½ mile (800m) beyond the village.

---

### Gallery Graves of the Clyde/Carlingford Group
### Identifying Features

- A large pear shaped, or oval or wedge shaped covering mound of stones and or earth.
- A rectangular burial chamber divided by transverse stone slabs into separate compartments.
- The chamber is lined with stone blocks, and roofed with stone slabs, or corbelled by a system of overlapping stones.
- The chamber is usually set near to one end of the cairn.
- The entrance opens into the middle of a curved façade with a boundary of upright stones continuing out some distance enclosing a forecourt.

## Outstanding Sites

### Cashtal yn Ard Chambered Cairn

Maughold, Isle of Man
OS 95, (1in 87), SC463892
A splendid example of a megalithic chambered cairn of Clyde-Carlingford type. Originally the covering mound was rectangular, about 100ft (30.4m) long and about 4ft (1.2m) high, lying roughly east to west, and contained by post and panel walling. These side boundaries were marked by lateral walls converging towards the east, and culminating in a horned forecourt which is almost square in plan. In the centre of the façade are the portal stones being the entrance to the burial chamber. The paved forecourt is bordered by six spaced orthostats or upright stones. The burial chamber is 38ft (11.5m) long separated by transverse slabs into five compartments. Some of the side slabs have been removed for house building. About 11ft (3.3m) behind the chamber is a mound of burnt shale surrounding a platform of horizontal stone slabs.

**Access**   The monument stands on high land north of Glen Mona, approached by a narrow country lane ¾ mile (1.2km) north of Dhoon Glen. Bear right after ¼ mile (0.4km) and proceed for 600yd (548m) to ford. Proceed left uphill for ½ mile (0.8km). Turn left along a track opposite a cottage to a stile by a copse of fir trees.

Alternatively from the bus and electric railway stop at Glen Mona, take the footpath opposite the Glen Mona Hotel past the railway halt to a ford and footbridge across the river. Then follow directions as above.

*Cashtal yn Ard Chambered Tomb*

### Pentre-ifan Burial Chamber

(DoE)
Nevern, Dyfed

OS 145, (1in 139), SN099370
The impressive remains of this burial chamber or cromlech are set on the gentle northern slopes of Carnedd Meibion Owen. The original long covering mound, now completely disappeared, was about 120ft (36.6m) long by 23ft (17m) broad. All the stones used are local unshaped igneous rocks. The central feature was a rectangular chamber constructed of large upright stones with an infilling of dry-stone walling. The chamber, which lies at the end of a semicircular forecourt, has two tall portal stones. The huge capstone, some 16ft (4.8m) long, rests on these and on another tall upright at the inner end of the chamber. The underside of the capstone is some 7½ft (2.2m) above the ground. On excavation, one of the other features revealed was a large stone to the east of the chamber.

*Pentre Ifan Burial Cairn*

**Access**  From the B4329 road, Haverfordwest to Eglwyswrw, proceed 1½ miles (2.4km) on a minor road north of the village of Brynberian. The site, which is signposted, is approached by a short footpath on the western side of the road.

Alternatively, the site can be approached from the A487 road 1½ miles (2.4km) east of Newport and then by minor roads for 2½ miles (4km).

**Cairn Ban Chambered Cairn**
Allt an t-Sluice, West of Whiting Bay, Isle of Arran
OS 69 (1in 66), NR991262
This isolated chambered cairn is situated some 900ft (274m) above sea level in the heart of the southern moorlands of the Isle of Arran. Its lonely position overlooking the east bank of the small stream, Allt an t-Sluice, has insured its preservation. The remains consist of a mound of stones some 100ft (30.5m) long and 60ft (18.3m) wide. The eastern end is composed of a semicircular façade and enclosed forecourt. The burial chamber, extending 15ft (4.5m) long and divided into three sections, is roofed by corbelling and a covering stone slab.
**Access**  Marked as a chambered cairn on the Ordnance Survey map Sheet 69. A track leaves the A841 at NR970214 running in a north-east direction, where it bifurcates after 2½ miles (4km). Bear left towards the Allt an t-Sluice and follow the stream through the afforestation for 1 mile (1.6km). Keeping the stream on the left-hand side the cairn is sited on the eastern slopes of the narrowing valley.

---

**Portal Dolmens
Identifying Features**

- Simple form of gallery graves found in Ireland and Wales, closely related to the Neolithic burial chambers of south-west England. Known as 'quoits' in Cornwall.
- A rectangular box-like chamber which has a 'portal' of two tall pillar stones at one end.
- The tomb may consist of at least three upright stones supporting one or more capstones.
- In many cases the long cairn has disappeared due to natural forces, or robbed for building material.
- Some remains have a strikingly dramatic appearance like a sculptured stone tripod.

---

**Outstanding Sites**

**Dyffryn Ardudwy Chambered Cairn** (DoE)
Dyffryn Ardudwy, Gwynedd
OS 124, (1in 116), SH589229
Set on higher ground over-looking the dunes of Morfa Dyffryn this Neolithic monu-ment consists of two chambers, the eastern one sited higher up the slope, and the lower western one which is the earlier construction. The latter tomb comprises a small rectangular stone chamber 9ft (2.7m) long, with two huge portal stones, a closing stone across the entrance, roofed with a capstone. The closing stone is set back so that the two portal stones form a kind of porch. The burial chamber had at one time been covered by an oval cairn of water-worn stones. All that remains today is the base of the cairn. Later on a larger stone burial chamber was constructed up the slope. It was 12ft (3.7m) long and 8ft (2.4m) wide with an end stone sup-ported by two wall stones on either side, and a low blocking stone within the entrance. At a later stage a wedge-shaped cairn was raised to cover both burial chambers.
**Access**  By a short signposted path from the A496 in Dyffryn Ardudwy village. The site lies behind the school.

### Lanyon Chambered Tomb (Lanyon Quoit) (NT)

Madron, Cornwall
OS 203, (1in 189), SW430337
This remarkable monument, the impressive remains of a Neolithic burial chamber, fell down in 1815, and was reconstructed with reduced height. Three huge upright stones support a giant capstone 19ft (5.8m) long. The faint remnants of a long north-east to south-west covering mound can still be seen. It measures 90ft (27m) by 40ft (12m). Some stones a little distance away at the southern end probably indicate another burial cist or grave.

**Access**   Situated on the northern side of the minor road from Madron to Morvah, and roughly half way between the two settlements which lie in the Penwith District of Cornwall.

*Lanyon Quoit*

### Trethevy Chambered Tomb (Trethevy Quoit) (DoE)

Darite, Cornwall
OS 201, (1in 186), SX259688
This elevated rectangular burial chamber, 7ft (2m) by 5ft (1.5m), is composed of seven tall stones standing over 9ft (2.7m) high. Resting in a sloping position is a massive capstone 12ft (3.6m) long which has a small hole at the highest corner. At its eastern end, a great doorstone divides the burial chamber into an inner compartment and an antechamber; the latter formed by the two end site stones. The doorstone has a small rectangular hole in the lower right-hand corner which allows for the passage of a body into the enclosed inner vault. There are slight traces of the original oval covering mound.

**Access**   Situated on the southern fringes of Bodmin Moor to the north of Liskeard. It can be approached from the A38 and minor roads to St Cleer and Darite, or from the B3254 to Darite or Tremar. The site direction is signposted at the approaches to the monument.

---

### Court Tombs
### Identifying Features

- Elaborate forms of gallery graves in Ireland, which seem to be closely related to tombs in south-west Scotland.
- A long, oval or wedge shaped covering mound of earth and stones.
- Three or four burial chambers entered from an open space or court, usuallly facing east.
- The court is usually flanked by a border of stones.
- There are variations of double, full and centre court tombs.

## Outstanding Sites

### Aghanaglack Double Court Tomb

Boho, County Fermanagh
OS Northern Ireland, New
Series, Sheet 17 (1in Sheet 7),
H098436. See map p76.
Set in a moorland and wooded
landscape, this very fine court
tomb has been used from time to
time as a rubbish dump. There
are two galleries about 20ft (6m)
long, each divided into two
compartments sharing a
common backstone. The court
to the north-east is roughly
horseshoe shaped, and the court
diagonally opposite is obstructed
by two low slabs of stone. It is
believed that the tomb dates
from the late Neolithic times.
**Access**   Proceed north-west
from Enniskillen via the A46 for
$1\frac{1}{2}$ miles (2.4km). Bear left on
the B81 for $1\frac{3}{4}$ miles (2.8km),
then take the minor road to
Boho. Continue to follow the
valley beyond the settlement for
$2\frac{1}{2}$ miles (4km) to a building

marked Dooletter on the map.
Turn right up the track and
keep right through a forestry
plantation for 1 mile (1.6km).

*Aghanaglack Court Tomb*

The monument is situated in a
clearing. The direction to the
site is signposted.

### Knockoneill Court Tomb

Swatragh, County Londonderry
OS Northern Ireland, New
Series, Sheet 8, (1in Sheet 2),
C820087
This tomb has a well preserved
forecourt $22\frac{1}{2}$ft (6.9m) in diameter sited in front of a burial
chamber. The vault is divided
into two compartments, together
with a small antechamber. At
the end of the gallery is an extra

chamber entered by wide
passage from the south-east. A
line of upright stones seals the
forecourt opposite the entrance.
Excavation has shown that the
forecourt was reused for burials
at a later time, and that the
whole tomb was covered by a
circular cairn, probably in the
Bronze Age.
**Access**   From the village of
Swatragh on the A29 Maghera

to Garvagh road, take the minor
road running west-north-west
for $1\frac{1}{4}$ miles (2km) to Knock-
oneill Bridge. Turn left beyond
the bridge and proceed by a
country lane for 1 mile (1.6km),
then bearing right for another $\frac{1}{2}$
mile (800m). The monument is
approached by means of a short
track and across a field. Marked
on the map as Chambered
Grave.

### Audleystown Double Court Tomb

Strangford, County Down
OS Northern Ireland, New
Series, Sheet 21, (1in Sheet 6),
J56 50
A partly restored wedge shaped

cairn is contained by a line of
dry-stone walling some 88ft
(26.9m) long. The tomb shows
similar features to the gallery
graves of the Severn/Cotswold
group of chambered graves,
including a wedge shaped cairn,

dry-stone walling and many
unburnt burials. There are
forecourts at each end of the
cairn that lead into galleries
with four paved sections each.
Some roof corbels are still in
position. On excavation, scat-

tered remains of over thirty skeletons were found, but only a small proportion of them showed signs of burning.

**Access**   From Downpatrick proceed for some 5 miles (8km) to a point where the main road swings away to the right. Take the by-road straight on, then left past Myra Castle, and head east towards Audley's Castle. The monument is situated two fields to the west of a lane running south from this by-road.

---

### Passage Graves
### Identifying Features

- A circular mound of earth or stone defined by a kerb of large stones.
- A round, polygonal or rectangular burial chamber with a corbelled roof.
- Entered from outside by a long narrow passage.
- The inner chamber may also have side chambers.
- The tombs usually built on hilltops in commanding positions, or often grouped in cemeteries
- Some wall stone decorations occur in the form of lozenges, spirals and zigzags.
- Found in Ireland, North Wales and Scotland, but there are many variants, particularly in Scotland, such as the Hebridean, Orkney-Cromarty, Shetland and Clava groups.
- Some passage graves have gallery grave characteristics.

---

## Outstanding Sites

### Camster Chambered Cairns
(DoE)
Lybster, Caithness, Highland Region
OS 11 and 12, (1in 16), ND260422, ND260440
In north-eastern Scotland, the chambered tombs known as the Grey Cairns of Camster look out across the bleak Caithness moorland northwards to the rough waters of the Pentland Firth. A small colony consists of two round cairns and a long horned cairn. A visitor needs to be supple or slight of stature to negotiate the narrow gloomy passages that lead into the hearts of the round and long cairns.

**Long Cairn**   This chambered grave has four horns and a covering mound measuring some 200ft (61m) by 65ft (19.7m). The triple sectioned chamber is attained by a passage from the long eastern side. The monument also has a small chamber

*Camster Round Cairn*

with a corbelled roof reached by a passage some 20ft (6.1m) long.

**Round Cairn**   The largest circular burial mound of loose rounded stones measures some 55ft (16.7m) in diameter, and stands 12ft (3.6m) high. The passage leading into the burial vault is partly obstructed by four pairs of projecting stone slabs. After negotiating the 20ft (6.1m) long passage, one notices that the first vault is roofed with flat stone slabs and the other two burial areas have a corbelled roof. For the unathletic explorer these chambers may be viewed through a modern porthole from the outside.

**Access**   The cairns lie on the western side of the minor road from Lybster to Watten, 6 miles (9.6km) north of Lybster. Marked on the map as Grey Cairns of Camster.

## Carnanmore Passage Tomb

Cushendun, County Antrim
OS Northern Ireland, New
Series, Sheet 5, (1in Sheet 1),
D218388
Lying at a height of 1,253ft
(379m) on the summit of
Carnanmore, in a fine moorland
setting, with superb views to
Torr Head, Fair Head and over
Rathlin Sound to Rathlin
Island. Conspicuously sited, the
cairn rises to a height of 15ft
(4.5m) and has a diameter of
75ft (22.8m). There are traces of
a stone kerb, and a passage 4¼ft
(1.4m) wide running south-west
for 10½ft (3.2m) from the
entrance to the chamber. The
rectangular chamber, roughly
5ft (1.5m) square, now open at
the front, is lined with upright
stones supporting a corbelled
roof and a capstone. One of the
exposed corbels has faint,
weather worn examples of
passage grave art, including two
groups of concentric circles, a
wavy line and other indefinite
markings. Another corbel close
by has cup marks picked into its
surfaces. There is evidence of

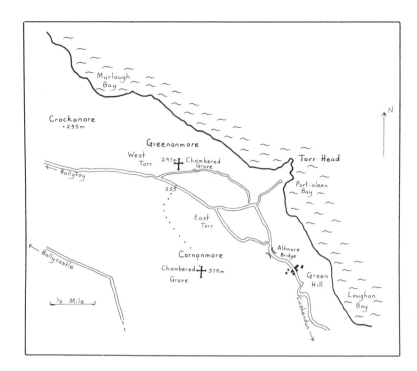

pieces of quartz — an important
clue in the identification of
passage graves.

**Access**   From the hill road
that passes between the summits
of Greenanmore and Carnanmore. This road with its outstanding coastal views travels

north from Cushendun to meet
the A2 to Ballyvoy. From the
highest point of the road, strike
south across the moorland,
gradually climbing to the summit of Carnanmore. Distance
from the road and back 2 miles
(3.2km).

## Maes Howe Chambered Cairn (DoE)

Stromness, Mainland Island,
Orkney
OS 6, (1in 6), HY317127 ·
Geology has been kinder to the
Orkneys than the Shetlands.
Sandstones have created a
landscape of long low hills and
gentle slopes. The favourable
soils enriched with glacially-
carried boulder clay have been
important to the inhabitants for
hundreds of years. The Orkneys
contain many archaeological
treasures, and in that context it
is one of the most interesting
areas in Britain. Neolithic
settlers used the quality of the

thinly bedded flat flagstones to
great effect in the construction of
their brochs and chambered
cairns.

A unique chambered cairn,
probably the last resting place of
kings or members of the ruling
class, is situated between Stromness and Kirkwall on Mainland
Island. This burial mound is
probably the finest example of
Neolithic craftsmanship in
Britain. Over the centuries it has
been pillaged by raiders,
particularly the Norsemen, who
looted the gold treasure and
other grave goods. These raiders
left fascinating calling cards in
the form of engravings and runic

markings scratched on the tomb
walls. Nearer our own time, it is
believed that structural damage
was caused by Victorian vandals
in 1861, who unthinkingly
destroyed the upper part of the
chamber roof. The vaulting has
now been replaced by a modern
concrete dome. The domed
mound of the chambered cairn is
115ft (35.2m) in diameter, approximately 24½ft (7.5m) high,
and is surrounded by a shallow
ditch 3ft 3in (1m) deep. The
central burial chamber is
reached by a passage 36ft
(10.9m) long which is lined by
great slabs of stone: note the
position of a door. The inner

sanctum is 15ft (4.5m) square, with the slabbed stone walls constructed without mortar, and rising to a corbelled roof supported by tall stone slabs in each corner. The chamber walls contain recesses which probably contained the burials and grave goods.

**Access**    From Scrabster, Caithness, by passenger/vehicle ferry to Stromness. The chambered cairn is situated just to the east of the southern tip of Loch of Harray. By road 5 miles (8km) north of Stromness, and 10½ miles (16.8km) west of Kirkwall via the A965. The key may be obtained from the farmhouse, and an admission fee is payable.

*Maes Howe Chambered Cairn*

*Mid Howe Chambered Cairn*

### Mid Howe Chambered Cairn
Westside, Rousay Island, Orkney
OS 6, (1in 6), HY371306
Situated close to the sea with fine views across to Eynhallow Island and Mainland Island. This monument is an impressive stalled cairn measuring 106ft (32.3m) long by 42ft (12.8m) wide. A straight chamber extending 76ft (23.1m) runs down the middle of the cairn, buttressed on either side by dry-stone masonry. The central passage is partitioned by upright slabs providing twelve burial stalls along each side. There are stone slabs in the recesses along the eastern side of the chamber. The chambered cairn is now safeguarded by a protective covering. Mid Howe has been called 'the great ship of death'.

On the benches between the stalls were found the remains of twenty-five human skeletons.

**Access**    From the Mainland of Orkney (Tingwall) to Brinyan Pier. Proceed west for 5½ miles (8.8km) by the B9064 road to Gue bridge. Bear left, and then first right along a track that follows the seashore.

### Taversoe Tuick Chambered Cairn
Brinyan Pier, Rousay Island, Orkney
OS 5/6, (1in 6), HY426276
The cairn belongs to the Camster group of chambered tombs with a mound measuring 30ft (9.1m) in diameter. It is one of the two two-storeyed cairns, situated in the Orkney Islands. The other is located on the Calf of Eday Island. The chamber is 12ft (3.6m) long, and 5ft (1.5m) wide and contains four compartments. The roof of the lower chamber is constructed of stone slabs which form the floor of the upper chamber. The upper chamber has two parts, one almost half the size of the other, and is reached by a passage 11ft (3.3m) long. Some distance away from the lower passage entrance is a small, oval rock-cut cist.

**Access**    From the Mainland of Orkney (Tingwall) to Brinyan Pier. Proceed west for ¾ mile (1.2km). The monument is sited on the north side of the B9064 road.

## Punds Water Chambered Cairn
Brae, Mainland Island, Shetland
OS 3, (1 in 2), HU325713
This area in the west of Mainland Island was the scene of widespread volcanic activity some 350 million years ago, when lavas were poured on to the ancient land surface or intruded along the joints in the rock. Within the last million years the climate became much

colder, which ultimately lead to the formation of an ice sheet over northern Europe. The glaciers advanced and retreated, subjecting the land to intense glaciation. The landscape of Shetland today is a countryside of streamlined hills, overlaid with a thin cover of grass, peat and heather and sprinkled with many small lochs.

At the southern tip of Punds Water is a large, well preserved chambered grave. The heel

shaped cairn has a long façade, over 50ft (15.2m) long, and a clover shaped roofless burial chamber. This is reached by a passage 12ft (3.6m) long from the centre of the façade.

**Access**  From Brae take the A970 for 3½ miles (5.6km), and turn left on a short by-road to Mangaster. Proceed for 600yd (548m), and walk due west across moorland for ½ mile (800m).

## Dwarfie Stane Rock-Cut Tomb
South of Bay of Quoys, Island of Hoy, Orkney.
OS 7, (1 in 7), HY243005
The island of Hoy (Norse for high island) has fine mountainous terrain worn by glacial action during the Ice Age. The tough pebbly sandstones give the island its distinctive appearance which results in some of the most beautiful scenery in the Orkneys. Travelling from Scrabster to Stromness, the boat passes the 450ft (137m) high isolated pillar of rock called the Old Man of Hoy, and the towering sea cliffs of St John's

Head. Inland, Ward Hill rises to 1,565ft (477m) and Cuilags to 1,420ft (433m). The island contains the only example of a Neolithic rock-cut tomb in Britain. The tomb lies on the opposite hillside beyond the steep south-eastern slopes of Ward Hill. Hollowed out of a block of sandstone, the tomb consists of a passage, 7½ft (2.3m) long, 2½ft (0.8m) high and 3 ft (0.9m) wide. There are two chambers, one on either side. It was originally sealed with a block of stone, which now lies just outside the entrance.

The stane is mentioned in Sir Walter Scott's *The Pirate* as a

favourite home of Trolld, the dwarf in the Norse Sagas.

**Access**  By boat from Stromness to Moness Pier, then follow the B9049 Lyness road for 1¼ miles (2km). Take the minor road to Rackwick for 1¼ miles (2km) to the point where it bends away to the right. Head across the moor due south for ¼ mile (400m). The site is signposted. The Dwarfie Stane is marked on the map. A passenger/vehicle ferry operates from Houton to Lyness. Then by the B9047 for a distance of 10½ miles (16.8km).

## Ben Langass Chambered Cairn
Loch a' Bharpa, North Uist, Western Isles
OS 18, (1 in 17), NF837656
Situated on the western slopes of a small oval shaped hill called Ben Langass, this chambered cairn overlooks that tiny ribbon of tarmac, the road south-west from Lochmaddy. As a solitary link with civilisation threading its way through countless lochs and lochans, it gives the impression that North Uist contains more fresh water than

land. This monument is one of many old remains sprinkled over the ancient ice-smoothed landscape of North Uist that has supported man for a long time. The cairn on Ben Langass is a circular heap of stones measuring some 78ft (23.7m) in diameter, and standing 14ft (4.2m) high. There is still evidence of the mound-retaining kerb in the form of small flat slabs. A well-preserved polygon-shaped chamber is entered by a passage from the east. The vault measures 9ft (2.7m) by 6ft

(1.8m) by 7ft (2.1m) high, and is constructed of large stone slabs with an infilling of drystone walling. The chamber is roofed by three large stone slabs.

**Access**  A vehicle ferry connects Uig (Skye) with Lochmaddy, and a service also operates from Tarbert (Harris) to Lochmaddy. From Lochmaddy take the A865 for 1 mile (1.6km), then turn left on to the A867 for 5 miles (8km). Proceed ¼ mile (400m) beyond the fifth milestone and walk upslope to the left for 300yd (274m).

### Clava Ring Cairn and Passage Graves (DoE)

Balnuaran, Culloden, Inverness, Highland Region
OS 27, (1in 28), NH756445

In Neolithic times the ritual beliefs associated with the burial of their dead probably had a profound effect on the lives of those early peoples. In archae-ological terms, the remains at Clava became one of the important sub-groups in the classification of chambered tombs. A colony of three chambered graves lie on the south-east bank of the River Nairn. The site contains two corbelled passage graves in round cairns, with entrance passages and burial chambers uncovered, and with an annular cairn situated between them. The ring cairn consists of a substantial border of stones contained by an outer stone kerb, and an inner line of upright stone slabs. The inner, almost circular area, apparently unroofed and with no access points, measures some 21ft (6.4m) at its greatest width. All three tombs are set within a circle of shapely standing stones with heights varying from 1ft (0.3m) to 7½ft (2.25m). It is possible that the stone circle was added at a later date during the Bronze Age.

**Access**   In the valley of the River Nairn 7 miles (11.2km) east of Inverness by the A9 and the B9006 road to Croy. Pass the Culloden battlefield, and turn right at Cumberland's Stone on-to a by-road. Cross the River Nairn and bear sharp right for ¼ mile (400m). The monuments lie to the right in an attractive leafy setting.

*Clava Stone Circle and Cairn*

### Corrimony Chambered Cairn (DoE)

Glen Urquhart, Inverness, Highland Region
OS26, (1in 27), NH381304

Situated on the banks of a small tributary of the River Enrick at the head of Glen Urquhart, this monument belongs to the Clava group of chambered tombs. An almost circular pile of rounded stones 60ft (18.3m) in diameter, and bordered by kerbing, sur-rounds a circular burial chamber 12ft (3.6m) in dia-meter. A low passage, possibly corbelled, leads some 23ft (7m) into the centre of the stone mound. The burial chamber is now roofless and the interior can be observed from above. The original capstone lying on the mound has engraved markings on its surface. Similarly, compared with the cairn at Clava, the monument is surrounded by a ring of stones, but Corrimony has eleven in number.

To digress for a moment. The road from the head of Glen Urquhart climbs over and descends to Strath Glass. The village of Cannich is the gateway to one of many of the mountain walker's promised lands — Glen Affric. Here in an area of great beauty is a wonderful panorama of rock, moorland, forest and water that complement each other perfectly. A walk from Cannich, through Glen Affric to Loch Duich, Shiel Bridge and beyond to Glenelg, is a true 'Road to the Isles', a challenging tramp of some 47 miles (75km). During the journey, one will always remember a night spent at Britain's loneliest Youth Hostel, Alltbeithe. It will be especially memorable as a remote simple shelter in the midst of these majestic mountains.

**Access**   West from Drumnadrochit. Take the A831 for 6¼ miles (10km). A signpost to the monument indicates a sharp turn left. Proceed on a by-road for ¾ mile (1.2km) to Corrimony Cairn. Or east from the village of Cannich on the A831 for 3½ miles (5.6km) to the signposted turning on the right.

## Skelpick Chambered Cairn

Strath Naver, Bettyhill,
Sutherland, Highland District
OS 10 (1in 10), NC723567
This long horned cairn is
situated on the banks of the
Skelpick Burn, a side stream
flowing from an area containing
innumerable streams and many
square miles of bog and moor.
Lying in a north to south direction, it measures some 200ft
(61m), and is entered by a
passage opening from the façade
at the northern end. The tomb
consists of three chambers which
gradually increase in size as one
proceeds into the cairn. The first
chamber is approximately 6ft
(1.8m) by 4ft (1.2m). The second
chamber is 10ft (3m) by 8ft
(2.4m) and the inner polygonal
chamber is slightly larger
overall. The two doorways
leading from the outer to the
middle chamber, and from the
middle to the inner chamber are
supported by long stone lintels.
The inner chamber is con-
structed of huge stone slabs with
a dry-stone infilling.

**Access**   Follow the estuary
south for 1 mile (1.6km) from
Bettyhill. Where the main A836
road crosses the river carry
straight on down the minor road
for 2½ miles (4km). Skelpick
Cairn lies across the field ¼ mile
(0.4km) to the east on the far
bank of the burn.

From the south by footpath
past Dun Viden broch to
Skelpick, 5 miles (8km) from the
B873.

---

### Entrance Graves
### Identifying Features

- Found in the Isles of Scilly, Cornwall and Wales.
- A circular mound of earth and stone rubble with an outer retaining wall of stones.
- The chamber opens directly from the side of the covering mound.
- The rectangular chamber is built of large stone slabs and roofed by huge capstones.

---

### Outstanding Sites

## Bant's Cairn Entrance Grave

(DoE)
Halangy Down, St Mary's, Isles
of Scilly
OS 203, (1in 189), SV911123
An impressive late Neolithic
tomb 40ft (12.2m) in diameter,
sited at the top of a slope overlooking the early village settlement and the Island of Tresco.
The tomb has an inner and
outer retaining wall which
probably indicates two periods
of construction. The entrance
leads in from the eastern side to
a rectangular chamber built of
stone slabs and roofed by four
immense capstones. This is
indeed a lovely setting, and
whether you are interested in
chambered graves or not, the
surroundings and the lovely
views are equally delightful.

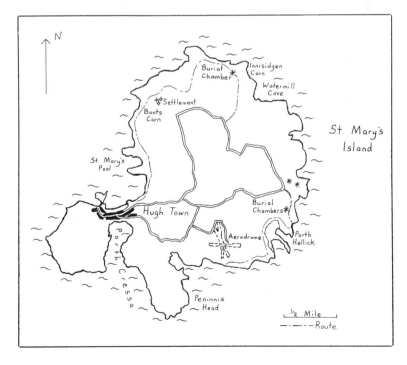

**Access**   On the north-west
corner of St Mary's Island near
the north end of the Golf Course
and overlooking the early village
settlement site. The cairn is signposted. Reached easily from
Hugh Town by pleasant by-
roads and footpath. Distance 1¾
miles (2.8km). You can continue
by footpath to Innisidgen Cairn
without expending too much
effort, and return to Hugh
Town. Complete walking
distance 3 miles (4.8km).

*Bant's Cairn*

### Porth Hellick Down Entrance Grave (DoE)

Porth Hellick Down, St Mary's,

*Porth Hellick Entrance Grave*

Isles of Scilly
OS 203, (1in 189), SV928108
This is another impressive late

Neolithic tomb sited on the tip of
breezy Porth Hellick Down.
Well restored, the grass covered
mound is 40ft (12.2m) in diameter, and contained by dry-
stone walling 5ft (1.5m) high.
The unroofed entrance is on the
western side and extends for 14ft
(4.3m). The passage bends into
the burial chamber, which is
about 12ft (3.7m) long and
roofed by four stone slabs.
**Access**   By signposted footpath
from the northern edge of the
tiny airport via Porth Hellick
Bay. The monument is situated
on rising ground to the right.
Distance ¾ mile (1.2km).
Alternatively, direct from Hugh
Town by road and footpath,
distance 1½ miles (2.4km).

### Tregiffian Entrance Grave (DoE)

St Buryan, Cornwall
OS 203, (1in 189), SW431244
This chambered tomb is situated
by the side of the B3315 road
which partly destroyed the
cairn. Excavations have shown
that this was originally a circular
mound with a possible diameter
of some 55ft (16.7m) bounded by

a kerb of stones. The burial
chamber which is on the
southern side is constructed of
stone slabs and walling stone
measuring 15ft (4.5m) long, 4ft
(1.2m) wide and roofed by four
capstones. Two urns were found
beneath the burial chamber
floor, one containing cremation
remains. A stone at the outer
eastern side of the entrance is

engraved with cup marks. The
present stone is a replica of the
original which is now preserved
in Truro Museum.
**Access**   Directly by the
southern side of the B3315 road,
Newlyn to Lands End. The site
is 1¾ miles (2.8km) south-east of
the village of St Buryan.

**Medway Graves
Identifying Features**

- Found in the Medway Valley in Kent.
- A burial chamber of massive upright stones in an H-shaped plan roofed by a huge capstone.

- Formerly covered by an elongated mound with a retaining kerb of large stones.

## Typical Sites

**Coldrum Chambered Tomb** (NT)
Trottiscliffe, Aylesford, Kent
OS 188 (1in 171), TQ654607
Set on the lower slopes of the North Downs the monument is a rectangular mound 70ft (21.3m) long by 55ft (16.7m) broad and lying in an east to west direction. Originally the mound was retained by a kerb of forty-one upright sarsen stones, of which seventeen have fallen on the slope and to the foot of the terrace, due to damage in the past by digging. At its eastern end stands the rectangular burial chamber which consists of four huge sarsen stones 13ft (4m) by 5ft (1.5m). It is believed that at one time the burial chamber was divided into two compartments by means of a holed stone. Excavations discovered the remains of twenty-two people of both sexes, long headed and short of stature, on stone paving in the north-west corner of the chamber. The skeletons displayed similar physical characteristics.

**Access**  Above Ryarsh Wood, east-north-east of Trottiscliffe village. The site can be approached by a footpath from the Pilgrim's Way, or by footpath and track from the village. Distances 600yd (548m) and almost 1 mile (1.4km) respectively

**The Chestnuts Chambered Tomb**
Addington, Maidstone, Kent
OS 188, (1in 171), TQ652592
This Neolithic chambered tomb has been severely damaged in the past, but has since been excavated and partially restored. Originally, a large mound of earth covered a burial chamber of sarsen stones some 12ft (3.6m) long, 7½ft (2.3m) wide and 9ft (2.7m) high. The chamber was divided into two compartments by a medial stone lying east to west, and enclosed by two large wallstones which supported two capstones. The wallstones were secured on the ground by blocks of local greensand stone. Both the eastern and western ends were blocked, and four large flanking stones formed a façade at the eastern end. The tomb was probably used for burials in the Early Bronze Age. Tiny bone fragments were discovered, being the possible remains of nine cremations and one or two children. Also found were three barbed and tanged arrowheads and a small pendant of fired clay.

**Access**  Situated at the western end of Addington village just off the Wrotham Heath road. The monument lies on private land and may be visited by permission of the owner at Rose Alba. There is a small fee payable.

CHAPTER THREE

# From Neolithic to Bronze Age

About 2,500BC immigrants came to Britain from the coastal areas of Northern Europe, particularly from the valley of the River Rhine, bringing with them a characteristic type of pottery vessel called a beaker. These so-called 'Beaker' people spread out across the lowland areas of Britain living a nomadic existence, raising stock and carrying on some simple cultivation. Their distinctive pottery vessels were copied, and variations on a similar theme occured in other regional areas of Britain. For example, in the north, the 'Food Vessel' users adapted the beaker pottery design and produced their own ornamented style of ware. The newcomers also brought with them a knowledge of metal working, particularly of copper and its alloy with tin, a combination known as bronze. Their religious ideas, and practices of crouched burials under small round barrows, were new to Britain, whose established Neolithic tradition was of worship at, and burial in, communal tombs.

The Beaker folk left very few traces of houses and settlements, but they did play an important part in the building and development of stone circles. They improved on the idea of Neolithic single-entranced henge monuments and built larger ones with two entrances. It is believed that they were concerned with the rebuilding and redeveloping of Avebury and Stonehenge, which seems to indicate a powerful chief-controlled society capable of organising the immense labour force required for these projects. The growth of this flourishing Early Bronze Age society is best represented in southern England by the great barrow cemeteries. The contents of the different types of round barrows have yielded distinctive evidence of material wealth from this culture. These magnificent burial mounds have yielded pottery, barbed flint arrowheads, bow wristguards, beautifully made stone axes, bronze daggers, beads fashioned in painted glazed

pottery, and in some cases some articles of worked gold.

By the end of the Bronze Age, skill in metalwork and metalworking techniques had reached a high level. Helped by continental influences there was a great variety of tools, weapons, personal ornaments and household equipment. The weapons particularly had become sophisticated in design, and included flanged, palstave and socketed axes, beautifully designed swords and pegged and socketed spears.

Towards 2,000BC the climate in Britain began to grow much drier and the sea level rose considerably, covering the coastal settlement strips. With the advent of warmer weather, the Beaker and Early Bronze Age people found that it was possible to move to higher ground, thus continuing their stockbreeding and nomadic existence. In contrast with the rich evidence of their culture obtained from the grave goods buried in barrow cemeteries, there are few remains of dwellings from the Beaker and Early Bronze Age periods. It is more likely that the wanderers lived in temporary shelters in the form of a rough hut or tent. There is evidence, after investigations of soil pollen analysis, that the main woodland clearance came in Bronze Age times. It is probable that after the trees were cut down, the stumps were burnt by piling brushwood round them. The wood ash provided a valuable fertilizer for the soil, but even so, this would only sustain a limited period of arable farming. As the lowland fields became exhausted, so agriculture increased on the margins of the higher land. In Late Bronze Age times, one can visualise a landscape of pastures and scattered dwellings interspersed by cleared patches of forest and small rectangular corn fields. Ploughing became more effective with the use of an improved plough called the ard. This implement, which could be pulled by oxen, made a wide furrow, and led to the formation of small squarish plots — the so-called 'Celtic' fields, which in many areas continued in use well into medieval times.

There are examples of Late Bronze Age sites in the Northern Isles, and evidence of settlements on the uplands of Bodmin Moor and Dartmoor. At Stannon Down on the western edge of Bodmin Moor, a number of stone hut circles have been investigated, together with field systems and boundary walls. It would appear that each of these Middle Bronze Age dwellings had a conical roof supported by a central pole, with the roof eaves resting on a low circular wall of stones. The fields were laid out in long strips separated by boundaries of loose stone. Other enclosures were built of a stronger walling, and these were most likely used for the holding of livestock. One interesting discovery was a system of stone chanelling in each hut for drainage purposes. In contrast to the looser pattern of settlement, are the groups of huts frequently enclosed by solid stone walls, known locally as pounds. It is believed that all the land on Dartmoor, roughly below the 1,300ft (400m) contour, was part of a planned system of sharing with separate parts marked by stone banks known as reaves.

Recent research has shown that Dartmoor was a forested upland until the Bronze Age. From this time, the removal of tree cover, followed by overgrazing of the higher land, together with the deterioration of the climate, led to the formation of peat and blanket bog. This cycle of events began to affect the settlement patterns generally throughout the upland areas of Britain.

For the inhabitants of Grimspound, 1,498ft (457m) high up on the eastern edge of Dartmoor, life became more and more difficult in an increasingly hostile climate. Cyclonic conditions of cold driving rain brought by strong winds, forced them to leave with their flocks and herds for new life in the lowlands. Grimspound became one of those abandoned sites, the remains of which can be visited today.

## HENGES

The Neolithic farmers adopted hilltops for the construction of enclosures surrounded by a ditch and bank, as convenient easily visible situations for social and economic reasons. Excavations on these sites, termed causeways camps, have indicated a string of pits dug in a seemingly disorganised fashion, containing household debris such as pottery, flints charcoal and human bone. It is possible that the burying of personal material was a form of insurance by these early people, whose very survival depended on the earth's natural forces. A storm, an earthquake, an attack by other tribes or by wild animals were ever present constituents in a hostile and demanding environment. The term, henge, was adopted from Stonehenge, where the standing stones were erected inside an earlier ditched enclosure, or causewayed type of structure. As time went on, and social life became more organised and settled, so these henges became peaceful meeting places, where goods were bartered and linking trade routes established. Excavations have shown that in their later phases, henges played their part in ritual ceremonies which involved the burial of human remains. Henges tend to occur in groups as there appears to be some connection in these focal points for the trading of stone axes and tools.

Henges are classified as Class I or Class II sites. and are found in many parts of Britain. The earliest phase of Stonehenge is included in the Class I period of time round about 2,800BC, although it is important to remember that the development of Stonehenge was spread over many hundreds of years after the earliest phase. Class I henges usually have a single entrance, and many include settings of timber or stone pots. Class II henges are larger monuments that usually have two or four entrances, and finds from some of these sites suggest that there were rituals involving the burial of human remains. It is believed that these later henges were constructed in the Early Bronze Age by the Beaker people.

## Outstanding Sites

**Arbor Low Henge** (DoE)
Monyash, Peak District, Derbyshire
OS 119, (1in 111), SK160636
This impressive monument is situated in an exposed position on top of one of the high limestone ridges some 1,231ft (370m) above sea level, the highest henge in Britain. The site has a more open aspect to the north-west and panoramic views to the distant gritstone edges. The henge lay on an important north to south trade route, and it was probably an important focal point linking Wessex with the Lake District. It is thought to have been built in the Beaker Period, the transition between the Neolithic Age and the Bronze Age. In its original state Arbor Low can be regarded as a member of the spectacular group of circle henges that include the complex sites of Avebury and Stonehenge.

Arbor Low is regarded as Class II henge with two entrances, one at the north-north-west, and one at the south-south-east. The bank with an external diameter of 295ft (89.9m) by 280ft (85.3m) and elongated to the north-east is 7ft (2.1m) high accompanied by a ditch 5ft (1.5m) deep. The flat

central area containing the blocks of limestone is 150ft (45.7m) by 170ft (51.8m). A large Bronze Age burial mound, now pitted from many previous diggings, is incorporated into the south-eastern edge of the surrounding bank. Two early Bronze Age food vessels and a cremation were found here in 1845.

It is believed that the stones in an oval setting, now recumbent on the central platform, were originally standing in shallow foundations. In time they tumbled down due to the

ravages of upland winters, and the later exploits of seventeenth-century wreckers who wished to destroy the sanctity of this pagan site. There are now forty-eight to fifty-one pieces of stone scattered irregularly near the edge of the ditch. It appears that the stones were not quarried on site, but are in fact large slabs of limestone obtained from a nearby area of 'limestone pavement'. Leading west from the southern entrance are the faint remains of a bank and ditch curving gradually towards Gib Hill burial mound. Today it is not

*Arbor Low*

certain if this ceremonial bank avenue ever led to the impressive tumulus.

It is probable that, as with other ancient sites, the Arbor Low temple was so designed that its entrances aligned with the sun and moon solstices.

**Access** Situated 1 mile (1.6km) east of Parsley Hay crossroads on the A515. Access to the site is via a farm track from the minor road to Youlgreave. The monument is signposted and there is a car park near to the farm. A short walk alongside a wall leads to the henge.

## Mayburgh and King Arthur's Round Table (DoE)
Eamont Bridge, Penrith, Cumbria.
OS 90, (1in 83), NY519285, NY523284

Just south of Penrith, near to the confluence of the rivers Eamont and Lowther and hemmed in by the macadam tracks of the M6, the A6, the A66 and the B5320, lie the henge monuments of Mayburgh and King Arthur's Round Table. Even outside the rocky mountainous areas, the digging of ditches and the raising of banks could not have been easy. At Mayburgh, however, no ditch was dug at all; but an equally laborious operation, the construction of a high rampart using large rounded stones, probably from the beds of the nearby rivers, was undertaken. Today this impressive site, regarded as a Class I henge, has a single entrance through the 18ft (5.4m) boulder bank from the east. In the flat centre of the interior stands only one of the four original stones. There may also have been a circle of standing stones at the foot of one side of the interior bank, although nothing now remains.

Close by, traffic rushes past without giving this tree-crowned bank a second look, but within, this ancient monument still manages to retain an air of mystery and solitude.

King Arthur's Round Table lies close to the junction of the B5320 and the A6, a short

*Mayburgh Henge*

*King Arthur's Round Table*

distance away from Mayburgh. There was only sufficient soft river silt to provide this monument with a 5ft (1.5m) high bank. At one time this Class II henge, some 35ft (90m) in diameter, supported two entrances, but due to damage to the site only the one on the south-eastern side remains. Like

Mayburgh, the bank rises in height towards this entrance.

Excavations have suggested that there may well have been a stone circle standing on the small platform between the bank and the ditch. Finds have also indicated that a trench dug into the central area had been used for cremation purposes. During medieval times the inner enclosure is known to have been used for games. The henge's fanciful title may have derived from the fact that the Cliffords of nearby Brougham Castle claimed descent from the Welsh kings and therefore from Arthur.

**Access** The monuments are within ½ mile (0.8km) of each other. Mayburgh may be reached from a stile to the south-west of the site, which is in turn approached from a cul-de-sac leading from the B5320 road. This access bends sharply away just before the bridge, and then runs parallel to the M6. Cars may be parked in this road. After viewing this site it is only a short walk down the B5320 to its junction with the A6, where a gate opposite some buildings gives access to King Arthur's Round Table.

**Ring of Brodgar Henge** (DoE)
Stromness, Mainland Island, Orkney
OS 6, (1 in 6), HY294134
This large, well preserved Class II henge is magnificently situated on a narrow finger of land separating Loch Stenness and Loch Harray. Brodgar is an impressive monument, and the second most northerly circle henge in the British Isles. Nearby is the unique passage grave of Maes Howe, and it is possible that the ceremonies at the neighbouring Orkney tombs and circle henges were inter-connected to some degree. Comparable associations of burial tombs and henges have been noticed with sites in Southern England, such as Marden in Wiltshire and Knowlton in Dorset. The ring of upright stones measuring 360ft (109m) in diameter still has twenty-seven standing out of the original sixty. They vary from a few inches to 15½ft (4.6m) in height, and are placed close to the inner edge of the 6ft (1.8m) deep rock cut ditch that is crossed by causeways at the north-west and south-east. Very little of the external bank remains. Four of

Ring of Brodgar

the stones carry separate individual carvings such as a runic symbol, an anvil, an ogham mark and cross; these were etched into the stone many years after their erection.

A solitary stone to the south-east of the circle henge may either have been part of an avenue of stones linking up with the Stones of Stenness henge, or may have acted as a boundary marker between the two sites.

The Ring of Brodgar may have been constructed in its particular geographical setting in order to make alignments on different positions of the moon.

**Access** Situated on Mainland Island to the west of the B9055 road, 1½ miles (2.4km) north-west of its junction with the A965 Kirkwall to Stromness road.

## STONE CIRCLES

A stone circle may be defined as a circular, or almost circular, setting of spaced standing stones thought to have been built by people of the Late Neolithic and Bronze Age. Although they are presumed to be successors of the henges, stone circles remain enigmatic structures. Many people have attempted to define their presence, their purpose and when they were erected. They were probably meeting places, and the finding of human remains in some of them reinforces the idea that the enclosures were also used for burial ceremonies and/or human sacrifices. It is possible that primitive peoples believed stone circles to be a link between crop and animal fertility, or symbols of sanctuary, where fire and death were offered in return for safety in a dangerous and uncertain environment. Their origins are still clouded in mystery, but it is now firmly believed that they are indigenous to the British Isles. They are spread all over the upland areas, with greater distributions in north-east Scotland, mid-Ulster, the Lake District and Cornwall.

As to their source, one explanation is that they developed from the henge monuments, with the banks and ditches giving way to a circle of raised stones. The sheer physical difficulties in henge construction using primitive tools to excavate hard rocky ground may have led to this development. It is interesting to note that an area which contains large stone circles will often also contain henges. It is also believed that stone circles, like henges, were used as centres where stone axe trading was carried out. The beautifully worked and polished stone axe was undoubtedly regarded as a very valuable object, a form of cult figure imbued with magical properties.

Many writers have made good arguments for the settings of the stone circles and the alignments of the stone to have been for astronomical purposes. Much research, with impressive mathematical calculations, has been carried out to support their theories. This, however, was probably only part of the function of stone circles, even though much has been made of the use of these monuments by the Druids for their ritual ceremonies. It must be remembered that some of these stone circles were raised long before the height of the Iron Age Celtic Druid culture.

Architectural variations include blocks of slate, slabs of flagstone, lumps of dolerite, boulders of granite and water-pocked monoliths of limestone. They remain as silent witnesses of ceremonies and rituals enacted by people long, long ago. They are well worth finding, situated as many of them are, amongst some of Britain's most beautiful scenery.

### Identifying Features

- A fairly common monument in the upland areas of Great Britain.
- A circular, almost circular, or oval setting of spaced, standing stones.
- The structure may be integrated with banks, ditches, single stones, or rows of stones, or other settings of stones.
- The stone circles vary greatly in diameter.
- The stones themselves vary greatly in size. They are usually locally obtained, but in certain cases may have been transported some distance.
- In other examples, the tallest stones flank an entrance to the circle, and the other stones are graded in height.
- The circles may have been used for astronomical purposes, with a tall stone used for sighting on natural features, or on the sun, moon and stars.
- In a few cases the stones are lying flat on the ground, possibly to show a ritual end to the life of a circle.

## Outstanding Sites

**Castlerigg Stone Circle** (DoE)
Keswick, Cumbria
OS 90, (1in 82), NY292236
The Castlerigg stone circle is
thought to be related to henges,
and is in all probability one of
the earliest examples in the
development of stone circles
built in north-west England.
Erected by people of the Late
Neolithic or Early Bronze Age, it
stands in an easily approached
position in a natural amphitheatre amongst the surrounding
mountains. The builders were
obviously impressed by the site,
a grassy shelf above the deep
wooded valley of the River
Greta, overlooked by the
Lakeland peaks of the Northern
and Derwent Fells. Although its
magnificent situation was an
important factor, we cannot be
certain of the circle's real
purpose. It may have been used
as a meeting place, for religious
ceremonies, or for axe-worship
and axe-trading. However, it is
likely that tracks connecting the
Langdale area with other stone
circles in the Lake District, and
the routes to the Irish Sea and
across to the Pennines, centred
on Castlerigg.

The circle is slightly oval with
a diameter of about 100ft (30m).
Of the thirty-eight stones which
stand in their original position,
five have now fallen. The stones
are not uniform in size, but there
is a definite entrance on the
northern side between two huge
stones 13ft (4m) apart, which
can be likened to the flanking
entrance stones found at other
henges. Within the circle on the
eastern side is a rough oblong of
ten stones, the purpose of which
still remains a mystery. It has
been suggested that the monument was used for astronomical
purposes, and that some parts of
the surrounding skyline were
used for astronomical sightings.
It has also been argued that
stone circles may have been
calendars to guide the early
farmers in sowing and
harvesting.

*Castlerigg Stone Circle*

**Temple Wood Stone Circle**
(DoE). See map p69.
Stockavullin, Kilmartin,
Strathclyde Region
OS 55, (1in 52), NR826979
The seaways along the north-
western coasts of the British Isles
encouraged the early people to
travel as far as the Northern
Isles. Land journeys over great
distances were out of the
question, as the forests, swamps
and mountains discouraged the
early settlers. No doubt these
folk in their fragile primitive
boats kept close into the shore,
not risking the dangerous
currents and whirlpools further
out amongst the islands. From
time to time in their wanderings
north, small settlements were
established, often few and far
between and set amidst barren
and wild surroundings of rock
and water. Occasionally, a
sheltered fertile spot was found
and the area was well settled by
the Neolithic people. Such a
region was the rich Kilmartin
valley, where many prehistoric
remains have been discovered,
including a fine linear cemetery,
a henge, standing stones and the
stone circle. Discoveries of
patterned stone slabs, the carved
shapes of bronze axes, beakers
and food vessels show a
flourishing settlement during the
Early Bronze Age.

The Temple Wood circle is
almost perfectly circular, some
40ft (12m) in diameter. Originally, there were twenty
upright stones, of which thirteen
now remain. Set almost in the
middle of the circle is a burial
cist comprising four stone slabs
minus its capstone, and
measuring 5ft (1.5m) by 3ft
(0.9m). In the south-eastern
corner there is one remaining
stone slab which possibly
indicates an entrance to the
circle. The position of the burial
cist may mean that the standing
stones were an outer kerb
surrounding a large burial cairn.

Traces of a cremation were found, and the cist probably contained a food vessel deposit.

It is likely that the monument was constructed during a period when burial customs changed from the large chambered tomb to simple interments in stone cists during the second millennium BC. The close proximity of a string of burial cairns in the Kilmartin area may also mean that the Temple Wood site was part of a gradual transition of burial cairn to stone circle.

## Druids Circle

Cefn Coch, Penmaenmawr, Gwynedd
OS 115, (1in 107), SH722746
See map p29.
Undoubtedly an excellent viewpoint, as this fine stone circle stands on a grassy saddle of the Cefn Coch ridge, some 1,300ft (396m) above sea level. People of the Bronze Age raised a bank of boulders around the ring of thirty stones, ten of which remain standing. There is an entrance, 8ft (2.4m) wide through the embankment at the south-west, which was guarded by a portal of two large stones. Some of the remaining stones are nearly 6ft (1.8m) high.

The Druids Circle seems to have been placed at the junction of ancient trackways where the stones stood conspicuously against the skyline. The granite uprights are not of local rock, but were probably carried from Snowdonia by the movement of glaciers. The centre of the circle contained a stone burial cist which held a large food vessel and a child cremation, and was surrounded by a scattering of quartz pebbles. North of this burial area was a similar urn with another child cremation, this time with a small bronze knife. A third pit some distance away contained a lining of whetstones and more human remains. The position of the standing stones and the

*Druids Circle, Penmaenmawr*

cremated remains of children has led to various explanations and folk tales concerning sacrifical ceremonies. Even so, the circle may have been a meeting place and religious centre. The surrounding moorland contains many ancient remains and trackways, occupied in earlier times by Neolithic people who fashioned stone axes at the nearby Graiglwyd axe 'factory'.

**Access**  From Penmaenmawr take the Sychnant Pass road to a point where it bifurcates at a central island. Just beyond this junction a minor road points towards the hills in a south-easterly direction. At the foot of the hill called Foel Lus a track-way climbs and swings past Ty'n-y-ffrith to Bryn Derwydd, and thence a westerly course to the stone circle. Distance from Penmaenmawr is nearly 2 miles (2.9km).

The site may also be reached via a maze of minor roads from the Conwy valley. For example, by twisting routes to Garnedd Wen (SH750738) or Tyddyn grasod (SH744746), and thence by delightful moorland paths. It is advisable to have a 1:25,000 Ordnance Survey map, sheet SH77/87, Second Series, for this expedition.

### Rollright Stones

Little Rollright, Long Compton,
Oxfordshire
OS 151, (1in 145), SP296308
Lying on the border of Warwickshire and Oxfordshire is a
stone circle known as the King's
Men, and marked as such on the
Ordnance Survey map. It is a
large circle of seventy-seven
stones composed of pock-
marked, weather-beaten blocks
of limestone. The circle is made
up of a variety of stones of
different heights and shapes, and
is about 100ft (30m) in diameter.
To the north across the road lies
a solitary stone called the King's
Stone, which is possibly
associated with the circle.
Standing about 8ft (2.4m) high,
it may have been used as a
sighting stone for astronomical
purposes.

Close by and east of the stone
circle are the remains of a burial
chamber called the Whispering
Knights. Notice how they
appear to be locked in conver-
sation! The three separate sites

*Swinside Stone Circle*

possibly date from the Early
Bronze Age.

**Access**   Situated to the west of
the A34, Shipston-on-Stour to
Oxford road, the monuments lie
on higher ground, 2 miles
(3.2km) south of Long Compton
village, and close by the minor
road linking the A34 and the
A44. A convenient layby allows
parking, and the sites, although

privately owned, may be
reached by short footpaths. A
small admission charge is
payable.

### Swinside Circle

Broughton in Furness, Cumbria
OS 96, (1in 88), SD172883

---

## STANDING STONES

---

Moving from the Late Neolithic times into the
Bronze Age, it is probable that the Beaker Folk
influenced the practice of erecting circles and
standing stones. In the main they are to be found
in the moorland and upland areas of Britain,
free-standing or in pairs or rows. The reason for
their existence is open to several interpretations.
They are at their most impressive when set on
open land against a background of rising terrain,
particularly seen against storm clouds. In County
Antrim, the mountain road travelling north-
west from Larne has a solitary standing stone, at
D336043, seemingly pointing the way through a
gap in the high land. So here is one explanation:
it acts as a landmark, a directional marker,

which guided travellers and traders through
difficult country such as forests, swamps or
mountains. Likewise it is noticeable how many of
these stones stand at the head of river valleys.
Seafarers would be guided into the calm sheltered
waters of Larne Lough using this distant monolith,
standing clear on the flat high plateau between
Agnew's Hill and Sallagh Braes. This mountain
road may have been a trade route eventually
linking up with other ways to the Tievebulliagh
Neolithic 'axe factory' in the north-east of
Antrim.

In North Wales a number of ancient trackways
defined by standing stones lead past mounds,
cairns and stone circles in the direction of Graiglwyd 'axe factory' behind Penmaenmawr. In
fact, some stone circles have centre pillars in
them which could be taken as directional
markers or landmarks for important prehistoric

routes. For example, Kerry Hill stone circle (SO158860), lies near the Clun-Clee trackway, an important prehistoric route between the Irish Sea and the Severn Basin. Standing stones may have been part of a stone circle, the other stones long since disappeared and the site covered over or ploughed in. As a solitary marker, the tall monolith may have acted as a pointer to a cult centre, a sacred place where religious ceremonies were held. Indeed, it is feasible that the stones themselves, whether alone or as part of a stone circle, may have been worshipped. They were thought to have magical powers, and were important factors in fertility rites.

It is certain that the strength and enthusiasm of religious feeling enabled these people to drag huge stones into position from a site some distance away. It has been suggested that another reason for this hard labour was to utilise the erected lines of stones, stone circles and standing stones as simple astronomical observaatories. Maybe the lines of stone rows or isolated pillars were used to fix a bearing on to a prominent landscape feature, such as a peak or pass, and then observing the full moon rising and setting behind it. Despite their lack of knowledge of mathematical calculations, it might just have been possible for our ancestors to assess these primitive observations to the point of estimating the time of an eclipse. What a dramatic event that would have been in the lives of these early people!

---

### Identifying Features

- The standing stones may be solitary, or more than one some distance apart, or in some cases a number of stones set in rows.
- The stone or stones may be part of an existing stone circle after the other uprights have long since disappeared.
- Many standing stones may be found in upland and moorland areas.
- Look for evidence of stone circles, stone rows, burial mounds or cairns in the vicinity of a standing stone.

- Many standing stones are aligned on natural features. Pairs of stones are common in the areas where circles and alignments are frequent. These are probably best regarded as short alignments.
- Many naturally sited stones are given fanciful names, and it should not be assumed that they are prehistoric monuments. For example, weather-eroded rocks, boulders, rocking stones and the sandstone sarsen stones called 'grey wethers', that litter the chalk downland of Wiltshire.

---

### Outstanding Sites

**The Devil's Arrows**
Boroughbridge, Ripon, North Yorkshire
OS 99, (1in 91), SE391666
Close to the busy A1 trunk road and subjected to the constant roar of traffic stand three massive standing stones. The tops of the stones are heavily grooved by weathering, although some believe the flutings were made for some unknown purpose by the people who erected them. They stand in a fair line on a north to south axis, and appear to be aligned to the religious sites at Thornborough and Hutton Moor east of Ripon, which include henges, a cursus and barrows. There were originally four stones, but one was believed to have been destroyed by treasure seekers in the sixteenth century. These huge monoliths of millstone grit were probably quarried near Knaresborough, and were most likely dragged 6½ miles (10.4km) with great effort to their present site. The largest stone at the southern end is 22½ft (6.85m), and proceeding northwards, the heights are 21ft (6.4m) and 18ft (5.4m) respectively.

**Access** On the western side of Boroughbridge, at a point before the by-road to Roecliffe passes beneath the A1. Two stones are situated in the field on the right and the third is beside the road on the left, partially hidden by trees. A closer examination of the two stones is possible, providing one remembers to keep close by the hedge, and taking care not to disturb growing crops.

**Rudston Monolith**
Rudston Village, Bridlington,
Humberside
OS 101 (1in 93), TA097677
This famous pillar of stone
stands in Rudston churchyard,
and is probably the tallest
standing stone in Britain, 25½ft
(7.7m) high. At its base it is 6ft
(1.8m) by 3ft (0.9m). It has been
said that there is a similar
amount underground.
Composed of gritstone, the
nearest source seems to be at

least 10 miles (16km) away at
Cayton. Clearly its significance
must have been great to justify
the tremendous labour and
ingenuity involved. The area
around this historic settlement
contains traces of three
enigmatic cursus monuments.
Observable only from the air, or
possibly from the church tower,
these Late Neolithic banked
earthworks lead into the valley
of the Gypsey Race, and appear
to point to the huge stone in the

village churchyard. There is a
smaller stone on the north-east
side of the churchyard, close to a
burial cist composed of sandstone slabs.

The stones were probably
erected in the Bronze Age, and
Rudston is an example of a
sacred pagan site being taken
over by the Christian church; in
this case just after the Norman
Conquest.

*Rudston Monolith*

*Clach an Trushal*

**Castell Bryn Gwyn Standing
Stones and Earthwork** (DoE)
Brynsiencyn, Anglesey,
Gwynedd
OS 114 (1in 106), SH462669
Two standing stones 13ft (3.9m)
and 10ft (3.0m) high respectively
are to be found close a to field
wall. It is possible that they are

the remains of a stone circle, and
are therefore a religious or ceremonial part of Castell Bryn
Gwyn earthwork. The site of this
latter monument is ¼ mile
(400m) to the north-east. The
earthwork is about 180ft (54m)
in diameter, enclosed by a bank
some 12ft (3.6m) high and 40ft

(12m) wide. Excavations have
shown that the site was begun
early, perhaps as a henge monument, but was made, remade
and adapted as a defensive
earthwork.
**Access**   1½ miles (2.4km) west
of Brynsiencyn village,
Llanidan, on the A4080. Take a

footpath heading north-east, some 300yd (274m) before the junction with the B4419 road. The standing stones lie a short distance along the footpath. Continue another 300yd (274m) further on to reach Castell Bryn Gwyn earthwork. Alternatively, approach from the by-road running north-west from Brynsiencyn to Caer Leb Iron Age Earthwork (SH473675). The footpath continues south-west to Castell Bryn Gwyn and the standing stones.

**Clach an Trushal**
Barvas, Stornoway, Isle of Lewis, Western Isles
OS 8, (1in 8), NB375537

**Callanish Standing Stones**
Callanish, Stornoway, Isle of Lewis, Western Isles
OS 8, (1in 8), NB213330

# BRITAIN'S GREAT CIRCLE HENGES

*Avebury Avenue*

*Avebury Stone Circle*

**Avebury** (NT and DoE)
Marlborough, Wiltshire
OS 173 (1in 157), SU103700
Just north of the Vale of Pewsey in Wiltshire and set below the western slopes of the Marl-borough Downs lies the mightiest stone circle henge in the British Isles. Avebury is one of the most impressive sites in Europe, lying at the centre of a network of ancient trackways that converged on this important meeting place. The monument probably dates from Late Neolithic times spreading into the Bronze Age. Finds of pottery suggest that the first phase of its construction was begun in the Late Neolithic period around 2,500-2,000BC, when the site probably consisted of three stone circles with the avenue of stones leading from the south-east. From pottery finds in the later levels it would appear that the Beaker Folk constructed an enormous bank and ditch, surrounding the stone circles and destroying the northern one. The raising of the bank may have taken place simultaneously with the completion of the final inner stone circle.

Standing on top of the outer mound it is staggering to imagine the fantastic physical effort needed to excavate the ditch, which even today, silted up, varies in depth from 23ft (7m) to 33ft (10m), and a ground level width of nearly 70ft (21.3m). The great bank of raised up material is still 18ft (5.5m) high in some parts.

One can only surmise that the surrounding area supported a fairly large population, who, driven on by religious or communal forces, laboured long and hard over many years, not only in the excavation of the ditch and the raising of the banks, but in the enormous task of dragging sarsen stones, some weighing in the region of forty tons, up and down slopes, and setting them accurately and firmly in their allotted positions.

The circle today encloses an area of some 28½ acres (11.5ha), large enough to contain the greater part of the modern village of Avebury. The great circle of stones round the rim of the inner enclosure may once have contained ninety-eight standing sarsens, of which only twenty-seven remain upright today. Blocks of concrete mark the positions of the missing stones. Of the two inner stone circles, the northerly one consisted of two circles, with an inner ring which once contained three large sarsens. Only two of these stones now remain upright. The southerly stone circle has a diameter similar to the northerly one, ie of over 300ft (103.6m), and which once probably contained over thirty sarsen stones. Today, five stones remain standing in the south-western segment close by the Marlborough road. The southern stone circle once enclosed a tall central stone pillar named the Obelisk. Near to the pillar's original setting is a line of small holes suggesting an enclosure of unknown purpose. Sadly, many of the fine sarsen stones were destroyed in the seventeenth century through a combination of religious beliefs and a desire to turn the land to profitable farming use. It is believed that some stones were heated, then split by the application of cold water, and finally pulverised with hammer blows.

Visitors approaching Avebury from the south by the B4003 road will be able to obtain a first class view of the avenue of paired stones. Look for the combination of pillar shape and lozenge shape which may be meant to represent male and female. It is believed that the rows of stones once led to the Sanctuary stone circle on Overton Hill (SU118679), close by the ancient track called the Ridgeway.

### Stonehenge (DoE)
Amesbury, Wiltshire
OS 184 (1in 167), SU123422
This is undoubtedly the most famous of British stone circles. Due to the tremendous number of visitors, access to the site is now via a subway from an assembly area containing vehicle park, refreshment and publication stalls. Close inspection of the stones is not possible as the central area is roped off.

The monument can be regarded as the ultimate design of a prehistoric religious circle, and despite its popularity, many visitors do not fully understand its complicated history. One great misconception is its presumed connection with the Druids. Although the great temple and other stone circles were used to celebrate solar and astronomical ceremonies, it should be stated that the Druid cult was not introduced into Britain until the stone circles were a thousand years old.

As a large church or cathedral is altered over the centuries, so Stonehenge has passed through similar architectural stages. In its earliest form, Phase I, constructed in the Late Neolithic Period, 2,700-2,500 BC, Stonehenge was a henge monument consisting of a ditch with an internal bank measuring some 325ft (100m) in diameter, with an entrance at the north-east facing the Heel Stone. This sarsen stone 16ft (4.8m) high probably dates back to this first phase of construction. Just within the interior bank is a ring of fifty-six small holes called Aubrey Holes, now marked by fillings of chalk. The purpose of these pits is unknown, although many of them held cremated remains. Also, on excavation of the ditch, examples of grooved pottery were found.

About 2,100 BC, the Beaker Folk constructed two parallel lines of earthen banks from Stonehenge. The Avenue ran north-east at first, then east and finally south-east to the River Avon, a distance of $1\frac{3}{4}$ miles (2.8km). Part of the ditch round the henge was filled in to widen the entrance to the Avenue. Then follows one of the wonderful mysteries that has teased minds for so long; some eighty-two blocks of stone,

*Stonehenge*

mostly blue speckled dolerite, were dragged up the Avenue to the earthwork henge. Unless these stones had been deposited in the area after glaciation (and this is considered improbable), this could only mean a tremendously difficult journey of 200 miles (322km) over land and water from the Preseli Hills in south-west Wales. These bluestones were shaped into rectangular blocks and erected in a double circle, but strangely the task was never finished.

About this time, 1,900BC, the task of erecting the bluestones was halted and decision taken to make the circle henge a really impressive temple — a centrepiece for the whole area. The bluestones were taken down and replaced by huge sarsen stones from the Marlborough Downs which were laboriously dragged to the site. The sides of the stones were pounded, dressed, rubbed smooth, and raised into the positions of a circle and an inner semi-circle that can be seen today. Tongues had been carved out of the top of the trilithon uprights, which would have fitted into sockets on the lintels — a marvellous prehistoric mortice and tenon joint. The design of the temple required the stones to be shaped to complement the curve of the circle and to heighten the feeling of persepctive. Also at this time two large uprights were raised to command the entrance to the monument. Only one still survives, fancifully called the Slaughter Stone.

A change of design came in the next phase when some of the original discarded bluestones were erected within the sarsen horseshoe of trilithons. Outside the great sarsen circle, a double circle of holes, called the Y and Z holes, were dug to accommodate the rest of the bluestones. But, for some unknown reason (perhaps a change of plan or lack of resources), these holes were not used. Finally, by 177BC, the bluestones were dismantled and erected as a circle of pillars inside the main stone circle, thus constituting a horsehoe of uprights within the five trilithons.

## ROUND BARROWS

It is true to say that the round barrows or cairns are the most common field monuments in England and Wales. Representing the Bronze Age, it has been estimated that many thousands survive. In most examples, the barrow consists of a circular grass-covered mound of earth and stone rubble, or a cairn of stones and boulders. Sometimes in stony areas, round barrows or cairns frequently have their circumference marked by a retaining kerb of stones. In the nineteenth century enthusiastic barrow diggers dug into the mounds, inexpertly in many cases, searching for believed caches of treasure. Their hurried excavations left the tops of the mounds scarred with shallow pits and depressions. Much damage was caused, precious objects simply disappeared, or were melted down, and valuable archaeological evidence was inadvertently destroyed.

Although there is little evidence of settlements, and of the domestic life of the Early Bronze Age, it is the provision for the dead that has revealed such a fascinating picture of their lifestyle. It is as well to contemplate the organisation of this society, which was able to design and carry out the construction tasks involved in the raising of these burial mounds. In southern England, the so-called 'Wessex Culture' erected several types of barrow which seem to represent the graves of important members of the tribal hierarchy. From the evidence we have, it is possible to picture the preliminaries, preparation and actual construction work involved in the erection of a round barrow. First of all, the siting of the burial mound was an important decision, although invariably the favoured positions were on or near hilltops, in upland country, or making use of rises in the terrain. It is also possible that the barrow had to be sited near a settlement, so that the mound was clearly visible, as it was a sacred place, or as a marker defining some form of tribal boundary.

The initial construction phase of the barrow may well have been the simple describing of a circle, using a cord tied to a central stake. Excavations have shown that in most cases, the turves were first removed from the barrow area surface. Also, that the grave or cist was cut into the ground or out of the rock, by the use of deer antler picks, deer and ox scapulae, stone and flint axes and even wooden shovels. Similar tools were also employed in excavating the ditches surrounding the barrows. Examinations of ditches have shown that they appeared to have been dug by different groups of labourers, as the various sections do not seem to join up properly.

Beaker burials consist of human remains buried in contracted positions, together with tools, weapons and food for the after-life. In some cases bodies were simply laid on the ground surface, lying on a bier of leaves or an animal skin, or placed in wooden mortuary houses. In Northern Britain, remains have been buried in tree-trunk coffins, or in stone-lined cists, where some of the slabs were engraved with cup and ring marks, spirals and other simple designs. It is possible that more than one burial was placed in the centre of the sacred area waiting for the time, when with due ceremony, the remains were covered by layers of turf, earth and stones. Throughout the Bronze Age the tradition of burying bodies became intermingled with cremation burials, and sometimes inhumation and cremation burials were interred in the same barrow.

Earth and rubble was used to raise the mound, such as limestone or chalk, usually obtained from the excavated ditch surrounding the barrow. Turves or boulders would be piled around the grave or cist, and basketloads of material from the ditch would be piled on to the cairn. In stony areas the cairn would be composed of boulders and large stones.

In the prosperous Wessex Culture of the Early Bronze Age, the barrows seem to represent the burial places of some powerfully organised society whose aristocracy were buried with elaborate rituals. Hence, the magnificent barrow cemeteries of Dorset and Wiltshire, which include different recognisable types, such as bowl, bell, disc, saucer and pond barrows. Excavations have indicated that sometimes the remains of adult males were interred in bell barrows, and as personal ornaments and household implements have been found in disc barrows, it has been assumed that female remains were buried there. Many barrows are still visible today despite centuries of farming. Sadly, in recent times, a considerable number of mounds were used as a ready-made training ground for military vehicles.

---

**Bowl Barrows**
**Identifying Features**

● Most areas contain examples of bowl barrows covering the whole of the Bronze and Iron Ages. Their surviving numbers run into many thousands.

● The bowl-shaped barrow is the most common type of round burial mound, the earlier ones usually having a surrounding ditch.

● A circular grass-covered mound of earth and stone rubble, or a rounded pile of stones and boulders.

● The mound may have been disturbed in the past, leaving pits and hollows, or a displacement and scattering of the stones and boulders.

● An outer retaining kerb of stones may still be visible.

● The mound may contain a stone-lined cist or burial compartment.

● They are generally sited in upland or moorland country like Exmoor. They are common on the chalk downlands of southern England and on the moors of north-east Yorkshire and Northumberland.

● In some cases the barrows are as small as 30ft to 50ft (9.1m-15.2m) in diameter, and others with larger dimensions exceeding 100ft (30.5m) in diameter may be up to 20ft (6.1m) high.

● The methods of interment may be of a crouched burial, or an extended inhumation, or a cremation placed in a pottery vessel.

● In the north some cairns contain interments with food vessels, and there are examples of cup and ring marks on kerbstones and cist slabs.

● In the Early and Middle Bronze Age the interments were accompanied by items of a personal and domestic nature, such as ornaments, weapons and tools.

## Outstanding Sites

**Setta Barrow,** SS726381
**Five Barrows,** SS732368
**Two Barrows,** SS748363
Simonsbath, Exmoor, Somerset
OS 180, (1in 163)
Standing high on the south-western edge of Exmoor, a ridgeway road offers a splendid opportunity to enjoy the commanding views south to the distant tors of Dartmoor and in the opposite direction, across the wooded valleys and sweeping upland of Exmoor to the superb northern coastline. The rounded hills display a canvas of curving contours that rapidly change colour as clouds hurry over them. When the sun is hidden, and storms threaten the hill tops, the dark shapes of the barrows rise boldly against the sombre lines of the moor.

The ridgeway followed by the county boundary between Devon and Somerset runs south-east along Bray and Fyldon Commons, and contains a string of burial mounds. Over the centuries Exmoor's barrows have been plundered by opportunists seeking caches of supposedly hidden treasure; but no doubt there are still more remote mounds waiting to be investigated. In your wanderering, go well prepared, as Exmoor is noted for its violent changes of mood and weather.

Setta Barrow sits prominently on the skyline, at an altitude of 1,555ft (474m), guarded by two satellite mounds. It is about 99ft (30.2m) across, 7ft (2m) high with a clear circle of retaining kerb stones and signs of a surrounding ditch. Rather imperiously, the county boundary wall cuts right through the centre of the barrow. Travelling a short distance south-east, the road bisects a second group of tumuli, and continues north of an extensive site marked Five Barrows, 1,618ft (493m) above sea level. In fact there are almost double that number at this impressive location, including one bell barrow. However, viewed from other moorland vantage points, it is interesting to note that only five can be seen. The site at Two Barrows (actually there are four), 1,585ft (483m) high, some 1¼ miles (2.0km) further on, offers another grand viewpoint overlooking the valley of Kinsford Water and the upper reaches of the River Barle.

**Access** From Simonsbath in the upper Barle valley, take the minor road south-west climbing over the moor for 3 miles (4.8km) to the ridgeway road at Kinsford Gate. The Two Barrows site lies ½ mile (0.8km) to the left, and to the right, is Five Barrows ¾ mile (1.2km) and Setta Barrow, 1½ miles (2.4km).

### Rillaton Barrow
Minions, Bodmin Moor,
Cornwall
OS 201, (1in 186), SX260719
The numerous Bronze Age antiquities on the higher land of the south-west peninsula are evidence of a flourishing pastoral society. The results of pollen analysis of the old land surface under barrows on Bodmin Moor point to a landscape of clumps of trees and open heathland. The Bronze Age people were farmers, and it can be assumed that they practised a shifting cultivation. It seems that the tree cover was reduced in one area and the land cultivated by means of a simple plough. The thin soils gradually lost their fertility and the people moved on, repeating in another spot. The effectiveness of man's interference with this forest cover brought about the growth of heathland, the degradation of the upland soils, and the rapid spread of blanket bog.

The forest clearances probably commenced in the late Neolithic period and continued throughout the Bronze Age. Upland settlement sites were accompanied by a range of ceremonial monuments and meeting places such as circular earthworks, burial mounds, stone circles and stone alignments. On Bodmin Moor a line of three stone circles called The Hurlers point to the hilltop and the commanding position of Rillaton Barrow. This Early Bronze Age round barrow, now consisting of a great ragged pile of stones, is about 120ft (36.6m) across and 8ft (2.4m) high. High on the eastern side of the mound is a rectangular stone-lined cist which contained a famous corrugated sheet gold cup, a single skeleton, a broken pottery vessel, beads of the blue glassy material called faience and an Early Bronze Age dagger. The cup, 3¼in (83mm) high, with a thin riveted handle, had quite an interesting history of travel, including a disappearance for some time. It was eventually recovered and is now to be found in the British Museum. The faience beads were probably made in the Eastern Mediterranean and most likely traded for local tin. The rich grave goods point to some similarity with the 'Wessex Culture' burials.

Nearer to our own times, in the 1830s, man's involvement once more brought distinct changes to the area. Mining operations scarred the eastern part of Bodmin Moor, for in the space of two decades, there were twenty-five mines at work exploiting the surface tin deposits and the rich veins of copper ore. However, after another few decades, the moorland slopes had returned to their former solitude, disturbed only by the breezy upland wind and the presence of sheep and buzzards. To the monuments of standing stones, barrows and hut circles, man has added the derelict engine houses of the former mines.

**Access**   The barrow is situated ¼ mile (400m) north of The Hurlers stone circles. From the road junction at Minions proceed north for ¼ mile (400m). Take the track to the left, and as it swings round to the north-west, bear left up to the barrow which lies on the highest ground.

## Loose Howe Round Barrow

Rosedale Moor, North York Moors, North Yorkshire
OS 94, (1in 86), NZ703008
There are very many Bronze Age barrows or howes on the North York Moors, and they are generally called by a word derived from the old Scandinavian for a low hill. Many have been damaged by nineteenth-century excavators searching for treasure, or robbed of stone for building purposes.

High on the Rosedale Moors at 1,400ft (427m) stands a barrow with an interesting history. This earthen mound is about 60ft (18.3m) in diameter, 7ft (2.1m) high, the whole defined by a retaining kerb, and set on a gently rising, heather-covered slope. On excavation by F. and H.W. Elgee in 1937, it was found to contain a dugout canoe coffin, 8ft (2.4m) long and 2ft 3in (0.7m) wide; the human remains had not survived. The only items recovered were a tiny piece of shoe with two lace holes, some linen fibre and the remnants of a bronze knife. There was evidence that rushes or straw had been placed in the coffin for the body to lie on, together with a straw or grass pillow. Close by lay another boat-shaped dugout canoe that had probably served as the lid of the coffin.

The use of these canoes may have been symbolic, representing the last journey of a chief. This assumption is possible as there is no navigable stretch of water near the barrow.

**Access**   From Rosedale village proceed up the valley for ¾ mile (1.2km). Bear right and take the road that climbs steeply on to Rosedale Moor for a distance of 2½ miles (4.0km). The barrow, which is named on the map, is situated on higher ground on the eastern side of the road.

Approached from the north it is 2 miles (3.2km) east-south-east of Rosedale Head.

## Nether Largie (North) Cairn

(Doe)
Kilmartin, Lochgilphead, Strathclyde Region
OS 55, (1in 52), NR831985
At one time the sea came right up to the present site of Kilmartin village, as the nearby raised beaches testify. Gradually the waters retreated, and in time a fertile valley emerged. The Kilmartin area was first settled by Neolithic people who came in from the sea, finding this sheltered and accessible spot protected from the fury of the Atlantic gales. They were

*Nether Largie Carved Axes*

followed by the Bronze Age people who exploited a local vein of copper ore and left evidence of their settlement in the form of burial cairns, stone circles and inscribed rocks. Subsequently, the area became an important meeting place of routes from the coast to Loch Fyne and further inland.

The Nether Largie (North) Cairn covers a burial chamber which can be entered from the top. The cairn is 70ft (21.3m) in diameter and 9ft (2.7m) high situated within a low rubble bank. The central cist has a covering slab bearing carvings of axeheads, as well as forty-one cup marks on its surface. An end slab of the cist has two axeheads carved on its inner surface. The carvings of the axeheads are probably symbolic, being too shallow to be of any use as bronze axe-head moulds. Perhaps they were inscribed to illustrate the importance of copper in the life and prosperity of this Bronze Age community and its chief.

**Access** The site is situated 8 miles (12.8km) north of Lochgilphead and 27 miles (43.5km) south of Oban. Proceed south of Kilmartin village for ½ mile (800m), and then turn right on a by-road to cross over the Kilmartin Burn. Vehicles may be parked at the foot of the lane which is the next turning to the right. The cairns are signposted at this point.

As well as the Nether Largie (North) Cairn, there are other monuments in the immediate vicinity, such as:

Nether Largie (Mid) Cairn (NR831984)
Nether Largie (South) Cairn (NR828979)
Glebe Cairn (NR833989)
Ri Cruin Cairn (NR826971)
Dunchraigaig Cairn (NR833968)
Temple Wood Stone Circle (NR827978)

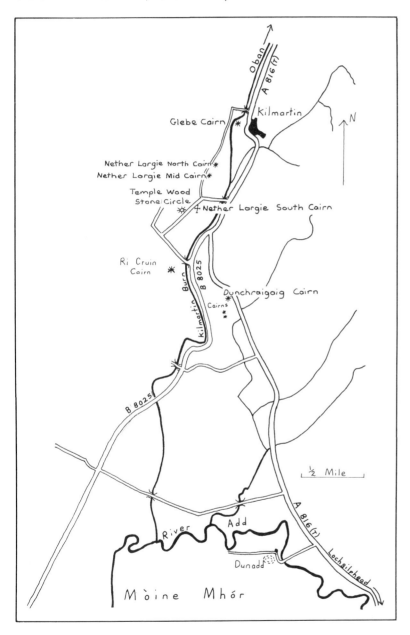

## Other Round Barrows
## Identifying Features

### Bell Barrows
● These spectacular barrows are constructed with a berm or platform between the mound and the surrounding ditch, and occasionally possess an outer bank.

● Some are more easily recognised than others, particularly those barrows with clearly defined berms, which are in some cases 12ft-15ft (3.6m-4.5m) wide.

● Some berms are level, others slope into the ditch, and others are raised above the level of the ground.

● The bell barrow has an average diameter of between 100ft-160ft (30.5m-48.8m).

● The mound usually contained cremated remains of a male adult, accompanied by rich grave-goods — the final resting place of a warrior chief.

● Mainly found on the chalk downlands of Wiltshire and Dorset, in south-east and south-west England, and in East Anglia.

● There are examples of bell barrows having more than one mound within the surrounding ditch.

### Disc Barrows
● This type of barrow consists of a wide inner platform containing a small mound.

● A circular, or sometimes oval ditch, accompanied by an outer bank surrounds the central area.

● Sometimes the central area supports twin tumps.

● The overall diameter of the disc barrow compares favourably with that of the bell barrow.

● The small inner mound usually contained evidence believed to be that of a female burial. Cremated remains were usually accompanied by such items as personal jewellery, pottery and household implements.

● They are normally located in the same areas as bell barrows.

### Saucer Barrows
● Usually a small barrow, consisting of a low shallow mound some 30ft-40ft (9.1m-12.2m) in diameter.

● The low central area is frequently enclosed by a ditch and outer bank.

● Saucer barrows are not very common, and excavations of a small number of mounds have revealed burials in some and cremations in others.

### Pond Barrows
● An uncommon form of barrow, examples of which are to be found among barrow groups in Wiltshire and Dorset.

● The barrow consists of a shallow circular depression surrounded by an outer bank, and varying in diameter from 30ft to 120 ft (9.1m-36-6m).

● Little is known about this type of barrow, but it may have been used for ritual purposes prior to interment or cremation elsewhere.

## Outstanding Sites

### Normanton Down Barrow Group (DoE)
Wilsford, Amesbury, Wiltshire
OS 184, (1in 167), SU120413 (centre)
South of Stonehenge, and across the busy A303, stretches a line of barrows roughly west to east, representing practically all the various types of 'Wessex Culture' burial mounds. Unfortunately, some of the examples

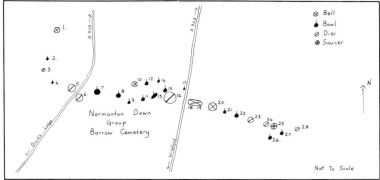

situated on the periphery of the line have been damaged or destroyed by farming. However, within the area contained by two rights of way there are a number under the protection of the DoE.

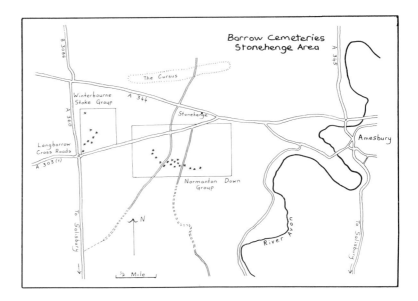

**Bell Barrow** (Number 1)
This impressive monument, situated some distance from the main sweep of mounds, is 174ft (53.5m) in diameter and 11ft (3.3m) high. On excavation it was found to contain male skeletal remains, two bronze daggers, an ornamented beaker and deer antlers.
**Access**  The barrow is situated to the north of the wood called Normanton Gorse, and may be reached by using the western of the two tracks leading south from the A303. After ¼ mile (400m), bear right across the field for 220yd (200m).

*No 1 Bell Barrow, Normanton Down*

**Disc Barrows** (Numbers 5 and 6)
SU116413 (centre)
These two superb disc barrows lie close together to the east of Normanton Gorse Wood, one on either side of the track. Number 5, situated on the western side of the right of way is 200ft (61.0m) in diameter and contained a cremation, beads of shale, amber and glazed pottery. Number 6, situated on the other side of the track to the south-east, was excavated to reveal a cremation burial. This disc barrow measures some 191ft (58.2m) across.
**Access**  From the A303 road take the western of the two tracks at SU118418, for 660yd (600m).

**Bowl Barrow** (Number 7)
This famous barrow, known as Bush Barrow, yielded a fascinating array of grave goods which must have represented the last resting place of a wealthy tribal chief. The skeleton of a tall man was accompanied by two bronze daggers, one with a wooden handle inlaid with tiny gold rivets, a bronze axe showing traces of fibre, a wooden and bronze shield and a polished stone macehead. Across his chest was a lozenge-shaped sheet of gold, which may have been an ornament attached to his clothes.

**Access** As for disc barrows 5 and 6. The bowl barrow lies some 115ft (35m) to the north-east of the latter disc barrow.

**Bell Barrow** (Number 10)
The monument is 135ft (41m) in diameter and 10ft (3m) high. The mound yielded a cremation burial with an incense cup, together with items of personal jewellery of amber and gold. Other objects recovered were gold-coated amber discs and a gold-covered cone.
**Access** This bell barrow lies east-north-east of the western-

most right of way across Normanton Down. As you walk towards the A360, the mound is situated some 282yd (258m) from disc barrow number 6.

**Saucer Barrow** Number 25
This is located towards the end of the barrow cemetery, being some 382yd (350m) east of the eastern right of way across Normanton Down heading for Springbottom Farm and Wilsford.

### Winterbourne Stoke Crossroads Barrow Groups (NT)

Winterbourne Stoke, Shrewton, Wiltshire
OS 184, (1in 167), SU102417
This barrow cemetery runs in a line north-east from the busy intersection of the A303 and the A360. From the crossroads the main distribution commences with a Neolithic long barrow, and is succeeded by a fine

selection of the major barrow types. To the north a small group lies close by the A360. The long barrow is some 240ft (73m) long and 10ft (3m) high. It contained the primary burial of a male skeleton, and six later burials, possibly of a family, interred with a food vessel and flint scraping tool.

Along the northern edge of the wood lies a Bowl Barrow, Number 1 and a Bell Barrow,

Number 3. Between these two mounds lies a Pond Barrow, Number 2, which overlaps the bell barrow. Bell Barrow, Number 3, some 180ft (54.9m) across and 12ft (3.7m) high was the source of a most interesting find. A wooden box holding a cremation was accompanied by a bone pin, tweezers and two bronze daggers.

The smaller group of barrows to the north of the long barrow

*Lambourne Bowl Barrows*

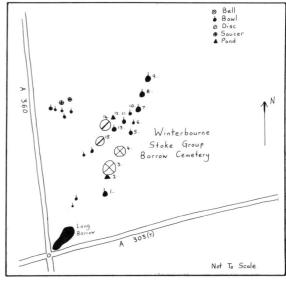

includes five bowl barrows and two saucer barrows, although one of the latter type is now very indistinct.

Barrow Number 14 is a large disc barrow measuring some 174ft (53m) across and displaying three burial tumps. All were found to contain cremated remains. Barrow Number 12 can be clearly identified as a pond barrow.

**Access**  There is an entry to the site by means of a gate, a few yards east of the crossroads on the A303.

## Lambourn Barrow Group

Lambourn Downs, Lambourn, Berkshire
OS 174, (1in 158), SU328829
This is another important barrow cemetery that contains examples of about forty barrows of the major round barrow types. They were numbered by L.V. Grinsell and H. Case. However, only the group set in two rows on the northern side of the sharp bend are accessible for inspection. The mound situated nearest the road is a Disc Barrow, Number 13. It measures some 100ft (30m) in diameter with a low central tump 1ft (0.3m) high. Walking up the track, the next monument is a Bowl Barrow, Number 9, that is nearly 60ft (18m) across and standing 6ft (1.8m) high. Here, excavation revealed a walled cist of sarsen stones containing a cremation in a collared urn, and covered by a capstone. Barrows Number 8 and 10 are of the twin

*Bowl Barrows, Lambourn*

bowl type enclosed by a single ditch. In fact, this combination extends to a length of nearly 100ft (30m). Furthest away from the road the last monument is a large disc or saucer barrow some 118ft (36m) in diameter. Instantly recognisable with its earthen tree ring bank is a ditched Bowl Barrow, Number 12 situated second in line nearest the road. It measures 70ft (21.3m) in diameter and stands 7ft (2.1m) high.

**Access**  Take the B4001 north from Lambourn village for 1½ miles (2.4km). Bear left, and proceed for 1 mile (1.6km) to a point just beyond where the road turns sharp left. Access to the site is via the track that carries straight on.

## INSCRIBED STONES — CUP AND RING MARKS

The subject of decorated stones, cist slabs and ornamented outcrops of natural rock has frequently given rise to controversy. Despite the numbers of examples found, and the volume of theories expounded, their significance and purpose remain a complete mystery. In Yorkshire, Northumberland, Scotland and Ireland, engravings have been found on rock outcrops and within cairns and round barrows; often in the graves of people buried with beakers and food vessels. Similarly, inscriptions have been discovered on stones in chambered tombs and on standing stones. Because these patterns are often connected with burial places, it may be assumed that the symbols have a religious meaning. The 'cup and ring' marks are certainly associated with the Bronze Age people, who may have regarded them as having magical properties. There is also a broad similarity between the cup and ring markings and particular patterns found in the famous passage of graves of the Boyne Valley in

Ireland. It has also been recognised that comparable designs occur in the passage graves of Spain and Portugal.

The main form of pattern design is a simple cup-like depression surrounded by one or more continuous or broken concentric rings. From the Early Bronze Age the designs were chipped into a softer stone surface, probably by means of a heavy stone tool or even a metal punch. It is assumed that the sculptor made a number of pick marks side by side, then joined them together by chiselling or rubbing down the ridge between them. The 'cup and ring' motif is the most common form, the cups being usually no more than 2in (5cm) in diameter. Occasionally there is a duct running into the cup.

Some of the depressions thought to be cup marks, are in fact hollows naturally formed by solution. The points to watch out for to determine if they are man-made are that the hollows tend to be smooth, wider than they are deep, hemispherical and regular. At the same time, it should be remembered that the uncovered engravings have been affected by the action of water and ice,

and the depressions have become shallower.

Many variations occur in the designs. In some cases a single symbol is found, and in others they include arches, incomplete circles, squares, ovals, grids and patterns joined up with radiating channels. Some of the distinctive features found on the northern and western edges of Rombalds Moor in West Yorkshire include the linking of pairs of concentric circles by ladder-like markings. Elsewhere, designs include spirals, and these are important because the spiral in art is one of the most commonly used symbols in prehistoric religion. As the engraving of the markings would involve a very laborious and lengthy operation, it is fair to assume that the symbols held some very special meaning for the Bronze Age people. Possibly, because these designs are connected with burial or sacred places, they may be a representation of Earth Mother, the giver of life, the rings depicting eyes and breasts. The concentric circles may also depict the sun, which being the source of heat, would be of particular concern to the Bronze Age people in a time of climatic changes.

---

### Cup and Ring Marks
### Identifying Features

● Some patterns consist of cup-like depressions pecked out of the surface of the stone or rock.

● The natural hollows caused by water action usually have steeper sides, whereas the man-made cups tend to be smooth, wider than they are deep, circular, and normally some $1\frac{1}{2}$-2in (4-5cm) across.

● Some of the cup-like hollows are surrounded by a number of broken or continuous concentric

rings, sometimes with a duct running into the 'cup'.

● Sometimes the cup and ring markings are linked together. Other variations in design include circles, half-circles, arches, grids, ladders and spirals.

● The carvings may be found on stones or cist slabs within cairns, or round barrows, and on boulders, natural rock outcrops and standing stones.

---

### Outstanding Sites

**Rombald's Moor**
Ilkley, West Yorkshire
OS 104, (1in 96)
In Mid-Wharfedale, an ancient prehistoric way crosses Rombald's Moor, and this was the route used by settlers from

Ireland who first brought the early bronze weapons to Yorkshire, They also brought rock carving in the form of cup and ring markings. These engraved stones are to be found along the northern and western edges of

Rombald's Moor, on Addingham High Moor, Green Crag Slack and Rivock Edge. The influx of fresh cultures brought in new ideas, and it is possible that with the spread of settlements each tribal group had its own emblem, such as a branching design, a ladder symbol or a swastika. In some cases the early cup and ring designs were incorporated with the later symbols or carved separately on nearby rock faces. It is possible that such markings originated to ensure good hunting, and to secure a happy and prosperous future in the next life. Rombald's Moor was the home of thriving communities as emphasized by the location of several stone circles. For example, Grubstones (SE136447), Twelve Apostles (SE126451), and Hawks-worth Moor (SE134435). Also one of a number of burial cairns to be found is known as the Skirtful of Stones (SE141445).

### Swastika Stone

Woodhouse Crag, Ilkley, West Yorkshire
OS 104, (1in 96), SE094470

The swastika symbol has always been regarded as a sign of good fortune. Although it is dated by some authorities to the Iron Age because of its likeness to Celtic art, its general appearance resembles the spiral motif that was popular in Cretan decorative designs. If assigned to the Bronze Age, maybe this design found its way to Wessex and thence to Mid-Wharfedale, where the spiral shape influenced and became incorporated into the existing symbols.

The swastika carving may be found etched into a flat slab of gritstone rock on the rim of the crags. An unsightly iron railing topped by barbed wire surrounds the original engraving, as well as protecting a replica on a separate slab close by.

*Swastika Stone, Ilkley Moor*

**Access**   From the railway station proceed uphill via Wells Road for a distance of 1¼ miles (2.0km). Just before the Panorama Reservoir, note the weather beaten wooden signpost on the left. From here a short track gives access to the moor. At the gate bear right and follow the path to Woodhouse Crag. Distance from the signpost is approximately ½ mile (0.9km).

### Panorama Stone

Ilkley, West Yorkshire
OS 104, (1in 96), SE115473

The carvings are an elaborate example of concentric rings and thin lines. Linking the rings are a variety of ladder markings unusual in rock carvings, and which are found in this district. In the lower half of the design the markings are of a simpler form, and may well be copies of the more complicated figure. Originally sited at Panorama Rocks, the carved stones may now be found set behind railings in a small public park.

**Access**   From the railway station proceed uphill via Wells Road. Bear right at the first junction. The monument lies in a small public park opposite St Margaret's Church.

### Badger Stone

Ilkley Moor, West Yorkshire
OS 104, (1in 96), SE110460

This cone-shaped rock has the whole of one side covered with a connected design. It has broad grooves, but incorporates the swastika complete with whorls. This is such a fine and interesting design that it is possible to see it as a ceremonial burial monument to a tribal chief.

**Access**   Climb on to Ilkley Moor via the old Keighley

Road. Note the small stream on your left as you ascend the slope. At a point just beyond the spring line bear east across the moor for some 550yd (500m). The hunt for this stone is an interesting diversion and well worth seeking out. Its position is marked on the OS 1:50,000 map.

### Boho Inscribed Stones
Boho, Toneel North Townland, Enniskillen, Co Fermanagh
OS Northern Ireland, Sheet 17, (1in 7), H113462
The engravings are to be found on outcrops of rock situated on a sloping pasture overlooking this rural hamlet. There are six stones, five with cup and ring markings. The largest of the rocks, 11ft (3.3m) long and over

### Other Carved Stones on Ilkley Moor
There are many examples of carved stones on the moor, which may be located after some patient and diligent searching.

Here are listed some other carved stones with their map references:

7ft (2.1m) high is fairly covered with the inscriptions, some of which join together. Nearby, the patterns on a smaller stone are deeply carved. Given good light conditions, the markings are seen at their best later on in the day.
**Access**   The settlement is situated in Toneel North Townland, 1½ miles (2.4km) north-north-west of Boho and 7½ miles

Doubler Stones west (SE072465)
Barmishaw Stone (SE112464)
Willy Hall's Wood (SE115465)
Hanging Stones (SE128467)
Pancake Stone (SE133462)
Idol Rock (SE132458)

(12km) west-north-west of Enniskillen. Take the lane running alongside the church for a distance of ½ mile (800m). This swings back on itself and continues to climb steadily uphill. The inscribed stones are in the field in front of the bungalow, the site being marked on the New Series map, Sheet 17.

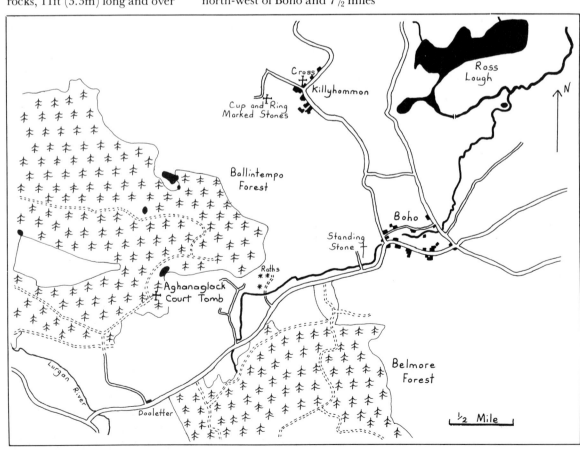

## Roughting Linn Inscribed Stone

Doddington, Berwick, Northumberland
OS 75, (1 in 64 and 71), NT984368
Lying close to the ramparts of an Iron Age Fort is an enormous tilted outcrop of sandstone. It rears above the grassy vegetation some 60ft (18.2m) by 40ft (12.2m) and its sloping surface is covered with a variety of engravings which include cup and ring marks, circles joined by grooves and flower-like designs.

*Roughting Linn Carved Stones*

Easily visible on one vertical surface is a finely engraved arch of three hollows and ridges.

Other fine examples of engraved rocks may be found after diligent searching at several places locally:
Doddington Moor (NU004317, NU009313, NU013328 — The Ringses)
Old Bewick hillfort (NU078216)
Lordenshaws hillfort (NZ054993)

**Access**  From the junction of the B6353 and B6525 roads west of the village of Lowick, proceed south for ½ mile (800m) to a crossing of minor roads. Bear right and continue for 2 miles (3.2km) along the lane. The site lies close to the junction of the lane with the track leading to Roughting Linn Farm. The rock outcrop is hidden behind the small copse of trees to the north-east.

## Cairnbaan Cup and Ring Markings

Lochgilphead, Mid Argyll
OS 55, (1 in 52), NR838910
This site contains fine cup and ring engravings with some symbols having four rings and radial grooves. There are also several smaller patterns including cup markings by themselves. Some of the separate symbols seem to be connected together by channels.

**Access**  The monument is situated some 2½ miles (4km) north-west of Lochgilphead via the A816 and the B841. The rock carvings, now protected by railings, may be reached by a short footpath.

Here are listed some other rock carvings in the locality with their map references:
Achnabreck (NR856906)
Kilmichael Glassary (NR858935)
Baluacraig (NR831970)

*Kilmichael Glassary Rock Carving*

# CHAPTER FOUR

# From Bronze Age to Iron Age

Towards the end of the Bronze Age, about 700BC, the upland and moorland areas previously favoured for settlement began to experience a deterioration of climate as the weather gradually became colder and wetter. The thin moorland soils were rapidly leached and the land was left impoverished. In time, these conditions led to waterlogged ground and the growth of blanket bog, peat, moss and heather.

The next important happening was the arrival of small bands of Celtic newcomers, who began to disturb the peaceful life of the native farmers and stock rearers, threatening their food supplies and livestock. Landing in south-east England, some groups eventually moved north using rivers to reach the north-east of the country and beyond. The most notable factor was their new knowledge of metal working, in particular iron. The production of iron is very different from that of bronze, for although the ore was far more easily available and easier to extract than copper or tin, iron was more difficult to forge, hammer and harden. The increased technical ability in iron-working gave the new arrivals a great superiority in the production of tools and weapons.

These settlers, named the Hallstatt people after the main excavation site in Austria, were the possessors of superior weapons, in particular heavy slashing swords that gave them a military advantage. This culture is also known as IRON A.

The introduction of iron marks a watershed in the history of mankind, altering the social structure and leading to an increase in strife and warfare. It became a period of great uncertainty for the indigenous Bronze Age people, and this unrest was destined to become the normal pattern of life in the Iron Age. Inevitably, skirmishes took place, the local inhabitants were quickly conquered, young men were killed and women and children carried off. In time the newcomers merged with the local population and the simple peasant life continued with a pattern of isolated farms and small settlements. A typical dwelling consisted of a circular structure with a central supporting rectangle of posts, and in some upland areas, mounds of small stones and stone slabbed troughs indicate the use of heated stones for cooking. Corn was grown and iron was worked in a number of communities. However, in such uncertain times it became necessary to defend the homesteads, and in a wider context, the earthen defences of forts began to appear on the upland vantage points. Some isolated lowland homesteads were defended by means of an artificial island, or crannog, constructed on timbers driven in or boulders placed in the shallow waters of a lake, estuary or marsh. In Ireland, another form of simple protected farmstead is the rath, usually a circular enclosure defended by a raised earthen bank. In some settlements another feature is the siting of an underground storage or refuge area called a souterrain or fogou.

The advent of defended houses is open to debate, but it is quite likely that the tradition of fortified vantage points, like hillforts, began in Bronze Age times. In Scotland, brochs were raised as places of refuge in uncertain times, and later on, the skill gained in dry-stone walling was used in the more peaceful purpose of building wheelhouses.

New settlers, called the La Tène culture (from the site on the shores of Lake Neuchatel in Switzerland), and usually referred to as IRON B, came to these shores after the Hallstatt immigrants. It would seem they were another group of Celtic tribes that had wandered throughout Europe and ultimately to south-east and north-east England. From an examination of objects recovered it was noted that this culture produced highly decorated metalwork with strong oriental styles and classical floral designs. Iron and bronze objects, such as shields, buckles, helmets, swords, sword-scabbards, mirror-backs and horse-harness were highly ornamented. This art almost died out with the Roman occupation, but fortunately survived in the upland regions of the west and north, and forms part of the heritage of Celtic and early Saxon England. Initially these new migrants settled in areas not colonised by IRON A. Also they spread westwards where they worked the iron ore deposits in the Forest of Dean. In time the two cultures merged together.

Throughout this period the scattered local population began to be gathered together in tribal groups, each led by their own chieftain. Uncertainty and danger went hand in hand with intertribal feuding and local wars, and it was only natural that each leader wanted to be the most powerful ruler. Further, the arrival of migrants from the Continent meant that homesteads and farms were under a new threat. It is believed that hillforts came into their own during this time. The hillfort idea developed from the principle of a refuge easily defended by an earthen rampart with a deep external ditch, and superbly sited to give a wide field of vision. The combination of good position and strong defences meant that any attacker would find the task an extremely difficult one. When trouble threatened, the chief and his people, together with their livestock and belongings, came into the fort for shelter. Gradually the hillfort design developed from a single ditch and earthen rampart, known as univallate, to another type consisting of two or more close set banks and ditches, known as multivallate.

There is a characteristic type of hillfort found in south-west Britain consisting of a relatively small enclosure defended by banks and ditches with each rampart separated by wide-spaced enclosures. This arrangement was probably planned for the protection of cattle.

Round about 150BC, a number of new immigrants landed in southern England, and are normally referred to as the Belgae or IRON C people. They originated from northern Gaul (northern France and Belgium), from an area between the Seine, the Marne and the Rhine. These colonists were probably the most important group to affect Britain in the early part of its history. The Belgae arrived with a distinct tribal structure and introduced a number of new techniques and ideas, including the use of the potter's wheel and a system of coinage. Most probably the first coins were imported from Gaul, but later British issues were minted illustrating the wealth of two rival tribes, and depicting a vine leaf and an ear of corn (or barley) respectively. Later issues of gold, silver and bronze coins often bear the names of their kings and of the tribal towns where they were minted.

The newcomers could also improve on the existing metal working skills and were able to produce ornamented ironwork and high quality tools. The availability and wide variety of the latter enabled the farmers to clear and cultivate the heavily forested land in the lowlands and river valleys, thus establishing farms and farming communities. Having initially settled in Kent round the Medway valley and on the Essex coast around Colchester, a study of the coin evidence shows that the Belgic communities spread on to the North Downs, the Chilterns and into Kent. North of the Thames they were known as the Catuvellauni and had established themselves as the most powerful tribe in the south-east, continually warring against their neighbours, the Trinovantes of Essex. The last band of Belgic invaders, known as the Atrebates, landed in southern England soon after Caesar's reconnaissance, and moved into Sussex, Berkshire and east Hampshire.

During this time of Belgic expansion, the native Iron Age people extended and strengthened the existing hillforts against the invaders. It is fairly certain that a number of hillforts were attacked and captured, slaves taken, and the sites occupied by the victors. However, the Belgic tribes did not specialise in hillfort building. Instead, they preferred to enclose large areas of land behind huge defensive dykes and natural features such as rivers, to create a Belgic *oppidum* or tribal capital. Examples of these dykes can be seen north of St Albans, Herts (TL183133), and west of Colchester, Essex (TL962242, TL958223,

TL966246, TL974246). The arrival of the new settlers in Britain may have been made easier by the previous spread of Belgic ideas by trade. This may seem to explain the reason for the Belgic immigrations, which began late in the second century BC and continued after the Caesarian invasions of 55 and 54BC. Finally, when the Roman expedition of AD43 overran the Belgic territory and destroyed their power for ever, the refugees fled before the disciplined might of Rome and moved westwards towards Devon, Cornwall and South Wales.

## IRON AGE SETTLEMENTS

Despite the worsening climate in Britain, with cooler and wetter conditions, day-to-day existence revolved around agriculture. The people moved down from some of the upland areas like Dartmoor and Central Wales to the lower slopes, but still well above the marshy and forested lowlands. In the Yorkshire Dales, particularly in upper Wharfedale, there are numerous examples of irregular fields and hut circles on the limestone terraces.

The houses themselves were usually circular, varying in diameter from 10ft to 50ft (3m to 15.2m) and constructed of a circle of spaced posts interwoven with laths and covered with clay. In other areas such as the west, square and rectangular timber-framed buildings have been identified. Another design was a circular ring of close-set posts placed in a trench, and rammed into position with a packing of stone. Sometimes there were two trenches running parallel several feet apart, and the space could have been filled with a barrier of sharp thorn bushes. A number of main load-bearing posts supported a conical roof that was most probably covered with turf or thatch.

In upland areas such as the south-west, Wales, the north country or Scotland, rough dry-stone walls were used instead of wattle and daub. There were variations here too, for in some cases double stone walls were constructed and the spaces filled with earth and stone rubble.

A central stone hearth provided warmth and cooking facilities, with the smoke most probably drifting round the interior of the hut before escaping through a hole in the thatched roof. There may have been wattle screens inside a house to form living compartments, and some huts were provided with drains, sumps and paved stone floors. The homestead or settlement would in many cases be protected from wild animals by means of a ditch and earthen bank, or by a stockade of stout timbers with a barricade of thorn bushes. In upland areas where stone was freely available, some settlements were enclosed by a stone wall like Bodrifty (SW445354) in Cornwall. Excavations have also revealed pounds for domestic animals, pits for the storing of grain, and other trenches for the disposal of household rubbish.

The lesser settlements of the late Iron Age seem to have been enclosed sites, having a small circular or oval enclosure with a single rampart and ditch. A regional type of this description is the 'round' found in Cornwall. Similarly, the courtyard house, where a number of huts were built within rounds in the Penwith district of Cornwall.

The influx of newcomers brought about unsettled conditions, and forced homesteads and nucleated settlements to take defensive measures. The idea of the bank and the palisade progressed into the development of hillforts, with their immense earthworks and ditches strengthened by wood and stone. However, although excavations of hillforts have shown the foundations of huts within the fort's defences, such as on the summit of Ingleborough (SD742746), it is believed that in many cases the hillfort was a temporary refuge for man and beast. Not only was it a secure place in times of trouble, but was also used as an encampment for pastoral activities during the summer months.

As with most Iron Age settlements, trackways led to small squarish plots, misleadingly called Celtic fields. In many areas of Britain, crops of barley, wheat and rye were grown in these small Celtic fields, particularly on chalk and other light soils. Deteriorating weather conditions gradually reduced the growing of cereal crops in the upland regions, and the people came to rely on stock rearing instead of arable farming. It is in these areas that many foundations of hut circles and walled enclosures have survived, especially in Dartmoor, Cumbria, Northumberland, north-west Wales, Yorkshire Wolds and the Peak District. The numbers of hut circles found in the lonely moorland wilderness of Sutherland have indicated that this area was occupied by ancient farming communities. All along the chalk hills from Sussex to Wiltshire and Dorset, the farms and fields patterns continued to thrive through the Iron Age and into the Roman period. In south-west Britain the same pattern emerges of huts, settlements and field systems. The fields were usually small and square to rectangular in shape, divided by banks of stone cleared from the plots. Recent field work on Dartmoor has shown that in many parts of the area, possibly all land below 1,300ft (396m) was part of a large allotment system marked out by linear banks of stone known as reaves. Lowland sites of circular or rectangular houses can often be detected when the plough turns up patches of dark soil, bits of pottery and burnt bone; or on grassland by the sharper outline caused by rings of lusher grass.

---

## Iron Age Settlements
## Identifying Features

### Houses
- They are circular in plan, although square or rectangular buildings have also been identified.
- On upland soils where nothing has been built since the huts disappeared, the ring grooves or stone foundations of the hut circles may still be seen on the ground, or by the outline of an earthen bank or ditch.
- In upland areas, the site of a hut may be indicated by a circular wall of tumbled stone, or a double-skinned wall with a rubble filling.
- The hut circles may contain a central hearth or hearths, and in others, examples have been found of drains, sumps and paved stone floors.
- In some cases, cells or small rooms may be detected in the thickness of the wall.
- In lowland areas, sites of homesteads may be detected on grassland by circular or rectangular ground impressions, and by the sharper outline caused by rings of lusher grass.

### Enclosures
- Some settlements were surrounded by a stone wall, some were enclosed by a palisaded bank and ditch, and others were undefended.
- Linear depressions may indicate the position of a former protective ditch or ditches.
- Within the interior of the enclosure there may be visible signs of storage or refuse pits.
- Old trackways and routes to the fields may be detected on the surface of the ground. The lines may show up more clearly in certain lighting conditions.

---

## Outstanding Sites

### Staple Howe Farmstead
West Hesterton, Malton, North Yorkshire
OS 101, (1in 93), SE898749
This small farmstead was established on top of one of the small chalk hills on the northern edge of the Yorkshire Wolds. The chosen site was a good defensive position with a level oval-shaped platform about 180ft (54.7m) long and 40ft (12.2m) wide. A timber stockade encircled the site which at first contained a single oval hut 30ft (9.1m) long and 20ft (6.1m) across; probably constructed of chalk rubble walls and a thatched gabled roof. Inside the dwelling were the remains of a hearth and clay oven. At a later date, two other round huts were constructed, and also one small square structure placed on the highest point of the enclosure, that may have been used as a granary. The round huts were constructed with timber post walls each having a central load-bearing support for their conical

thatched roofs. Both dwellings appeared to have south-east facing porches, and the one at the western end of the enclosure had a diameter of 30ft (9.1m). On excavation, large amounts of burnt grain, animal bones, (both wild and domesticated), bone gorges for fishing, pottery, iron and bronze objects were found on the farm site.

**Access**   The farmstead is situated south of the A64 in Knapton Plantation, nearly 1½ miles (2.4km) west from West Hesterton. A footpath leads to the site from the main road.

### Kestor Pound and Settlement
Teigncombe, Chagford, Devon
OS 191, (1in 175), SX665867
Dartmoor is one of the areas of hard igneous rock that makes up the south-west peninsula. In the north, the granite rises to its highest point, High Willhays, 2,038ft (622m) above sea level. Today it is mostly trackless moorland, bleak and inhospitable; a place of creeping mists, dark areas of peat and troublesome sections of bog.

Yet Dartmoor was for a long time a home of early man, who inhabited the lightly wooded uplands as the lower slopes and valleys were clothed in impenetrable forests. The moor is littered with evidence of their occupation throughout many centuries, such as stone circles, hut circles, barrows and settle-ment patterns. Also, man has worked the rich deposits of tin, copper and lead since the Bronze Age.

Kestor settlement and accompanying field systems are to be found on the eastern fringe of Dartmoor, scattered on the northerly slopes of the hill dominated by Kestor Rock. There are stone foundations of more than twenty-two circular huts, 20-33ft (6-10m) in diameter, whose walls were almost certainly constructed of blocks of granite. The roofs covered in thatch or turf were probably supported by an inner ring of posts. On the North Teign River side of the present road lies a round pound measuring 110ft (34m) across and containing one large hut 37ft (11m) in diameter. On excavation there was evidence that the building was occupied by a blacksmith who carried out iron workings here, as there were signs of a furnace as well as traces of slag. Nearby there seem to be two parallel trackways that could be associated with this area of ancient settlement. In the surrounding fields the plough soil overlies peat, suggesting that conditions were already deteriorating on the moor during Iron Age times.

**Access**   West of Chagford village bear left at the road fork and proceed by a narrow twisting by-road to Teigncombe and Batworthy. After the former, the lane climbs steeply and becomes unfenced as it crosses the lower slopes of Kestor where many of the huts and field systems are situated. Distance from Chagford, 3 miles (4.8km).

### Greaves Ash Settlement
Linhope, Ingram, Northumberland
OS 81, (1in 71), NT965164
The border county of Northumberland is an area of great natural beauty, rich in wild life and with a wealth of historical and archaeological interest. The great dome of the Cheviot Hills, with the highest point reaching 2,676ft (815m), is a smooth barren surface covered with thick deposits of deeply furrowed peat hags. The region is in fact a deeply dissected volcano with the centre composed of a large mass of pink granite.

The Cheviot area contains many examples of hillforts, settlements and terraced cultivation strips. The Iron Age people cleared the forest and settled on the lower hill slopes above the marshy river valleys. One such site, called Greaves Ash, is situated at Linhope, in the valley of the River Breamish. There are large groups of hut circles spread over a wide area, contained within three separate enclosures, and with evidence of field boundaries close by. The westerly group is enclosed by a large double boundary wall, with the inner one having an entrance on the east, and the outer one having three entrances. A short distance away to the east is another group of huts and courtyards, and there is yet another group to the north east. The outer walls of this settlement are remarkable for their construction with many large boulders collected locally. Some of the standing walls are 6ft (1.8m) thick, and excavation has indicated some huts with a diameter of 25ft (7.5m) having paved floors and a simple internal partition. The settlements probably commenced in the Iron Age and continued into the Roman period.

**Access**   Proceed west from the

A697 by minor road to Ingram. Continue up the rapidly narrowing valley to leave the main stream and climb uphill to Hartside, where cars may be parked on the grass verge.

## Gray Coat Settlement and Homestead

Dod, Hawick, Borders Region
OS 79, (1in 69), NT471052,
NT471049
Hawick lies in the picturesque valley of the River Teviot at the centre of an intensively farmed area. It is famous for its high-quality woollen goods industry, for its busy auctions of farm livestock, and of course, its fervent support for rugby football.

To the south-west rises the bleak head of Teviotdale where once-barren windswept moorland is now covered by dark armies of ubiquitous conifers.

In the border foothills south of Hawick, between the encroaching forests of Craik and Wauchope, plentiful evidence of habitation may be seen, as hill top forts guard the access to

secluded valleys and settlements flank the lower slopes.

At the end of a narrow by-road and situated on the summit ridge of a hill spur overlooking Dod Burn lies the site of the Gray Coat settlement and homestead at 1,239ft (378m). The more northerly feature shows surface remains of a double stockade which combines in a curve on either side of the entrance. Within the enclosure, which measures some 155ft (47.1m) by 124½ft (38m), are signs of the surface foundation groove of a circular dwelling 50ft (15.2m) in diameter. Along the ridge, about 300yd (91m) to the south are the remains of a tumbled wall, almost rectangular in shape, measuring 348ft (106m) by 200ft (61m). This enclosure contains surface signs of about eight circular wooden houses, including three that are

similar to the dwelling found in the single enclosure to the north.
**Access** The site lies 6¾ miles (10.8km) south-south-west of Hawick. From the centre of the town on the A7 road, take the first minor road left, past the church after crossing the Slitrig Water. Follow this by-road climbing steadily past Pilmuir and Dodburn to the farm buildings at Dod. Leave the road and proceed left on a track for a few yards before ascending right on a path above a copse of trees. The settlement and homestead lies on the ridge above to the right.

This ancient route which continues over Dod Rig to Swire Knowe, at 1,506ft (459m) and down by Braidleyhope to the Hermitage Water is called the Thieves' Road.

## Burwens Settlement

Crosby Lodge, Crosby Ravensworth, Cumbria
OS 91 (1in 83), NY622123
This district around the Lyvennet Beck has long been settled in by man, with numerous sites in the vicinity of Crosby Ravensworth village. Sherds of Beaker pottery have been recorded from cairns on Crosby Ravensworth Fell and numerous bronze objects found in the immediate area. The Romans drove a road from Low Borrow Bridge in the Lune Valley, and passing near to Ewe Close Iron Age settlement,

before continuing north to Brougham. The region of the upper Lyvennet is said by some to be the home of a British King Urien Rheged, a descendant of a Celtic chieftain living during the time of the Roman occupation. The barren nature of the ground has preserved the signs of man's involvement, such as the cairns, settlement patterns and Celtic fields from agricultural development. In the neighbourhood of the ancient cairn of Robin Hood's Grave, is an ancient dyke believed to be the boundary of a former deer park, another factor in the

preservation of ancient settlements.

Burwens settlement is a roughly rectangular area of about 1 acre (0.4ha), enclosed by a stone rubble wall and containing the remains of a number of roughly circular buildings with courtyards. Some of the huts are small, and probably would not have required a main load-bearing post for the conical roof. An entrance to the enclosure leads off the northerly pointing farm track and splits into two interior pathways. In the south-eastern-segment of the enclosure there

Beyond the farm is a private road, no cars allowed, which means a short walk of ¾ mile (1.2km), to the ancient settlement. Just before Linhope, a path begins from the boundary

of a cleared patch of woodland. After a few yards, follow the earthen banks left up the gentle slope to the settlement site.

are the lower foundation walls of a rectangular shaped building, possibly of Scandanavian origin. Its walls appear to have been constructed of two facings of stone slabs infilled with earth and stone rubble. Any gaps between the slabs were completed with dry stone walling. To the east and north of the settlement are traces of low field walls which may be the boundaries of an earlier field system.

**Access**   The site may be approached by footpaths on either side of the Lyvennet Beck, starting at Town Head or by the bridge just south of the village of Crosby Ravensworth. From either of these points follow the course of the stream for ¾ mile (1.2km) to join a farm track to Crosby Lodge. After crossing the stream proceed for ¼ mile (400m) and the settlement site lies on the left-hand side of the track.

### Grimspound Settlement

Hameldon Tor, Widecombe-in-the-Moor, Devon
OS 191, (1in 175), SX701809
This elevated site lies at 1,476ft (450m) above sea level, amongst barren expanses of heather and surrounding rock tors.

This settlement for pastoralists and herdsmen consisted of a number of dwelling huts and a few more used as store houses and animal shelters. There were about sixteen circular huts of varying diameters from 8ft to 15ft (2.4m to 4.5m) with strong outer walls some 3ft 6in (1.07m) thick. The houses were roofed with turves or thatch supported above the walls on upright timber posts. The huts used for habitation contained traces of hearths, cooking pits and benches. The settlement was enclosed by a stout stone boundary wall with an entrance on the eastern side, and although reconstructed in parts, may originally have been much wider than it is now. The area enclosed within the boundary wall is about 4 acres (1.6ha), and outside the pound there are traces of four or five animal corrals.

**Access**   The shortest walk is from a minor road at SX698808, just over 1¼ miles (2km) from its junction with the B3212. Approaching from the east there are paths from Heathercombe, distance 1¼ miles (2km), and from north of Natsworthy Manor, distance 1½ miles (2.4km).

---

### Courtyard Houses
### Identifying Features

- Round the interior edge of this open unroofed area were round dwellings, store houses and animal shelters, partly built into the thickness of the bank.

- A roughly circular earth and stone structure with a single entrance leading into a central paved courtyard.

---

### Outstanding Sites

### Carn Euny Settlement (DoE)

Brane, Sacreed, Penzance, Cornwall
OS 203, (1in 189), SW402288
This small settlement, situated on western facing slopes, is 2¾ miles (4.4km) from the sea cliffs at Aire Point on the Penwith peninsula. In the Bronze Age people lived on this site in round timber houses with thatched roofs; although all traces of them have long since vanished, there is a posthole stone, a padstone for a roof support, to be found

*Carn Euny Settlement*

off-centre in one of the existing huts. This indicates that the houses were rebuilt in stone over the foundations of the previous ones. The four courtyard houses were roughly circular earth and stone structures, with a single fairly wide entrance leading into a central courtyard. Two of the dwellings clearly show a room on either side of the courtyard, which could mean that the courtyard itself was roofed. One of the courtyard houses overlies an impressive fogou: a curving stone-lined trench, roofed with stone slabs and covered over with earth, which may have been used as an underground cold-storage area, or as a refuge by earlier inhabitants. This runs for a distance of 66ft (20m), and there are indications that the passage itself was constructed in two periods.

**Access** The ancient

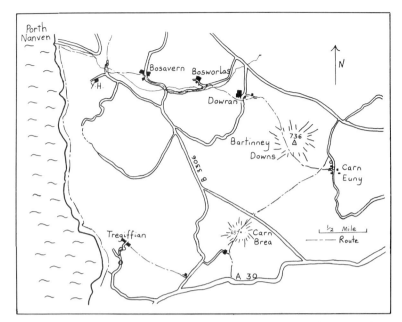

settlement is situated amid a network of narrow country lanes between the A3071 and the A30, 1½ miles (2.4km) from the village of Sancreed. The

winding access road stops at the hamlet of Brane. Please use the parking facilities. There is then a short walk of about 550yd (500m) to the site.

### Chysauster Courtyard Settlement (DoE)
Chysauster, Gulval Downs, Penwith District, Penzance, Cornwall
OS 203, (1in 189), SW472350
This ancient corner of Britain

ends a short distance away in the storm-beaten, shelterless granite cliffs of Lands End. The Atlantic Ocean has long been an aid to the movement of peoples, trade and ideas. The remains of these people, in the form of megaliths,

field patterns and settlements, lie scattered across Penwith's upland landscape. Other relics of the past are the stream-side humps and hollows of long abandoned tin workings; for it was the lure of this mineral that first attracted trade with Mediterranean peoples.

At Chysauster, the well-preserved remains of an Iron Age village lie along the gentle slopes of a remote hillside. Within the settlement enclosure are four pairs of roofless dry-stone-constructed houses which stand on either side of a kind of street. Externally, each building is roughly oval in shape, and all the rooms, both round and long, are contained in the thickness of the massive outer wall. Access to the living quarters in the round room is from a central irregularly-shaped courtyard, the entrance to which is

*Chysauster*

sheltered from the prevailing wind. Generally, this round room is opposite the passage to the courtyard from outside. All the houses were probably laid with paved floors and a drainage system, with one house in particular (Number 6) having a sump for the collection of water. Some of the rooms have padstones or bases for roof supports. Each croft seemed to have its own cultivable plot, and the surrounding area contains the remains of field systems. The outlines of at least two more houses can be traced outside the main group. The inhabitants of Chysauster, although primarily farmers, probably streamed for tin from the little river at the foot of the hill. In the south-eastern corner of the village complex is the partially excavated remains of a fogou.

**Access**   From Penzance take the A30 east, and then the B3311, St Ives road. At Badger's Cross, turn left on to a narrow lane for $1\frac{1}{2}$ miles (2.4km) where a signpost indicates the footpath to the site. There are parking facilities. The settlement may also be approached from the B3306, St Ives to St Just road south-west of Zennor.

**Percy Rigg Iron Age Village**
Kildale, North Yorkshire
OS 94, (1in 86), NZ608116
At the end of a minor road crossing Kildale Moor, opposite Lonsdale Plantation.

## CELTIC FIELDS AND LYNCHETS

In establishing their fields, the Iron Age farmers collected the numerous boulders lying on the surface of the ground, and arranged them to form small rectangular plots. These fields were then ploughed using the simple ard, which only scratched the thin soil. One-way ploughing was totally insufficient, and so the plots would have to be ploughed in a criss-cross fashion in order to create some tilth of soil. After constant ploughing, even on gentle slopes, the soil would gradually creep down and bank up against the field boundaries. These would be reinforced, so that in time a series of fields, bounded in some cases by quite high banks or lynchets, would be super-imposed on the land. In some areas there is evidence of an ancient farming heritage, which may date from the Iron Age to Medieval times, over which now a pattern of post-medieval stone walling can be recognised.

---

### Celtic Fields and Lynchets
### Identifying Features

- These are squarish to rectangular plots ranging in size, usually, from $\frac{1}{4}$ to 2 acres (0.1-0.8ha).
- The field boundaries are usually marked by ditches, low banks or walls of stone.
- After constant ploughing, even on gentle slopes, the soil would creep down forming terraced banks or lynchets.
- The fields may have a few circular hut foundations scattered amongst them.
- The ancient fields and lynchets may date from the Iron Age to Medieval times.

---

### Outstanding Sites

**Grassington**
Wharfedale, North Yorkshire
OS 98 (1in 90), OS Outdoor Leisure Map, 'Malham and Upper Wharfedale', SE003648, SE004660, SD995662

On the limestone terraces in the Craven district of Yorkshire, numerous places preserve clues of Iron Age settlement. On the limestone plateau north of Grassington there are a variety of ancient field patterns, their bare ribs of boundary walls or banks standing out on the thin upland soils.

Commencing just north of Bank Lathe there are fine

impressions of rectangular fields and circular hut enclosures. A little further north on Sweetside there are a number of rectangular fields, between 320 and 390ft (97-118m) long and about 75ft (23m) wide. A little way to the west, on Lea Green, there are even larger rectangular fields, 500ft (152m) long, and about 205-290ft (62.4-88.2m) wide. At the northerly part of the Lea Green area there are clear evidences of stone hut foundations within an enclosing wall. This points to the site of an Iron Age village settlement which probably existed into Roman times.

**Access** Proceed up the main shopping street in Grassington, bear left at the north end and then take the second lane on the

*Celtic fields, Grassington*

right. Take the left fork almost immediately and climb gently to a junction of tracks. Bear right and then left on an indistinct footpath. The first field systems lie on the other side of the stone wall to the right. For Lea Green,

turn left at the north end of the main shopping street; continue to the end of the road and take the footpath straight on at the sharp corner. Keep to the upper route when the footpath divides after a few yards.

## Fyfield Down

Avebury, Wiltshire
OS 173, (1in 157), SU140712, SU142709

The history of the local fieldscape is plainly visible on the chalk surface of Fyfield and Overton Downs. The area contains many examples of rectangular Celtic fields, some with boundary banks that fall 9ft (2.7m) to the next plot. Linking the fields are many ancient

trackways that are clearly etched into the chalk surface. The term 'Celtic' is a somewhat misleading term, for the small rectangular enclosures have been an integral part of farming practice from the Bronze Age to Roman times. In fact, the whole area is a complex system of field patterns overlain by medieval ploughlands and modern pasture.

This archaeologically

important landscape, which is now a Nature Reserve, is also littered with giant sarsen stones, the grey 'wethers', used by the prehistoric builders of Avebury and Stonehenge.

**Access** There are many walking routes to reach Fyfield Down, including:

**a** From Overton Hill on the A4. After 1¾ miles (2.8km), bear right at a junction of tracks, and then keeping the wood on the left, proceed to a point just beyond a copse on the right. Distance 2¾ miles (4.4km).

**b** From Avebury village, follow a straight track east-north-east across Avebury and Overton Downs, and as above, passing the wood on the left to a point beyond a copse on the right.

**c** Ridgeway path walkers coming south may deviate at Rough Hill, and walk south-east to the east of New Totterdown.

*Celtic fields, Fyfield Down*

### Winspit

Worth Matravers, Swanage, Dorset
OS 195 (1in 179), SY975761, SY976765, SY977770, SY980772
1:25,000 Outdoor Leisure Map, 'Purbeck'

From 1,200 BC onwards, the Celtic warrior farmers brought the Iron Age to Britain from northern Europe, and soon dominated Wessex. Their great hillforts of Eggardon and Maiden Castle still look across the countryside of twentieth-century Dorset, regarded by many as one of the loveliest of the English shires. Its rolling chalk downs and breezy heathland enfolds sleepy stone-built villages with charming names and a wealth of archi-ectural treasures. More breathtaking still is the Dorset coastline, with its plunging hill crests cut shear by the pounding sea; where the pebble-laden waves are shaping the cliffs into caves, arches and stacks.

Equally clear, on the downs and hillsides, are the strip lynchets, patterns of ancient field systems used by farmers, it is believed, from the Iron Age to medieval times. One has only to study the Ordnance Survey map to see the frequency of their locations. For example, south of Worth Matravers, there is ample evidence of field systems on the hillside slopes of the two little valleys running down to the sea, notably at East Man and West Man.

**Access**    From Worth Matravers, a footpath accompanies the stream along Winspit Bottom to Winspit. Turn east along the coastal path for ⅝ mile (1km), and then bear north up the next valley, Seacombe Bottom, to a point where it bifurcates. Keep to the left fork for a gentle climb and return to the village, to complete a short circular walk. Total distance 2½ miles (4km).

### Manifold Valley

Oldpark Hill, Manifold Valley, Grindon, Staffs
OS 119, (1in 111), SK107532,
1:25,000 Outdoor Leisure Map, 'The White Peak'

This area is one of those country-side delights that could remain comparatively unknown to a good many travellers. Surely, when discovered, they ask themselves the question: 'Why has it taken so long to find this delectable spot?' The limestone hills of the Staffordshire Moorlands, green and tidy, are crossed and chequered by walls of white stone. In this limestone landscape the dales, worn deep and sinuous by the rivers, constitute the features.

Below the great grey limestone outcrop of Beeston Tor (where in a cave, Saxon jewels and coins have been found), the River Hamps, after taking a circuitous route from its source on the dark flanks of the Morridge, finally joins the River Manifold. Both watercourses are unusual among rivers, as from time to time they disappear and flow underground. By the side of the river is a tarmac path, the remains of the track of the Leek and Manifold Valley Light Railway. This line, with a 2ft 6in gauge (0.8m) and Indian-style locomotives, was never a commercial success and, sadly, closed in 1934.

Climbing the steep grassy

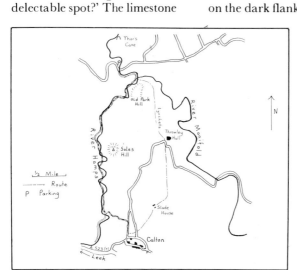

*Lynchets, Manifold Valley*

path to the road above Beeston Tor, one can look across the valley to the heights of Oldpark Hill and Soles Hill, the latter reaching 1,163ft (355m) above the dale. In the little green fold of the land on the eastern side of Oldpark Hill, a track climbs up to Throwley Hall. When the sunlight is at the right angle the lynchets stand out clearly on the eastern side of the track.

**Access** There are steep and narrow roads into the dale from Grindon and Wetton with a parking spot at Weags Bridge. There are several alternative walking routes:

**a** From Hulme End down the Manifold Valley. Distance 5 miles (8km).

**b** From Waterhouses, north up the valley of the River Hamps. Distance 3½ miles (5.6km).

**c** A circular walk goes from Calton, by track to Slade House and bridle way and footpath to Throwley Hall. A footpath descends through a thin line of trees and into the dry valley where the lynchets become evident. Continue down to Beeston Tor Farm. Return along the Hamps Valley to a point just before the last bridge over the river, about ½ mile (800m) from the main A52. Strike uphill to the east, and meet a track which zigzags to the left of a small copse to reach a lane into Calton. Distance 5½ miles (8.8km).

Lynchets, Knipe Scar

Lynchets, Hethpool

### Knipe Scar

Hawkswick, Littondale, North Yorkshire
OS 98, (1in 90), SD964701, 1:25,000 Outdoor Leisure Map, 'Malham and Upper Wharfedale'
An irregular pattern of small walled fields and lynchet banks. The lynchets may be observed from the minor road to Hawkswick.

### Hethpool

Elsdon Burn, Kirknewton, Wooler, Northumberland
OS 74, (1in 70), NT892287 and NT894288
Long banks of lynchets are visible on the southern slopes of White Hill north of Hethpool.

**Access** Via a narrow road from Kirknewton.

### Wharton Hall

Kirkby Stephen, Cumbria
OS 91, (1in 84), NY768063
A series of fine hillside lynchets to the west of Wharton Hall in the valley of the River Eden. They extend up to the railway.

**Access** By farm track from the A685, at a point 1 mile (1.6km) south from the centre of Kirkby Stephen. Continue for just over ½ mile (800m), and the lynchets may be observed on the hillside directly ahead. The area may also be approached from Bullgill at NY767052, and track to beyond Wharton Hall. Distance ¾ mile (1.2km).

## Knighton Bushes

Ashbury, Oxfordshire
OS 174, (1in 158), SU299833
This is the centre of a large area of Celtic fields, somewhat reduced by ploughing, which stretch northwards towards the Ridge Way. From this prehistoric trade route, a number of ancient trackways travel south through this old farming landscape.

**Access**  This is a circular walk of great interest to include a number of ancient sites. From the north-eastern corner of Ashbury village, a footpath leaves the B4507, to ascend past a thin line of trees before joining a track over Odstone Hill. Bear right and walk up to the Ridge Way. Turn left and after a few yards you will encounter the chambered long barrow named Wayland's Smithy. Continue for another $1\frac{1}{4}$ miles (2km) to view Uffington Castle Iron Age hillfort, and the nearby famous chalk-cut figure of the White Horse. Turning south a path

passes Idlebush Barrow and crosses Woolstone Down into an area of ancient field systems. Turn right and follow the county boundary footpath to Knighton Bushes; note the field systems on the right. Return via Knighton or Odstone Down to the Ridge Way, and descend via Kingstone Combes to Ashbury. Total Distance $8\frac{1}{2}$ to 9 miles (13.6 to 14.4km).

## Butser Ancient Farm Project

Petersfield, Hampshire
OS 197, (1in 181), SU719207
This large area of downland is now part of a Country Park run by the Hampshire County Council. On high ground there are many traces of habitation and cultivation, including three defensive dykes, burial mounds, Celtic fields and ancient trackways. The Ancient Farm Project is a very interesting experiment using methods, crops, materials and livestock that would have been known to Iron Age farmers.

**Access**  A footpath leaves the road cutting on the A3, 3 miles (4.8km) south-south-west of Petersfield and heads north-west. After $\frac{1}{4}$ mile (400m), when the path turns westwards, continue north-west to the triangulation point on the flat summit of Butser Hill, 888ft (271m) high. From here proceed north-north-east for a $\frac{1}{4}$ mile (0.4km) to the site. Alterna-

tively, the Ancient Farm Project site may be reached by minor roads west of Butser Hill, and from road junction, SU715175 if approaching from the south.

The site is open daily during the summer months (except Mondays) from 2pm to 5pm, and on Sundays, 11am to 1pm and 2pm to 5pm. There is a small entrance charge and explanatory literature is available.

## Woolbury Ring (NT)

Stockbridge, Hampshire
OS 185, (1in 168), SU384347
The Celtic fields are to be found on the eastern side of Stockbridge Down. The fields extend

downslope from the Iron Age fort of Woolbury Ring. The ancient farming pattern is indicated by dykes on the western side; their purpose was, in all probability, to separate grazing

areas from ploughed sections. Access may be obtained from any number of points on the A272, 1 mile (1.6km) east of Stockbridge.

### Smacam Down

Cerne Abbas, Dorset
OS 194, (1in 178), SY660993
On Smacam Down there is a small dry valley with a good field system. On the adjoining northerly hill spur at SY657994 are the remains of a well-preserved Bronze Age settlement with a hut circle 35.5ft (11m) in diameter. Another area of ancient fields lies on the northern edge of the settlement.
**Access**   The field system in the dry valley may be viewed from the footpath off the A352 at SY664992, and the settlement may be approached from the track in Higher Hill Bottom and up the hill slope to the left.

### Valley of Stones

Littlebredy, Portesham, Dorset
OS 194, (1in 178), SY597877
The valley contains some fine examples of field systems within an area of approximately $1\frac{1}{4}$ acres (0.5ha). The boundary lynchets are 7 to 10ft (2.1 to 3m) high.
**Access**   By footpath from Littlebredy Farm, $\frac{3}{4}$ mile (1.2km) south of Littlebredy village, or into the Valley of Stones from ithe crossroads on Portesham Hill. It is just a short walk either way.

### Selside Shaw

Selside, Horton-in-Ribblesdale, North Yorks
OS 98, (1in 90), SD775780,
1:2,500 Outdoor Leisure Map, 'The Three Peaks'
Running south from the above map reference, below the line of trees of Bent Hill Wood, is a wide area of ancient field systems. They also extend across the road and the railway line. The Celtic fields were probably farmed by people who lived in round huts, each one contained within a walled enclosure at SD777772.
**Access**   The field systems may be observed from the farm track to Colt Park, or from the side of the B6479, or from the bridge over the railway.

## SOUTERRAINS OR FOGOUS

These are names given to galleries created by lining a trench with large slabs of stone, roofed with capstones, and the whole structure covered over with soil and turf. The passages are often curved, open at each end, and usually contain a side gallery or galleries. There has been much discussion as to the function of these structures; but it is now believed that they served as a place of refuge in times of danger, and more likely, as well-ventilated underground storage areas. They would act as a form of prehistoric refrigerator for salted meat, fish and milk products.

In County Down, Northern Ireland, Drumena Cashel (J311340) is a stone-walled rath or defended farmstead. Within the enclosure is a well-preserved souterrain with a passage 50ft

*Drumena Cashel*

(15.2m) long and 7ft (2.2m) high leading to a rectangular chamber measuring 16ft (4.8m) by 6ft (1.8m). The stepped entrance is modern, with the original narrow one leading in at right angles to the passage and facing the chamber.

---

**Identifying Features**

- A feature associated with certain settlements, and known generally as souterrains or in Cornwall as fogous.
- They are underground galleries floored and roofed with stone slabs.
- The main passage, which may be open at each end, is often curved, and usually has a side gallery or galleries.
- Their purpose is unknown, but they may have been used as underground storage areas, or possibly as places of refuge.

## Outstanding Sites

### Halligye Fogou
Garras, Helston, Cornwall
OS 203, (1in 190), SW714238
This curved underground stone-lined passage, running east to west, is 54ft (16.4m) long. The interior is pitch-black so a torch is necessary. At the eastern end of the main gallery, another impressive passage runs off at right angles, with the northern end now blocked. At the western end of the main gallery, a short length of tunnel runs south-west. Near the entrance to this side tunnel, and partially obstructing the main gallery is a block of stone. The purpose of this is uncertain.

**Access**    The village of Garras on the B3293, lies some 4¼ miles (6.8km) south-east of Helston. From the village take the by-road to Mawgan and then the first lane on the right for ½ mile (800m). At the junction with another track coming in from the left, take the short stretch of footpath opposite which leads to the fogou.

### Culsh Souterrain (DoE)
Tarland, Grampian Region, Scotland
OS 37, (1in 42), NJ505055
Set between the valleys of the Don and Dee lies a pleasant and fertile vale called the Howe of Cromar. Tarland, the largest settlement, still retains its old-world charm set around a quiet central square. The vale is surrounded by the foothills of the Grampian Mountains, and was long a settlement area for early man, with plentiful evidences of stone circles and burial cairns. A short distance to the north-east of the village is the site of a souterrain. The curving passage which extends for several yards is built of irregular blocks of stone and roofed by huge lintels. This is a good example to visit, but take care as it is very dark inside and so a torch is necessary.

**Access**    It is situated next to Culsh Farm and adjacent to the B9119 road, some 2½ miles (4km) north-east of Tarland.

### Carlungie Souterrain (DoE)
Newbigging, Monifieth, Tayside Region, Scotland
OS 54, (1in 50), NO511359
Although well set out, and the details carefully preserved, this souterrain is roofless. The lay out is by no means simple, having a main curving gallery some 150ft (45.6m) long with a number of smaller and narrower passages leading off it. Excavations have indicated that a number of hut dwellings were situated on the periphery of the site, and the souterrain may have been an underground storehouse for the settlement. But was this the real purpose? Imagine this complex roofed, giving an area of curving underground passages, where a number of people could shelter when danger arose. To hide in a pitch-black subterranean hole, where your enemy could simply light a fire at the entrance and suffocate you, does not seem realistic. Perhaps the inhabitants designed the souterrain with branching passages in order to store different kinds of foods, each in its own allotted space.

**Access**    The souterrain is situated 4 miles (6.4km), north-east of Monifieth. On reaching the A92 at the Mains of Ardestie, turn right and proceed to the first minor road on the left. The site is signposted. At the end of this road, a short footpath leads left across the field to the souterrain.

*Carlungie Souterrain*

**Mains of Ardestie Souterrain** (DoE)
Mains of Ardestie, Monifieth, Tayside Region, Scotland
OS 54, (1in 50), NO502344
This is another example of a roofless souterrain, consisting of a curving passageway 80ft (24.4m) long, with what seems to be a stone drain running down the middle. Excavations have uncovered the foundations of hut dwellings, and the site may have been occupied during the Iron Age and some time beyond. The inclusion of the passage drain may support the belief that livestock were held in the souterrain, and that fish or molluscs were kept in the stone-lined trough on the bank outside the passage.

**Access** The souterrain is situated 2¼ miles (3.6km) north-east of Monifieth. Take the B962 to the junction with the A92. Turn left for a few yards and access to the site is by signposted footpath from the north side of the main road.

## HILLFORTS

Since the end of the Iron Age, two thousand years of farming, animal husbandry and settlement has removed much of the evidence of early man's occupation of the land. The long-lasting features of the Iron Age that have survived as part of the present landscape are the deep grass-grown ditches and weathered earthworks of the hillforts. The passage of time has silted up the defensive trenches; grasses, bushes and trees have in some cases overgrown the site. Nevertheless, throughout Britain there are more than 2,500 embanked and ditched enclosures as man-made features of the landscape; many are situated on upland vantage points. At first glance a good number appear as a natural part of the terrain, so beautifully do they seem to fit in with the lie of the land. Many of them are located in situations of incomparable scenic beauty; the contour-hugging ramparts offering a wide sweep of far-reaching views. Probably the best description of a hillfort is an enclosure, apparently fortified, for use as a cattle compound or a settlement varying from several dwellings to something the size of a small town. The purpose was seldom purely military, but they were usually sited to gain the maximum military advantage. On the southern chalk downlands of Britain some of the hilltop settlements are likely to have been associated with sacred places as well as with cattle raising. It is possible that they simply carried on the tradition of causewayed camps, using the elevated sites as meeting, ritual and trading places for the benefit of the surrounding scattered population.

The first farmers of the Iron Age lived on undefended sites, whether as single homesteads, farms or hilltop villages. The principal characteristics of the British Iron Age can be recognised as the results of three main waves of continental immigrants from about 700BC, namely IRON A, B and C. It is possible that as the first group of migrants, IRON A, spread north so the farms and settlements began to be defended, but nobody can be absolutely certain. There would appear to be a strong possibility that the great majority of hillforts were built to defend the inhabitants against attacks from neighbouring communities, whether those inhabitants were established settlers or newcomers. In its simplest form the defence was a palisade or stockade of heavy timbers set in a trench interlaced with wattles and thorny material. The hillfort's strength was in using the lie of the land to make it very difficult to attack, and also to make the enclosed area safe by erecting ramparts and digging ditches. The material excavated from the ditch was used to build up the rampart mound, thus making the simplest type of hillfort with a single earthwork and ditch. This type of fort is known as univallate.

On examination of the earthworks it would appear that posts were set along the inner edge of the ditch, and a second row of timbers were then placed behind them. The two lines of posts were lashed together and the gap filled with earth, turf and rubble. In upland areas stone blocks were used to face the outside edge of the earthen mound.

The second influx of Celtic people, IRON B, not only brought with them metal-working skills, but also the practice of using the sling as a weapon. This new technique in warfare may have led to the improvement in defences, such as the development of two or more closely set banks and ditches, known as multivallate. Some of these larger hillforts had a comparatively intricate defensive system in which the entrance gate or gates were guarded by multiple trenches and wooden towers (long since gone) which exposed the attackers to cross-fire from slingers. In some cases there were quite wide spaces between the ramparts, and it is believed that they were designed for holding livestock. This could happen when the animals were gathered in prior to their movement to lower pastures, or in a time of uncertainty. So the picture is one of defended settlements, many of them on vantage points, used on a temporary or permanent basis for settlement and livestock protection.

These fortified camps were in their turn menaced by another group of invaders who spread slowly outwards from south-east England in the last century BC. This third continental influence, known as IRON C, introduced the use of coinage and wheel-turned pottery. They did not seem to carry on the tradition of hillfort building, but preferred to construct a system of linear earthworks particularly in the lowlands, to protect their tribal capital or *oppidum*.

Another type of defensive site running throughout the Iron Age and possibly also used in the Late Bronze Age is the promontory fort. Inland, if the sides of a hill-spur were steep enough to give a natural defence, a ditch and earthworks were constructed across the neck of the spur. A headland jutting out to sea also provided a good defensive site; an ideal, if breezy, spot was protected by the cliffs. A rampart or ramparts were constructed in a variety of ways, including simple stone walls, stone-faced earthen ramparts and simple earthworks. In Shetland, these forts are small in area and occur in two kinds of location: on cliffed headlands or promontories and on small islands in lochs or sheltered voes.

## Hillforts
### Identifying Features

● These familiar ancient monuments are generally found throughout the British Isles, many conspicuously sited amidst splendid scenery.
● A hillfort is an enclosure, apparently fortified, sited in a position to achieve the ultimate defensive advantage, and usually not less than ½ acre (0.2ha) in enclosed area.
● Some of the hillforts were established in the Bronze Age, and continued as a characteristic feature of the Iron Age.
● In some cases the forts are defended by a single rampart of earth and/or stone rubble, with or without a trench or ditch, and following the contours of the hill. These hillforts have one or two entrances.
● Later developments produced two or more ramparts with accompanying ditches, and with elaborately defended entrance points.
● Some forts are dramatically situated on headlands or on hill spurs protected by ramparts as well as by the existing natural features, such as cliffs and steep slopes.
● Where there were no hills, some forts were built on low ground with particularly strong ramparts and heavily defended entrance points.

● Some forts are sited on hill-slopes with widely spaced earthworks. These are located in the south-west of England, and are regarded as non-defensive forts, probably constructed as cattle enclosures.
● In the upland areas where stone was plentiful, many of the defensive walls were constructed of stone or a core of earth and stone rubble faced with stone blocks.
● At some of the hillfort sites in Scotland, there is evidence that the defensive walls have been vitrified, due to being deliberately or accidentally fused into a solid mass by burning.
● Many of the earthworks and ditches are still massively impressive, despite the ravages of time, weather and farming operations. In other examples the earthworks have been lowered and the ditches silted up, so that now only a faint outline exists on the ground. These are well worth exploring all the same.
● The evidence from excavations carried out within the interiors of some hillforts has indicated that they were inhabited, but whether this was a permanent or seasonal occupation is a matter for conjecture.

## Outstanding Sites

### Old Oswestry Hillfort

Oswestry, Shropshire
OS 126, (1in 118), SJ296310
This splendid fortress with its multiple ramparts occupies a commanding position just north of the town, and overlooking the rich farmland to the east. In parts it has a formidable system of seven earthworks enclosing an area of 12½ acres (5ha). It is believed that the first occupants built a number of circular timber-framed huts on an undefended site. Some time after the houses had been deserted,

two earthworks were thrown up round the contours of the hill, accompanied by ditches and entrances on the eastern and western flanks. These earthen defences were strengthened by stone facings front and rear to protect a group of circular stone dwellings. After this phase, it appears that the inner rampart was enlarged, and two further lines of banks and ditches were constructed around the hill.

After strengthening the western entrance passage with a facing of stone, two massive

earthworks were raised around the base of the hill. Supporting banks were erected on either side of this entrance, probably as extra protection for the weak point, and also to uphold the unstable material of the upper earthwork. The humps and hollows caused by these supporting earthworks should not be mistaken for cattle enclosures. Fragments of pottery have been discovered in the interior of the fort, which was probably deserted at some time during the Roman period.

This ancient fortified enclosure has acted as a true landmark through the centuries. Wat's Dyke, an early eighth-century Mercian linear earth-work, of an earlier date than King Offa's frontier, was constructed right up to the ramparts of the Iron Age fort at Old Oswestry.

**Access**  Just a mile (1.6km) north of the centre of Oswestry. From the site of the railway station bear right at the junction, and proceed along the A483 Llangollen road. Take the second turning on the left and carry straight on for ½ mile (800m). Parking space is limited on this narrow lane.

*Old Oswestry Hillfort*

### Tre'r Ceiri Hillfort

Llanaelhaearn, Lleyn Peninsula, Gwynedd.
OS 123, (1in 115), SH373446
This impressive, well preserved fort is dramatically situated on the most easterly of the three peaks of Yr Eifl — the 'town of the giants', 1,503ft (458m) high. The well constructed dry-stone walls of hard igneous rock trace an irregular oval, some 947ft (289m) long and 328ft (100m)

wide round the summit. The wall is still in good condition, but varies in thickness from 7ft (2.1m) to 11ft (3.4m). In places along its northern side the parapet walk and access ramps up to it still exist. Steep tracks slant up the hillside to approach the main gateways at the west and south-west sectors. There are also three narrow gateways, and very surprisingly, the one on the northern side still retains the

lintel stone *in situ*. A hillside spring some little distance beyond the main entrance on the western side probably provided a reliable water supply.

Originally, the enclosure held twenty round houses, but during the Roman period the number of dwellings increased to about one hundred and fifty. The foundations of many of these dwellings remain visible. During the later period the houses were constructed with a central partition, and varied in shape from round to roughly rectangular. The fort's exceptional state of preservation is probably due to the fact that it was occupied during the Roman period and escaped the usual fate of slighting. Around the sides of the hill and below the ramparts are many traces of small enclosures or paddocks, which were probably used for holding livestock. A Bronze Age cairn of earlier times is to be found at the highest north-easterly point of the fort's interior.

The inevitable question will be asked as to why this stone-walled enclosure was erected on such a bleak inhospitable summit surrounded by rocks and heather. It has been suggested that Iron Age farming communities in the surrounding lowlands organised their own territorial units, with each unit possessing its own hillfort. The original Iron Age settlers had brought with them the techniques of hillfort design and construction, and faced with increasing attacks from Ireland, built a secure stronghold in which they could safely shelter.

*Entrance to Tre'r Ceiri Hillfort*

As no evidence has been found to indicate that the inhabitants of Tre'r Ceiri was occupied with arable farming, it may be assumed that the people were engaged in stock rearing. Therefore, the hilltop enclosure would not only be a refuge in time of trouble; bearing in mind its exposed position, it would also serve as a temporary settlement during the summer months while their flocks and herds roamed the hillside pastures.

**Access**   Take the B4417 Nefyn road for ¾ mile (1.2km) from the village of Llanaelhaearn. The rocky slopes of Yr Eifl rear up on the right-hand side. Parking space is limited near to the start of the path. The route is clearly marked on the ground as it climbs to a grassy plateau. Bear right and continue steeply up to the south-west entrance of the hillfort. Distance from the road, 1 mile (1.6km).

The fort may also be approached from the village of Llithfaen, via a track which leaves the B4417 on the right just before the crossroads. Thence by footpath in a north-easterly direction. Distance 1½ miles (2.4km).

### Carrock Fell Hillfort

Mosedale, Near Mungrisdale, Penrith, Cumbria
OS 90, (1in 83), NY342336

The summit of Carrock Fell, at 2,174ft (663m), contains the scattered ramparts of a once important Iron Age fort. It occupies an irregularly shaped enclosure of some 5 acres (2.0ha), measuring about 800ft (243m) from east to west, and at its narrowest point, about 230ft (70m) from north to south. The fort utilises the contours of the hill with the stone rampart running fairly level at its east end, and rising to the higher western section. The wall, now a broad band of stones, is interrupted by a number of gaps; although there appear to be two main entrances, one at the western end and another halfway along the southern side. Tracing the line of the collapsed wall, the best fragment of original masonry is to be found along the northern side. Inside the fort there is no evidence of hut circles, only a cairn is to be found at the eastern end, now hollowed out as a shelter. However, there are signs of settlement in the form of burial cairns in the valley of Carrock Beck to the north. Maybe these contained the remains of people whose fortress refuge stood on the hilltop. Thus situated, Carrock Fell hillfort dominated a wide area of countryside to the

*Arthur's Stone, Neolithic burial tomb, Dorstone, Herefordshire*

*Bryn Celli Ddu Chambered Cairn, Anglesey*

*Standing Stone, Uyeasound, Unst, Shetland*

*Old Oswestry Iron Age Hillfort, Shropshire*

east and north. No doubt it became an important defensive point in the territory of the Brigantes and an obvious target for the advancing Romans. Its subsequent storming and capture by them meant that its defences were slighted in such a way that the fortress would never be of any use again. The gaps in the northern and eastern sectors of the wall may be the result of this deliberate dismantling, and removal of demolished material.

**Access** From the hamlet of Mosedale follow the minor road north for approximately 1 mile (1.6km), to a point just beyond the entrance to Stone Ends Farm. Where the stone wall on the right bends away, look for a parking spot on the grassy verge. Away to the left is a small quarry and the faint remains of the former Carrock End Mine. Walk towards the quarry and bear round the right-hand side to climb the slope on a path through the bracken. This path,

called 'Rake Trod', climbs into a steep grass gully, where one has the choice of climbing directly upwards, or working through the low crags on the left. From the head of the gully continue uphill to follow a cairned route to the east peak, passing a shooting butt and a sheepfold on the way. Distance from the road 1¼ miles (2km) and 1,400ft (427m) of ascent.

## White Caterthun Hillfort
(DoE)
Bridgend, Brechin, Tayside Region
OS 44, (1in 50), NO548660
A visit to the foothills north of Brechin gives the visitor the opportunity of studying two hillforts, namely the White Caterthun and the Brown Caterthun.

The conspicuous White Caterthun fortress, 978ft (298m) above sea level, is nearly oval in shape and the massive ruined stone walls enclose an area measuring about 500ft (152m) by 230ft (70m). Of the two impressive ramparts, the inner one may originally have measured 40ft (12m) and the outside one 20ft (6m) thick. It is important to remember that the rubble from them has spread over a present width of about 100ft (30m). An entrance lies amongst the boulders in the south-east sector of the inner

*White Caterthun Hillfort*

wall. The interior of the fort contains a well, probably of similar age. Moving out from the centre of the fort the next feature beyond the tumbled walls is a low bank that encircles the hilltop with an accompanying inner ditch. Further down the hillside there are the remains

of two further earthworks with a ditch between them. It is not certain which lines of defence were completed first, except that the massive stone walls were probably constructed with a timber framework.

## Brown Caterthun Hillfort
(DoE)
OS 44, (1in 50), NO555669
The remains of this neighbouring hillfort, 943ft (287m) above sea level, lie ¾ mile (1.2km) to the north-east. The

gentle hill slopes are encircled by six lines of fortification which are quite difficult to interpret and may be explained by the possibility of a number of different periods of construction. Commencing at the lower slopes

of the hill is an earthwork with an external ditch, pierced by a number of entrances. Moving upslope one encounters another earthwork seemingly without a ditch, also having several entrances. Next come two earthworks containing nine entrances accompanied by a central ditch. Close to this line of fortification are the tumbled remains of a once formidable stone wall, some sections composed of huge boulders protecting its outer edge. Finally, a ruinous stone rampart guards the summit enclosure, which is entered by a single entrance in the northern side.

**Access** The forts lie some 5 miles (8km) north-west of Brechin. Take the minor road via Little Brechin, ignoring the turning to Tigerton about 1¾ miles (2.8km) beyond, and proceed straight on towards Bridgend. At the top of the rise there is a parking spot and signposted directions to both hillforts. White to the left and Brown to the right. There is a footpath to the top of the White Caterthun, about 400yd (360m) away. Also a footpath leads to the Brown Caterthun, in about 800yd (720m).

### Yarnbury Castle Hillfort

Winterbourne Stoke, Wiltshire
OS 184, (1in 167), SU035404
This outstanding hillfort is situated on high ground above the Wylye valley on the southern edge of Salisbury Plain. Particularly impressive are the two inner ramparts, 25ft (75m) high protected by deep ditches, but with only faint outlines of a third outer earthwork, and altogether enclosing an area of some 26 acres (10.5ha). The entrance set on the eastern side was through a gateway and passage protected by strong inturned banks and by another earthwork placed across the entrance approach. This had the purpose of deflecting a direct advance on the one weak spot in the fort's defences.

Before the construction of the larger fort, a small fort of 10 acres (4ha) occupied the interior area, protected by a single V-shaped ditch 12ft (3.6m) deep with an entrance on the western side. Its earthen rampart had a facing of timbers. Remains found point to the possibility of occupation by the Belgae and on into the Roman period. The Romans were probably responsible for the small external enclosure on the western side of the fort. Note the ridges and depressions on the eastern side of the enclosure which are the relics of sheep pens from an annual sheep fair in more modern times.

**Access** The hillfort is situated 2½ miles (4km) west of Winterbourne Stoke via the A303. Turn right at a point where a track linking the villages of Chitterne and Stapleford bisects this busy main road. If approaching from the Wylye valley main road intersection proceed for 1½ miles (2.4km) and take the track on the left.

### Mam Tor

Castleton, Derbyshire
OS 110, (1in 111), SK128838
The village of Castleton, situated on the northern edge of the limestone area of the Peak District, derives its name from Peveril Castle, an eleventh-century stronghold placed in a commanding position on the south side of the village. It is a popular spot for visitors, as the locality has a number of caves open to the public.

The surrounding scenery is particularly attractive due to the geology of the area. To the south lies a high limestone plateau, much quarried and mined in the past. To the north, the Back Tor ridge from Mam Tor to Lose Hill overlooks the fertile Vale of Edale, and beyond, to the dark sombre mass of Kinder Scout, composed largely of a coarse feldspathic sandstone-millstone grit. This is a sterile desert of fringing gritstone tors, and an inner heart of groughs and boot-sucking peat — the first or last obstacle for Pennine Way walkers!

At Castleton, the western side of the valley is dominated by Mam Tor, a hill composed of alternating bands of sandstones and shales and known as 'shivering mountain'. This description is emphasised by the huge landslip scar on its south-eastern face. It is believed that the exposed hilltop of Mam Tor 1,696ft (517m), once supported a sizeable population, as investi-gations have produced evidence of occupation with postholes, hearths, charcoal and pottery. The fragments of ware, rough and gritty, have been attributed to the Late Bronze Age or even earlier. It would also appear that a number of platforms were cut into the hillside to the east of the summit, and these most likely served as foundations for hut dwellings. The defences consist of a single earthwork strengthened by a stone facing with entrances at the north and south ends, and accompanied by a ditch and outer bank. The rampart can be traced following the contours around the hilltop and enclosing an area of aproximately 15 acres (6ha).

It is believed that the hillfort

*Mam Tor Hillfort*

defences were raised at a later date by the Brigantes, as a protective measure to safeguard their flocks and herds from raids from other tribal factions; or as a defensive measure against the threat of Roman attack.

**Access** By a well-marked footpath from the car park off the minor road over Rushup Edge to Edale from the A625. Proceed to the far end of Mam Tor summit and bear sharp left along the hillside to follow the rampart and ditch overlooking the Vale of Edale. Look out for the hut platforms on this side of the hill within the enclosure.

## SHETLAND ISLES

Some 200 miles (320km) north of Aberdeen lie the Shetland Isles, a collection of four main and hundreds of smaller islands, of which only sixteen are now inhabited; a thin straggle of deeply indented land lying north to south and in constant harmony with the sea. In fact, at one point called Mavis Grind (from the Norse *maev eiths grind*: the gate of the narrow isthmus), the Atlantic Ocean and the North Sea are little more than 100yd (91m) apart. The grain of the Caledonian rocks runs north and south through the mainland and North Isles. The land has been streamlined smooth by glacial ice action, with hundreds of small lochs, streams and marshes scattered over the moorlands. Trees are few, and those that have been planted are carefully protected against the weather and the ravages of sheep. Shetland has no mountains compared with those on the Scottish mainland, but in Ronas Hill, 1,486ft (450m), there is a granite mass that leaves the visitor with a sense of wonder at the extensive views from its tundra-like summit where arctic-alpine flora can be found.

Shetland's most spectacular feature is its coastal scenery. Continually battered by the sea, the coastline is a wealth of headlands, cliffs, clefts or geos, caves, arches, stacks and fjord-like voes. The sea supports whales, common and grey seal, and the sea coasts and moorlands abound with a great variety of birds. It is a remarkable sight to see the cliffs and ledges stacked tier upon tier with guillemots, razorbills, kittiwakes, fulmars, puffins, gannets and shags. At certain times of the year it can be quite unnerving to be 'dive-bombed' by terns and worse still by great skuas — so take a walking stick and a hard hat!

Down by the sheltered voes are small strips of carefully farmed fields, and it is in such places that early man attempted to wrest a living amongst the bare hills and on poor soils. Shetland has a wealth of archaeological remains, some difficult to reach, many well preserved, and others not so good but in fine settings. Most of them are accessible to the explorer who is prepared to go on a little expedition to seek them out. This is great country; a journey to these fascinating islands will be well rewarded, whatever the interest of the visitor. For our purposes Shetland is a microcosm of the Neolithic, Bronze Age and Iron Age periods. There are fine examples of chambered tombs, standing stones, stone circles, aisled round houses and brochs, while some features, such as burnt mounds are unique to Scotland.

# BURNT MOUNDS

These monuments appeared towards the end of the Bronze Age, and most examples are kidney-shaped in plan. The mounds are composed of a large pile of burnt stones generally quite small in size. When excavated most of these mounds contained troughs made of flat slabs of stone. The Iron Age people at the time had no suitable vessels in which to cook large pieces of meat, so they devised a clever way of overcoming the problem. The trough would be made watertight with moss and clay, filled with water and the joint of meat placed in it. In the meantime stones would be heated and placed in the trough, eventually bringing the water to boiling point. To keep the water boiling, fresh hot stones would be placed in the trough from time to time. It was a long-drawn-out business, but the diners would eventually be rewarded with a cooked piece of meat — no doubt a welcome change of diet.

---

### Identifying Features

- Composed of a large kidney-shaped pile of small burnt stones.
- Unless destroyed or removed, most mounds contain a trough of flat slabs of stone.
- Traces of hearths may be found.
- There is usually a water supply close by.

---

## Outstanding Sites

**Crawton Burnt Mound**
Crawton, Sandness, North Mainland, Shetland.
OS 3, (1in 2), HU214577
A very large kidney-shaped mound 56ft by 48ft (16.8m by 14.4m) and 5ft (1.5m) high. There appears to be no sign of a trough, and the immediate surroundings are rather boggy.
**Access** Take the main A971 road leading to Sandness, and the many small crofting communities that overlook the island of Papa Stour. After crossing the lochan-spattered moorland beyond Bridge of Walls, take the first minor road to the right and proceed for 1 mile (1.6km). Look out for a public telephone facility, and then take the next track on the left. The burnt mound lies a short distance on the left of the track to Ness.

**Burnside Burnt Mound**
Burnside, Hillswick, North Mainland, Shetland.
OS 3, (1in 2), HU280784
Although damaged, this crescent-shaped mound still stands 4ft (1.2m) high and measures 36ft by 27ft (11m by 8m). In the hollow centre of the mound there can still be seen the stones edging the cooking trough.
**Access** Take the A970 to within $\frac{3}{4}$ mile (1.2km) of Hills-wick. Turn right on to the B9078, Esha Ness road. Proceed for just over $\frac{1}{2}$ mile (1km) to a track leading to a dwelling marked Burnside on the map. The burnt mound is beside the track on the right.

**Quendale Burnt Mound**
Quendale, Toab, South Mainland, Shetland
OS 4, (1in 4), HU385128
You will need to be a little more adventurous to locate this site; but given a fine day, you will be rewarded with good views. The mound is situated on a hillside, and away from any good water supply, which is unusual. The roughly oval heap of stones measures 50ft by 27ft (15m by 8m), and stands 5ft (1.5m) high. On the north side may be seen the remains of a stone slab cooking trough.
**Access** Proceed $1\frac{1}{4}$ miles (2km) north from Sumburgh Airport on the A970, to a track leading west to the Coastguard Station on Ward Hill. Walk up the track and continue a little north of west for a distance of just over $\frac{1}{4}$ mile (0.5km). The mound lies on the hill slope overlooking the Bay of Quendale.

## AISLED ROUND HOUSES AND WHEELHOUSES

During the period of the Scottish Iron Age in the second century AD, the characteristic brochs which had served as fortified farms were allowed to fall into decay with the return of settled conditions. Many were pillaged of stone for the building of large stone roundhouses in the lee of the broch. The wheelhouse culture is a phenomenon of the Shetlands and the Hebrides; they do not exist in that form in the Orkneys. It has been suggested that the aisled round house was the next progression in design from the traditional Bronze Age stone huts. The original timber roof supports which may have proved inadequate were replaced by stone pillars. This led to the development of the pillars being connected to the outer wall with stone lintels. In time, the aisles became blocked with the stone partitions forming seven or eight roofed living recesses. This radial construction, like the spokes of a wheel, has given the name of 'wheelhouse' to these dwellings. It seems that a family unit was involved in the building of a wheelhouse, whereas a broch would have involved much greater labour resources, such as several family groups working together.

---

**Identifying Features**

**Aisled Round Houses**
- Circular houses within an enclosing stone wall.
- The roof was supported by a ring of stone pillars.
- The house contained a central hearth.

**Wheelhouses**
- These are circular houses with seven or eight roofed living recesses separated by stone partitions.
- The inner stone walls supported the roof and the centre of the building usually contained a hearth.

---

### Outstanding Sites

**Jarlshof Settlement** (DoE)
Jarlshof, Sumburgh, South Mainland, Shetland
OS 4, (1in 4), HU397096
This most famous of British archaeological sites has evidence of settlement including Neolithic, Bronze Age, Iron Age, Viking, medieval and the late sixteenth century. Superbly sited at the tip of South Mainland, it looks out across sheltered West Voe to the mass of Sumburgh Head and beyond to distant Fair Isle.

The practice of building brochs during the late Iron Age as defensive homesteads seemed to be relatively short-lived, and may only have covered a span of two or three centuries. They served the purpose, in a time of emergency, as strongly built farmhouses, protecting large numbers of people. With the return of settled conditions, from the end of the Iron Age into the Roman period, many brochs were abandoned and allowed to fall into decay; or their stone was used for the building of dwellings inside and outside the reduced towers.

At Jarlshof there is a portion of an aisled round house constructed within the courtyard round the base of the broch. Owing to the later building of wheelhouses only the northern and eastern curve of the main wall still stands 6ft (1.8m) in height. Originally, this dwelling was circular in design measuring internally nearly 32ft (9.6m) in diameter. The interior enclosing wall contains a number of alcoves which were used as store or fuel cupboards. Below them, the floor surrounding the inner edge of the wall is paved; the edge can be recognised by a line of upright stones. There is part of an oblong cooking hearth visible in the unpaved area of the floor. An upper wall ledge or scarcement probably supplied the support for a mini-roof covering the paved area. A line of timber posts driven into the ground around the edge of the inner paving would also hold up the roof. In time the design of the aisled round house improved, and pillars of drystone construction replaced the timber posts to support an enlarged roof span, and separating the interior of the house into a number of radial interconnected compartments.

On the westward side of the broch, and situated in the centre between the aisled round house and the sea, are the remains of two later wheelhouses. There are also lesser preserved examples inside and outside the remains of the broch. The best preserved wheelhouse is the central dwelling on the western side, and built partly within the side of the aisled round house. This radial structure has several dry-stone partitions, with each compartment paved with stone slabs. A kerb of upright slabs marks the boundary between the paved surround and the central court. The complete interior measures 24ft (7.2m) across which was originally entered by a passage roofed by large stone lintels. This former entrance, which included wall sockets for a door bar, is now blocked. Visitors can now enter the wheelhouse on the north-west side by means of a secondary doorway. The official publication on Jarlshof is an excellent means of studying in greater detail the long history of this fascinating site.

**Access**   Situated at the southern tip of South Mainland. Continue on the A970 past Sumburgh Airport to just before the hotel. A signposted footpath indicates the short walk to the site.

*Jarlshof Settlement*

**Kilpheder Aisled Round House**
Daliburgh, South Uist, Western Isles
OS 31, (1in 32), NF735205
This is a well preserved example, with a stout circular stone wall enclosing a courtyard, 29ft (8.8m) in diameter. About 11ft (3.4m) from the interior edge of the wall are eleven squarish dry-stone pillars set in a circle. The remaining courtyard area contains a hearth.

**Access**   Vehicle ferry from Oban to Lochboisdale, South Uist. Then by the A865 to Daliburgh. At the junction with the B888 proceed straight on taking the second turn on the right after ¾ mile (1.2km). Where the road peters out turn left, and follow the track south-south-west across the machair. On meeting a track from Kilpheder proceed west-north-west for 220yd (200m). Distance from Lochboisdale, nearly 5 miles (8km).

## BROCHS

During the first century BC, new settlers arrived in the Hebrides with new ideas and the skill of building with dry-stone. They developed the construction of an extreme form of defended homestead to a considerable height in the shape of circular dry-stone towers. These forts, known to archaeologists as brochs (from the Norse term meaning a fortified place), probably developed in Skye and spread rapidly through Orkney, Shetland, Caithness, Sutherland and the Western Isles. The main requisite was a good supply of building stone; eminently suitable were the flagstones of Orkney and Caithness. As a typical example, a broch tower consisted of an encircling wall rising from a wider foundation, some 12ft (3.6m) thick and narrowing somewhat towards the top of the structure. The height of the walls, rising to over 40ft (12.2m), suggests the purpose of a useful watchtower. Chambers led off the single small entrance passage providing a guard room and access to an internal staircase. At a certain distance above ground level, the character of the broch wall changes, becoming hollow, and invariably containing a spiral stairway that cuts through a number of level galleries.

Within the court there probably stood dwelling platforms supported by timbers at one side and resting on ledges of stone protruding from the inner face of the broch. Some brochs have extra defensive qualities within the wall, such as narrow passages allowing a defender to bar the way, and spaces in the floor of the gallery so that an intruder could be speared from the gallery above. In Shetland, as many brochs were situated at strategic sites along the shore, it is clear that the inhabitants feared an attack from the sea.

In troubled times a broch would seem to have been an ideal place to shelter. At the approach of the enemy the local inhabitants would have had time to offer a few rude gestures and quickly retire to safety within. In those days, attackers would simply not have had the technology to gain access. However, I am sure that the Romans, with their siege equipment and technical skills would have made short work of any broch.

### Identifying Features

- Found in the north of Scotland, and in the western and northern Isles.
- They are regarded as another form of defended homestead.
- The broch wall is a dry-stone structure, circular in plan, usually about 15ft (4.5m) thick, and from 30ft to 40ft (9m-12.2m) in internal diameter.
- The height of the brochs cannot be stated with accuracy, but were probably on average some 20ft to 43ft (6m-13m) in height.
- Access is by a single entrance through a solid masonry base. Above, the encircling wall is hollow, containing galleried passages that are connected by an internal staircase.
- The interior probably sheltered a number of lean-to dwellings.
- A typical broch situation is on higher ground overlooking good farming land.

### Outstanding Sites

**The Broch of Mousa** (DoE)
Sandwick, Mousa Island, South Mainland, Shetland
OS 4, (1in 4), HU457237
The broch on the island of Mousa stands today almost complete and is regarded as the finest example of its type in Britain. It is just over 43ft (13m) tall, which is probably nearly its original height. The tower has a solid base measuring 50ft (15m) in diameter with the lower part of the walls 15ft (4.5m) thick enclosing a central courtyard 20ft (6.1m) in diameter. The whole building is of dry-stone construction using locally obtained flags from the thin-bedded series of the Old Red Sandstone rocks.

At the top of the tower the width is 40ft (12m). The building has a profile like a stubby bottle-oven kiln, wider at the base, then tapering and swelling out again. There is a single entrance from the seaward side leading to the inner court-yard, its passage 4ft (1.2m) wide and 16ft (4.9m) in length. Originally there was a door half-way along the passage to prevent unwanted visitors gaining access to the interior. Within the solid wallbase are three oval-shaped cells with corbelled roofs. These are reached from the inner court through narrow doorways. At a later date these recesses were partly covered by the construction of a wheelhouse wall. At a height of 7ft (2.1m) and on the same level as the lower scarcement, the broch wall is of hollow construction to the top of the wall. Within this hollow wall are six galleries

bonded together by lintels of large stone slabs, so that the roof of each gallery forms the floor of the one above. A steep narrow stairway leaves from an opening 7ft (2.1m) above the level of the interior courtyard floor and spirals up through the galleries to the top of the wall. The interior court of the broch may once have held a wheelhouse-like building raised at a later date. There may have been dwellings outside the broch, and as an added defensive measure, a stone rampart was raised across the narrow part of the small headland on which the broch stands.

**Access**  The broch is situated on the west side of the island of Mousa, some $1\frac{1}{2}$ miles (2.4km), from Sand Lodge, South Mainland, from where a boat can be hired. (Details published locally.)

*Broch of Mousa*

### Clickhimin Broch and Wheelhouse (DoE)
Lerwick, Mainland Island, Shetland
OS 4, (1in 4), HU465408
Excavation evidence here points to the fact that the upper stonework of the broch was dismantled, and the inner courtyard raised and drained. The stone was then used to construct a wheelhouse wall within the broch courtyard. It contained a recess in the north wall which was probably used for storing fuel such as peat. The dwelling would have contained radial stone partition walls forming living areas, that looked out on to a central court containing a cooking hearth. Some post holes were discovered a little distance in towards the centre of the court, which

*Clickhimin Broch and Wheelhouse*

indicates that timber uprights were placed in position to support a storeyed building with upper floors. The official publication on Clickhimin is an excellent means of studying in greater detail the history of this interesting site.

**Access** The site is situated at the southern end of Loch of Clickhimin, on the south-western outskirts of Lerwick, via the A970 road to the south. The monument is signposted.

**Dun Telve and Dun Troddan Brochs** (DoE)
Glenelg, Kyle of Lochalsh, Highland Region, Scotland
OS 33, (1in 35), NG829173, NG834172

These two well-preserved brochs are fine examples of defensive dwellings situated in a beautiful and remote glen facing the Isle of Skye. Gleann Beag is fertile, and it may well be because of this that it was inhabited for at least two thousand years. The narrow road hugs the riverside and curves through woods of alder and hazel. The fine shape and symmetry of these two monuments are testimonials to the skill and workmanship employed in the construction of these dry-stone buildings.

The tower of Dun Telve Broch reaches a height of 33ft (10m), and by the entrance the

*Dun Telve Broch*

base wall has a thickness of 13ft (3.9m). Galleries spiral up within the thickness of the double wall which tapers to become a single wall at the top. The inner court is about 30ft (9.1m) in diameter, from which position two scarcements may be observed.

Dun Troddan Broch is popularly ranked as the third-best preserved broch, with a wall

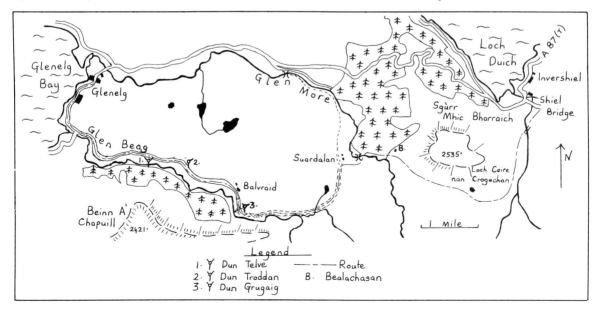

Legend
1. Ỿ Dun Telve
2. Ỿ Dun Troddan
3. Ỿ Dun Grugaig
------ Route
B. Bealachasan

which rises to a height of 25ft (7.6m), and a similar thickness of masonry at the entrance as that of its neighbour, Dun Telve. The broch contains wall cells, three galleries, stairway and scarcement, and the courtyard is about 28ft (8.4m) in diameter.

**Access**   Access is from Shiel Bridge, via Bealach Ratagan (Ratagan Pass), and the old Military Road to Glenelg. Distance 9 miles (14.4km). Proceed left at the fork, continue through the village, along the shore of Glenelg Bay, and in $1\frac{1}{4}$ miles (2km) turn east up the Gleann Beag road. From this point the distance to Dun Telve is $1\frac{3}{4}$ miles (2.8km), and to the site of Dun Troddan is $\frac{1}{2}$ mile (800m) further up the valley.

For enthusiastic hill walkers there is a moderately strenuous trek of 13 miles (21km), which includes interesting mountain scenery with ever-changing views. Leave the A87 on the old road to Glenshiel Lodge. Turn left and follow the path on the east bank of the Allt Undalain Cross by a wooden bridge to climb steadily at first and then steeply bearing west round the shoulder of Sgurr Mhic Bharraich to Loch Coire nan Crogachan. Beyond lies the Sound of Sleat and the mountains of the Isle of Skye. The path descends past a waterfall and through a ravine to a stretch of moorland. Follow the river valley and head towards a house in the distance marked Bealachasan on the map. At the house, cross the stream, through a forest gate, and bear left downhill following the fence to meet a forestry road. Continue on this forest road until you observe a bridge on your left over the Glen More River. Cross this bridge and turn right along the river bank for a few yards, then bear west to reach a large walled enclosure. Turn left and follow the wall to a farm building marked Suardalan on the map. A barely visible track passes to the west of this small farm building and proceeds uphill to the west of Torr Beag. This way gradually improves to descend to the valley of the Abhainn a Ghlinne Bhig, and passing the site of Dun Grugaig to the building marked Balvraid on the map. Dun Troddan is 1 mile (1.6km) and Dun Telve is $1\frac{1}{2}$ miles (2.4km) from here. From the latter, the distance to Glenelg is 3 miles (4.8km).

# DUNS

As the broch was an extreme form of defended homestead, so duns (Gaelic, *dun:* a fort or fortified dwelling place), in the main also belong to the homestead category. Hundreds of these fortified dwellings are to be found in Scotland. There are several types from plain dry-stone circular or oval structures without galleries, to substantial dwellings with an entrance door, passages and internal steps. Some of the encircling walls are massively built; so strong are they that they were used and re-used over many centuries. Like hillforts, many of the Scottish duns are situated on prominent vantage points amid spectacular and rugged scenery.

## Identifying Features

- They are found in south-west Scotland, and in the western highlands and islands.
- They may be regarded as another form of fort or fortified homestead.
- They may be similar in design to hillforts, having a thick stone wall protecting an enclosure which housed hut dwellings.
- The duns may be oval, circular or rectangular in shape.
- In other examples, the massively-built dry-stone wall may be 16ft (4.8m) thick; it may be pierced by a door opening, and contain passage ways and steps to the top of the wall.
- It is more than likely that they were occupied at various intervals over the centuries, before, throughout and after the Roman period.
- Many duns are situated in isolated places amongst rugged mountains. To locate some of them entails one of the more challenging aspects in discovering and understanding the countryside.

**Outstanding Sites**

**Dun Carloway** (DOE)
Carloway, Stornoway, Isle of Lewis
OS 8, (1in 8), NB189412
Although robbed of its stone in the past, the remains of this well-preserved broch still clearly show its internal construction. At the base the overall diameter is 46ft (14m), the wall measures about $11\frac{1}{2}$ ft (3.5m) across, and the inner court is 24ft (7.2m) across. The entrance passage with its cell is in good condition, and the galleries within the double wall are accessible by a stairway from a wall chamber at ground level. As with the Mousa broch, the inner and outer walls are held together by lintels, so that the roof of each gallery forms the floor of the one above. The corbelling of the lower part of the wall suggests that the interior of the broch was used to support either a floor or a roof for a courtyard dwelling.

*Dun Carloway Broch*

**Access**   Vehicle and passenger ferries run from Ullapool to Stornoway, $3\frac{1}{4}$ hours, and from Uig (Skye) to Tarbert (North Harris), 2 hours. The broch is situated on the western side of Lewis, 15 miles (24km) north-west of Stornoway. Take the A858, and bear left on a byroad $1\frac{1}{4}$ miles (2km) from the head of Loch Carloway. The monument is located at Doune Carloway, about 660yd (600m) from the junction with the main road. There are parking facilities nearby.

**Dun Grugaig**
Glasnakille, Elgol, Isle of Skye, Highland Region, Scotland
OS 32 (1in 34), NG535124
The route down the Strathaird peninsula winds round the head of Loch Slapin and ends at Elgol. From this point the visitor is close to obtaining the classic view of the Cuillin Hills. For explorers who would like an open look at them, an interesting footpath leaves the village and heads north contouring above the shoreline of Loch Scavaig. Given good weather, this route offers a marvellous oportunity to view one of the most famous mountain skylines in Great Britain.
   The peaks take their name from *Kjöllen*, the Old Norse for 'keel-shaped ridges'. The hills of the Black Cuillin ARE NO PLACE FOR THE INEXPERIENCED WALKER. Spires and pinnacles of rock soar into the sky, ravines and gulleys bar progress, and ridges are so narrow in places that you can literally put your hands on the top, and look over to a drop of many many hundreds of feet. From Glen Brittle a path leads into Coire Lagan, the tiny lake surrounded by savage cliffs that are draped with large expanses of scree. The most spectacular of these is the Great Stone Shoot which drops some 1,500ft (457m) from the summit of Sgurr Alasdair.
   A through walk of nearly 11 miles (17km) from Elgol to Sligachan Hotel via Camasunary, Loch na Crèitheach and Glen Sligachan, will certainly give the walker a good impression of these magnificent mountains. But remember, you must return to Elgol village if you wish to explore Dun Grugaig.
   On the eastern side of the Strathaird peninsula, some $1\frac{3}{4}$ miles (2.8km) from Elgol, lies the site of Dun Grugaig. This is a small but strongly fortified rectangular dun situated on a headland overlooking the entrance to Slapin and Erisort sea lochs. A massive defensive wall on the western side 15ft (4.5m) thick traces a rectangular course, with an interior measurement of 50ft (15.2m) by 25ft (7.6m). The entrance is also

on the western side with the remains of a gallery in the wall still visible above it. Within the courtyard there is an opening in the wall which is the stairway access to the upper gallery.

*Dun Grugaig*

**Access** Situated 16½ miles (26.4km) south-west of Broadford via the A881 to Elgol and thence by narrow road to Glasnakille. Park by the public telephone box, and turn south along the shore road. The road twists sharply and then passes a white cottage on the right. Look for the next 'Passing Place' sign, and go left towards the sea down a grassy gully. Beware of the crevice and cliffs; it is not a place to bring gambolling children and people of a nervous disposition. Although the remains are slight the place has a distinctive atmosphere.

**Dun Mhuirich**
Tayvallich, Knapdale,
Lochgilphead, Strathclyde
Region, Scotland

OS 55, (1in 58), NR722845
This dun is situated on an excellent defensive site above the water of Linne Mhuirich. A

*Dun Mhuirich*

fairly well preserved wall, in parts 7½ft (2.3m) thick, encircles a rocky eminence, and forming an enclosure measuring some 53ft (16.1m) by 42ft (12.8m). There are traces of an outer defensive wall around the dun, except on the eastern flank, where there is a steep drop down to the shore. Also, the foundations of dwellings may be recognised close to the outer wall.
**Access** The dun is situated some 14 miles (22.4km) west of Lochgilphead near to the Sound of Jura. Take the A816, B841 and the B8025 to Tayvallich. The dun lies close to the east side of the road, some 2 miles (3.2km) south-west of the village.

**Kildonan Bay Dun**
Kildonald Bay, Campbeltown,
Strathclyde Region, Scotland
OS 68, (1in 65), NR780277
This galleried dun, in a fairly

good state of preservation, is situated close to the shore line of Kildonald Bay on the eastern side of the Mull of Kintyre. The defensive wall is roughly oval in

shape and contains an interior courtyard which measures some 70ft (21.3m) by 40ft (12.2m). The wall is not of uniform thickness, varying in width from

5ft 6in (1.7m) to 14ft (4m). It accommodates an entrance passage, a mural cell and an opening to a double stairway. The dun was probably constructed in the Early Iron Age.

**Access**  The monument is situated 6½ miles (10.4km) north-east of Campbeltown via the B842. It lies close to the road 1¾ miles (2.8km) beyond Peninver Bridge. Marked as 'Dun' on the 1:50,000 map.

### Queen's View Dun
Loch Tummel, Pitlochry, Tayside Region, Scotland
OS 43, (1in 48), NN864602
This dun is marked on the 1:50,000 OS map as 'Homestead'. The lower courses of the wall are fairly well preserved, being some 10ft (3m) thick, and the interior enclosure measures about 55ft (16.7m) in diameter.

**Access**  It is situated in the forest only ¼ mile (0.4km) north of the B8019, and just a short distance from the Visitors Centre and the famous view-point over Loch Tummel.

Approaching from the Pass of Killiecrankie, proceed beyond the hotel, take a forest track on the right and then a footpath. The dun is situated in a forest clearing on the route of an overhead power line.

## CRANNOGS

These are small defended artificial islands built on a foundation of brushwood and logs or peat and large stones, and further supported on piles driven into the shallow waters of a lake, estuary or marsh. The word crannog is derived from the Irish word *crann*, a tree, meaning either the use of wood in its construction, or relating to the profusion in the growth of trees and shrubs on its surface.

The artificial island would be occupied by a circular timber-framed, grass or turf roofed house, and although in time the house would rot away, the crannog island would last forever. It is believed that many such homesteads were in use until medieval times. A causeway of stones led from the shore to the island, laid in such a way as to be slightly submerged at normal water level. Boats were usually docked in a small sheltered enclosure on the open water side. Some crannogs were surrounded by a strong protective stockade or by a stone wall.

### Identifying Features

• Now generally recognised as small tree or scrub-covered circular or oval-shaped islands.
• Occasionally known to have been located in estuarine waters or in areas of former marshland, but usually found in lakes.
• Many of the existing lake crannogs lie in shallower water up to varying distances offshore.
• Many crannogs have disappeared due to drainage and peat cutting operations. At a distance it may not always be possible to distinguish the difference between a natural island and an artifical one.
• Although only a few sites have been excavated, these monuments are of archaeological interest due to the preservation of many objects by the wet peat.

### Outstanding Sites

**Lough-na-Cranagh**
Townland of Cross, Fair Head, Ballycastle, Co Antrim, Northern Ireland
OS, NI 5, New Series, (1in 1), D178427
This well-preserved example of a crannog, although unexcavated, lies in Lough-na-Cranagh, a small lake set in a green bowl among the hills. The oval-shaped artifical island rises from

the water to a height of 6ft (1.8m) and is enclosed by a boulder wall. The interior measures about 87ft (27m) by 118ft (36m), mainly grass-covered at its northern tip and decorated by a small clump of weather-beaten trees at its southern end.

Loch-na-Cranagh

**Access**    The site is some 4½ miles (7.2km) east-north-east of Ballycastle. At Ballyvoy, take the minor road straight on, and then the first by-road on the left. Continue directly along this lane through the hamlet of Craigfad, and then turning sharp left to end at a small scatter of houses. Here parking space is available. The site lies ¼ mile (400m) to the north by footpath. For a clearer view of the crannog it is necessary to leave the path, proceed left through a gate and down the sloping meadow.

### Loch Bruicheach Crannog
Druimkinnerras, Kiltarlity, Beauly, Inverness, Highland Region
OS 26, (1in 27), NH455368
This remote site is tucked away in the hills between the Boblainy Forest and Eskdale Moor south of the River Beauly.

The footpath leads towards the northern shore of Loch Bruicheach and to the location of the crannog. Although there is little information available about the site, it appears that the top surface of the crannog was vitrified. Perhaps when the island dwelling was destroyed by fire, it may in turn have set alight the timber framework of the foundation, producing fierce internal heat that fused the materials together.

**Access**    Leave the A833 on the minor road to Kiltarlity and Culburnie. After closely following and crossing the stream, leave the minor road ½ mile (800m) beyond the bridge at NH485414 and take the narrow lane running south-west across Culburnie Muir to Druimkinnerras. Bear left towards the dwelling marked Knockvuy on the map, where the track ends. From this point, a path leads south, then south-west, and continues south climbing the valley on the east bank of the stream towards Loch Bruicheach. The site of the crannog is marked on the 1:50,000 map. Distance from NH485414 is 3½ miles (5.6km).

### Drumgay Lough Crannogs
Enniskillen, Co Fermanagh, Northern Ireland
OS, NI 17, New Series, (1in 7), H2447
The sites of four crannogs are marked on the New Series map and may be seen to lesser and greater advantage from the minor road to Ballinamallard, 2½-2¾ miles (4-4.4km) north of Enniskillen. The countryside around Lower Lough Erne, Fermanagh Lakeland, contains numerous examples of lake crannogs.

### Loch Arthur
Beeswing, Dumfries, Dumfries and Galloway Region
OS 84, (1in 81), NX903690
Situated close to the north-west shore of Loch Arthur. Access by footpath.

### Lochrutton Loch
Lockfoot, Dumfries, Dumfries and Galloway Region
OS 84 (1in 74), NX898730
The circular crannog is situated in the middle of the loch. It can be seen from the minor road running south from the village of Lochfoot.

# RATHS

Looking at the place names on a detailed map of Ireland, one cannot fail to notice the mention of the word 'rath'. They are the sites of simple protected farmsteads comprising a circular area of varying size with a raised earthen bank. The ditch or ditches from which the material was obtained was usually filled with water, and access to the interior platform was by means of a causeway. Raths have a long history extending over thousands of years from the Neolithic to the Early Christian period and into medieval times. They are most numerous amidst the lush green lowland meadows and easily recognisable anywhere in the country. Also found in Ireland are elaborate stone versions of the rath or ring fort with staircases and chambers within the walls. Stone-walled forts are usually termed 'cashels' and sometimes 'cahers'. Whereas earthen forts were usually constructed from the material dug up from the ditches or trenches, the walls of stone forts are built of stones collected from the surrounding area.

## Identifying Features

- They are the sites of simple protected farmsteads, and can be seen almost anywhere in Ireland.
- Some were constructed prior to the Iron Age and many others are of the Early Christian period.
- They comprise a circular area of varying size with a raised earthen bank protected by a ditch.
- Access to the interior platform is by means of a causeway.
- The distribution pattern of raths is mirrored in the present-day landscape of rural Ireland by its mosaic of farms and scattered homesteads.

## Outstanding Sites

### Budore Raths

Budore, Crumlin, Co Antrim, Northern Ireland
OS, NI 14, New Series, (1 in 6), J234763
These raths are situated close together, with the univallate type to the south having a diameter of 120ft (36.5m) and its ditch almost filled in. The second rath, 40ft (12.2m) away is bivallate, with an interior diameter of 90ft (27.4m). The inner ditch is well-preserved and, although partly silted up, has a depth of 13ft (3.9m). The central enclosure has a raised aspect which is probably due to a subsequent levelling of the inner earthwork. It is possible that the second rath is of medieval origin because of its

*Budore Rath*

clear outline and good condition.

**Access**    The raths are located by the side of a minor road east of Thompson's Bridge, and some 6 miles (9.6km) east of Crumlin. Take the A52 from Crumlin to Nutts Corner, then the B101 for $1\frac{3}{4}$ miles (2.8km). Turn left along the B154 for $\frac{3}{4}$ mile (1.2km), and then right for $\frac{1}{2}$ mile (800m). The raths lie close to the junction of a farm lane with the minor road.

### Livery Hill Rath

Livery Hill, Stranocum, Ballymoney, Co Antrim, Northern Ireland
OS, NI 5, New Series, (1 in 3), D014 296
This is a tree-fringed site in an attractive setting on the banks of the Bush River. A fairly large enclosure is contained by a single substantial earthen bank, with entrances on the western and eastern sides. However, there is a possibility that one of the entrances was made at a later date. The rath is protected by an encircling ditch except on the northern side where there is a steep drop down to the river. The interior is grazed by cattle and is free of vegetation.

**Access**    Situated $5\frac{1}{4}$ miles (8.4km) north-east of Bally-money via the B147. Turn right entering Stranocum on to a by-road. The site lies on the left-hand side of the road opposite a road junction, and nearly $\frac{1}{2}$ mile (800m) from the village.

### Rough Fort Rath (NT)

Bessbrook Bridge, Limavady, Co Londonderry, Northern Ireland
OS, NI 4, New Series, (1 in 2), C658230
This circular tree-fringed rath is in fairly good condition with a deep ditch and steep earthen bank protecting the enclosure which is relatively free of undergrowth.

**Access**    Situated by the side of the main road, 1 mile (1.6km) west of the centre of Limavady. The rath lies $\frac{1}{2}$ mile (800m) west of the crossroads of the A2 and the B69, by the junction of a farm lane to Moneyrannel.

### Tullaghoge Rath

Township of Ballymully Glebe, Cookstown, Co Tyrone, Northern Ireland
OS, NI 13, New Series, (1 in 5), H825744
The overall diameter of the twin-ringed rath or ring fort is about 270ft (82.3m), with a wide space between the two banks. The outer earthwork is about 6ft (1.8m) high and the inner bank rises about 10ft (3m) above its encircling ditch. It is believed that the original entrance was situated on the northern side.

Although the site is now over-grown with trees, it has always been recognised as the inaugur-ation site of the O'Neills, and the capital of medieval Tyrone. The 'Kings Stone' which once stood inside the rath was destroyed in the sixteenth century.

**Access**    From Cookstown take the main Dungannon road south for nearly $1\frac{3}{4}$ miles (2.8km). Just past Kings Bridge over the Ballinderry River, bear left on a secondary road to a road junction. Do not turn sharp left, but head slightly south-east for 1 mile (1.6km) to cross over the Killymoon River and on to Tullaghoge. A track heading north from the village gives access to the ring fort which is sited on a low hill 300ft (91.5m) high.

### Knockans Rath

Knockans, Cushendall, Co Antrim, Northern Ireland
OS, NI 5, New Series, (1 in 3), D226263
This rath is centred on a small rock outcrop at the foot of the steep northern slopes of Lurigethan. Well sited at 320ft (110m) above sea level, the rath commands extensive views sea-wards and overlooks Glen Ballyemon. The rampart contours round the rock outcrop to form an oval-shaped enclosure with rising ground at its north-eastern end. The rampart, which is plainly seen along the northern side, is not visible on the southern side, and was probably destroyed by the line of the present road.

**Access**    From Cushendall take the B14 Ballymena road climbing steadily for just over $1\frac{1}{2}$ miles (2.4km). Turn left along a byroad, and the site which is easily accessible, is a short distance along on the left.

*View from Carrock Fell Iron Age Hillfort, Cumbria*

*The Vallum, Hadrian's Wall, Northumberland*

Hardknott Roman Fort, Cumbria

Portchester Roman Shore Fort and Medieval Keep, Hampshire

# CHAPTER FIVE
# The Romans

The reasons for Caesar's invasions of Britain in 55 and 54BC are not clear. From his base in southern France he had already subdued the Gaulish tribes of France and Belgium. From the information he received from traders and merchants from Britain, it is possible that he feared an alliance of the British tribes, now grown more powerful, and their Continental cousins. His excursion across the seas to an unknown land to extend the frontiers of Rome might suggest that no obstacle could hold back the career of this ambitious nobleman. In 55BC he took tremendous risks, setting out on a military expedition late on in the year; in fact, in 54 his fleet was badly damaged by wind and tide. After the capture of the fortress of the Catuvellauni, Caesar decided that Britain was not a conquest priority, as his ambitions would just as easily be furthered by subduing Gaul.

When Caesar had departed, the Catuvellauni gradually expanded their territory at the expense of their weaker neighbours, despite the treaties with Rome promising to protect them. After the death of their leader, Cunobelin, the Catuvellauni at once conquered more territory in southern Britain. This expansion led to the capture of the last remaining strongholds in southern Sussex, and an envoy fled to Rome for help.

Claudius became emperor and his own precarious future was upheld by the loyalty of his troops. Rome's eyes were once more directed towards Britain, always considered to be unfinished business after Caesar's excursions. Further weight was added to the belief that here was now a hostile power on the frontiers of imperial Rome, and that retribution was necessary to satisfy the country's treaty obligations. The Senate was also impressed by the thought of crossing the sea, and so here was an ideal opportunity for Claudius to gain the virtue and prestige of military success by conquering the whole of Britain.

The reasons for the decision to invade may be too complex to dismiss with such a simple explanation. Perhaps it was the need for an imperial victory or to settle scores with the Catuvellauni and the Druids, or to reap the reward of Britain's great mineral wealth, or to find work for the surplus legions sitting on the banks of the Rhine — whatever the reasons, the time was right.

An army consisting of four legions under the command of Aulus Plautius (II Augusta, IX Hispana, XIV Gemina and XX Valeria, and auxiliaries), about 40,000 men in all, was assembled at Boulogne and embarked for Britain.

It would appear that the only landing place of the Roman army in AD43 that has been clearly identified was at Richborough in Kent. The landing was unopposed, but on moving inland to the Medway, the Britons attacked, and in one of the battles their leader Togodumnus was killed. Within days, the Romans crossed the Thames and occupied the Catuvellaunian capital at Colchester.

It became clear to the Britons that this time Roman rule was to be permanent. After the departure of Claudius, the army was divided into three battle groups, with a fourth staying behind in their newly captured base. Legion II was despatched to the south and south-west where it had to overcome severe resistance before capturing the Isle of Wight, as well as defeating the inhabitants of some twenty hillforts, including Maiden Castle and Hod Hill.

Legion IX headed towards the north-east to be based at Lincoln, with Legion XIV advancing through the Midlands with its early fortress at Wroxeter near Shrewsbury. During this period of consolidation, it would appear that the Rivers Severn and Trent formed natural boundaries, behind which was established a network of roads and forts.

In any captured territory, the policy of the Romans was to install native rulers, who, in return for protection, were allowed to run their own affairs, providing they maintained their allegiance to Rome. This proved to be an economical method of controlling a new province with a minimum of manpower, and enabled the provincial governor to manage with a small administrative staff.

However, trouble was never far away, as the other former ruler of the Catuvellauni, Caractacus, had escaped and joined the Welsh tribes of the Silures and Ordovices. Eventually he fled north and was finally captured with the help of Cartimandua, Queen of the Brigantes, who was an ally of Rome. He had much success in guerrilla warfare in the earlier years, but chose to engage in a full-scale battle against the disciplined might of the Roman army, and was completely defeated. Caractacus was eventually captured and displayed at Rome.

In East Anglia the Roman administration treated the Iceni as a conquered nation incorporating their territory into the province. The people, under the widowed Queen Boudicca, rebelled against Roman rule. Their ranks were swelled by the Trinovantes, who were furious because their lands around Colchester had also been seized. At first, the rebels were very successful, destroying Colchester, London and *Verulamium* (St Albans), and massacring many of their inhabitants. With part of Legion XI ambushed by Boudicca and the infantry wiped out, Suetonius Paulinus, the governor, decided to retreat to relatively open country between Towcester and Atherstone. Having chosen an advantageous site, Paulinus, gathered what forces he could together and faced the rebels. Inevitably, this wild native rabble was no match in a set-piece battle controlled by the well-trained Roman army. The Britons were very heavily defeated, the remnants fled in disorder, and Boudicca committed suicide.

It was understood in Imperial Rome that Britain could only be ruled if a more understanding approach was adopted.

In AD67, Legion XIV Gemina was tempor-arily withdrawn, and between AD71 and 74 the governor Petillius Cerealis, with the replacement Legion II Adiutrix, marched north to Lincoln to deal with a serious Brigantian revolt. Cerealis campaigned against the Brigantes who probably made their last stand at Stanwick, near Scotch Corner.

Cerealis took few steps to hold the region and the only new fortification known is the legionary fortress at York. This site grew in importance over the years, and the defences were substantially increased and strengthened.

Julius Frontinus, the new governor, realised that as the power of the northern Brigantes had been broken, he could deploy his forces in the delayed task of subduing the Silures of Wales. The campaign was carefully planned and new forts were built at Neath and Caerleon, with the remaining territory being controlled by a number of other forts set at short intervals and manned by auxiliary detachments.

Gnaeus Julius Agricola, who arrived in AD78, is the best known governor of Britain, as the result of the biography left by his son-in-law Tacitus. He placed the seal on the Roman occupation of Britain. Firstly he moved into Wales and completely defeated the Ordovices, advancing into Anglesey. Forts were established to control the main routes, giving clear evidence of the man's strategic genius. With the establishment of Chester, the military control of the area was now complete. Agricola also imposed his high standards on the reform of the administration, curbing the existing tax excesses and abuses.

In AD79 Agricola and his army were on the march again, and the routes of his advance may be marked by the two principal Roman roads into Scotland, one on the west on the line of the A6, and along the Lune and Eden valleys, the other on the east from York through County Durham and Northumberland.

Now, as a result of these advances, a new generation of fortresses was required, in addition to numerous auxiliary forts, including the most northerly legionary fortress for the twentieth Valeria Victrix at Inchtuthill on the banks of the Tay. Here, it was said, was the spot that Agricola chose as the centre of his proposed operations against the Scottish tribes. The climax of his campaign in the north was a decisive victory over the Caledonian tribes at a site called *Mons Graupius*, reputed to be at Bennachie in Aberdeen shire.

During the winter of AD84-5 Agricola was recalled to Rome after serving a long term as governor. He was an outstanding figure, remembered as a great soldier and builder of roads and forts, who was capable of seeing beyond the battle, to the settlement and peaceful administration of a conquered territory.

However, Emperor Domitian turned to Britain for reinforcements, and Britain had to provide one legion, Legion II Adiutrix and numbers of auxiliaries for campaigns on the continent. Thus a withdrawal was gradually made to the line of the Solway-Tyne. The northern fortress of Inchtuthill was abandoned, although this decision may also have been hastened by the action of warring tribes, and there is evidence that some forts were violently attacked and burnt during the withdrawal.

In northern Britain the peace was tenuous, and the frontier now was the Stanegate, Agricola's road across part of the Tyne-Solway isthmus. In the same decade the consolidation of the three remaining army bases took place: the legionary fortresses at York, Chester and Caerleon. The defences were made stronger and more permanent by the addition of stout masonry walls, and were equipped with internal towers, which probably meant that the period of mobile warfare was over for the foreseeable future.

Emperor Hadrian visited Britain in AD122, just after another serious war in northern Britain had successfully concluded. It was then decided to construct a defensive barrier far stronger than had been built elsewhere in the empire.

As a result, the wall named after the emperor was built from the Tyne to the Solway Firth, acting as a fortified base line for the northern garrison. The route takes advantage of the nature of the landform, especially in the central sector where it occupies the summits of the basaltic ridges of the Whin Sill. The wall was constructed by the Legions II Augusta, VI and XX each being allotted various sectors. Consequently, the rate of progress was rather uneven, with the wall in one sector having wider

foundations than the superstructure. Milecastles and turrets were built at regular intervals and the wall was further strengthened by a ditch and earthwork on the southern side, known as the vallum. Allowing for alterations in design, apart from the reconstruction of the turf wall in stone which was done later on, the whole project took about four years to complete. By all accounts, it was a wonderful achievement by an army of soldier-labourers, some 10,000 to 15,000 in number.

In AD139 Hadrian died and was succeeded by Antoninus Pius. The governor Lollius Urbicus advanced into lowland Scotland and won the necessary victory over the Scottish tribes. This enabled him to establish new frontier controls on the narrow neck of the Forth-Clyde line. There was no system of milecastles, and the garrison forts, thinly manned due to shortage of troops, were placed closer together compared with those on Hadrian's Wall.

In AD155, a serious revolt, possibly by the Brigantes, meant that reinforcements were needed and the Antonine Wall garrisons were moved south, leaving the barrier temporarily unmanned. Although southern Scotland was reoccupied and the wall reinforced, events in the Roman Empire saw the moving of more troops from Britain to Gaul.

Another crisis in AD163 saw the final abandonment of southern Scotland and the Antonine Wall. There was more unrest elsewhere in Britain, and the northern tribes destroyed parts of Hadrian's Wall, burning many of the forts to the ground, destroying the *vici*, the civilised villages, and annihilating the inhabitants. Order was slowly restored and by AD208 the Wall and most of the ruined forts were rebuilt. Scotland was invaded again and from AD213-70 peace reigned in northern Britain, including more settled times in the territory of the Brigantes.

A very significant event was the granting of Roman citizenship to all freeborn men and women. Although taxes were increased, it meant that the population enjoyed greater privileges. Soldiers could now buy land, and marriage with the local people was legally allowed.

Settled conditions never lasted, and there was increasing insecurity in south-east England due to the Saxon raids. These raiders from northern Germany attacked the shores and plundered the settlements, and so forts were constructed at vital points along the coastline. These were to be known later as the Saxon Shore defences.

In AD286, Carausius declared himself emperor of Britain and northern Gaul, but after he was murdered later that year, Constantius recovered Britain and set about the task of rebuilding parts of Hadrian's Wall, some of the Pennine forts and the legionary fortresses at Chester and York. With the return of Britain to the empire, prosperity and settled times returned. This state of affairs continued under his son, Constantine, until his death in AD337. Shortly afterwards trouble flared up once again on the northern frontier with attacks by the Picts and Scots, who destroyed several outpost forts on the Wall. Order was restored by the emperor Constans, but changes in leadership during the next few years led to a weakening of the garrison in Britain.

Perhaps this was one of only several factors that combined to make the opportunity ripe for the barbarian invasion of AD367. In the north overwhelming and concerted attacks by the Picts, Scots and Saxons overran Hadrian's Wall despite its defenders, and in the south, the Count of the Saxon Shore was killed in action.

For the next two years chaos reigned throughout the land, and it was left to Theodosius to come to Britain with army reinforcements to restore the situation. The Wall was repaired, together with some forts, and signal stations were built along the Yorkshire coast. This increased security restored the *status quo* and towns and villas began to prosper once more.

In AD383 Magnus Maximus rebelled against Rome, and although he was quickly defeated, the regiments taken from these islands never returned. Further weakened, Britain was subjected to increased attacks, particularly on the Welsh coast by the Irish. Further attacks threatened Rome and more of the garrison left Britain. In AD407 Constantine III removed the last remaining troops to Gaul where there were very serious disturbances. After his death, the next emperor, Honorius, told the British settlements to look to their own defence.

So after a period of nearly four hundred years, the Roman occupation had created and developed a civilised and prosperous province. Trade flourished, technology improved and the admini stration maintained law and order, despite lengthy periods of fighting on the northern frontiers and intermittent attacks along the coastline.

We have much to thank the Romans for in the field of organisational and administration thoroughness, their policy of strong defences, and the establishment of settlements, farms and villas linked by good communincations. All combined to constitute a solid platform for the very gradual emergence and growth of the British nation. Fortunately there is still much evidence of their long stay to study, admire and enjoy. They were a fascinating and unique people, who transformed a turbulent land of warring tribes, in the lowland areas particularly, into an ordered prosperous society.

## ROMAN FORTS AND FORTRESSES

The Roman army had a number of types of encampment: the permanent auxiliary garrison, the great legionary fortresses, the marching camp for overnight stops on campaign, the practice camp for military training, and the small guard post called a fortlet. The permanent forts were the bases of the Roman forces, particularly auxiliary units, quartered there for policing and supervision of the newly conquered tribal territory. Generally the shape of the fort was like that of a playing-card with straight sides and rounded corners. The first permanent establishments were built in turf and timber, ranging in size from $2\frac{1}{2}$ to 8 acres (1 to 3.2ha), with a protective ring of ditches. Set at intervals along the earthen ramparts were towers and gateways also constructed of timber. Later on, the defensive mounds were strengthened by a stone wall set into the outer face, usually 15ft (4.5m) high with a battlement at the top. The

*The Granary, Housesteads Fort*

timber towers and gateway were also rebuilt in stone; the towers placed at each rounded corner and also between the corners and the entrance gates. Roman forts had four gateways, consisting of one or two arched carriageways. These vaulted portals were flanked by guardrooms, and closed with thick iron-bound wooden doors.

The function and layout of an auxiliary fort like Housesteads, (NY790688) was basically the same as in a permanent legionary fortress, but on a smaller scale. Inside, the area was divided up by streets and passageways. The commandant's house (*praetorium*), the headquarters building (*principia*), the hospital (*valetudinarium*) and the granaries (*horrea*) were placed in the centre, and the back and front areas of the fort contained the barrack blocks, stables and workshops. Against the walls would be latrines and cooking ovens. The earliest internal buildings were of timber construction, wattle and daub, to be rebuilt later in stone. In some forts, the important central buildings were built in stone, while the barracks were of timber construction on stone foundations.

A single barrack block was divided into ten sections, with each section containing one *contubernium* or tent unit of eight men. The centurion and his junior officers had the privilege of larger living quarters at one end of each barrack block. There were no mess-room facilities, the soldiers cooked their food individually or in little groups, and ate, slept and kept their weapons and equipment in their barrack rooms. Every fort

was provided with its own bath-house, but this major installation was often sited outside the fort. Also outside the fort was the parade ground (*campus*) and the civilian village (*vicus*). The soldiers garrisoned in the forts acted as guardians of the law in the surrounding district, as well as being engaged in mining, quarrying, farming, road engineering and tax collecting.

Legionary fortresses were of similar plan to the auxiliary forts, but much larger in area, being able to hold a legion of six thousand men in some 50 acres (20ha). Although there were a number of temporary legionary bases, there were only three permanent legionary fortresses in Britain, all rebuilt in stone: York (*Eburacum*), Chester (*Deva*) and Caerleon (*Isca*).

When the Roman army was on campaign or military exercise, there was a real need to defend itself on overnight stops. The marching camp was pitched around the spot chosen for the commander's tent. A ditch usually 3ft (0.9m) wide and of the same depth was dug around the complete site, although sometimes this was not done when the ground was hard. The material from the excavation was thrown up on the inside to form a 5ft (1.5m) high bank, and 5ft (1.5m) wooden palisade stakes were planted on the top and tied together. These poles were carried by the soldiers, as part of their standard marching equipment, which also included three days' food supplies and weapons.

*Legionary barrack block, Caerleon*

In some cases the shapes of the marching camps are irregular due to the type of terrain they were passing through. But the general design was that of long straight sides, rounded corners and wide entrance gaps. These gates were usually defended by *claviculae,* which are curved extensions of the rampart, or by *titula,* which are short sections of rampart and ditch set before the gateway. As part of their training the soldiers also built practice camps, mostly much smaller, and generally lacking the long lengths of earthen defences. Also, the ramparts tended to be smaller in height, as these camps were never meant to be occupied.

Fortlets were small forts, usually defended by an earthwork, a ditch or ditches, and entered in most cases by a single gateway. Their purpose was to fill the gaps between the larger forts, and although their size varies, each post probably held from between fifty to one hundred soldiers.

---

## Forts and Fortresses
## Identifying Features

### Permanent Auxiliary Garrison Fort
● The early forts were built with earth and stone rubble ramparts, and defended by encircling rings of ditches and banks. They ranged in size from $2\frac{1}{2}$ to 8 acres (1 to 3.2ha).
● Within the ramparts timber buildings were constructed. Towers and gateways were also first built of timber.
● Later, in some cases, the earthen rampart was cut back and a stone wall raised in front of it. This was usually about 15ft (4.5m) high.
● Later on, some forts had a tower at each rounded corner and between the corners and the entrance gates.
● Generally, each fort had four gateways normally protected by towers and flanked by guard rooms. Later on, these were rebuilt in stone.
● The interior was divided into streets and passageways.
● Where constructed, the main stone-built buildings, such as the commandant's house, the headquarters building and granaries were placed in the centre of the fort.
● Around these buildings were situated barrack blocks, stables and workshops. Sometimes, they were of timber construction of stone foundations.
● Where included, the bath-house and parade ground were usually sited outside the fort.

### Legionary Fortress
● A larger version of the auxiliary garrison fort, and capable of holding a legion of six thousand men.
● The fortress was defended by strong stone curtain walls that replaced the earlier earth and timber ramparts.
● Interval towers and bastions were also added to strengthen the fortifications.
● The fortress contains a similar range of internal buildings, later rebuilt in stone.
● The three permanent bases, later rebuilt in stone, were at Caerleon, Chester and York.

---

## Outstanding Sites

### Ardoch
Braco, Dunblane, Strathallan, Tayside Region, Scotland
OS 57/58 (1in 54/55), NN839100
The earthworks of the Roman fort at Ardoch are truly magnificent, and as the remains are extensive, a little more time spent here will be amply repaid.

There are at least three super-imposed forts at Ardoch together with a large annexe, and five different marching camps. The only visible evidence of all these temporary camps is located on the west side of the 130 acre (52ha) enclosure. A section of the rampart and titulum may be observed to the right, as the B827 road cuts through the camp, some 220yd (200m) from its junction with the A822.

The original fort at Ardoch was founded by Agricola, but all the visible ramparts and ditches probably belong to the Antonine period. However, the first Antonine fort was reduced in size and has two further ditches dug into the end of the larger enclosure. The north-west corner of the fort is a good vantage point for a study of the extent of the fort's defences. The earthworks are remarkable, still standing bold and resolute at a height of 6½ft (2m). Along the north and east sides are five superb ditches with firm causeways striding impressively across them from the gateway openings. The two outer ditches to the north and east may have been part of the defences of the first century fort. Look for the extra protection provided by a curve in the outer ditch on the eastern flank.

**Access** The site lies on the north-eastern edge of the village of Braco above the River Knaik,

*Ardoch Roman Fort*

situated in Strathallan, some 6¾ miles (10.8km) north-east of

Dunblane via the A9 and the A822.

## Low Borrowbridge, Auxiliary Garrison Fort
Lune Valley, Tebay, Cumbria
OS 91, (1in 89), NY609013
This isolated fort's function was to keep the Lune valley open, and to protect the lines of communication to Brougham,

Ribchester, Watercrook, and maybe to Brough via Crosby Garrett. It occupies a dramatic position in the Lune gorge, and is situated on a little plateau above the river. The site is closely bypassed by the M6, and almost cut by the main

*Low Borrowbridge Roman Fort*

railway line.

The area of the fort is about 3 acres (1.2ha), large enough for an infantry battalion of 500 men. There is also a possibility of cavalry stationed there from evidence provided by a tombstone (unfortunately now lost). The long axis of the fort lies north and south, with the side gates closer to the southern ramparts than to the northern ones. The western defences, which stand out clearly above the general level of the interior are pierced by a single gateway. Within the ramparts nothing is visible, and it would appear that ploughing has obliterated evidence of its internal buildings. The fort now visible is unlikely to have been the first one on the site.

**Access** The site is situated 2¼ miles (3.6km) south of Tebay, via the A685 Kendal road. The disposition of the fort is not easily recognisable at valley level, and it is better to view it from an elevated position. On descending to the bridge over Borrow Beck, stop half-way down the slope opposite a gate, and take the hillside track overlooking the stream. From this vantage point a splendid view can be obtained, not only of the site of the Roman fort, but of the Lune valley and the sweeping slopes of the Howgill Fells.

If wishing to view the site from a closer angle, take the first turning left over the bridge on the minor road to Sedbergh.

This passes under the M6 and the railway, and curves round the eastern limits of the fort. Permission should be obtained from the farm on the right-hand side of the road.

### Hod Hill, First Century Fort
Stourpaine, Blandford Forum, Dorset
OS 194 (1in 178), ST855107
The Iron Age hillfort is set in a splendid commanding position 470ft (144m) high overlooking the confluence of the Rivers Stour and Iwerne.

The Romans attacked the defences in AD44 and the inhabitants were forced to surrender. Afterwards the Romans constructed a fort inside the north-west corner of the existing ramparts. Their defensive lines consisted of chalk blocks faced on both sides with turf, and wide enough at the top to take a patrolling walkway. Despite the ravages of ploughing over the centuries the ramparts still stand about 5ft(1.5m) high at the north-east corner. Three ditches, about 5ft (1.5m) deep were excavated outside the rampart with a flat platform 55ft (16.5m) wide separating the two outer trenches. The fort had entrances in the north-west corner on the southern and eastern sides with convenient causeways spanning the ditches. Excavations revealed that the interior contained foundation holes for timber-framed buildings which probably housed a garrison of some 800 soldiers.

**Access**   The village of Stourpaine lies on the A350, some 3 miles (4.8km) north of Blandford Forum. In the village take the first turning left, then right and continue straight on across the stream and ascend by the track to the south-east corner of the hillfort. Pass through the pre-Roman defences and walk towards the Roman fort. The circular depressions and platforms on the ground indicate the position of the Iron Age huts.

### Whitley Castle Fort, Auxiliary Garrison Fort
Whitlow, Alston, Cumbria
OS 86 (1in 83), NY695487
Whitley Castle Roman fort is sited at an altitude of 1,050ft (320m), on the upper slopes of the beautiful valley of the River South Tyne. The rhomboid-shaped enclosure sits atop a hillock surrounded by a magnificent system of banks and ditches. In fact, the south-west side has as many as seven ditches with steep earthen banks protecting the rampart around the enclosure. The ground outlines in the interior indicate the position of the main buildings, particularly the headquarters block. The fort was probably built in the second century, with the later addition of a stone wall to the earthen rampart. Although little is known about the history and purpose of the fort, an inscription from the site mentions its garrison, at one period, as being the Second Cohort of Nervii from the lower

*Whitley Castle Roman Fort*

Rhine. It is thought that this lonely fort may have been constructed to protect lead mining operations in the locality. The line of the Roman road (Maiden Way), from Kirkby Thore to Carvoran, passes on the east side of the fort.

**Access** Permission to visit the fort should be obtained from Whitlow Farm just to the south-east of the site. Follow the A689, Alston to Brampton road for 2 miles (3.2km). The track to the farm bears sharp left after crossing Gilderdale Burn.

Alternatively, proceed along the road for another ½ mile (800m), and park opposite Castle Nook Farm. The Pennine Way footpath is reached by means of a dilapidated stile on the north-west side of the stream. Walk through a jungle of grass to cross the stream, and then on to the track that climbs easily around the western perimeter of the fort. From this elevated position, a clear view can be obtained of its western and south-western defences.

## Hardknott Castle, Auxiliary Garrison Fort (DoE)

Hardknott Pass, Eskdale, Cumbria
OS 89, (1in 88), NY218015, OS 1:25000 Outdoor Leisure Map, 'The English Lakes', South West Sheet

A visit to this fort will certainly stir the imagination, for it is one of the most outstanding remains of the Roman army in Britain. Scenically and strategically it is magnificently placed on a high spur overlooking Eskdale. To the north the crags of Bell Stand fall to the valley floor and the view beyond encompasses the Scafell range. The word Hardknott is of Norse derivation, meaning 'the rocky or craggy hill'. The Roman name was *Mediobogdum*, 'the fort in the middle of the curve', a reference to its position in relation to the Esk below. Evidence from excavations revealed that the fort was built in the second century, and finished under the reign of Hadrian. It was garrisoned by auxiliary infantrymen, the fourth cohort of Dalmatians from Yugoslavia. A bleak spot indeed for men used to the Mediterranean sun on their backs.

The track from the road to the fort passes the remains of the externally sited bath-house. The building, *balneum*, consisted of a furnace and a suite of three rooms of differently graded temperatures. Now, only the lowest courses of the brick-built stoke hole survive. Close by is a circular hot-room with a flue.

The path continues to the fort walls and the south gate, with no evidence of guard rooms. The walls, made of local stone with an earth bank behind them, now stand to a height of 8 to 10ft (2.4 to 3m). In each corner are the foundations of the angle turrets. The other gaps in each straight side, which mark the position of the gates, have double portals, except the north gate which has a single portal. All the stone above the slate course has been rebuilt in modern times from fallen masonry. Lying around are blocks of red sandstone used in the construction, that must have been brought in from the coastal outcrops.

The centre of the fort contains the Headquarters building with L-shaped store rooms and administrative rooms. The remains of the commandant's house lie to the west of the HQ, the whole building appeared to be unfinished. To the east lies the granary with its internal floor supports and loading platforms. The remaining interior space would have been occupied with wooden barrack blocks.

Hardknott has the best preserved Roman parade ground in Britain. This levelled area, partly cut out of the hillside, may be reached by walking 220yd (200m) from the east gate. Note the raised mounds at its edge marking the site of the commander's rostrum.

**Access** Approached by a narrow mountain road from Little Langdale via the Wrynose Pass, or up the Duddon valley from the south to Cockley Beck Bridge. Then a steep twisting climb to the summit of the Hard Knott Pass. From the west, the road quietly follows the valley of the River Esk to Whahouse Bridge, and then a short steep ascent to the fort.

There is an exciting approach to the Roman fort whichever direction you choose.

## Marching Camps
### Identifying Features

- The usual design was that of long, straight sides, rounded corners and wide entrance gaps.
- The defences consisted of an earthwork topped by a palisade, and an outer ditch.
- The gateways were usually defended by *Claviculae* (curved extensions of the rampart and ditch, or by *titula* (short sections of rampart and ditch in front of the gateway.
- In some cases, the marching camps have an irregular outline due to the type of terrain locally.

## Outstanding Sites

### Y Pigwn Marching Camp

Trecastle, Powys, Wales
OS 160, (1in 140), SN828312
Outdoor Leisure Map 1:25,000, Brecon Beacons National Park (Western Area).
Long distance walkers on the Cambrian Way (a mountain route from Cardiff to Conway), may pass through the area having tramped over the Black Mountain (Carmarthen Vans) to the south. The surrounding countryside is wild, unspoilt and lonely, and the marching camps lie at an altitude of 1,353ft (412m) on the northern edge of Mynydd Myddfai.

There are two camps, one inside the other, belonging to the first years of the Roman conquest (AD47-78). It is more than likely that the marching camps were only occupied for short periods during those initial campaigns. The Roman road from Brecon to Landovery passes right alongside the site, and here the agger is clearly preserved in places, 15ft (4.5m) wide.

Along the south-eastern side, the earthworks have been destroyed by lead workings. However it is possible from this angle to observe the southern corner mound of the inner camp, and the now overgrown line of the ditch which actually encroaches upon the line of the outer camp's south western earthwork. This is positive proof that the inner camp was constructed at a later date. The outstanding visible remains are to be found along the north-western edges of both camps. Note the well-preserved remains of the earthworks of both camps, and the north gate and *clavicula*, a curved extension of rampart and ditch protecting a gateway, of the inner camp.

**Access**   From Trecastle take the A40 westwards for 4 miles (6.4km). Immediately before Halfway, bear left on a minor road out of the valley that climbs and twists for $1\frac{3}{4}$ miles (2.8km). Turn left at the junction and proceed for another $\frac{1}{2}$ mile (800m) to Hafod-fawr farm. It is a 1 mile (1.6km) walk from here to the Roman camps.

### Rey Cross Marching Camp

Bowes Moor, Bowes, Co Durham
OS 92, (1in 84), NY901124
At the highest point of the Stainmore Pass 1,468ft (447m) above sea level lies one of the best preserved marching camps. The visitor can trace its defences easily on foot, as most of the rectangular outline of earth-works are visible. It probably marks the line of the first century campaign of Cerealis and the XI Legion against the Brigantes in AD72 and 73.

*Rey Castle Marching Camp, North Gate*

There is a lay-by on the south side of the A66, park and then cross over to the northern side. Walk along the grass verge in an easterly direction for approximately 230yd (207m), ignoring the rounded depressions to the left. You will easily be able to make out the easterly defensive earthwork. Turn to the north and follow the ramparts for most of its playing-card shape. There are no less than nine gateways each defended by a *titulum* (a short detached stretch of rampart and ditch protecting the gateway of a marching camp). Except where parts of the earthworks have been destroyed by quarrying (south-west section), or sunk into marshy ground (north-west section), the surviving defences show up clearly; they are 20ft (6.0m) wide and sometimes 6ft (1.8m) high. The remains of the marching camp have become part of the sombre, open moorland surrounding it.

**Access**  Summit of Stainmore Pass, on the A66, Penrith to Scotch Corner road, 6 miles (9.6km) west of Bowes.

## Pennymuir Marching Camp

Kale Water, Hownam, Borders Region, Scotland
OS 80, (1in 70), NT754140
This is the largest and best preserved marching camp, enclosing 42 acres (17.0ha), with impressive ramparts, 15ft (4.5m) wide, 4ft (1.2m) high, and a clearly visible ditch. The defensive earthworks survive everywhere except in the south and south-eastern sectors, with a particularly outstanding section nearest the road junction. Of the six original gates, two on each long side and one at each end, five survive together with their *titula*.

In the south-east corner lies a smaller camp, constructed at a later date with a well preserved western rampart, together with three of the original six gates. There are faint traces of two other camps to the east of the road.

**Access**  From the junction of the A6088 and A68 west of Carter Bar, take the A68 north for 3 miles (4.8km), then turn right. Proceed for 4 miles (6.4km) to a crossroads, and continue straight ahead for nearly 1¼ miles (2km) to a road junction. The two camps lie immediately south of the crossroads. If approaching from the north, leave the B6401 at Morebattle and follow the valley of the Kale Water south to Hownam. Continue south through Chatto and take the next turn right to Pennymuir. The distance from Morebattle is 8 miles (12.8km).

---

## Practice Camps
### Identifying Features

- Although some practice camps were of normal size, generally they are smaller, and lack long lengths of rampart.
- The earthworks tended to be smaller in height.

- In some examples defences were strengthened, or mounds raised to support the heavy Roman siege machines.
- The camps would be used for military training exercises.

---

## Outstanding Sites

## Woden Law Practice Camp

Tow Ford, Kale Water, Hownam, Borders Region, Scotland
OS 80, (1in 70), NT768125
The earthworks lie to the east and south of the oval-shaped, pre-Roman hillfort. Its defences were strengthened, and then a little distance away on the north, south and east sides, three ditches and two earthworks were constructed. There is evidence to show that the outer bank was engineered to take the heavy Roman catapult machines. Also, further away on the eastern slopes of the hill, there are other siege lines; some running north to south, and another set running across the south-eastern sector. The nature of these earthworks suggests that they were constructed as part of

training exercises for the Roman soldiers, who were presumably quartered in the camps at Pennymuir.

**Access**   From Pennymuir Roman Camps proceed south-south-east on the minor road (the Roman road Dere Street), to Tow Ford. At the road junction beyond the Kale Water stream, take the footpath that climbs steeply to reach the depression between the two hill summits. From this point, a short walk to the south-west leads to the Woden Law earthworks, 1,388ft (423m) above sea level. Distance from Penymuir road junction is 1¾ miles (2.8km).

A circular walk can include Pennymuir, Woden Law and Dere Street, to the Main watershed of the Cheviots. Then south along the Pennine Way to the Roman Camps at Chew Green, passing enroute the site of the Roman signal station. Return via Coquet Head, Whiteside Hill, Nether Hindhope and Tow Ford. Distance 10½ miles (16.8km).

---

**Fortlets**
**Identifying Features**

- A small rectangular area usually defended by an earthen rampart, a ditch or ditches.
- Access to the interior is by a single cause-wayed entrance.
- Found on the lines of communication between the bigger forts.

---

## Outstanding Sites

**Kaims Castle Fortlet**
Orchill, Braco, Tayside Region, Scotland
OS 58, (1in 55), NN861129
The well preserved remains of this fortlet lie on a natural mound, with the turf rampart still 3ft 3in (1.0m) high, and enclosing an area 70ft by 73ft (21.2m by 22.1m). The entrance causeway may be located on the south-eastern side crossing the encircling ring of two ditches. The fortlet lay on the line of the Roman road linking Ardoch and Strageath, which still survives as a low mound between the modern road and the entrance. The fortlet probably belongs to the Antonine period, but it is probable that the first structure on the site was built by Agricola.

**Access**   The fortlet may be approached from the A822, 3½ miles (5.6km) south of Muthill. The earthworks lie on the western side of the road behind a cottage. Access to the site is through a field gate and down a short length of track.

**Castle Greg Fortlet**
Camilty Hill, West Calder, Lothian Region, Scotland
OS 65, (1in 61), NT050592
The very well preserved ramparts of this fortlet, still standing up to 3ft 3ins (1.0m) high, defend an enclosure 150ft by 120ft (45m x 36m). The rampart is encircled by two ditches, cut by an entrance causeway on the eastern side. It may have been built at the end of the first century, as its position is some distance away from the known route of any Roman road.

**Access**   It lies 3½ miles (5.6km) south-east of West Calder via the B7008, and ⅝ mile (1km) north of its junction with the A70. The Roman earthworks lie 165yd (150m) on the east side of the B7008, on the edge of a plantation. Good footwear will be required to combat the long grass and wet ground.

**Durisdeer Fortlet**
Durisdeer, Carronbridge, Dumfries and Galloway Region, Scotland
OS 78, (1in 68), NS903048
The fortlet lies above the north bank of the Kirk Burn, on the line of the Roman road from Nithsdale to Clydesdale. It must have been a lonely outpost, guarding a lonely road through the rolling rounded masses of the Lowther Hills. The Roman fortlet stands prominently on a small ridge, the site seemingly levelled before building commenced. The earthen rampart, 27½ft (8.8m) wide, encloses an area 105ft by 60ft (32.0m by 18.0m), and access to the interior is by a single

entrance on the north-eastern side. There is a single ditch encircling the rampart, and the causeway entrance is protected by a detached stretch of ditch.
**Access** Leave the A702, 2¾ miles (4.4km) north-north-east

of Carronbridge, and bear right on a minor road to the village of Durisdeer, just over 1 mile (1.7km) ahead. Take the track past the church for ½ mile (0.8km), then the left-hand turn when the track divides. Con-

tinue for 660yd (0.6km), and the fortlet lies on the left. Beyond the site, the track now called the Well Path, makes for the pass and descends to the valley of the Potrail Water.

## Other Roman Forts and Camps

**Tomen-y-Mur**, Auxiliary Fort
Trawsfynydd, Gwynedd, North Wales
OS 124, (1in 116), SH707387

**Castell Collen**, Auxiliary Fort
Llandrindod Wells, Powys, Central Wales
OS 147, (1in 128), SO 055628
Ask permission to visit at the farm.

**Brecon Gaer**, Auxiliary Fort
Brecon, Powys, South Wales
OS 160, (1in 141), SO002297

**Burnswark**, Practice Siege Camp
Ecclefechan, Dumfries & Galloway Region, Scotland
OS 85, (1in 75), NY185787

**Caernarfon** (*Segontium*), Auxiliary Fort
Caernarfon, Gwynedd, North Wales
OS 115, (1in 107/115), SH485624

**Old Carlisle**, Auxiliary Fort
Wigton, Cumbria
OS 85, (1in 82), NY260465

**Lanchester** (*Longovicium*);
Auxiliary Fort
Lanchester, Co Durham
OS 88, (1in 85), NZ159469

**Piercebridge**, Auxiliary Fort
Darlington, Co Durham
OS 93, (1in 85), NZ210157

**Binchester** (*Vinovia*), Cavalry Fort
Bishop Auckland, Co Durham
OS 93, (1in 85), NZ210314

**Cramond**, Auxiliary Fort and Supply Base
Cramond, Edinburgh, Lothian Region
OS 66, (1in 62), NT189769

**High Rochester** (*Bremenium*), Auxiliary Fort
Rochester, Redesdale, Northumberland
OS 80, (1in 70), NY833986

**Redesdale Camp**, Marching Camp
Rochester, Redesdale, Northumberland
OS 80, (1in 70), NY827988

**Cawthorn**, Practice Camps
Cropton, Pickering, North Yorkshire
OS 100, (1in 92), SE784900

## ANTONINE WALL

The reasons for the construction of this wall are unknown. Maybe the emperor's desire for a quick and spectacular military achievement in order to enhance his political career in Rome, or perhaps the control of the warring tribes of southern Scotland, and the consequent consolidation of the Empire's northern frontier, were the main factors. Using the supply base of Corbridge on Hadrian's Wall, the Roman forces under Lollius Urbicus advanced into southern Scotland, and the whole of this area was captured and refortified. An area stretching northwards to Perth was restored to the province, and new forts were constructed along the roads

previously built by Agricola. The forts were the bases to control the local tribes and the new frontier line, which ran along the central valley of Scotland from the Forth to the Clyde.

The Antonine Wall is a much simpler structure than Hadrian's defensive barrier. Probably constructed between AD139 and 142, the Wall stretches for 37 miles (59.3km) from Bridgeness on the Forth to Old Kilpatrick on the Clyde. The rampart was built up of cut turves, most certainly to a height of 10 to 12ft (3.0 to 3.6m) on a heavy stone base usually 14ft (4.2m) wide. It was about two-thirds the width of Hadrian's Wall, and the heavy foundations of boulders and dressed kerbstones aided stability and also drainage. The use of turf has posed a difficult question to answer; the most likely reason for its use was a desire to complete the work quickly.

Nevertheless, it is not so unusual, as turf and timber barriers were commonly used elsewhere in the empire; and the building of a stone rampart like Hadrian's Wall was the exception rather than the rule.

Along the top of the rampart there may have been a patrol walk protected by a timber breastwork. On the northern side of the turf wall, and separated from it by a flat open space or berm about 20ft (6m) wide, lay a wide and deep ditch. This varied in size, from 40ft (12m) wide and 12ft (3.6m) deep in the east, to generally half that size in the western part.

The soldiers lived in forts, between sixteen and nineteen in number, placed on average at intervals of roughly 2 miles (3.2km) apart. Most of the forts had turf ramparts and ditches, although two had stone walls. The designs of the main buildings, and the materials used, were similar to those used in the forts of Hadrian's Wall. However, greater planning and insight had gone into the siting of the Antonine forts, as all but one faced north, with the principal buildings lying across the long axis of the fort. To the side of each Antonine fort lay an enclosure, often of similar size as the fort, which housed the bath-suite, workshops and storehouses. A supply road, or Military Way, which serviced all the forts, ran along the whole southern length of the Wall. Compared with Hadrian's Wall, only seven fortlets or milecastle-type structures have so far been discovered, as well as only six beacon-platforms which would be used for signalling.

This new frontier barrier was built by soldiers of the three legions, XX Valeria Victrix from Chester, VI Victrix from York and II Augusta from Caerleon. Units from the legions divided the construction of the turf mound and ditch between them, each building lengths of 3 to 4 miles (4.8 to 6.4km) or even less. Evidence concerning their participation has been found in the form of inscribed stone tablets that mentioned the particular legion and the distance covered. For example, one inscription, now in the Hunterian Museum of the University of Glasgow, reads: 'For the emperor Caesar Titus Aelius Hadrianus Antoninus Augustus Pius, father of his country, a detachment of the Twentieth Legion Valeria Victrix built 3,000 ft.'

This second massive construction project by the Romans can be seen as a failure, for its usefulness can only be counted in terms of probably less than twenty years. After thirteen years the Antonine Wall was temporarily abandoned due to a native rebellion. There are some clues that certain forts were first destroyed by the Roman garrison before evacuation. The wall was re-occupied in about AD158, and again abandoned after further enemy attacks not long after AD160; although it has been suggested that it was not because of pressure from local tribes, but by direct orders from Rome after the death of Antoninus Pius.

## Antonine Wall Sites

**Rough Castle Fort** (DoE)
Bonnybridge, Falkirk, Central Region, Scotland
OS 65, (1in 61), NS843798
The fort built against the turf rampart covers 1.5 acres (0.6ha), and is thus one of the smallest on the Wall. The Wall mound and ditch forming the north side are well preserved, as are the earth defences and ditches on the other three sides. The northern side consists of the mound of the Antonine Wall. 60ft (18.3m) beyond the ditch

and upcast mound lie the defensive pits called *lilia*, arranged in staggered rows in order to make a crossing difficult. Originally they were a little deeper and each pit would probably have contained a sharp stake vertically implanted in the bottom. The whole area would have been camouflaged with brushwood, twigs and leaves — an unpleasant surprise for any enemy attacker.

Behind the ramparts of the Antonine Wall lay the head-quarters building, commandant's house, and the barracks; the latter was separated from the important buildings by the Military Way. Outside the eastern defences of the fort was an annexe defended by a rampart and ditches. This enclosure contained the soldiers' bath-house. The fort was garrisoned by men of the Cohors VI Nerviorum (from the Lower Rhine).

Along the Wall a short distance westwards can be seen

two low mounds 330yd (0.3km) apart. These were probably beacon platforms used for signalling. On excavation, the nearer platform revealed its stone foundation 18ft (5.4m) square with traces of considerable burning.

A fine section of the ditch and the Wall lies a short distance away to the west in front of the parking area.

**Access** The site can be reached by following the B816 to High Bonnybridge, and then turning right towards Bonnybridge. Just before the canal bridge turn right, and follow this road which becomes unmade after crossing the railway line. Continue along it and over a cattle grid to a small parking area. The monument is also signposted in the centre of Bonnybridge.

*Rough Castle, Antonine Wall*

**Watling Lodge** (DoE)
Tamfourhill, Falkirk, Central Region, Scotland
OS 65, (1in 61), NS865798
Although the Wall mound has suffered badly from ploughing, there is a fine example of the Antonine ditch which still survives some 40ft (12.2m) wide and 15ft (4.5m) deep. It is still easy to judge the effectiveness of this man-made obstacle when standing at the foot of the slope.

**Access** Travelling west from Falkirk on the A803, turn left on the B816 High Bonnybridge road running alongside the Forth and Clyde Canal. After nearly ¾ mile (1.2km), the road turns sharp right along Lime Road. The ditch lies behind trees on the left (DoE signposted).

**Tentfield Plantation**
Tamfourhill, Falkirk, Central Region, Scotland
OS 65, (1in 61), NS855798
Continue westwards along the B816, Lime Road, for ½ mile (0.8km). Turn right at the crossroads. The monument is signposted on the left. For 1 mile (1.6km) westwards there is a walk well worth undertaking despite the undergrowth. The Wall and ditch remain in good condition, and this section also contains two beacon platforms attached to the rear of the ramparts. These are difficult to make out during the summer months, but they stand out more prominently in the winter time. The first platform lies 520ft (160m) past Lime Road, and the second beacon site is 130ft (40m) east of the railway crossing.

# SIGNAL STATIONS AND WATCH TOWERS

One of the key factors in the Roman defensive strategy was their warning system of any impending attack. Good vantage points were selected, the ground was cleared and an earthen platform was raised. The site was usually defended with an earth rampart and ditch. A wooden tower was constructed, probably with two or three storeys, from the top of which the surrounding area could be surveyed. Also, messages were transmitted using fire, smoke and semaphore.

Stretching west from Perth, the Gask Ridge overlooks Strathearn to the south, and north to the foothills of the Highlands. Here, the Romans constructed a line of watch and signal towers in the first century as part of a system of frontier control protecting the fort at Strageath (NM898-189. The line of towers stretching for 8 miles (12.8km) to the east was connected by a Roman road. Today, seven sites are visible, although only the remains of two of them are worth inspecting. Each signal station consisted of a central, almost circular platform surrounded by a rampart about 10ft (3.0m) wide, and a ditch of similar width. There is a single entrance facing north. The inner platform would have been the base for a timber signal tower about 12ft (3.6m) square.

In the late fourth century, a number of well-defended stone signal stations were built along the north Yorkshire coast. Here, the tower was also surrounded by a wall and corner turrets, in order to withstand attacks on the small garrison. In the event of a raid, alarm signals were sent to a mobile force, such as a unit of cavalry, stationed just inland.

## Identifying Features

- A central, almost circular platform enclosed by an earth rampart and a ditch or ditches.
- Usually, there is a single causewayed entrance.
- The interior would have been the support base for a wooden tower.
- A number of well-defended stone signal stations were built along the North Yorkshire coast.

- The tower was surrounded by a square compound and enclosed by a strong wall. It was defended by four angle bastions, and entered by a single fortified gateway.
- Outside the walls a single ditch encircled the defences. A wide berm separated the walls from the ditch.

## Outstanding Sites

**Barcombe Hill Signal Station**
Barcombe Hill, Thorngrafton Common, Bardon MIll, Northumberland
OS 86, (1in 77), NY783668
This signal station stands within the defences of an early British fortification. The roughly circular enclosure, some 40ft (12m) across, is situated within the fort's north-west corner. There is a turf-built rampart, an outer ditch and a possible causeway on the north-eastern side. The ramparts of the prehistoric fort curve round in a D-shape to the south. The site commands a spectacular view overlooking the Stanegate road, the Roman settlement and fort of *Vindolanda* and to the Wall in the north.
**Access**   Leave the B6318 almost 2 miles (3km) east of the Youth Hostel and Information Centre at Once Brewed. Turn right on a by-road to Bardon Mill and continue for nearly ¾ mile (1km) to a junction. Take the footpath opposite and climb the hill slope beyond. At the top, bear left and walk a short distance along the escarpment to the site.

### Parkneuk Watch Tower

Innerpeffray Wood, Kinkell
Bridge, Auchterarder, Tayside
Region, Scotland
OS 58, (1in 55), NN916185
The site, although situated in a
forest clearing, is not easily seen
in summer months, due to a
luxuriant, and usually very wet
growth of long grass. At other
times the rampart, ditch, outer
bank and causeway are clearly
visible. The latter is situated on
the north side facing the line of
the Roman road.
**Access**   Take the B8062,
Auchterarder to Crieff road.
The site lies 1¾ miles (2.8km)
north of Kinkell Bridge. At a
sharp left-hand bend, there is a
forestry track on the right. Walk
for a few yards to a clearing, and
the site lies just to the right.

### Sma' Glen Watch Tower

Fendoch, Buchanty, Crief,
Tayside Region, Scotland
OS 52, (1in 55), NN907285
The well-preserved remains of
this signal tower consist of a
rampart and single ditch.
**Access**   Just north of the
junction of the A822 and the
B8063 on the left of the road.
Access by footpath.

### Black Hill Watch Tower

Meikleour, Blairgowrie, Tayside
Region, Scotland
OS 53, (1in 49), NO176391
The signal tower site situated on
top of a large mound, is
encircled by a low rampart,
ditch and outer bank. The ditch
is crossed by an entrance
causeway to the north.
**Access**   Proceed east from
Meikleour on the A984, cross the
A93, and take the first track on
the right after ½ mile (800m).
Turn left at the end, and
proceed for 220yd (200m) to the
mound in the wood on the right.

### Muir O'Fauld Watch Tower

Muir O'Fauld, Kinkell Bridge,
Auchterarder, Tayside Region,
Scotland
OS 58, (1in 55), NN982189
At this site the outer mound,
ditch and rampart are clearly
visible. The causeway also clear,
faces the line of the Roman road
to the north.
**Access**   From Auchterarder
take the B8062 to Kinkell
Bridge. Turn right and proceed
for 3¾ miles (6km). At
NN986191, there is a sharp
right-hand bend. Walk
westwards along the track for ¼
mile (400m), and the site lies to
the left just before a gate.

### Roper Castle Signal Station

Stainmore, Brough, Cumbria
OS 92, (1in 84), NY882111
On a clear day, the slight mound
of this signal station can just be
observed on the skyline, west-
south-west from the Bowes Moor
Site. Pick a good day for a
moorland trudge to this lonely
spot. You will need to be
equipped with strong boots, a
1:50,000 OS map and a
compass. The remains are very
similar to the Bowes Moor site,
but do not expect to see a castle!
**Access**   From the junction of
the minor road to Kaber with
the A66 at NY874128, compass
bearing 154° SSE across Black
Riggs. Distance 1⅛ miles
(1.8km). Alternatively take the
minor road to Kaber from the
A66. After 1¼ miles (2km) turn
left and proceed for another ¼
mile (400m). A rough track
heads south-east and east across
Millstone Howe where it peters
out after ½ mile (800m). The
route lies across Moudy Mea,
with a compass bearing 110°
ESE. Distance from the minor
road at NY855121, is 1¾ miles
(2.8km).

### Scarborough Signal Station

Castle Cliff, Scarborough, North
Yorkshire
OS 101, (1in 93), TA0589, AM
This signal station was sited on
the edge of the headland overlooking the bay. Originally there
was a small enclosure about
100ft (30m) square with corner
turrets, and a central stone
platform upon which the tall
stone tower was built. No
Roman stonework is now visible,
but the outline of the signal
station has been shown in
concrete. Furthermore, part of
the once encircling ditch has
been cleared out on the southern
and western sides.
**Access**   Situated on Castle
Cliff, close to the ruins of a
medieval chapel and Henry II's
twelfth-century keep. The site
lies on the edge of the cliff.

### Turret 45a, Hadrian's Wall
(DoE)

Walltown, Greenhead,
Northumberland
OS 86, (1in 76), NY673663
Although it was later to become
part of Hadrian's Wall, this
turret was probably built
initially as an observation tower.
The original frontier along the
Stanegate road did not have a
good view to the north, so this
stone tower was built in a
commanding position on the
Walltown crags. Its structure
offers sufficient evidence to
verify the fact that it preceded
the Wall. The tower is 19ft
(5.7m) square with a single
entrance on the southern side.
**Access**   Take the B6318 east of
Greenhead for ½ mile (800m).
Turn left, follow the DoE signs,
and then bear up the slope to the
right to reach turret 45a.

## Goldsborough Signal Station

Goldsborough, Whitby, North
Yorkshire
OS 94, (1in 86), NZ835152
Roman watch towers or signal
stations were usually constructed
to a standard pattern, but the
site at Goldsborough was one of
a series of solid stone structures
built along the north Yorkshire
coast. Strong foundations were
built to support a tall stone
tower, which perhaps stood 80ft
(24m) high. Surrounding the
tower and separated by an inner
courtyard, was a stout encircling
wall with defensive turrets at
each rounded corner. Immediately beyond the outer wall was
a level area, and a final protective ditch. Access to the interior
was provided by a gateway
along the southern side of the
wall. There is no longer any
stonework visible, only a
prominent mound. During the
latter days of Roman rule in
Britain the towers were
attacked, and at Goldsborough
dramatic evidence illustrated
the dangerous times. Excavators
found the skeleton of a short
man, his hand twisted behind
him, lying across a fire hearth.
The remains of another man lay
at his feet, covering the skeleton
of a large dog. Perhaps the dog
had died trying to save its
master.

**Access**   The hamlet of
Goldsborough lies to the north of
the A174, some 5 miles (8km)
north-west of Whitby. Turn
right off the main road just
outside the village of Lythe and
follow the minor road to
Goldsborough. From the hamlet
take the footpath to Kettleness,
and after a $\frac{1}{4}$ mile (400m) the
site lies just to the east of the
route.

## Brownhart Law Signal Station

Pennine Way, Chew Green,
Cheviot Hills, Borders Region,
Scotland
OS 80, (1in 70), NT790096
Close by the Pennine Way
footpath on the border between
England and Scotland. The
remains consist of the low bank
of a turf rampart encircled by
two ditches, except on the south-
eastern side where there is only
one ditch. The single entrance
faced the line of the Roman
road, Dere Street.

**Access**   A gate in the border
fence gives access to the site from
the Pennine Way footpath. The
Roman signal station lies just
north of the point where the
border fence veers south-west to
Brownhart Law.

Although there is not a great
deal to see, a visit gives an
opportunity to enjoy the view of
the valleys and hills west of the
watershead. Pennine Way
stalwarts en route for Kirk
Yetholm will pass the site. Those
with enough strength left to look
up may only give it a cursory
glance. Distance from Byrness is
$6\frac{1}{4}$ miles (10km).

There is a circular hill walk of
$10\frac{1}{2}$ miles (16.8km) from the
valley of the Kale Water to the
north, taking in Pennymuir
marching camp, Woden Law
practice camp, Dere Street,
Brownhart Law signal station
and Chew Green Roman camps.
Return via Conquet Head,
Whiteside Hill and Nether
Hindhope.

## Bowes Moor Signal Station

Stainmore, Bowes, Co Durham
OS 92, (1in 84), NY929125
There are a number of Roman
remains on Stainmore, one of
the principal routes across the
northern Pennines. On the
summit of the pass at Rey Cross
lie the well-preserved ramparts
of a marching camp, constructed
in AD72 during the campaigns
against the north British tribes.
Later on, forts were built at
Brough guarding the western
route, and at Bowes commanding the eastern approaches.
Between the forts and across
Stainmore, the Romans
constructed a number of signal
stations in order to relay
messages by smoke and
semaphore. The remains of the
Bowes Moor Signal Station consist of an earthen rampart,
some 10ft (3m) thick
surrounded by a V-shaped
ditch. The excavated material
was thrown out on to the outer
edge of the ditch, and this can be
seen to good effect on the
northern side. The causeway to
the interior is situated on the
southern side nearest the main
road. The enclosure would have
held a timber signal tower.

**Access**   The signal station is
situated a short distance to the
east of Bowes Moor Hotel,
beyond the fence on the north
side of the A66. There is a
convenient lay-by and parking
space opposite.

## SAXON SHORE FORTS

A line of coastal defence forts were built by the Romans in the third century, to combat increasing attacks from Germanic sea-raiders. They stretched from the Wash to the Isle of Wight, and were strong-points built on a different design to the usual rectangular shape. Their stone walls were tremendously strong, probably 30ft (9m) high, and mostly without an earth bank behind them. They were further strengthened by projecting towers.

### Outstanding Sites

**Pevensey Saxon Shore Fort**
Pevensey, Eastbourne, East Sussex
OS 199, (1in 183), TQ644048
This is one of the most impressive of the Saxon Shore forts, and was built by the Romans in the early fourth century. The fort, known to the Romans as *Anderita*, is unusual in that it is oval-shaped, enclosing an area of about 9 acres (3.6ha). In Roman times it was built on a small peninsula jutting out to sea, and the water lapped the south wall with a harbour on the east side. There are impressive remains of the walls between the west gate and the east gate, but the only remains on the southern side are two bastions that became part of the defences of the later Norman castle. The west gate is particularly impressive, being flanked by two huge bastions, with the remains of guardrooms on either side of the entrance. Following the line

*Pevensey Saxon Shore Fort*

of the defences from the west gate, there were three bastions, followed by a splendid length of wall, its masonry well-preserved with many facing stones. The position of a small postern gate comes next, followed by a tree-covered fallen section, and then a further length of wall incorporating three more bastions.

**Access**   In the village of Pevensey, between Eastbourne and Bexhill. The site lies close to the A27, Polegate to Pevensey road.

**Burgh Castle Saxon Shore Fort**
Burgh Castle, Belton, Great Yarmouth, Norfolk
OS 134, (1in 126), TG475046, AM
Known as *Gariannonum* in Roman times, this was the furthest north but one of the Saxon Shore forts. It was probably built in the latter part of the third century (earlier than Pevensey), and was occupied into the early fifth century. The fort was rectangular, and although the west wall facing the River Waveney has disappeared, there are sections along the other sides that stand to an impressive height of about 15ft (4.5m). An approach by the footpath to the south-east corner enables the visitor to study a short section of wall: a length majestically standing, a section crazily leaning and a part fallen. Examine the former, complete with facing flints, and note the red brick bonding tiles separating them. The tiles were used as levelling courses during construction, when sections of the wall were built by different work-gangs.

Another fascinating piece of building evidence emerges after studying the bastions, shown clearly on the leaning tower in the north wall. It would appear that after about 7½ft (2.3m) of wall had been built, the order came to add bastions to strengthen defences. Therefore, the lower courses of the bastions simply rest against the wall, while the upper masonry courses of the wall and tower are bonded together. Also, there are circular depressions on the tops of the bastions used for supporting Roman artillery or ballistae — heavy weapons for discharging, amongst other things, iron-headed bolts.

**Access**    Take the A12 Lowestoft road south for 1½ miles (2.4km). Turn right at the roundabout, signposted to Burgh Castle, and travel for another 3¼ miles (5.2km). Either approach the site by footpath north of the church, and south along a line of trees, or down a track south from the church and due west by footpath.

**Porchester** (*Portus Adurni*)
Portchester, Portsmouth, Hampshire
OS 196, (1in 180), SU625406
This site, at the head of Portsmouth harbour, probably contains the best preserved Roman remains in Britain.

Except at the north-west corner, where Henry I erected a great keep in the twelfth century, the magnificent defences are complete. The flint wall separated by courses of stone and red bonding tiles still stand 20ft (6m) high, together with fourteen hollow bastions of the original twenty. These towers were designed to take ballistae, and these pieces of Roman artillery were probably supported on timber flooring. Of the four gateways, the north and south entrances were only narrow posterns. Along the east and west sides the gateways were defended by sections of inturned wall. Today, only the lower courses of the west gate are visible, for on the opposite side, the Roman east gate was built over in medieval times. South of the Landgate on the west side, where excavation has taken place, the original inner width of the Roman wall can be seen.

**Access**    The site lies at the head of Portsmouth Harbour between Fareham and Portsea Island. It is signposted on the A27 as it passes through the suburb of Portchester.

**Lympne** (*Portus Lemanis*)
Lympne, Hythe, Kent
OS 189, (1in 173), TR117342
Known today as Stutfall Castle, the remains are scattered forlornly on a hillside slope that has been much disturbed by landslips. The wall originally enclosed a site of about 10 acres (4ha), and some isolated sections are about 25ft (7.5m) high and 13ft (3.9m) thick. Although the site does not offer the same quality of evidence when compared with the other Saxon Shore forts, it is nevertheless an interesting spot to visit — it certainly has an atmosphere all of its own.

**Access**    Make for the village of Lympne, on the B2067, 3 miles (4.8km) to the west of Hythe. the site may be approached by footpath at the end of the road to Lympne Castle. The right of way continues down the hill slope towards the Royal Military Canal.

**Richborough** (*Rutupiae*)
Sandwich, Kent
OS 179, (1in 173), TR325602, AM
This was originally the bridgehead site for the invasion army of AD43. Later, the area became a great store base, and then the chief port of Roman Britain. About the middle of the third century, triple ditches were excavated to surround a signal tower on three sides. Late in the third century, the massive walls of the Saxon Shore fort were built. They were probably 30ft (9m) high, faced with squared stones and interspaced by courses of bonding tiles. Today, many lengths of wall still stand up to 20ft (6m) high. The bastion on the north wall has a narrow postern opening, and the west wall has a gateway defended by guard chambers. Only one of these is now visible.

**Access**    Situated 1½ miles (2.4km) north-north-west of Sandwich. Take the A257 Canterbury road, and bear right on to a minor road just before the level crossing.

## HADRIAN'S WALL

This remarkable monument has attracted the attention of countless people throughout the ages, and is a fitting memorial to the skill, tenacity and tremendous organisational ability of the Romans.

After the initial expeditions by Julius Caesar in 55 and 54BC, it was left to Claudius to conquer the southern part of the country some ninety years later. The narrow isthmus between the Solway Firth and the estuary of the Tyne was not reached by the Romans until AD78, when Julius Agricola became Governor of Britain. He advanced deep into Scotland, particularly up the lowland east coast, and around the highland mass to Inverness. As he advanced, a network of roads was created to link up the forts and to enable his army to move easily and quickly.

One of these roads was the Stanegate (the name given to it in the Middle Ages means Stone road), which became the base for Agricola's advance into Scotland. After the recall of Agricola to Rome, plans for further conquests in Scotland were abandoned, and the Romans withdrew to the line of the Stanegate. This east to west road, connecting Corbridge *(Corstopitum)* with Carlisle *(Luguvallium)* was the important link, and it became the new frontier across the Tyne-Solway gap as more forts were built at regular intervals along it.

In AD118, soon after Hadrian became emperor, there was a major rebellion by the tribes of northern England and southern Scotland. In AD122, soon after order had been restored, Hadrian visited Britain to study the situation for himself. Presumably it was as a result of these disorders that Hadrian decided to deal effectively with this part of northern Britain. As the Empire was experiencing frontier problems in Europe, Hadrian's policy was to establish clear static boundaries and frontiers, such as a sea, river or a permanent artificial barrier. He decided to create an effective frontier by the construction of a wall from sea to sea; a demarcation line that would divide the Romans from the barbarians. The existing system of a fortified road like the Stanegate was insufficient. The need was for a barrier that would allow the army to supervise the movement of people, prevent petty raiding, hinder large-scale attacks, and encourage the peaceful settlement of the province right up to the frontier-line. The construction of the Wall was an attempt to strengthen the Stanegate

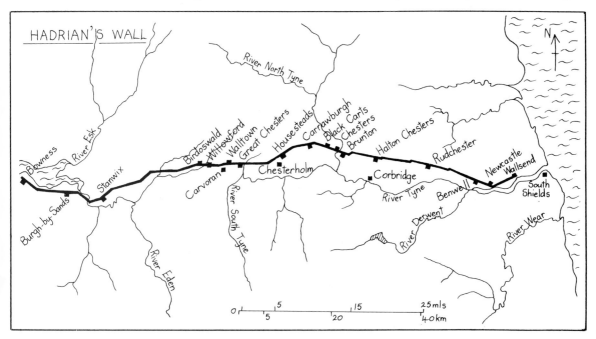

*Hadrian's Wall, Housesteads Fort*

system of small forts and watchtowers, and was planned with the existing system in mind, about a mile or so north of the Stanegate forts. The Wall was planned to be 80 Roman miles or 73½ English miles (117km) long. It was to be a stone wall 10ft (3m) wide and about 20ft (6m) high, from Wallsend-on-Tyne to the River Irthing. West of the latter point, the Wall was to be of turf, with a base width of 20ft (6m) and a height of about 17ft (5.1m) topped by a timber defence work.

The Wall was accompanied by a ditch on the northern side, except where cliffs made it unnecessary. Spaced at intervals of about one Roman mile (1620yd) were small forts or milecastles which contained living quarters for a small number of soldiers.

The milecastle walls were of stone on the stone wall and turf on the turf wall. These small forts were built on the wall with double gates at front and rear, and access was defended by a watch tower or observation towers. Between each milecastle were two turrets built of stone and measuring about 14ft (4.2m) square internally.

In the central section, the Wall made use of the Whin Sill, a volcanic outcrop forming a line of northern crags. In the east, the Wall ran on the north side of the Tyne valley, crossing the North Tyne by a bridge at Chollerford. From this point the Wall climbed steadily to the crags at Sewingshields, Hotbank, Highshield and Peel to

Winshields, the highest point on the Roman Wall at 1,230ft (345m), and descended gradually to the River Irthing. It continued westwards on the north side of the Irthing gorge, passing on the northern side of Carlisle, across the River Eden at Stanwix, and along the Solway marshes to the sea at Bowness on Solway.

Although the Wall itself ended at Bowness on Solway, a number of milecastles and towers have been traced further along the Cumbrian coast, and this system of control may have continued as far south as St Bees Head. These milecastles had turf walls and possibly timber living quarters, and, as they were protected by the sea, had only one gateway. The towers, acting like the observation turrets on the central section of the Wall, were built of stone. Milecastles are now numbered from the east, and the same number, followed by a or b, is given to the turrets on the west side of each milecastle.

The Wall was constructed by various detachments from Legions II Augusta, VI Victrix and XX Valeria Victrix. These work gangs were divided into groups, some on the turrets and milecastles, others on the breast-work of the Wall, and others on digging the ditch. The Wall is not of uniform construction throughout its length, due to the different work rates of the gangs involved. Many of the turrets and milecastles had been built to the wider dimensions and were completed first, so in some sections you have a narrow wall on narrow foundations, and in others, stretches of narrow wall on broad

*Headquarters building, Chesters Roman Fort*

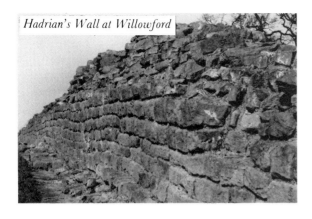

*Hadrian's Wall at Willowford*

foundations. Also many of the turrets and milecastles had first been built to the wider dimensions. In some places the uneven join can be seen where one labour force met the work of another gang. The turf Wall was rebuilt in stone at at later date with a width of 9ft (2.7m).

The ditch also varied in width, but was generally V-shaped with the excavated material banked upon the north side, with a distance of about 20ft (6m) between the excavation and the Wall. Along the craggy parts of the Whin Sill, the ditch appears only where there are gaps in the ridge.

Soon after the work started in about AD122 under the supervision of the governor Aulus Platorius Nepos, a decision was taken to move the main army formations to the Wall and to house them in newly-built forts. Originally there were twelve forts which eventually rose to sixteen. At about the same time, or shortly after, other decisions were made to decrease the width of the Wall from 10ft (3m) to 8ft (2.4m), and to construct an earthwork known as the vallum a short distance south of the frontier line, and running roughly parallel to it.

The vallum was probably constructed at the time when the decision was taken to move the forts on to the line of the Wall. The strategy behind this idea was to create a barrier to the south protecting the military area from surprise attack by the still troublesome natives from the south. The vallum consisted of a large ditch protected by linear banks and could only be safely crossed by causeways. These crossing points to the forts were guarded by strong entrance gates on the northern side of the vallum. This formidable obstacle is yet another outstanding achievement of Roman engineering, and there are still some fine sections to be seen along this remarkable frontier line.

After the Wall and vallum had been constructed, a well-engineered road was laid down between the two sets of defences. Known as the Military Way, the route was stone-lined and surfaced with gravel, and was so well built that it was still in use by pack-horse trains in the mid-eighteenth century. Today, it is grass-covered, but can easily be traced in certain parts, especially west of Housesteads.

Although the legionaries built the Wall, the ramparts were probably manned by regular auxiliary detachments drawn from the tribes of the Empire's frontier regions. There is evidence that the Wall had a defensive breastwork, with the stone section possibly having a crenellated parapet, and the turf section having a stockade of timber posts. These units were stationed in the forts to the rear, and the Wall served as a frontier look-out and as a means of protective cover. The Wall was never meant to be a fighting platform to defend against an attack, but a base line from which to sally forth and engage the enemy in the open.

The main purpose of the Wall, ditch and vallum was to form a barrier between hostile northern tribes, but allowing the peaceful movement of people, and the growth of civilian settlements outside the military forts. The Wall remained the northern frontier during most of the period of the Roman occupation, except for occasional incursions into Scotland which left it unmanned. By the end of the fourth century it was largely deserted, as greater dangers nearer home threatened the stability of the Roman Empire, leading to the final removal of troops from Britain, leaving its cities and settlements alone and undefended.

Today, there are substantial remains of this remarkable monument. The central section cresting the dramatic outcrops of the Whin Sill affords views second to none in the British Isles. It is a memorable experience to stand on these blue-grey dolerite crags and follow the Wall as it snakes over a succession of rises and dips.

## Hadrian's Wall
### Features of Special Note

- In the central part of its course there are many fine lengths of Wall, some sections standing to a height of 7 to 8ft (2.1 to 2.4m), eg Walltown (NY673663)
- There are sections where the Wall is broad 10ft (3m) on a broad foundation, and sometimes narrow on a broad foundation.
- The facing stones front and rear were cut to a particular size, approximately 6in (0.15cm) high, 10in (0.25m) wide and 20in (0.5m) deep. The stone used was quarried locally.
- Lime was burnt and mixed with sand and gravel for mortar.
- Rubble bonded with mortar or clay made up the central core.
- The Wall was mainly built by detachments from legions II Augusta, VI Victrix and XX Valeria Victrix.
- Each legion constructed certain sections of the Wall, the soldiers divided into small work-gangs under the direction of their own officers.
- There are obvious junctions and offsets where lengths of the Wall were joined together. The end of a completed section was marked in places with inscribed centurial stones, eg at Black Carts (NY885713).

## Hadrian's Wall Sites

**Walltown** (DoE)
Walltown, Greenhead,
Northumberland
OS 86, (1in 76), NY673663
Here is a magnificent section of the Wall, in parts still standing 7 to 8ft (2.1 to 2.4m) high, extending for some 400yd

(366m) west of the turret signalling tower, number 45a. The Wall winds its way round the rock outcrops known as the Nine Nicks of Thirlwall, and where the slope dips steeply, the inner blocks of stone are stepped to ensure stability.

**Access**    From Greenhead, proceed ½ mile (800m) east on the B6318, to a signposted minor road on the left. Follow the DoE signs, and then bear right up the slope. Further on, keep to the right of the trees, which brings you in line with turret 45a.

**Black Carts**
Walwick, Chollerford,
Northumberland
OS 87, (1in 77), NY884713
Here is a stretch of Wall 656ft (200m) long and 8ft (2.4m) high incorporating turret 29a. It is a point of reduction from the broad Wall to the narrow Wall, with the turret walls built on the broad gauge. This portion was obviously rebuilt at a later date, as one centurial stone was used in the reconstruction of the north face. It is located in the middle of the bottom course of the north wall. Usually, these stones were placed on the south face as a record of construction by a particular unit of soldiers.
From this point, there are good views of the vallum and ditch; the latter is to be seen to

good advantage on the other side of the lane.
**Access**    Some 2½ miles (4km) west of Chollerford. The section

of Wall is visible on the right-hand side of the B6318, and access is from the narrow lane running north.

*Centurial Stone, Black Carts*

## Hotbank Crags, Housestead Crags and Cuddy's Crags

Housesteads Roman Fort, Roman Wall, Northumberland OS 87, (1in 77), NY775685
This section westwards from Housesteads Roman fort runs along the crest of the rocky outcrops of Housestead Crags, Cuddy's Crags and Hotbank Crags, 1,074ft (327m).

On Housestead Crags look for the sections of slightly different widths due to the separate sections of each legionary working party. Also to be seen here are the remains of milecastle 37 built by Legion II Augusta. At Rapishaw Gap, a natural fault in the Whin Sill, the Pennine Way leaves the Roman Wall and heads north towards Wark Forest, the Cheviot Hills and Kirk Yetholm

*Hadrian's Wall at Cuddy's Crags*

for its final 58 miles (93.6km).
**Access**  Visitors may accompany this fine section of Wall from Housesteads, where there is a car-park alongside the B6318. Alternatively, a circular walk may be undertaken from the car-park at Steel Rigg (NY751677), following the Wall overlooking Crag Lough, and climbing up to Hotbank and

Cuddy's Crags to Housesteads fort *(Vercovicium)*. Continue over Kennel Crags to a gateway in the Wall, and return by fieldpath north of the crags. The route crosses the Pennine Way through Peatrigg to the minor road, and left to the car-park at Steel Rigg. Distance 6¾ miles (10.8km).

## Brunton

Chollerford, Northumberland OS 87, (1in 77), NY921698
This is a section of broad Wall 10ft (3m) wide resting on a broad foundation. This is interesting, because only a short

distance east at Planetrees, the structure is only 6ft (1.8m) thick.
**Access**  The site may be reached by a short footpath from the A6097, a few yards south of the junction with the B6318. The Wall enters turret 26b on

one side in its 'broad' form, 10ft (3m) wide, and leaves on the other side in its 'narrow' form 8ft (2.4m) wide. There is limited parking space.

## Planetrees

Chollerford, Northumberland OS 87, (1in 77), NY929696
This stretch of Wall, 165ft (50m) long, is an example of the point of reduction from the broad wall

to the narrow wall. The latter is only 6ft (1.8m) thick, with the masonry resting on a broad foundation that incorporates a drainage culvert.
**Access**  This site is situated ⅝

mile (1km) east of the crossroads between the A6079 and the B6318. There are some stone steps over the wall on the right-hand side of the road.

### Hadrian's Wall Forts

Corbridge *(Corstopitum)*, Military Supply Depot
Hexham, Northumberland OS 87, (1in 77), NY982648

Chesters *(Cilurnum)*, Cavalry Fort
Chollerford, Hexham, Northumberland OS 87, (1in 77), NY912702

Chesterholm *(Vindolanda)*, Fort and Civilian Settlement
Chesterholm, Twice Brewed, Northumberland OS 87, (1in 77), NY771663

Housesteads *(Vercovicium)* (NT), Fort and Civilian Settlement
Housesteads, Northumberland OS 87, (11in 77), NY790688

South Shields *(Arbeia)*, Fort and Supply Base
South Shields, Tyne and Wear OS 88, (1in 78), NZ365679

Birdoswald *(Camboglanna)*, Fort
Gilsland, Brampton, Cumbria OS 86, (1in 76), NY615662

---

### Hadrian's Wall Milecastles
### Identifying Features

- Small forts or milecastles, providing accommodation for a small number of soldiers and their equipment, were constructed at intervals of one Roman mile, 1,620yd (1.55km).
- They measure about 50 to 60ft (15 to 18m) wide, and 55 to 75ft (16.5 to 22.5m) long.
- The visible remains contain two gateways, one through the Wall and one to the rear.

- Each of the legions constructed milecastles in their own style, and this is noticeable in the form of the gateways, where certain features can be attributed to a particular legion.
- Within the interior the outline of a stone barracks building may be identified, eg Poltross Burn, milecastle 48 (NY634662).

---

## Milecastle Sites

### Castle Nick, Milecastle 39
Steel Rigg, Once Brewed, Northumberland
OS 86, (1in 77), NY760677
Milecastle 39 measures 62ft by 50 ft (18.6m by 15m) approximately, with side walls 7ft (2.1m) thick. The gateways opposite to each other in the north and south walls are built with small masonry. The northern gateway was most likely topped by a tower, built on a broad gauge foundation. To the west of the milecastle the Wall is built on a narrow gauge foundation. The interior of the milecastle held a timber barrack building against the east wall and a small store hut against the west wall.
**Access**   Turn north off the

Milecastle 39, Castle Nick

B6318, opposite the Northumberland National Park Information Centre. There is a

car-park at Peel Rigg. Walk east along the Wall over Steel Rigg for ⅝ mile (1km) to the site.

### Poltross Burn, Milecastle 48
Gilsland, Northumberland
OS 86, (1in 76), NY634662
One of the best preserved milecastles on the Wall. It measures 70ft x 60ft (21m x 18m). In the north-east corner a stairway leads up to the

ramparts, and there are the remains of an oven in the opposite corner. The side walls built by men from Legion VI are of the broad gauge, but there is a junction of the narrow gauge Wall on a broad foundation on either side of the milecastle.

Within the interior are the outlines of two stone barrack blocks.
**Access**   Take the B6318 from Greenhead, and turn left just before the railway bridge in Gilsland. The site is signposted.

### Housesteads, Milecastle 37
Housesteads, Thorngrafton, Northumberland
OS 86, (1in 76), NY785687

### Cawfields, Milecastle 42
Cawfields, Haltwhistle, Northumberland
OS 86 (1in 76), NY716667

### Harrow's Scar, Milecastle 49
Birdoswald, Gilsland, Cumbria
OS 86, (1in 76), NY620664

## Hadrian's Wall Turrets
### Identifying Features

- Two turrets were built between each milecastle, one third of a Roman mile apart, and were constructed of stone.
- Externally they measure 20ft (6m) square, and 14ft (4.2m) square internally.
- Each turret recesses about 6ft (1.8m) into the thickness of the Wall.
- The entrance to the turret was a door on the south side.
- On the stone Wall, each turret contained a stone platform with four or five steps; some still survive. This probably formed the support for a timber ladder or stairway to the wall top. On the turf Wall most of the turrets contained a low stone platform, but without steps.
- Most of the turrets would have had a hearth, where the soldiers could cook their food and keep warm.
- The turrets were used as regular observation posts on the Wall.

## Turret Sites

### Brunton, Turret 26b
Chollerford, Hexham, Northumberland
OS 87, (1in 77), NY921698
To the west of the turret, the Wall was constructed in its broad gauge 10ft (3m) wide. On the turret's eastern side the Wall is in its narrow form of 8ft (2.4m) wide. The turret still exhibits its door-sill with pivot hole, and the interior contains the lower half of a corn mill and an uninscribed altar. The turret was constructed by a work-gang from Legion XX.
**Access**  Take the A6079 south of Chollerford, a few yards from its junction with the B6318. There is a small parking place close by the entrance to the site on the left.

*Turret 26b, Brunton*

### Black Carts, Turret 29a
Walwick, Chollerford, Hexham, Northumberland
OS 87, (1in 77), NY885713

### Coesike, Turret 33b
Sewing Shields, Haydon Bridge, Northumberland
OS 86, (1in 77), NY821705

### Denton Hall, Turret 7b
Denton, Newcastle upon Tyne
OS 88, (1in 78), NZ198655
Alongside the A69, some 330yd (300m) west of the Ring Road South roundabout.

### Willowford, Turret 48b
Willowford Farm, Gilsland, Cumbria
OS 86, (1in 76), NY625665
This turret lies nearer to the farm.

### Willowford, Turret 48a
Willowford Farm, Gilsland, Cumbria
OS 86, (1in 76), NY630663
Note that the side walls are built to the broad gauge. This turret lies nearer to the minor road.

### Walltown, Turret 44b
Walltown Farm, Greenhead, Northumberland
OS 86, (1in 76), NY680666

### Banks East, Turret 52a
Banks, Lanercost, Brampton,
Cumbria
OS 86, (1in 76), NY575647
This is on the turf Wall, with a
well-preserved plinth joined on either side by the stone Wall.
The interior of the turret
contains a raised platform where
the soldiers would have cooked
and slept. A piece of the turret
masonry lies nearby.

**Access** Situated alongside the
minor road running north of the
River Irthing, 1½ miles (2.4km)
east of Lanercost. From
Brampton, the site lies 3½ miles
(5.6km) to the north-east.

---

## Hadrian's Wall — The Ditch
### Identifying Features

- The width of the ditch varied, but usually it was about 27ft (8.1m) wide and 10ft (3m) deep.
- Its profile was V-shaped with a drainage channel at the bottom.
- The excavated material was thrown on to the northern bank.
- A section of ground called a berm, or open flat space, separated the ditch from the Wall, usually a distance of up to 20ft (6m) in width.
- Where there are cliffs, the ditch only appears at gaps in the Whin Sill.
- In other places, the ditch was not completed due to the incidence of solid rock. For example, at Limestone Corner (NY875716).

---

## Ditch Sites

### Wall Fell
Portgate, Hexham,
Northumberland
OS 87, (1in 77), NY965692

### Black Carts
Walwick, Chollerford, Hexham,
Northumberland
OS 87, (1in 77), NY885713

### Sewing Shields
Sewing Shields, Haydon Bridge,
Northumberland
OS 87, (1in 77), NY813704
Section of ditch west from
Coesike Turret to site of
Milecastle 34.

### Peel
Twice Brewed, Haltwhistle,
Northumberland
OS 87, (1in 77), NY750676

*Black Carts Ditch, Hadrian's Wall*

---

## Hadrian's Wall — The Vallum
### Identifying Features

- The vallum was a very effective obstacle marking the boundary of the military zone.
- It consists of a flat-bottomed ditch 20ft (6m) wide at the top, 8ft (2.4m) wide at the bottom, and 10ft (3m) deep.
- There are two mounds 20ft (6m) wide, 6ft (1.8m) high, one on either side, and set back 30ft (9m) from the lip of the ditch.
- Access across the vallum was by means of heavily defended causeways. For example, one such crossing point was at Benwell (NZ215646).

**Vallum Sites**

**Heddon-on-the-Wall**
Newcastle-upon-Tyne,
Northumberland
OS 88, (1in 78), NZ138669

**Wall Fell**
Portgate, Hexham,
Northumberland
OS 87, (1in 77), NY964691

**Carrawburgh**
Chollerford, Northumberland
OS 87, (1in 77), NY871714

**Cawfields**
Haltwhistle, Northumberland
OS 87, (1in 76), NY717666

*Vallum at Carrawbrough*

## PUBLIC BUILDINGS AND VILLAS

After the initial opposition to the Romans and later periodic uprisings from the Welsh and northern tribes, attitudes began to mellow and the Romans effectively spread their policies. The local population, particulary in the lowland areas of central and southern Britain, quickly realised the benefits of being part of the Roman Empire. However, the area in the far north of England and southern Scotland never became a settled part of the province, and remained a military zone.

By the fourth century, there was at least one important town at the centre of some twenty-eight administrative units throughout those parts of conquered Britain, excluding the frontier area in the north. These tribal capitals (*civitas*) served any number of smaller settlements within their area: for example, the Coritani, a tribe living in the East Midlands, had their capital at *Ratae Coritanorum* (Leicester). From the earliest days of their development, these capitals were laid out with a regular street plan. They contained important buildings, such as the meeting hall (*basilica*), the temple, the baths and the market place (*forum*). As the centre of the town's activities, the *basilica* and *forum* were

usually sited at the intersection of the main streets. The *basilica* was a long hall with semi-circular or rectangular ends, where meetings were held and ceremonies enacted. It lay along one side of the forum, which was a rectangular open market place surrounded by a colonnade. Behind the colonnade were small rooms used as shops, workshops and eating places.

The main styles of temple were the classical, the Romano-Celtic and the Mithraic. The classical temple was an elevated rectangular platform with a row of columns supporting a porch. The shrine was approached by a flight of steps. At the foot of the steps there was an altar for public sacrifice. The Romano-Celtic temple, which was the most common type, consists of a ground plan of two squares, one inside the other. The inner room was the shrine (*cella*) surrounded by a colonnaded wall and covered portico. The Mithraic temples were usually quite small rectangular buildings with an apse or a recess at one end where the altars were placed. The body of the temple was divided into three parts longitudinally. Just inside the entrance would be a small annexe screened off from the main part of the temple.

Mithraism was a Roman adaptation of an ancient religion from Persia. It was a cult of special importance to senior officers in the army. The god represented the victory of the soul after death. Mithraism was also popular with merchants because it represented honesty and fair-dealing. The *mithaeum* had a dark interior with only a little light coming through a number of small upper windows. This tended to heighten the air of mystery and awe surrounding the ceremonies. Furthermore, a lamp behind the altar enhanced the effect by effectively illuminating the relief in the recess. The slaying of the wild bull was Mithras's greatest task which represented the releasing of creative power for mankind. The cult was only open to men, who had to undertake certain initiation tests, some symbolic, some by physical ordeal. On passing the tests successfully, the follower could take part in the sacred banquet, believing that this action would ensure a better life in the next world. It has some affinities to freemasonry with the passing of different grades by the initiates, and also to Christianity, as it promised believers everlasting happiness and salvation in the life hereafter.

The bath suite was a most essential part of Roman life, not only providing communal washing facilities, but also providing a place where people relaxed, conversed and took exercise. Some of the buildings were magnificently decorated and the interior must have been in complete contrast to the conditions in which most ordinary people lived. The Roman bath system, of which the modern equivalent is the Turkish bath, consisted of a series of rooms heated to different temperatures.

The water and the rooms were heated by the Roman hypocaust system. The floors were supported on short pillars of brick and stone. Then the hot air from the nearby furnaces circulated around the pillars, and subsequently escaped up the wall-flues to the air outside. A fine example of a public bath-suite is to be found at Wroxeter *(Viroconium Cornoviorum)* near Shrewsbury, the tribal capital of the Cornovii (SJ565087).

During the Roman occupation, in the country areas, many people would still live in the type of house common in the Iron Age period; a circular building with mud or wattle walls, supporting a turf or thatched roof. In the remote upland areas, stone-built round houses of the Bronze Age tradition continued to be a common feature.

Each *civitas* capital was a self-governing community with its own local council of at least a hundred members, who were residents or natives of that town. These local councils were therefore responsible for most aspects of day-to-day life. There were laws to uphold, taxes to collect, corn to store, mines to oversee, public baths to heat, and so on. Local jobs made profits and the officals were able to ensure a very comfortable life for themselves. Their accommodation was a considerable improvement on the round and oblong thatched-roof huts of people living in the country districts.

The prosperity of a town depended on the richness of the surrounding countryside. In some areas, large and prosperous Roman villa estates grew up. Although these properties would suit the status of a *civitas* offical, there is evidence that estates in Britain might also have belonged to high officals from other parts of the Empire. The province would appear to have been an ideal exile for some of Rome's unwanted senators. These comfortable villas were developed on well-chosen sheltered sites. The basic design is an oblong block in which several rooms lead off a long corridor, and in some examples short wings were added on either side. In other cases, the blocks of rooms were grouped around one or more courtyards. Some villas had living quarters for more than one family, and separate buildings to house farm labourers and slaves.

Those sites that date from the third and fourth centuries usually include hypocaust heating systems, and have mosaic floors laid in the principal rooms. A bath-suite or house was also normal. For example, Chedworth near Northleach in Gloucestershire (SP053135), had damp-heat (Turkish style) and dry-heat (Swedish sauna style) baths. The great beauty of the mosaic patterns seem to portray the character and lifestyle of the families who owned and lived in the villa. The main themes of the tesselated floors were taken from the characters and traditions of classical mythology, concerning Orpheus or scenes from Virgil, perhaps. For example, in the apse of the dining-room at the Lullingstone villa (TQ530650), there is the abduction of Europa by Jupiter in the guise of a bull.

## Roman Temple Sites

### Temple of Mithras
Carrawbrough, Chollerford,
Northumberland
OS 87, (1in 77), NY859711, AM

The remains of this small
mithraic temple are located just
outside the south-western limits
of the Roman fort of *Brocolitia*.
Originally founded at the
beginning of the third century, it
was extended to its present size
of 36ft by 15ft (10.8m by 4.5m)
later in the same century before
being destroyed, probably by

*Temple of Mithras, Carrawbrough*

Christians. At the northern end
stand three splendid altars
dedicated to Mithras, the
westernmost one depicting the
god with a halo. In all
probability, there would have
been a relief illustrating the bull-
slaying ceremony in the recess
behind the altars. Today, the
three altars are copies; the
originals are in the University
Museum, Newcastle-upon-
Tyne. The central aisle of the
temple, now represented by

concrete posts, was originally
flanked by raised platforms
where the worshippers waited.
Just inside the entrance of the
building was a small ante-room
which was equipped with a
sunken pit, used for one of the
less attractive initiation
ceremonies, when the initiate
was probably buried alive for a
short while. Also down the
central aisle stand four small
altars, and the desecrated statues
of the two torch-carrying
acolytes, Cautes and
Cautophates, who represent
light and life, and darkness and
death, respectively.

**Access** The site is situated 3¾
miles (6km) to the west of
Chollerford on the B6318. From
the car-park alongside the
Roman fort of *Brocolitia*, take the
path following the eastern side,
then proceed along the southern
rim to the little temple. 150yd
(136m) to the north of the
temple, lies the well and shrine
of the nymph Coventina, where
votive offerings of coins,
brooches and bronze pins were
made.

### Benwell Temple
Benwell, Newcastle-upon-Tyne,
Northumberland
OS 88, (1in 78), NZ217646, AM
Today, the remains of the tiny
temple dedicated to the native
god Anociticus or Antenociticus
lie tucked away amongst the
modern buildings of a housing
estate. The low walls trace out
the shape of a small rectangular
structure, 23½ft by 15ft (7.1m by
4.5m), terminating in a semi-
circular apse at the southern
end, and an entrance along the
lower eastern side. The altars on
the site are replicas, and the
originals are now in the

*Benwell Roman Temple*

University Museum, Newcastle-upon-Tyne, together with the splendidly-sculptured head of the god himself with large eyes and wavy snake-like hair. This remained a local deity, and was probably highly revered by the units stationed in the fort of Condercum.

**Access**   Situated in the suburb of Benwell 2 miles (3.2km) west of the centre of Newcastle. The site is signposted to the south of the A69, and may be located on the left-hand side of Broomridge Avenue in a space between two houses.

### Maiden Castle Temple
Winterborne Monkton,
Dorchester, Dorset
OS 194, (1in 178), SY671884,
AM

Towards the end of the fourth century, during a time when Christianity and Pagan religions were being practised, a typical Romano-Celtic temple was built in the north-eastern sector of the existing hillfort. The remains indicate a square central shrine (*cella*) facing east surrounded by a precinct and outer wall. On the north side is a tiny structure which is believed to have been a simple dwelling for the resident priest. The deity worshipped at the temple is not known, although finds have included a statuette of a horned Celtic bull-god.

**Access**   Leave the A354 just south of Dorchester, where a signposted route on the right leads to the famous Maiden Castle hillfort. Approach through the west gate from the car-park, and walk east across the interior to the temple site. Distance from the centre of Dorchester is 2½ miles (4km).

## Roman Villa Sites

### Chedworth Roman Villa
(NT)
Yanworth, Northleach,
Gloucestershire
OS 163, (1in 144), SP053135

This is one of the finest villa sites in Britain, beautifully situated in the wooded upper reaches of the River Coln. Chedworth is an excellent topographical example, as it lies within a small hollow, protected by hills on the north, west and south sides. It has a fine open aspect to the east, looking across the valley and its stream.

*Hypocaust, Chedworth Roman Villa*

The first building work was begun in the early part of the second century, and consisted of two buildings on the west and south. During the next century, these blocks were rebuilt after a fire. The site as seen today, and now set out on three sides of a courtyard, belongs to the early fourth century. The last building work consisted of a number of rooms along the north side. Altogether, the villa contained over thirty-six rooms. In the west wing are to be found fine examples of mosaic flooring executed by the Cirencester school of mosaicists.

Further along the west side is a damp-heat Turkish-style bathsuite, containing an *(apodyterium)*, a *(tepidarium)*, a *(caldarium)*, and a *(frigidarium)*. There are examples of hypocaust pillars, pilae, flue tiles and a mosaic floor to be seen. Tucked away in the north-west corner of the site is a sacred shrine to the water nymphs of the spring — this source still supplies water today.

Firstly, along the north wing can be seen the position of the original bath-suite, which was later demolished, and the block converted to the Swedish-style dry heat type in the fourth century. Continuing along the north side, further rooms were added in the third century, but in one room only do the hypocaust pilae remain. After the fourth-century improvements to the bath-suite, the rest of the block was extended, terminating in a large reception room heated by a channelled hypocaust; a colonnade was also erected.

**Access** The site may be approached from Fossebridge on the A429 by narrow country lanes. Ignore the turning to the village of Chedworth, and proceed straight on. Turn sharp right to cross the River Coln and ascend to the T-junction. The village of Yanworth lies to the right, but bear left, and continue for 1 mile (1.6km) to descend to the river again. The villa, signposted, lies straight ahead beyond the road junction. Distance nearly $3\frac{1}{2}$ miles (5.4km).

From the north, leave the A436 south of Andoversford, through Withington and Cassey Compton. Distance: nearly 6 miles (9.3km).

From the village of Chedworth by footpath: take the lane east, climbing to a sharp right-hand bend, where a path strikes due north alongside a track coming in from the left. After a short distance the path descends through Chedworth Woods to meet a country lane. Bear left and walk for a few yards to the villa. To vary the return route, turn right on leaving the villa and pass beneath a disused railway track. After a few yards, head left and follow the path through the woods. Beyond, the route continues through the eastern end of a small copse, and then above the line of the old railway track back to the village. Distance: 2 miles (3.2km).

## North Leigh Courtyard Villa
East End, Stonesfield, Charlbury, Oxfordshire OS 164, (1in 145), SP397155, This villa reached the height of its prosperity in the fourth century, when it had rooms and corridors occupying three sides of a courtyard, and an entrance gateway along the south-eastern side. The walls of the final building and small parts of earlier masonry are visible along the west and north-western sides. Further investigation has revealed building extensions in the south-western corner, and along the north eastern side,. verified by aerial photography.

The first room to visit, which is under cover, is the dining room in the north-west corner of the villa. The room is floored with a three-coloured geometric mosaic, probably laid by the same Cirencester craftsmen who operated at Chedworth. It is exciting to note that the hypocaust is in excellent condition, and that the pilae can be seen where a section of the floor has been removed. Along the north-western wing in which the villa's living quarters could be found, there are rooms cotaining channelled hypocausts. In the northern corner, the original baths, probably constructed in the second century, became part of an extensive bath-suite containing ante-rooms heated by channelled hypocausts, and two semi-circular plunge pools.

**Access** The villa may be approached by footpath from the southern end of the village of Stonesfield, south-east of the church of St James. A footbridge crosses the River Evenlode, and the path continues for 220yd (200m) before veering south-east to join a lane. Cross over the railway bridge and take the next turning to the left to reach the villa site. Distance to and from the village is $2\frac{1}{4}$ miles (3.6km). The village of Stonesfield lies on the route of the Oxfordshire Way, a long-distance footpath of $67\frac{1}{4}$ miles (107.6km), from Bourton-on-the-Water to Henley -on-Thames.

By car, take a narrow minor road west, and then south from Stonesfield, to cross the railway and the river. Turn immediately sharp left along the river to the signposted entrance drive to the villa. Alternatively, leave the A4095, 3 miles (4.8km) north-east of Witney. Ignore the turning to North Leigh, and take the minor road to East End. Beyond, the villa is signposted to the right.

## Other Villa Sites

**Beadlam,** Helmsley, North Yorkshire
OS 100, (1in 92), SE634842

**Bignor Courtyard Villa,** West Burton, Arundel, West Sussex
OS 197, (1in 181), SU988147

**Fishbourne Palace,** Chicester, West Sussex
OS 197, (1in 181), SU841047

**Littlecote Park,** Chilton Foliat, Hungerford, Wiltshire
OS 174, (1in 157), SU298708

**Rockbourne,** Fordingbridge, Hampshire
OS 184, (1in 179), SU120170

**Brading,** Sandown, Isle of Wight
OS 196, (1in 180), SZ599863

**Lullingstone,** Eynsford, Sevenoaks, Kent
OS 188, (1in 171), TQ529651, AM

**Great Witcombe**
Brockworth, Gloucester
OS 163, (1in 143), SO899142, AM

## Roman Towns and Fortress Walls

**York,** *(Eburacum),* Legionary Fortress, Colonia and Military Capital
York, North Yorkshire
OS 105, (1in 97), SE603523
Situated in the gardens of the Yorkshire Museum, on the north bank of the River Ouse, is a magnificent stretch of fourth-century fortress-wall, ending at the spectacular remains of the Multangular Tower. This very well-preserved structure is a polygonal tower of 35ft (10.5m) high with fourteen sides. To the right of the tower is another fine section of fourth-century curtain wall with well-preserved facing stones and bonding tiles. A small gateway by the side of the tower gives access to the legionary fortress, where there is a fine section of the interior wall standing.

Visitors are able to walk along the fortress walls from Bootham Bar to Monk Bar. The defences continue to the east angle tower, and to another length of curtain wall 16ft (4.8m) high.

York Minster was built on the site of the Roman fortress's headquarters building *(principia).* Following vital preservation work in the late 1960s, when the Minster had serious foundation problems, the excavations revealed a great deal of evidence concerning the Roman building. Now, there is a splendid museum in the Minster's Undercroft, where sections of Roman walls may be examined. While you are there in this unusual museum, note the number of column bases, and superb colourful fragments of Roman painted plaster. The illustrations include architectural details, a human figure, a theatrical mask and birds.

**St Albans** *(Verulamium),* City Wall
OS 166, (1in 160), TL137067
Although the facing stones have disappeared, the remains still stand 8 to 10ft (2.4 to 3m) high. The wall is built of flint with triple courses of tiles running horizontally through it. Originally, the wall stood about 20ft (6m) high, and was protected by a ditch, now tree-covered. A little way along are the foundations of projecting bastions. These were probably bonded into the wall later on in the fourth century.

The city-wall is situated some 770yd (700m) south of the Verulamium Museum in the direction of the abbey.

**Caerwent** *(Venta Silurum),* Tribal Capital
Caerwent, Caldicot, Newport, Gwent
OS 171, (1in 155), ST469905

**Aldborough** *(Isurium Brigantium), Tribal Capital*
Aldborough, Boroughbridge, North Yorkshire
OS 99, (1in 91), SE405665

**Lincoln,** *(Lindum)*
Lincoln, Lincolnshire
OS 121, (1in 113), SK977718

## Bridge Abutments

**Willowford**, Gilsland, Cumbria
OS 86, (1in 76), NY623665

**Chesters**, Chollerford, Hexham, Northumberland
OS 87, (1in 77), NY914701

**Piercebridge**, Darlington, Co Durham
OS 93, (1in 85), NZ211157

## Bath Houses

**St Albans** *(Verulamium)*, Hertfordshire
OS 166, (1in 160), TL136069
The remains constitute part of the bath-suite of a large, second-century town house. There is a large mosaic pavement with a hypocaust heating system beneath it.
**Access** The site, which is 440yd (400m) south of the Verulamium Museum, is signposted from the car-park.

**Bath** *(Aquae Sulis)*, Avon
OS 172, (1in 156), ST7564

**Bearsden**, Glasgow, Scotland
OS 64, (1in 60), NS525721

**Chesters** *(Cilurnum)*, Chollerford, Hexham, Northumberland
OS 87, (1in 77), NY913701

**Wall** *(Letocetum)*, Lichfield, Staffordshire
OS 139, (1in 120), SK098066

**Wroxeter** *(Viroconium Cornoviorum)*, Shrewsbury, Shropshire
OS 126, (1in 118), SJ565087

**Ravenglass** *(Glannaventa)*, 'Walls Castle', Ravenglass, Seascale, Cumbria
OS 96, (1in 88), SD088959

**Lancaster**, Castle Hill, Lancaster, Lancashire
OS 97, (1in 89), SD474620

**Leicester** *(Ratae Coritanorum)*
OS 140, (1in 121), SK582045
Near the church of St Nicholas. Fine Stretch of Roman masonry called the Jewry Wall. The wall is part of the exercise hall *(Palaestra)* of the Roman baths.

**Binchester** *(Vinovia)*, Bishop Auckland, Co Durham
OS 93, (1in 85), NZ209313

**Ebchester** *(Vindomora)*, Mains Farm, Ebchester, Co Durham
OS 88, (1in 78), NZ102556

## Roman Lighthouse

**Dover** *(Dubris)*, Kent
OS 179, (1in 173), TR326418
The Pharos is situated in the grounds of Dover Castle close by the church of St Mary. Only the lower 42ft (12.6m) are original

Roman work. The octagonal-shaped tower was built with an inner core of flint rubble, and faced with dressed stones with tile bonding courses. The upper 20ft (6m) is entirely medieval.

**Access** Situated on the eastern side of Dover. From the town centre, take the A258 for ½ mile (800m) up Castle Hill road.

## Roman Shrine

**Scargill Moor**, Bowes, Co Durham
OS 92, (1in 84), NY998104
Situated amidst wild moorland south of Bowes. Two shrines, one circular, the other rectangular, were both dedicated to Silvanus or his local variant, Vinotonus. They were raised by senior officers stationed at Bowes to

honour the moorland god. An altar from the circular shrine, erected by the prefect of the first cohort of Thracians, is now displayed in the Bowes Museum at Barnard Castle.
The shrines are located on the west bank of the East Black Sike just south of its meeting with Eller Beck. The circular shrine is

clearly visible, and the more northerly rectangular one is now marked by a heap of stones.
**Access** From Bowes, take the minor road south crossing over the River Greta. After ½ mile (800m) turn left and proceed for ⅝ mile (1km). Footpaths head south for Farewell and The Combs on Scargill Low Moor.

On reaching Eller Beck follow the stream in a south-westerly direction to its meeting with the East Black Sike tributary. To incorporate a circular walk, follow the course of the Eller Beck to the west keeping to the northerly arm where the stream bifurcates. On reaching a number of old mine shafts head north-east and then north on a right of way to the minor road and into Bowes. Total distance is 5½ miles (8.8km).

## Roman Amphitheatres

**Caerleon**, Newport, Gwent OS 171, (1 in 155), ST339906 Caerleon was the base of the 2nd Legion Augusta established by Frontinus in AD74. The early fort was defended by a stockaded earthwork and an outer ditch. Within the ramparts the buildings were mostly of timber. During the second century, the earthwork was revetted with stone externally, and the important buildings were reconstructed in masonry.

The oval amphitheatre was built in about AD80 just outside the south-west wall of the Roman fort. The arena was hollowed out of a sloping site and the excavated material was piled up round it. This earthen bank was supported internally and externally with stone walls. The inner surface was covered with plaster, and the outer wall was buttressed at regular intervals. It is believed that the external walls reached a height of 32ft (9.6m). Timber seating was erected on the earth banks, and it has been estimated that it seated about 6,000 spectators.

As was the usual Roman practice, the task of construction was carried out by various units of the legion. On completion of a section, the detachment inscribed its name upon a piece of masonry. Of these record stones four are visible, and if you are successful in finding them, their markings are very faint. The two easiest to find are set into the inner wall on either side of main western entrance into the arena.

The central eastern and western entrances are larger and more elaborate. Broad stairways led down to a small room which opened on to the arena. At the foot of the steps, side staircases led up through brick archways, one to a box for important visitors, and the other to the spectators' seats. The small rooms served as waiting chambers for competitors. The amphitheatre was probably used as an area for gladiatorial combat, animal baiting, troop training and weapon handling.

**Access**    The Roman fort and amphitheatre are situated on the western side of Caerleon. If approaching from the south, the road crosses over the River Usk and becomes part of a one-way system. Turn left opposite the museum, and the sites are on the edge of a wide expanse of playing fields.

Roman Amphitheatre, Caerleon

**Chester**, (*Deva*)
Chester, Cheshire
OS 117, (1in 109), SJ408661
This was the site of the largest
amphitheatre in Roman Britain.
Today, only the northern half
can be seen beyond Newgate.
Excavations have shown that the
original timber structure was
replaced by stone after a few
years. The arena wall is well-
preserved, with entrances on the
north and east. In the former,
the stone gateposts for the
entrance doors are still visible
next to the arena wall, as well as
one flight of steps leading up to
the seating accommodation.
Close by is a small room that
probably housed a statue
dedicated to the various
activities in the arena. The
eastern entrance consists of a
passageway with steps down to a
waiting room. Stairs on either
side would have led to an
enclosure for honoured guests
and also to the main seating
area. Today, only one very worn
flight of steps is visible. The
spectators would have sat on
wooden seats raised on banks
around the arena.
**Access**   Close to the River
Dee, and near to St John's
Church. The site lies at the south
side of the junction of Vicars
Lane, St John Street and
Souter's Lane.

## ROMAN ROADS

By the time the Roman legions landed in Britain,
they had become extremely skilled at building
roads. The famous Appian Way, to name but
one example, extended its well-paved surface
from the city of Rome to the surrounding hills.

There were three main reasons for the expansion
of the Roman Empire. First, increased political
status; secondly, increased wealth; thirdly, the
obsessive determination to spread abroad the
ideas and ideals of Roman civilisation. The
strongest weapon in the pursuit of these tasks was
the might of the Roman army. In the first
instance, as the legions advanced, the roads were
created for military purposes. The troops were
able to move quickly in a newly-conquered
territory, securing and establishing the area with
good lines of communication. Once peace was
established, the roads became part of a wider
network of routes connected with the economic
development of the country.

In AD43, the Roman army moved into south-
east Britain from their beachhead and supply
base at Richborough in Kent. Initially, the
legions made use of the many existing Iron Age
paths and trackways in their general advance
across the Medway and Thames to Colchester.
After a period of consolidation and regrouping,
the Roman legions were ordered to advance in
various directions, and to construct military
roads as they advanced. In the early days of the
invasion, the XXth Legion remained at Colchester.

The IXth marched north, laid Ermine Street
and built a fortress at Lincoln. The IInd fought
their way south-west to Dorchester and on to
Exeter, and the XIVth moved north-west towards
the Midlands, and engineered Watling Street.

Once southern England was subdued and
fortresses built in the Midlands and the north,
Agricola struck swiftly at the far north of
England and made deep advances into Scotland.
Eventually the time came when the Roman
army was stretched to its limits, its forces were
depleted thanks to other troubles throughout the
Empire, and there was a subsequent withdrawal
to the line of Hadrian's Wall.

It is well worthwhile remembering the spectacular successes of the legions' soldiers and
engineers. Probably most of the major roads
were built in the first hundred years of the
conquest of Britain. It is, however, estimated
that the approximate total mileage constructed
during the Roman occupation is about 10,000
miles (16,000km). In the early years of the
campaigns, the Roman surveying parties and
work-gangs were under constant danger of
attack. They planned and laid highways with
great skill through hostile and difficult country:
hills and moors were crossed, forests cut through,
marshes negotiated, rivers and streams bridged
and forded.

In the early days the Romans took full advantage of the existing ancient routes along the
ridges; although these were often primitive, they
were quickly converted to Roman standards. On
new roads, the surveyors laid out sections in
straight lines, with sighting points established on

areas of higher ground. Most probably, beacons were lit to assist the surveyors in their work. It is interesting to note that Roman roads always make their important turns at the high points. Roman roads are characterised by long straight alignments, but this is not always the rule; if obstacles lay in the path of a road, then minor deviations were made, and the alignments would consist of a series of short straight lengths.

Along the line of the road a strip of land would be marked out, and the forest and undergrowth removed and burnt. Down the middle of the cleared strip an embankment would be raised using material obtained from ditches or pits on either side of the mound. This embankment, or *agger*, to give it its Roman name, was constructed with a well-drained base. Its size varied greatly both in width and height, and its composition could be just earth, or stones and other material.

Along major routes, the *agger* was often 5ft (1.5m) high and 40ft to 50ft (12m to 15m) wide. In many cases the surface layers consisted of successive layers of small stones, crushed chalk or flints thoroughly rammed down. The road surface was often steeply cambered. The impact of Roman roads, although built so many centuries ago, remains very clear today. Many of our modern main roads follow the routes laid down by Roman surveyors and engineers; two famous examples are Watling Street and Ermine Street. Minor roads on their Roman foundations also trace unerring straight lines across the countryside. Others hide their former status in the guise of tracks, bridleways and footpaths. The remnants of an *agger*, or a terraced hillside zigzag, illustrate another example of the engineering skill of these conquerors who changed the communications face of our land.

---

## Roman Roads
### Identifying Features

- Usually built in a series of straight sections.
- These alignments usually made important turns at sighting points on higher ground.
- Roman roads were not always straight, especially in hilly country, or following the course of a river valley.
- The composition of each road foundation varied considerably.

- In some cases, a foundation bed of a large stone was covered with layers of rammed down chalk, flints, small stones or fine gravel.
- Many Roman roads were often built on raised embankments or *aggers*. In some cases ditches ran along either side of the mound.
- Hillsides were negotiated by terraces or zigzags.

---

### Sites of Roman Roads

**Ackling Dyke**
Sixpenny Handley, Blandford Forum, Dorset
OS 184, 195, (1in 179), SU016163
This is a fine stretch of Roman road running on a well-embanked causeway in a north-east to south-west direction across the rolling downland. It is one of the best surviving pieces of Roman road in Britain, with a massive *agger* 40ft to 50ft (12m to

15m) wide and 5ft to 6ft (1.5m to 1.8m) high.
**Access**   Turn right off the busy A354, Salisbury to Blandford Forum road, at Handley Hill, on to the minor road, B3081. Proceed for 550yd (500m) to the location of the Roman road.
**Walks   a**   From the minor road at SU016163, there is a short walk along the *agger* north-east to Oakley Down Bronze Age barrow cemetery, with its

fine group of six disc barrows. Distance, there and back, 2 miles (3.2km).
**b**   From SU016163, follow the line of the Roman road south-west to Badbury Rings. For the greater part of the journey the route uses existing rights of way. Do not forget to arrange to be picked up, otherwise it is an 18 mile (28.8km) round trip!

## Wade's Causeway (DoE)

Wheeldale Moor, Goathland,
North Yorkshire
OS 94, (1in 86), SE805975
The line of this Roman road,
'Wade's Causeway', can still be
followed across the North York
Moors to Whitby. A well-
preserved section of its
foundation layers can be seen
exposed on Wheeldale Moor.
The original road surface of
gravel or small stones has been
eroded away over the centuries.
There are some kerb stones still
in place, and also traces of
culverts put in for drainage.
**Access** The site may be
approached by minor roads
south from Egton Bridge or
Grosmont in the valley of the
River Esk. After crossing
Wheeldale Gill, proceed for $1\frac{1}{4}$
miles (2km) and look for the
DoE signpost on the left. Follow

Wade's Causeway

the exposed part of the road for
$\frac{3}{4}$ mile (1.2km).

Or, follow the Lyke Wake
Walk footpath from Eller Beck,
and across Howl Moor from the
east, to a point where the long

distance moorland way crosses
the line of the Roman road just
above the valley of the Wheeldale Beck.

## Peddars Way

Fring, Snettisham, Norfolk
OS 132, (1in 124), TF737336
This track, known as the

Peddars Way, has been used
through the ages as a pilgrims'
route, a market route and a
drove road. Previously, the

Peddars Way

Romans converted this existing
Bronze Age trackway for their
own use, as part of their
communications system in East
Anglia. The road runs north-
west across Norfolk from Coney
Weston, Suffolk, to Holme next
to the Sea on the coast. Between
the villages of Anmer and Fring
there is a section now followed
by trackways and green lanes.
East of Red Barn Farm the *agger*
is well preserved, up to 45ft
(13.5m) wide and 1ft to 2ft (0.3m
to 0.6m) high.
**Access** Take the minor road
running south-west from the
village of Fring. After 550yd
(500m), at the point where it
crosses over the Peddars Way,
bear left, and walk along the line
of the Roman road. The location
lies $3\frac{3}{8}$ miles (5.4km) east of
Snettisham.

## Doctor's Gate

Coldharbour Moor, Glossop,
Derbyshire
OS 110, (1 in 102), SK 093932;
1:25,000 Outdoor Leisure Map,
'The Dark Peak'.

The Roman road ran in a north-westerly direction from Brough (*Navio*) to their fort *Ardotalia* north of Glossop. At Doctor's Gate Culvert, a narrow path leaves the A57 and crosses the stream where there are signs of a bridge embankment on the western side. The track climbs gradually to Doctor's Gate, 1,654ft (503m), and it is along this section that the best preserved remains are to be found.

At the beginning of this century the remains were much more impressive, with a cutting through the peat 50ft (15m) wide, and a paved way nearly 5ft (1.4m) wide. The road was edged with gritstone slabs 2ft (0.6m) long and standing 6in (0.15m) above the surface of the road. Today, the line of the road cutting through the peat is still visible, but the paved way is only 3ft (0.9m) wide with occasional standing kerb stones.

**Access**   From the summit of the Snake Pass on the A57, Glossop to Sheffield road, walk north-east along the Pennine Way for 440yd (400m). Bear right at the point where a shallow depression marks the line of the Roman road. The narrow paved sections lie a short distance down the gentle slope.

From Doctor's Gate Culvert take the signposted path on the

*Doctor's Gate*

north side of the A57. The path crosses the stream and gradually ascends to where the narrow paved sections become visible.

## Holtye

East Grinstead, East Sussex
OS 187, (1 in 171), TQ 462388

A secondary road was constructed by the Romans from London through the Weald and to the South Downs at Lewes. It passed through an area important for iron-working, timber and corn. A short length

of the road surface has been exposed just south of the crossroads on the A264 at Holtye. Preserved by the Sussex Archaeological Trust, a small section has been stripped of its overlying soil to expose the original rutted iron slag surface. At other points along the road's course scattered remains of iron

slag metalling have also been found.

**Access**   A signposted right of way leads from the A264, Royal Tunbridge Wells to East Grinstead road, 1 mile (1.6km) west of the B2026 to Hartfield, and 110yd (100m) east of the inn at Holtye.

## Pitchford

Shrewsbury, Shropshire
OS 126, (1 in 118), SJ 525025

This is part of a Roman road running south-west from Wroxeter. South of Pitchford village the route leaves the minor road, and continues first as a rutted track, and then as a green lane between hedgerows. On approaching the dingle, the track bends away to the right with a gate at the end of the copse. Do not walk as far as the gate, but strike to the left through thick undergrowth. There is a fine modern

footbridge of motorway proportions spanning the water-course; from the far end of the bridge walk upstream for a few yards towards the line of the Roman road embankments and stone bridge abutment.

This deep little ravine must have provided a problem for the Roman engineers. It would appear that there are a number of bridge approaches, with the first construction work in the form of a terrace 40ft (12m) wide. This was overlaid on its eastern side by an embankment which carried a later road

surface. Along this line on the south bank are the remains of a stone bridge abutment with its original rubble core still standing to a height of 10ft (3m). The exterior stonework does not seem to be up to the Roman standard, and it is possible that the bridge supports were roughly rebuilt at a later date. I also suspect that the builders of the modern footbridge supports on the southern bank reused some pieces of Roman masonry. There are no signs of a bridge abutment on the north side of the stream. Later still, the

Romans constructed a second, larger embankment which can be seen today high above the dingle on the southern bank. The northern part is also visible, but difficult to observe with its covering of undergrowth. The later road surface is situated slightly east of the stone abutment, and as no bridge has survived, it is assumed that it was probably a timber structure.

Beyond the dingle to the south, the line of the Roman road is traced by the hawthorn hedgerow. Halfway up the field, the hedgerow has been grubbed out up to the metalled road.

From the sharp corner, the modern road follows the line of the ancient route towards Church Stretton and the prominent hills of the Lawley, Caer Caradoc and Ragleth. Obviously, these were excellent siting points for the Roman road surveyors and engineers.

Note that luxuriant summer undergrowth makes it difficult to see the features clearly, so choose a time when the vegetation has died down. Also young trees have been planted recently on the later Roman road embankment, and in a triangular patch of ground above the south bank of the

stream. Very soon, this fine outline will be hidden from view.
**Access**   Take the A458 south-east from Shrewsbury, just over 4 miles (6.7km) from The Column. Take the minor road to the right, signposted to Pitchford. $\frac{1}{4}$ mile (400m) south of the village the line of the Roman road slants away on the right as a rutted track lined with hedges. Or, from Acton Burnell, take the Frodesley road for $\frac{5}{8}$ mile (1km), to a sharp left-hand bend. From this point, follow the fence down the field to the right towards the hedgerow and the dingle beyond.

*Roman bridge abutment, Pitchford*

*Roman road embankment, Pitchford*

## Wrynose and Hardknott

Wrynose, Little Langdale, Lake District, Cumbria
Hardknott, Cockley Beck, Lake District, Cumbria
OS 90, (1 in 88); Outdoor Leisure Map 1:25,000, 'The English Lakes', SW sheet.
NY294033-215013
The Roman road can be first traced on the ground above the present Wrynose Pass road at the Pedder Stone below Hollin

Crag. It continues up the pass and crosses the modern road at the Three Shire Stone. In Wrynose Bottom it may be observed as a 24ft (7.2m) wide embankment on the north side of the River Duddon for almost a mile (1.5km). A good view of it may be obtained from the ridge up to Little Carrs, namely, Wet Side Edge.

From Cockley Beck the line of the Roman road continues down

the Duddon Valley to Black Hall, and ascends to the summit of Hard Knott Pass in a series of zigzags. This route can be followed by footpath. The Roman road crosses over to the north side of the modern road at the summit, continues on that side to the Roman fort, Hardknott Castle, and then descends to Eskdale.

## Dere Street

Woden Law, Hownam,
Cheviots, Borders Region,
Scotland
OS 80, (1in 70), NT772122-
770128
A fine *agger* 2ft to 3ft (0.6m to
0.9m) high on the saddle
between Hunthall Hill and
Woden Law. The line of the
Roman road may also be seen
both as a terraceway and a large
*agger* on the east and north-east

slopes of Woden Law. The agger
is up to 30ft (9m) across.

## Dere Street

Crailinghall, Jedburgh, Borders
Region, Scotland
OS 74, (1in 70), NT690217-
662239
A green lane follows the line of
the Roman road.

## Dere Street

Soutra, Oxton, Lauder, Border
Region, Scotland.

OS 66, (1in 62), NT464567-
472553
The road, about 20ft (6m) wide,
lies on a terrace which varies in
width from 30ft to 55ft (9m to
16.5m). Do not confuse the
Roman road with the course of a
more recent road. Approach
from just beyond Soutra Aisle,
the medieval hospice on the
B6368 road, ³/₄ mile (1.2km)
south-west of its junction with
the A68.

## Maiden Way

Melmerby Fell, Cumbria
OS 86, 91, (1in 83), NY645325-
695487
This isolated Roman road ran
from the Eden valley near
Appleby to Hadrian's Wall.
Sections of this ancient route
across the high Pennine moors
are traceable with examples of
terraceways and *aggers*. The
Way passes through a lonely
landscape of heather, grass, moss
and bog. In the summer months
the air is beset by midges and
flies, all determined to make
your journey one of utter misery.
On Melmerby Fell, the Roman
road passes Meg's Cairn
(NY657374), in the form of a
fine *agger*, 2ft to 3ft (0.6m to
0.9m) high and 21ft (6.3m) wide,

with large stones at the sides,
before descending sharply to the
west of Brown Hill. The views
from the escarpment on a clear
day are supremely expansive.
Far below, a patchwork quilt of
fields and hedgerows stretches
away to the distant horizon of
Lakeland peaks. To the north,
the Maiden Way continues
down Melmerby Rigg as a green
track, in some places showing its
smaller surface layers, and in
others, worn down to its rough
stone foundations. Approaching
Rowgill Burn (NY673413), the
embankment for a bridge can be
clearly seen on its south bank.
**Access** Rowgill Burn:
Approaching Hartside Cross, 3³/₄
miles (6km) from Alston on the
A686, take the track just past a

long thin plantation on the left.
Walk for 550yd (500m), and
take the footpath that descends
south-south-east to Rowgill
Burn.
To Meg's Cairn: Approaching
from the village of Ousby in the
Eden valley. Proceed to Townhead, and take the left-hand
track where the road bifurcates.
Immediately on crossing Ardale
Beck, leave the track and climb
steeply to Man at Edge. The
footpath assumes a northerly
direction to reach the
escarpment edge at Meg's
Cairn. Follow the Maiden Way
for a short distance across the
plateau. Distance to Meg's
Cairn from Townhead is 3 miles
(4.8km).

## Blackpool Bridge

Blakeney, Gloucestershire
OS 162, (1in 156), SO653087
A well-preserved section of a
paved Roman road through the
Forest of Dean. Although only
8ft (2.4m) wide, it is carefully
built with kerb stone settings.
**Access** Situated 2 miles
(3.2km) north-west of Blakeney.
Take the B4431, and then the
scenic road to Soudley. The
section of Roman road is beyond
the railway bridge on the left.

## Bignor Hill

South Downs, West Sussex
OS 197, (1in 181), SU970128-
945110
Fine remains of *agger*.

## Sarn Helen

OS 115, 124, (1in 116); 1:25,000
Outdoor Leisure Map,
'Snowdonia National Park',
Bala.
Line of Roman road running to
the east of Manod Mawr, below
Carreg y Fran, Rhyd yr Helen

towards Bont Newydd. Good
signs of cuttings, terraces and
zigzags.

## Water Newton

Cambridgeshire
OS 142, (1in 134), TL108989-
121970
Ermine Street, now seen as a
mound, crossing the site of the
Roman town of *Durobrivae*. A
footpath between Water Newton
and Castor crosses the line of the
Roman road.

## High Street

Martindale, Eastern Lake
District, Cumbria
OS 90,(1in 83); Outdoor Leisure
Map 1:25,000, 'The English
Lakes', NE Sheet.
This road was probably a pre-
Roman trackway that was
improved for infantry and packhorses. It traverses the High
Street range of hills in a north-
east to south-west direction,
passing over a number of
summits above 2,000ft (609m).
There are occasionally faint
traces of low *aggers* between
grassy ditches or terraces on
Brown Rigg on Barton Fell, and
then running as a hollow-way to
the north-western slopes of
Loadpot Hill (NY475216-
455185). Looking south at the
Straits of Riggindale
(NY439123), where the track
divides into two, the lower one is
the real old route. Beyond High
Street, the Roman road
descends with some terracing
direct to Troutbeck, the route
being clearly visible as a line of
finer turf.

High Street

## Blackstone Edge

Near Littleborough, Lancashire
OS 109, (1in 101), SD973171
Many writers have concluded
that the well-preserved remains
of the road on Blackstone Edge
are of Roman origin. It is
maintained that the route was
constructed as a trans-Pennine
link between two forts. This road
is also marked on the Ordnance
Survey maps as a Roman road.
However, evidence by a
Rochdale historian, James
Maxim, concludes that this
section of slightly cambered
sandstone setts was probably
built under the First Turnpike
Trust Act of 1735, following the
line of the original packhorse
road across the main Pennine
watershed. The pattern of
construction is certainly akin to
the early packhorse and cart
roads. Today, a stretch of the
road echoes to the tramp of
walkers following the line of the
Pennine Way long-distance
footpath.

### Craik Cross Hill

Raeburnfoot, Esdalemuir,
Dumfries and Galloway Region,
Scotland
OS 79, (1in 69), NT264004-
321063
This section from Mid Raeburn

Farm to Craik Moor, a distance
of 5 miles (8km) in a south-east
to north-west direction.
Remains of road metalling,
*aggers* and terracing. Beyond the
summit of Humphrey Law is a
remarkable cutting where a

wide area of peat 5ft (1.5m)
thick was removed down to the
shale bedrock (NT285028).
There is the possible site of a
Roman signal station on the
summit of Craik Cross Hill.

## Roman Milestones

### Middleton

Kirkby Lonsdale, Cumbria
OS 97, (1in 89), SD624859
Situated on gently rising ground
to the east of the River Lune,
and close to the A683. In 1836 it
was moved a short distance from
its original position, having been
discovered and re-sited by
William Moore. The Roman
markings briefly indicated 'MP
L111', 53 miles (84.8km),

presumably from Carlisle.
Further inscriptions were added
by Moore recording its discovery
and setting up.
**Access** A right of way leaves
the A683 just south of the church
at Middleton. The milestone is
visible on the higher ground a
few yards from the main road.
Distance: 6 miles (9.6km) north
of Kirkby Lonsdale, and $2\frac{1}{2}$
miles (4km) north of Barbon.

*Roman milestone, Middleton*

### Stinsford

Dorchester, Dorset
OS 194, (1in 178), SY709913
Situated on the south side of the
A35, $1\frac{1}{4}$ miles (2km) north-east
of the centre of Dorchester. The
uninscribed milestone, not quite
in its original position, stands
nearly 6ft (1.75m) tall at a point
where the minor road continues
to Stinsford village.

### Temple Sowerby

Temple Sowerby, Penrith,
Cumbria
OS 91, (1in 83), NY620264
Protected by an iron cage, this
milestone, in its original
position, stands forlornly on the
edge of a lay-by.
**Access** By the north side of
the A66, $\frac{1}{2}$ mile (800m) south-
east of Temple Sowerby.

### Chesterholm

*Vindolanda* Roman Fort,
Northumberland
OS 87, (1in 77), NY772665
This fine cylindrical milestone
can be seen, uninscribed,
standing in its original position
close by the Bradley Burn. The
present track running past the
milestone represents the line of
the Stanegate, the Roman road

from Corbridge to Carlisle.
**Access** Follow the signposted
route from the B6318 at Twice
Brewed to *Vindolanda* Roman
fort and civilian settlement.
From the car-park entrance
walk down the track in an
easterly direction for 330yd
(300m). The milestone lies on
the north side between the two
streams.

*Roman milestone, Chesterholm*

# ROMAN GOLD MINE

**Dolaucothi** (NT)
Pumpsaint, Lampeter, Dyfed, Wales
OS 146, (1in 140), SN565405
Before the coming of the Romans, the local people had discovered placer deposits of gold washed down into the gravel of the River Cothi. After the arrival of the Romans, gold-bearing pyrites were extracted, first by means of open-cast workings, then from underground galleries. A fort was established on a site now under the present village of Pumpsaint, for the protection of the soldiers and the skilled engineers. The Romans improved the technique of open-cast working by constructing a system of aqueducts and hillside reservoirs, sometimes through solid rock. Both the Rivers Annell and Cothi were tapped for water, which was channelled for distances of between 4 to 7

*Dolaucothi Roman Gold Mine*

miles (6.4km to 11.2km) to the site. When the surface deposits were exhausted, shafts and tunnels were dug, and in one of these galleries a piece of timber waterwheel was discovered.
**Access**   From the A482, Lampeter to Llanwrda road, $\frac{1}{2}$ mile (800m) south-east of the village of Pumpsaint. Site signposted.

From the National Trust information hut follow the red arrows up the hillside, and into the wood to the Roman mining entrances. Nearby is an earth bank, with a red and blue marker post, which was the site of a water storage area. Follow the blue markers to trace the line of the aqueduct. Keep to the marked paths — it is much safer!

# CHAPTER SIX
# The Dark Ages

During their period of occupation the Romans were never able to control the warlike activities of the Picts, although they subdued Scotland for a short time and made brief incursions into the country. The northern tribes continued to harass the forts and garrisons on and near Hadrian's Wall, occasionally forcing the Romans to abandon their prestigious frontier line. Also at this time newcomers from Ireland, the Scotti (hence the later name of Scotland) were attacking the western seaboard. They eventually gained a foothold in the north-west, and even combined with the Picts to attack the Romans. Inevitably, increased settlement brought the Picts and Scots into conflict with each other over territorial rights, until they united in the ninth century.

The Romans did not simply abandon Britain in one operation. Their legions were gradually withdrawn to meet the threat of barbarian invasions of their own homeland. By the end of the fourth century Britain came under increasing threat from Scottish, Pictish and Anglo-Saxon raiders. At the beginning of the fifth century, Constantine III withdrew the few remaining soldiers to defend Gaul. He failed, and the local communities were told by the emperor Honorius to look to their own defences.

The result was a series of struggles for supremacy between various British factions. According to British and Anglo-Saxon tradition, it was at this critical point in history that a local leader called Vortigern (Great King), invited to Britain some Anglo-Saxon mercenaries from northern Europe Europe for the protection of his followers. The Angles came from an area now known as Schleswig-Holstein, the Saxons from north-west Germany, the Jutes from northern Denmark, and the Frisians and the Franks from the Low Countries. These pagan newcomers had their own way of life, which had not been influenced by Roman ways and culture. Eventually the Anglo-Saxons revolted, possibly because the Britons were unable or unwilling to pay for their services, and sent for more of their kinsfolk from the Continent.

By the end of the fifth century their numbers had grown considerably. Vortigern was defeated, and south-east Britain was put to fire and the sword. Throughout this period, despite this conflict, there were still many Romano-British communities who managed to maintain their civilisation and keep alive their Christian faith. There was an opposition movement against the Anglo-Saxons under the leadership of one Ambrosius Aurelianus, and continued by Arthur. As the invaders marched westwards, the Romano-British forces commanded by Arthur won a famous victory. The exact site of this battle is not known, although there is a strong possibility that it took place at Liddington Castle, a prominent Iron Age hillfort near Swindon in Wiltshire (SU209797). As a result of this encounter Arthur managed to stem the Saxon advance, and won a peace which lasted for a number of decades. Very few facts are known concerning Arthur; historical sources report that he was

*Liddington Castle*

158

later killed at the Battle of Camlann, but even this is uncertain, as its location has been difficult to place. Whatever the facts, Arthur has earned a place in history, and even more in legend, with tales of chivalry and knightly deeds of valour.

The early poetic references to Arthur do not mention southern England, but point to Cumbria and the ancient kingdom of Rheged around the Solway Firth. Although it cannot be proved, there does seem to be a case for thinking that the story of Arthur centred around the battles for supremacy between the northern British tribes at the time of the Roman departure. The various tribal leaders took over the former Roman strongholds and set up their kingdoms around them. The Roman fort of Birdoswald on Hadrian's Wall was called *Camboglanna* (the crooked bend), and it is possible that the word Camlann was derived from this name. It is an exciting thought that Arthur's last great battle in the west may have been fought on the heights overlooking the River Irthing.

Gradually, the Anglo-Saxons reasserted their ascendancy, and by the end of the sixth century had swept into the west country, capturing the settlements of Bath and Gloucester. Their foothold in south-eastern and southern England had become established. In AD597, the church sent St Augustine to Kent to revitalise the Christian beliefs still held by some of the Romano-British; at the same time Christanity was also making converts from paganism, starting with the royal families, followed by their retainers and the rest of the people. Aethelbert of Kent was the first English king to be converted to Christanity.

Meanwhile, other parts of the country were being colonised by different bands of Anglo-Saxon settlers, who were not always well disposed to one another. Each group was led by a warrior chief, and consolidated the newly won territory; with the influx of more followers the group spread out into the surrounding area. Each of the warring factions developed separate kingdoms over a period of two centuries. Eventually, the kingdoms were unified into seven, the Heptarchy, and England was controlled by the most powerful — in succession, Kent, East Anglia, Northumberland, Mercia and Wessex.

In the north of England, the sixth century saw the beginning of the Anglian kingdom of Northumbria. Strong British resistance resulted in a slow rate of progress, but the Anglo-Saxons gradually extended their influence across the Pennines. Numerous isolated settlements continued to hold out, but eventually the kingdoms of Rheged (Dumfries, Galloway and Cumbria) and Elmet (South Yorkshire) lost their independence.

The latter part of the seventh century saw the rise to power of the Anglian kingdom of Mercia, a combination of many different tribes of the north and west Midlands. King Penda waged war on his Northumbrian neighbours, and Mercia's power flourished as many smaller kingdoms came under its domination. The ferocity of the Mercian conquests was typified by the violent leadership and immoral life-style of King Athelbald. He can be regarded, in many ways, as one of the last of the great conquering barbarians. This period of savage upheaval was followed by the ordered rule of King Offa, the first Anglo-Saxon king to be regarded as a major political figure. He ruled for thirty-nine successful years, a ruthless leader who was not averse to getting rid of rivals; a dictator, who maintained his supremacy until his death.

Until the end of the eighth century England was still divided into the four great kingdoms of East Anglia, Northumberland, Mercia and Wessex. After the death of Offa the power of Mercia declined, and this was followed by the ascendancy of Wessex (West Saxons). It is important to note that until AD878 only Wessex reigned supreme. The eclipse of the other great kingdoms began in the 790s, when a dark cloud appeared over the development of Anglo-Saxon civilisation in the shape of the Vikings. In the north, the religious settlement of Lindisfarne was sacked, plundered and desecrated after one of many hit and run attacks along the coast. Later on, in a change of tactics, the Danish war bands came ashore and moved quickly and decisively across northern and eastern England. Between AD865 and 880, the Danes conquered Northumbria, eastern Mercia and East Anglia. A giant foothold had easily been achieved, and the newcomers were intent on staying permanently.

Danish settlements were soon established down the eastern side of England.

Following their colonisation in the north and east, the Danes turned their attention towards the West Saxons, and a series of battles and skirmishes took place between the two sides. In the winter of AD870, the West Saxons faced the invaders at Ashdown on the Berkshire Downs. After fierce fighting, in which the young Alfred distinguished himself, the Danes were defeated and retired to the east. The Saxons had found a worthy champion and it was not long before Alfred was crowned king. However, the victory was short-lived, for the reinforced Danish army beat the Saxons at the next encounter, and Alfred was forced to pay the victors large sums of money as tribute. The Danes led by Guthrum pretended to go away, but instead carried out a series of cat-and-mouse attacks, always maintaining the upper hand. After a number of reverses, Alfred went into hiding in the lonely Somerset marshes in order to build up his forces. Patiently he waited, secretly sending out messages for support throughout the area. His couriers established the enemy's movements and strengths and also led in reinforcements to his camp along the secret footpaths through the marshes. When all was ready he emerged with a strong army, and decisively counter-attacked the Danes at the battle of Edington (in Wiltshire).

Alfred secured a peace treaty with Guthrum, with an agreed frontier along the line of Watling Street. To the east of this line the Danes were allowed to settle and farm the land in the region known as the Danelaw.

After the death of Alfred, his son Edmund began the process of restoring all the lands seized by the Danes. His successor, Athelstan of Wessex, became the first king of a united England who governed Saxon and Dane alike. His campaigns took him into the north of England and Scotland where the Anglo-Saxons defeated the forces of a number of minor rulers. Athelstan reigned for fourteen years and died in October 939 at the age of forty-four. In Northumberland there were many political stirrings, for the local chiefs had first acknowledged Athelstan's half-brother Eadred as their ruler, then invited the Norseman, Eric Bloodaxe, to be their king. Eric ruled North-

umbria from his capital at York, and the city became a very important trading centre — a gateway between Scandinavia and Anglo-Saxon England. Although Eric left to roam the seas as a slave-trader, he returned, only to be betrayed and killed on the moorlands of Stainmore.

Edgar was then crowned king, and reigned at a time that can be regarded as the golden age of Anglo-Saxon England. His death at the early age of thirty-two led to events that heralded a period of great hardship and uncertainty for England. Edgar's young son Edward became king, but inter-family rivalries and intrigues led to his murder in suspicious circumstances. This enabled his ten-year-old half brother Ethelred to ascend the throne. From the beginning, the portents for his reign were hardly auspicious; crops failed, famine struck and disturbances arose. Throughout his rule, Ethelred's life was one of hardships and difficulties. The word 'Unready' is the modern form of *Unraed*, meaning 'no counsel', for he was a man who chose his advisers badly, and who acted on bad advice. In all fairness his nickname should have been 'Unlucky', because he arrived on the scene at a time when England was hard-pressed by concerted, well-led Danish attacks. His councillors advised him to seek peace, and to negotiate the payments of huge sums of money (Danegeld) to the enemy. Although tribute was paid at regular intervals and great quantities of provisions were made available, the Vikings still continued to rob and slaughter the people.

The Danish leader, Swein Forkbeard, attacked eastern England forcing London to surrender and Ethelred to flee into exile in Normandy. Swein was accepted as king, but his rule was short-lived, and in 1014 he was succeeded by his son Canute. Ethelred returned to England, only to die two years afterwards. His son Edmund gained some early successes against a second Danish army led by Canute, but ultimately was defeated at the battle of Ashingdon in Essex. Canute was succeeded briefly by Harthacanute, but in 1042 England returned to Anglo-Saxon rule under Edward the Confessor, the son of Ethelred. For many years Edward had lived in Normandy, and on his death in 1066, Norman ties with England were already well established.

## SAXON PLACE NAMES

After the departure of the Romans, intermittent raids by Saxon pirates were followed by larger scale settlement by more of these determined invaders from northern Europe. The incomers, Angles, Saxons and Jutes, collectively for convenience known as Saxons, followed their own coastlines before making the short sea-crossing to Britain. They probably travelled in 60 to 80ft (18m to 24m) long wooden boats each propelled by thirty oarsmen. They continued to sail inshore before entering the many navigable rivers and estuaries that divide Britain's eastern coastline. The Saxons and the Jutes settled in the south and south-east, and the Angles in the east and north. Once ashore, the new settlers quite likely would have used the major Roman routeways to penetrate an unfamiliar land.

For example, in the fifth and sixth centuries, the north-east Midlands was an area settled by Anglian people who were able to take best agricultural land. In northern England, after Anglian settlements had been made on the Yorkshire Wolds, the colonists eventually spread westwards into the valley lands of the River Ouse. This was followed by the establishment of the Anglian kingdom of Northumbria that stretched from the Tweed to the Humber. The subsequent defeat of the British kingdom of Elmet enabled the Anglians to penetrate further inland and colonise the lower sections of the northern dales, via the river valleys of the Tyne, Wear, Ure, Nidd, Wharfe and Aire to name but a few. Some of these venturers passed over the Pennines, through the Aire Gap into the Craven limestone area, and down into the Ribble valley. The settlers cleared spaces in the woodland, and it is interesting to note that the most numerous settlements lie in the Vale of York and in the lower Pennine dales.

The interpretation of place-names has played an important role in the understanding of landscape history. An understanding of the subject has never been a straightforward matter, and in recent years there has been a more critical approach to the problem. The quest is full of pitfalls, for it is essential to know the earliest surviving form of the place-name to make an interpretation with some degree of certainty. In a general sense, place-names in many localities give clues regarding their former woodland cover. The names were given by the first Saxon settlers, who made small or large clearings in the dense forests that covered the valley floors and the lower hill slopes. The places cleared of trees and undergrowth were named -*leah,* and these settlements can be recognised by names ending in the modern day form of -ley. To confuse matters, however, the name could also mean a glade or open space in the forest that required little clearing, and in some cases, the element -*leah* was used to denote meadow or pasture-land. Most likely the -ley settlements began as small communities of more than one family. This was essential for the heavy work of clearing, breaking and tilling the new ground. Other present-day names which have some connection with former woodland end in -leigh, -hurst and -stock.

Roaming bands of settlers continued to move inland from the east, exploring the river valleys and making use of the major Roman roads. The later groups preferred more open ground above the flood levels of the valleys, and their enclosed homesteads developed into village settlements with the suffix element -*tun.* The meaning of the word -*tun* may well have been to denote an outlying farm attached to an original homestead. These settlements can now be recognised by names ending in -ton. Another common element found in place-names is the ending -*ham.* The original meaning is thought to refer to flat land close to a river or stream, or in the bend of a river, where the type of land would be pasture or water-meadow. The element -*wickham* may mean Saxon settlement in large Romano-British villages: a combination of the Saxon -*ham* and the Roman *vicus,* a village. The -*wickham* and -*ham* names are often found to occur in close association with the Roman roads and settlements.

The -ing element contained in some place-names, and thought to be part of a later phase of settlement, is derived from the Saxon word -*ingas* which means people. This would imply that these settlers in a particular area were the followers or relations of the original tribal chief.

The -ing, -ingham and -ington names also seem to show a strong correlation with the river networks. The element -*wic* frequently denotes a dairy farm or cattle farm, so that -wick is particularly common where cattle farming has played an important role.

Many of the place-names of the homes and settlements that include the elements -*leah*, -*ham* and -*tun*, also contain personal names or words describing the topography of the site.
For example:
Aldgyth's -*leah* (a woman's name)
   Audley in Cheshire. SJ795505
Beorg-*tun*: tun by a hill or barrow
   Broughton in Buckinghamshire. SP895401
Maer-*ham*: ham by a mere

Marham in Norfolk. TF708097
(The lake is no longer there)
Brorda's -*leah*: clearing belonging to Brorda
   Bordley in Yorkshire. SD942649

---

**Identifying Features**

**The Saxons** (Angles, Saxons and Jutes)

Place-name element -leah
Present day place-names ending in -ley
Small or large man-made clearings, or glades in woodlands.
- Some settlements took on personal names.
- Other names record a description of the site.

---

**Examples of Descriptive Names**

Brilley (Hereford/Worcs) leah A place cleared by burning
Mearley (Lancs) A boundary leah
Mawsley (Northampt) leah by a gravel ridge
Oxley (Staffs) leah or clearing for oxen
Tansley (Derbys) A branch leah; a valley branching off the main dale
Shipley (Derbys/Yorks) A leah

or pasture for sheep
Buckfastleigh (Devon) The leah (probably forest) of the stronghold of the male deer
Stanley (Durham) A stony leah
Birtley (Durham) Beorhte leah: a bright leah
Bromley (Middlx) leah where brambles grew
Pateley Bridge (Yorks) Pæth leah: leah by a path
Ripley (Yorks) Ripel -leah: a leah that has the shape of a strip
Bulkeley (Chesh) Bulluca -leah: a bullock pasture

**Examples Based on Personal Names**

Granta's leah Grantley (Yorks)
Bettu's leah Betley (Staffs)
Illica's leah Ilkley (Yorks)
Fremi's leah Frimley (Surrey)
Onna's leah Onneley (Staffs)
Otta's leah Otley (Yorks, Suffolk)
Beage's leah Beeley (Derbys)
Blecca's leah Bletchley (Bucks)

---

**The Saxons** (Angles, Saxons and Jutes)

Place-names elements -ham, hamm
Present-day place-names ending in -ham, -ingham
Homestead, village or land belonging to a homestead or village, a water meadow close to a river, in the bend of a river.

- Some settlements took on personal names, the followers of a leader or tribal chief -Ing, -Ingas. (The Saxon word meaning the people of, the followers of)
- Other names record a description of the site.

---

**Examples Based on Personal Names**

Godalming (Surrey) Godhelm's

people
Ovingham (Northampt) The ham of Ofa's people
Brantingham (Yorks) The ham

of Brant's people
Addingham (Cumb/Yorks) The ham of Adda's people
Wolsingham (Durham) The

ham of Wulfsige's people
Raveningham (Norfolk) The ham of Hræfn's people
Mendham (Suffolk) Mynda's ham
Massingham (Norfolk) The ham of Mæssa's people
Wymondham (Leics/Norf.) Wigmnund's ham
Buckingham (Bucks) The hamm of Bucca's people

## Examples of Descriptive Names

Stittenham (Yorks) A place with a steep slope
Stamfordham (Northumb) The ham at the stony ford
Selham (Sussex) The ham by a sallow copse
Reedham (Norfolk) The reedy ham or hamm

Langham (Dorset) The long ham, village or homestead
Thornham (Kent) The ham where thorn bushes grew
Marsham (Norfolk) The ham by a marsh
Graffham (Sussex) The ham by the grove

---

The place-name element -Wicham
Present-day place-names ending in -Wicham
- In some cases this element is found in close association with Roman roads and settlements.

Wickham (Berks) a dwelling-place, a dairy farm
Wykeham (Lincs) a dwelling-place, a manor

---

## The Saxons (Angles, Saxons and Jutes)

Place-name element -tun
Present-day place-names ending in -ton
A homestead or village established above the flood levels of the valleys, or to denote an outlying farm attached to the original homestead.
- Some settlements took on personal names.
- Other names record a description of the site.

---

## Examples Based on Personal Names

Luddington (Lincs), The tun of Luda's people
Gossington (Gloucs), The tun of Gosa's people
Winlaton (Durham), Winelac's tun
Marchington (Staffs), The tun of the Mercham people
Tufton (Hamps), The tun of Tucca's people
Kellington (Yorks), The tun of Cylla's people

Eckington (Derbys), The tun of Ecca or his people
Hardington (Somerset), The tun of Heardred's people
Godington (Oxfordsh), The tun of Goda's people

## Examples of Descriptive Names

Rudston (Yorks), Rode — stan: place near a rood stone
Ryton (Durham), Ryge — tun: a rye farm
Bickerton (Chesh), The tun of the beekeepers

Warton (Lancs), Weard — tun: a look-out place
Norton-in-the-Moors, (Staffs), The north tun, a homestead or village north of another
Leverton (Lincs), The tun where rushes grew
Horton-in-Ribblesdale (Yorks), Horh — tun: the tun on muddy ground
Kempston (Bedfords), The tun by the bend (of the River Ouse)
Cheddleton (Staffs), The tun in a narrow valley

## SCANDINAVIAN PLACE-NAMES

After the wars between Alfred and the Danes, the Scandinavians retired to the east of the agreed boundary line, the former Roman Watling Street. In this territory of the Danelaw the Danish Vikings shared out the land, and gradually became assimilated with the Anglo-Saxon people. This was possible because there was plenty of good land to cultivate, the way of life was similar, and the two peoples could probably understand each other's language. Peace in the Danelaw encouraged trade, and there was a steady flow of immigrants, mainly from Denmark but also from Sweden and Norway. This influx of people prompted the development of settlements, and the number and extent of these suggest the presence of many thousands of colonists in north and east England.

The density of Scandinavian settlement in eastern England is most clearly reflected in the numerous place-names in the area from Grimsby to Leicester, throughout Yorkshire, and particularly in East Anglia. The familiar place-name ending -by from *byr*, is the old Scandinavian word for village or settlement.

For example:

Brumby (Lincs), Bruni's *by* SE893097
Dalby (Yorks), *by* in a valley SE638711

Sometimes the names that have survived in use are a mixture of Scandanavian and English, so-called hybrid names.

For example:

Swaton (Lincs), Swafa's tun: TF133375
Thurmaston (Leics), Thormodh's tun: SK610095

---

**The Scandinavians**

Place-name element *by*
Present-day place-names ending in -by.
The word means a village, settlement or homestead.
- Some settlements took on personal names.
- Other names record a description or topographical feature concerning the site.

---

**Examples Based on Personal Names**

Asgarby (Lincs), Asgar's by
Naseby (Northamptons), Hnæf's by
Oadby (Leics), Audhi's by
Bilby (Notts), Bille's by
Scalby (Yorks), Skalli's by
Rollesby (Norfolk), Hrolf's by
Sulby (Isle of Man), Solabyr: Sola's farm
Jurby (Isle of Man), Jngvar-byr: Invar's home
Colby (Isle of Man), Kollabyr: Kolli's farm
Scholarby (Isle of Man), Skollabyr: Skoll's farm

**Examples of Descriptive Names**

Kirkby (Yorks), A village with a church
Waitby (Cumbra), A wet homestead
Hunsonby (Cumbria), The by of the dog keepers
Langwathby (Cumbra), The by at the long ford
Raby (Cheshire), A by near a boundary mark
Selby (Yorks), The by near to the sallow copse
Grenaby (Isle of Man), Gren-byr: The green farm
Dalby (Isle of Man), Dal-byr: The croft in the glen

---

**The Scandinavians**

Place-name element *-toft*
The word means the site of a homestead and its outbuildings.
The first element is usually a personal name or an adjective, and these settlements are chiefly found in East Anglia, the East Midlands and in Yorkshire.

## Examples

Lowestoft (Suffolk), Hlodhver's toft
Langtoft (Lincs, Yorks), The long toft
Sibbertoft (Northamptons), Sigbiorn's toft
Wibtoft (Warwicks), Vibbe's toft
Blacktoft (Yorks), Blaca's toft
Altofts (Yorks), Old toft
Wigtoft (Lincs), The toft by the creek or lake

---

### The Scandinavians

Place-name element -*thorp*
A very common name in the Danelaw.
The word means an outlying farm dependent on an early settlement, or a small settlement colonised at a later date from a larger one.
The first element is frequently a personal name. In many cases a distinguishing first element has been added to an original -*thorp*.

---

## Examples

Westhorpe (Suffolk), West thorp
Towthorpe (Yorks), Tofi's thorp
Swinthorpe (Lincs), Suni's thorp
Swinethorpe (Lincs), Svein's thorp
Ravensthorpe (Northampts), Hrafn's thorp
Pensthorpe (Norfolk), Pening's thorp
Oakthorpe (Leics), Aki's thorp
Fridaythorpe (Yorks), Frigedaeg's thorp
Calthorpe (Norfolk), Kali's thorp

---

### Scandinavian and English Hybrid Names

These words have the Scandinavian (mainly Danish) personal name as the prefix, and the final element Tun is the English word for homestead or village, -ton.

## Examples

Grimston (Leics), Grim's tun
Swaton (Lincs), Swafa's tun
Kedleston (Derbys), Ketel's tun
Ouston (Northumberland), Ulf's tun
Rolleston (Staffs), Hrolf's tun

---

At the beginning of the tenth century a new Scandinavian invasion began with the landing of Norwegians from Ireland. The Norse were great travellers, having migrated from Norway to Orkney and Shetland, thence to Ireland and the Western Isles. The Norwegian Vikings not only colonised the remote Scottish islands, but sailed on to Iceland, Greenland and eventually to America. Later generations travelled across the Irish Sea to settle in the Isle of Man, the Lake District, and much of northern England west of the Pennines. They even crossed the high moors into the South Tyne valley, and infiltrated into Yorkshire, capturing the city of York. This important settlement was the king-pin of the Irish-Norse kingdom, and lasted until the middle of the tenth century, when the last Norse king Eric Bloodaxe was slain on Stainmore.

There was very little conflict of interest between the Norse and the Anglo-Danish people already settled in the lowlands and in the valleys. The Norwegians preferred the hill lands and the higher dales above the limits of the forests. Their way of life was very similar to that in the valleys and mountains of western Norway. In the summer months their flocks of sheep and herds of cattle were grazed on the higher hill-slopes, and then kept on the lower slopes during the rest of the year. This rotational use of pasture-land is emphasised by the word ending in -*saetr*, a pasture, a shieling: this now appears as -sett, -seat, -satter and -side. For example: Gunnerside, (Swaledale, Yorks) SD950982; and in Wensleydale, (Yorks) with the settlements of Burtersett, Marsett, Appersett and Countersett. These summer pastures were also called -*erg*, which was a Norse-Celt variant derived from the Celtic *airge* or *airidh*, a shieling. For example, Sizergh (Cumbria) — Sigridhr's *Erg*, SD498879. Seasonal settlements with a temporary shelter used by shepherds or cowherds were often called *-skali*, now found as -scale. For example, Scales (Cumbria), NY343269, Scholes (Yorks), SE375370 and Barden Scale (Yorks), SE052567.

Place-names ending in -by and -bie from the Scandinavian *-byr* are found in the Northern Isles, and in south-west Scotland around the Solway Firth; an indication that these areas were also settled by the Scandinavians, mainly Norse and possibly a few Danes. For example, Gillesbie (Dumfries and Galloway), NY165915, Warmanbie, NY195690, and Sibbaldie, NY146877.

Natural features appeared prominently in the Norse language, and these have now enriched our everyday speech, particularly in the north of England, such as in the form of fell, beck, gill, rigg, tarn, mere, moss, moor, heath and ling. The Norse word *-thwaite*, generally denotes a forest clearing just above the valley floor. For example:

Langthwaite (Yorks) — NZ005025
   A long thwaite or clearing
Satterthwaite (Cumbria) — SD339924
   A clearing or thwaite by a shieling
Braithwaite (Cumbria) — NY232236
   A broad thwaite or clearing
Swinithwaite (Yorks) — SE044892
   A thwaite cleared by burning.

---

**The Scandinavians** (Norwegians)

Place-name element *-thwaite*
A common word ending in the north of England. The word means a forest or woodland clearing on the lower slopes of the valley.
Sometimes the homesteads took on personal names.

---

**Examples:**

Yockenthwaite (Yorks), Eogan's thwaite
Warberthwaite (Cumbria), A thwaite with a hunting or fishing shed
Thornthwaite (Cumbria), A thwaite where thorn-bushes grew
Slaithwaite (Yorks), A thwaite where sloes grew
Lowthwaite (Cumbria), A clearing or thwaite on a hill
Linthwaite (Yorks), A thwaite where flax was grown
Huthwaite (Yorks), A thwaite or clearing on a spur of land
Gunthwaite (Yorks), Gunnhild's thwaite
Branthwaite (Cumbria), A broom-covered thwaite

*Yockenthwaite, a Norse settlement with later packhorse bridge*

Between the eighth and eleventh centuries the Scandinavians raided and settled in many lands. Archaeological evidence suggests that by AD850 there was already a substantial settlement of Norse colonists in Orkney and Shetland. The settlement probably occurred after many previous trading ventures, as the islands were obvious ports of call, with the help of seasonal prevailing winds. The Norsemen left records of their exploits in the sagas, such as the *Orkneyinga Saga*, which also tells of political upheavals in Norway where the ruler Harald Fairhair attempted to unify the whole of the country. In AD872 these troubles caused a great number of Norsemen to leave their native land for greater freedom in the Northern and Western Isles of Scotland. Once established they returned to their Viking way of life, not only raiding the British coastline, but also making repeated attacks on their former homeland. In the latter case, Harald Fairhair responded to these incursions by mounting an expedition, and quickly brought Orkney, Shetland, the Hebrides and the Isle of Man under his domination. Orkney and Shetland became completely Norse, but in the Hebrides and the Isle of Man the inhabitants retained their culture, with the Gaelic language persisting and influencing the Norse tongue.

The Norsemen left a mark on almost every aspect of life in Orkney and Shetland still visible today. Most noticeable is the tremendous number of Norse place-names. Practically every physical feature was named by the Norse, and the homesteads and farms were named from their territorial situations or they took on personal names. In Orkney alone it has been estimated that nearly all farm names are of Norse derivation. The abundance of Norse place-names points to a considerable migration over a relatively short period, and in the case of farm names illustrates the outward growth of settlement from the original favoured sites.

In Orkney and Shetland the *-byr* name means a 'farm' and this particular element is related to the Danish place-name in England ending in -by. In the islands it may be -by or -bie.

**Examples**

Dounby (Orkney), HY295208
Houseby (Orkney, Stronsay), HY673216
Houbie (Shetland, Fetlar), HU623907
Kirkaby (Shetland), HP568063
Tiptoby (Shetland, Fetlar), HU609909

As previously mentioned, the word ending *-saetr* is commonly found in the Northern Isles in the form of -setter, where the original element means a homestead.

**Examples**

Winksetter (Orkney), HY341165
Garthsetter (Orkney), HY255278
Setter (Shetland, Yell), HU460820
Hestinsetter (Shetland), HU293453

Other very common name elements are *-geo*, meaning a cleft in the rocky coastline, from the Norse *-gja*; *-wick*, meaning a bay or inlet, from *-vik*; *-skaill* and *-quoy*, meaning a cattle enclosure from *-kvi*.

Other Norse words, such as *-land*, *-gardr* and *-bolstadr*, which refer to sites of attractive farmland, have given rise to the name elements -land, -garth and -bister. These words are indicative of early Norse settlement in the ninth century when colonisation was probably at its most expansive.

**Examples**

Fladdabister (Shetland), HU434325
Starkigarth (Shetland), HU431297
Holmsgarth (Shetland), HU465425
Houlland (Shetland, Yell), HU502802
Symbister (Shetland, Whalsay), HU539622
Bimbister (Orkney), HY325167
Wasbister (Orkney, Rousay), HY395328
Burraland (Shetland), HU225497
Sandgarth (Orkney, Shapinsay), HY526155

# SAXON CHURCHES

The Christian faith was probably introduced to Britain in the second century AD. Later, when the Saxons arrived in south-eastern England, there can be little doubt that they found Christianity well-established among the Romano-British population. There has been very little evidence to show that churches were already built to serve the Romano-British upper classes, but if they were, they were probably built of timber. After the arrival of the Saxons it is likely that the Christian belief continued side by side with pagan worship. Cemeteries provide important evidence, with grave goods in pagan graves, and a lack of articles together with an east to west orientation in the Christian interments.

At the end of the sixth century Pope Gregory sent Augustine and a band of monks on a mission to England. He landed in Kent and presented himself to King Aethelbert, who was impressed with Augustine and his followers with their vestments, silver cross and other symbols of the Roman Church. After the baptism of the king, Augustine converted the royal household, the retainers and gradually the local population, both Saxons and native British. Paganism still survived throughout the Anglo-Saxon period, and the worship of such things as mountains, streams, hills and woods continued to flourish and played a part in the day to day life of the Anglo-Saxon peasant.

It was during the time of Christian expansion in the south-east that Celtic monks from Iona had established a monastery at Lindisfarne under Aidan. The process of converting the kingdom of Northumbria to Celtic Christianity had begun. Monasteries were built at Jarrow and Monkwearmouth by the Northumberland nobleman Benedict Biscop in the late seventh century. This was the golden age of Northumbria; a time of great artistic, spiritual and intellectual attainment personified by the saintly hermit Cuthbert, and England's first great historian, the Venerable Bede.

One of Augustine's followers, Paulinus, left Canterbury to begin his mission in the north of England, and so began the clash between the Celtic Church and the Roman Church. There was a struggle for supremacy, and the issue was debated at the Synod of Whitby in AD664. After much discussion and heated argument the followers of Rome carried the day, and the Celtic Church retired, defeated, to the far west.

Meanwhile Christianity was making progress throughout the rest of England, and by the late seventh century, the structure of the English Church had been established.

Anglo-Saxon churches were first built after the arrival of Augustine, but these buildings were mostly confined to the south-east. Basically, they were small missionary churches, plain, and of simple design. They were built of stone, high in proportion to their size, and with comparatively thin walls; on average only 2ft 6ins (0.8m) thick. They took their form from the Roman basilica, and in some cases, they re-used Roman materials, such as tiles, bricks and masoned stone; for example, the lonely church of St Peter-on-the-Wall, at Bradwell-on-Sea, Essex, TM031081.

A number of features are characteristic of Anglo-Saxon churches. The church walls are often set on flat plinths, and the exterior surfaces are sometimes decorated with horizontal courses of stone moulding, called string courses. The churches are mostly built of irregular-coursed masonry. The interior is usually divided into two compartments, a small rectangular nave and an even smaller chancel arch. The simple plan sometimes contains a side chapel or chapels called porticus. The most visible features are doors, windows and quoins. The latter provides a very useful clue in proving the existence of a Saxon church — quoins form a distinctive pattern of stonework strengthening the corner of a building.

## Saxon Churches
## Some Identifying Features

### Quoins
- They are dressed stones found at the angles of a building.
- There are three main types of quoins:

  **a** Stones placed alternately, a long side next to a short side.

  **b** Large stones set at random, at irregular intervals.

  **c** The use of tall upright stones, alternately placed next to short horizontal stones.

### Windows
- The sides of the windows slant towards the interior of the building, either as single or double splays.
- The windows can be round-headed, square-headed or triangular-headed.
- In some areas the windows can be narrow

vertical slits or of a keyhole shape.
- Belfry windows often have baluster pillars, or small columns of stone, sometimes wider in the centre that at the ends.

### Doors and Arches
- The doorways are usually massive and round-headed.
- Arches are often constructed of through-stones passing through the width of the wall.
- Sometimes a wedge-shaped stone is used as an arch.
- Door jambs are laid partly of through stones and upright stones.
- The entrance is often decorated with a stripwork of stone moulding to emphasise the opening.

### Outstanding Sites

### Church of St John the Baptist
Escomb, Bishop Auckland, Co Durham
OS 92, (1in 85), NZ189301
This splendid little church is one of the best preserved Anglo-Saxon churches in Britain. Although now surrounded by modern housing development, it retains a simple beauty and an air of tranquillity. Apart from a short period in the nineteenth century, it has been used for worship since the late seventh century. There are two round-headed Saxon windows on the south side of the nave, and two square-headed windows on the north wall; all splayed internally to admit more light. There is one more window as old as the church in the west gable wall. The original nave window jambs have vertical grooves used for shutters before they were glazed. These window jambs have through-stones laid alternately upright and flat — 'Escomb-

*Escomb Anglo-Saxon Church*

fashion'. Five other windows date variously from the thirteenth to the nineteenth centuries.

The walls are constructed of large squared stones, but nearer the top the smaller stones are of Roman origin obtained from the nearby fort at Binchester. Look for the tell-tale criss-cross diamond pattern on the stones. The building's corner stones or quoins are large and are placed alternately one long side next to a short side. The north wall has two square-headed doorways, with the easterly one blocked up. Originally this led to a small side chapel or porticus. In the more westerly doorway, note the way the jambs are morticed into the door head.

There are other points of interest worth looking for;

notably, a stone used by the Saxon builders set upside down on the east end of the outside north wall. It reads, LEG VI, (the Sixth Legion). There is a semi-circular Anglo-Saxon sundial, with a snake-like pattern, still in its original position to the east of the porch on the outside south wall.

Inside, the lofty nave has a fine chancel arch, almost certainly Roman, and most probably taken from Binchester — look at the arrangement of the stones in the jambs. There is

a small area of original cobbled flooring to be found at the west end of the nave, and the very old carving of a cross on a stone behind the altar.

**Access** The church is situated in the centre of the village. It lies at the end of a minor road $\frac{3}{4}$ mile (1.2km) north of its junction with the B6282, and 2 miles (3.2km) west of Bishop Auckland. A notice on the gate informs visitors that the key may be obtained from a house opposite.

### Church of St Peter on the Wall

Bradwell-on-Sea, Maldon, Essex
OS 168, (1 in 162), TM031082
This remarkable Saxon building stands above the Essex marshes, on the promontory between the estuaries of the Blackwater and the Crouch.

It is believed that the building dates from the latter part of the seventh century, and is known traditionally as the Church of St Cedd. The saint was bishop of the East Saxons, and was granted the site of the old Roman fort of *Othona* for the establishment of a new church. Cedd's masons built a small nave, a western porch, side chapels, (one on the north side, one on the south), and an eastern apse. Only the nave

stands today with the ends of the apse walls still visible. In the interior, the pilasters or wall piers carry a considerable number of Roman tiles in the fabric. Also inside can be seen the heads of the three arches which separated the nave from the apse — look for the line of Roman tiles. Other interesting details to spot are the quoins, which consist of very large stones set at random at the exterior angles of the building. There are three of the original windows in good shape, two in the south wall and one in the north. Around the square-headed west door are traces of the original porch. The building eventually became derelict, and was in fact used as a barn for many years up to 1920, (note the repaired parts

of the south wall where the farm carts were trundled through). Now renovated and reconsecrated, this outstanding Saxon church is a joy to behold — a popular spot for visitors in summer-time.

**Access** From Maldon take the B1018 and then the B1010 to Latchingdon. A by-road leads east in a series of sidewinding turns for $9\frac{1}{2}$ miles (15km) via Lower Mayland to Bradwell-on-Sea (which is not by the sea). Take the signposted lane east from the parish church, and walk for 2 miles (3.2km) along the line of the Roman road to the Saxon church. Bradwell may also be reached by the B1021, $8\frac{3}{4}$ miles (14km) north of Burnham-on-Crouch.

### Chapel of St Laurence

Bradford-on-Avon, Wiltshire
OS 173, (1 in 166), ST824609
This ancient chapel, situated on the north side of the River Avon, is thought to have been founded by St Aldhelm at the beginning of the eighth century. However, some experts have dated the whole building to the tenth

century, and others have stated that only the upper parts were erected at that time. No one is absolutely sure of the period of construction.

The chapel is of handsome proportions, being tall and narrow, with a simple high-roofed nave and small chancel. The chancel arch is also tall and

narrow, a plain solid-looking structure, with the arch resting on through-stone supports, and surmounted by a decoration of convex reeding or moulding. There is a surviving chapel or porticus on the north side but the one on the south side has been demolished.

Other points of interest are

the three double-splayed windows, and, set high on the east wall of the nave above the chancel arch, are the famous Bradford Angels. These splendid stone carvings were originally positioned lower down, and probably hovered above the arms of a Crucifixion which has now vanished. Outside there is a pattern of stone pilaster stripwork that decorates the sides and corners of the building. These shallow rectangular columns end at a bold string-course which serves as plinth for a blank arcade of round arches on pilaster columns.

In the mid-nineteenth century, this Saxon masterpiece was rescued, restored and rededicated after serving as a dwelling and a school.

**Access**  This fine ancient monument is situated opposite Holy Trinity Church, its location being well signposted in the town. Bradford-on-Avon lies some 8 miles (12.8km) south-east from the centre of Bath, via the A363 Trowbridge road.

## St Peter's Tower
Monkwearmouth, Sunderland, Tyne and Wear.
OS 88, (1in 78), NZ402577
The west tower and some stone carvings are all that remains of the monastery founded in the seventh century. The west tower and the west wall of the nave cover almost the whole period of Anglo-Saxon church building. St Peter's church stands alone on the north bank of the River Wear surrounded by housing development.

**Access**  Proceed north from the centre of Sunderland on the A1018. After crossing the north bridge turn right on to the A183, and continue for 660yd (600m). Turn right on a side road to the church.

## All Saints Church Tower
Earls Barton, Northampton
OS 152, (1in 133), SP852638
This church which stands prominently in the centre of Earls Barton is noted for its magnificent late tenth-century Anglo-Saxon tower. The tower may be divided into five sections, with each stage decreasing in size. The crenellated upper part probably dates from the fifteenth century. The four Anglo-Saxon stages are separated by simple string-courses, and each section is extensively decorated with pilaster strips. On the south face of the tower the lowest stage has a double round-headed window ornamented with rounded side shafts. Note the carved crosses on the heads, and the circular stone with a similar carving. On the second stage there is a row of semi-circular pilasters resting on a solid-looking string-course. On the south side of the tower at this level is a round-headed door opening — a strange place for a door so far off the ground. The third stage is somewhat over decorated by vertical pilaster stripwork supplemented by two rows of diagonal strips. The belfry stage has sets of five narrow windows with rounded heads separated by cylindrical shafts. The western tower door has a rounded arch resting on heavy through-stones. Look for the fine decoration on these imposts. The angles of the tower are bonded with fine examples of long and short quoining.

**Access**  The church is situated 4 miles (6.4km) south-west of Wellingborough, via the A45 Northampton road, then by side road to the centre of the village.

## Church of St Peter Saxon Tower (DoE)
Barton-on-Humber, Humberside
OS 112, (1in 99), TA035219
The main attraction here is the superb tenth-century Anglo-Saxon church tower, now in the care of the Department of the Environment. The original chancel was destroyed in the fourteenth century, and a new church was built on to the eastern side of the tower. The two lower stages of the tower date from the tenth century, and the upper section was built later in the eleventh century, probably at the time of the Norman Conquest. The tower has two entrances, a triangular-headed door on the north side (now blocked up), and a round-headed one on the south side. Both doorways are simple, solid-looking structures, with the jambs constructed with through-stones laid alternately upright and flat. Both archways rest on heavy, protruding stones. The doorways fit neatly between the pilaster stripwork that decorates the north and south sides of the tower. Above the doorways, the stripwork terminates into round arcades, and then the pilasters

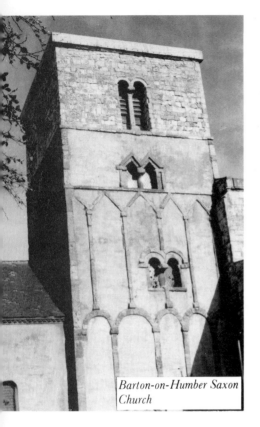

Barton-on-Humber Saxon Church

continue from the top of each arch to triangular-headed arcades headed by a string-course. Also above the doorways are fine double-headed windows with baluster pillars surmounted by heavy moulding.

The Anglo-Saxon belfry, or middle stage of the tower has double triangular-headed windows in all four walls. Now only two are visible, as the one on the western side is now occupied by a clock, and the eastern one is now within the nave. The corners of the tower are strengthened by the slim lines of long and short quoins, and its appearance is heightened because the strip-work stands out clearly against the plaster background. The upper part of the tower has a further set of three double windows.

The little narrow annexe has long and short quoins, and may be older than the tower itself. It has a blocked round-headed

doorway, and above are signs of two circular windows. The north and south walls of the annexe both contain one round-headed window.

Inside the tower, notice the fine arches with their jambs and through-stones, and headed by wedge-shaped stones or voussoirs. A stone carving of a man's head can be seen above the eastern arch. The original chancel was probably not much larger than the surviving western annexe. All the evidence so far points to the fact that the tower was originally the main body of the church.

**Access**   The church lies on the eastern side of the town, 10 miles (16km) north of Brigg. Follow the A15 and then the B1218 into the centre of Barton. Turn right, and then left at the next crossroads. The church lies 330yds (300m) ahead on the right, but is currently under repair and closed to visitors.

### St Andrew's and St Peter's Churches
Bywell, Corbridge,
Northumberland
OS 87, (1in 77), NZ048615,

NZ049614
These two churches containing Anglo-Saxon work are situated within sight of each other in the village of Bywell, on the north

bank of the River Tyne, 12 miles (19km) west of Newcastle-upon-Tyne. Access from the A695 or the A69 and then by the B6309.

### St Patrick's Chapel and Church of St Peter
Heysham, Morecambe,
Lancashire
OS 97, (1in 94), SD409616
The small ninth-century chapel of St Patrick stands on a headland overlooking Heysham Sands and Morecambe Bay. The ruins are those of a simple one-roomed rectangular building. There are side alternate quoins, a south doorway with a decorated round head and heavy jambs. Close by are a number of rock-cut graves which

add to the atmosphere of the site.

Below the headland lies the parish church of St Peter which contains a number of Anglo-Saxon features: namely, the west wall of the nave, the east wall above the chancel arch, the ends of the south wall, the blocked west door, and a doorway in the north wall. Inside the church, in the south aisle, is a splendid hog-back tombstone, which is decorated with a hunting scene; a fascinating frieze of men and animals upon its sides. The

Scandinavian sculptor obviously had a sense of humour as he carved the ends of the tombstone with the figures of strange bear-like creatures. There is also the base of a ninth-century cross-shaft in the churchyard beside the path.

**Access**   From the A589, follow the road to Heysham village, and the signs to St Peter's church. The tiny chapel ruins are situated on the headland above St Peter's churchyard.

## St Gregory's Minster, Kirkdale

Beadlam, Helmsley, North Yorkshire
OS 100, (1in 92), SE677857
Set in a beautiful situation alongside Hodge Beck, this small church contains many items of interest for the visitor, notably its Anglo-Saxon sundial above the south doorway, which is probably the most complete and best preserved example; its approximate date is AD1055-6. The inscription in translation reads: 'Orm, the son of Gamal, obtained the church of St Gregory when it was broken and ruined, and had it renewed from the ground in honour of Christ and St Gregory, in the days of Edward the King and Tosti the Earl'. Above the dial are the words 'This is the day's sun marking at every hour'. The dial itself is divided into ninety minute sections from 6.00am to 6.00pm. There is a special mark for daytime at 7.30am. Below

*Anglo-Saxon Sundial, Kirkdale*

the carving are the words 'Hawarth made me and Brand, priest'.

The nave is basically Anglo-Saxon with some fine long and short quoins outside at the west end. Note the west doorway, the chancel arch jambs, and the re-used Saxon cross-shafts in the south wall of the nave and in the west wall north of the tower. Inside the church there are two decorated stone coffin lids; the Cedd Stone, of the tenth century, with a fine interlace

pattern; and the Ethelwald Stone, of the eighth century, with the carving of a cross and scrollwork.

**Access** The church lies 1½ miles (2.4km) east of the village of Beadlam via the A170 and a by-road.

Just south of the church, by the ford, is an old quarry and two openings of a cave. Animal bones found here were identified as lion, bear, tiger, elephant, bison, hyena and many other species.

## Other Sites

**All Saints Church**
Wing, Aylesbury, Buckinghamshire
OS 165, (1in 146), SP880225

**Church of St Mary**
Stow, Lincoln, Lincolnshire
OS 121, (1in 104), SK882819

**Saxon Cathedral, North Elmham** (DoE)
North Elmham, East Dereham, Norfolk
OS 132, (1in 125) TF988217

**St Mary's Church and Odda's Chapel** (DoE)
Deerhurst, Tewkesbury, Gloucestershire
OS 150, (1in 143)
St Mary's SO870299
Odda's Chapel SO869298

**All Saints Church**
Hough-on-the-Hill, Grantham, Lincolnshire
OS 130, (1in 113), SK923463

**St Wystan's Church**
Repton, Derby, Derbyshire
OS 128, (1in 121), SK303272

**All Saints Church**
Brixworth, Northampton, Northamptonshire
OS 141, (1in 133), SP747712

**St John the Baptist**
Barnack, Stamford, Cambridgeshire
OS 142, (1in 123), TF079050

**St Mary's Church**
Beachamwell, Swaffham, Norfolk
OS 143, (1in 124), TF751054

*Saxon stair turret, Hough-on-the-Hill*

**St Andrew's Church**
Great Dunham, Swaffham,
Norfolk
OS 132, (1in 125), TF873147

**St Mary's Church Tower**
Ovingham, Prudhoe,
Newcastle-upon-Tyne,
Northumberland
OS 88, (1in 78), NZ085637

**St Andrew's Church**
Greensted, Chipping Ongar,
Essex
OS 167, (1in 161), TL538030
A church with a unique wooden-
walled nave (restored).

*Beachamwell Saxon Church*

## ANGLO-SAXON CROSSES AND SCULPTURES

The physical survivals of the Anglo-Saxon period, fragmentary as they are, are enough to indicate a highly-organised civilisation based on village and small town communities. The earliest examples of free-standing crosses were probably wooden ones, erected after the appearance of Augustine in southern England. In many cases, the crosses were set up to indicate places where local people could gather and listen to the preaching of the gospel. Understandably, wooden crosses have not survived, but there are many examples of free-standing carved stone crosses to be found from the Midlands to the north of England.

The sculptor's art came to the Anglo-Saxons from the Mediterranean, and this inspiration produced a rich heritage of elaborately carved designs. These Anglo-Saxon carvings generally fall into three main divisions: the Northumbrian, the Mercian and the West Saxon (Wessex). The former can be recognised by its vinescroll panels, in which birds and animals are arranged in a pattern of vine leaves and branches. The creatures are often to be seen biting or pecking the fruit. The design may be further ornamented by an intertwining pattern called interlace. Sometimes this intertwining takes the form of an animal's body.

The golden age of the Northumbrian tradition was between the seventh and eighth centuries, after which it faded only to revive under Scandinavian influence between the late ninth and eleventh centuries. Two famous examples of this type of sculpture are to be found at Ruthwell (Dumfries and Galloway) and at Bewcastle (Cumbria), NY565746.

Mercian sculpture exhibited an architectural style which combined both figure work and abstract design. There were a considerable number of crosses produced in the region, which was doubtless due to the plentiful supply of good stone suitable for carving. The crosses date from the ninth to the eleventh centuries.

Between the tenth and eleventh centuries, a famous school of carvers at Winchester, in southern England, developed a neo-classical style from Continental inspirations. It became one of the most important in Europe, and an outstanding example of their work is the angel carvings from Bradford-on-Avon (Wiltshire), ST824609. Outside Wessex, Scandinavian ideas rejuvenated Northumbrian sculptures with the use of various creatures set in intertwining patterns. A fine example depicting figural compositions from Norse mythology is the Gosforth Cross (Cumbria), NY072036.

## Anglo-Saxon Crosses and Sculptures
### Identifying Features

These Anglo-Saxon crosses and sculptures may contain a small number or a great variety of the following designs:

**Northumbrian Style** (late seventh or eighth centuries)
● Tall graceful crosses with vinescroll panels, birds and beasts, figure subjects, interlace and linear patterns.
● The ornamentation was often accompanied by runic inscriptions.

**Anglo-Scandinavian Style** (ninth to eleventh centuries)
● A rejuvenation of the Northumbrian tradition with Scandinavian ideas.
● Richly decorated designs, with intertwining animal ribbon, birds, beasts, figures, ring-chain patterns, interlace and runic markings.
● Stones containing carvings that have attempted to reproduce Viking Jellinge style ornament, such as opposed beasts, dragons and interlace.

**Mercian Style** (ninth to eleventh centuries)
● The cross-shafts have rounded, slightly-square or tapering rectangular profiles.
● The border designs include interlace, plaits, and chain-link, and the panels contain richly decorated figure work, geometric patterns and types of scrollwork.

**Wessex Style** (late tenth to eleventh centuries)
● A naturalistic style of carving from Continental ideas — the 'Winchester School' of carving, eg the Bradford Angels, Bradford-on-Avon.
OS 173, (1in 166), ST824609

**Ringerike Style** (early eleventh century)
● Foliage patterns with long twisted leaves, added to carvings of beasts and ribbon animals, eg Old St Paul's Cross, Museum of London, London Wall.

## Outstanding Anglo-Saxon Crosses

### Gosforth Cross
Gosforth, Egremont, Cumbria
OS 89, (1in 88), NY072036
This is truly one of the finest examples of tenth century Anglo-Scandinavian art in the country. This graceful tapering sandstone pillar stands 15ft (4.5m) high, with the lower rounded section of the shaft rising to a square upper part supporting a small ring-head.

The latter is the only Christian element, apart from the figure of Christ with uplifted arms carved on the east face. The typical Scandinavian ring-chain patern, as found in the Isle of Man, is much in evidence along the shaft, and the upper panels are crowded with scenes, some of which may relate to Norse mythology. The position of the Christian element amongst the

Scandinavian images may accurately convey the state of religious turmoil at that time.
**Access** The cross is located in St Mary's churchyard on the eastern side of the village of Gosforth. Leave the main A595 and proceed through the village, then bear left towards Wellington.

### Bakewell, Derbyshire
OS 119, (1in 111), SK216685
This cross with a partly broken head is a fine example of ninth-century Mercian work. The remaining section of the cross-head displays a mounted figure riding over a dragon on one side,

and a crucifixion scene on the other. The shaft face below the horseman depicts a creature at the head of a fine column of wonderfully carved spiral scrolls. On the reverse side of the shaft there are vinescrolls, with more scrollwork running down the

sides of the shaft.
**Access** The cross, protected by a neat railing, is situated in the churchyard of All Saints Church in the middle of the town.

### Bewcastle Cross

Bewcastle, Brampton, Cumbria
OS 86, (1in 76), NY565746
This historic hamlet is set in typical border country, remote and quietly serene. The Roman fort, built in about AD120, was an isolated outpost of Hadrian's Wall, and linked to that northern frontier line by a supply road. Over the centuries, the Roman stones have been incorporated in many of the local dwellings and farms, including the church. Anglo-Saxons and Scandinavians settled here, and it is possible that this magnificent sandstone column may have been erected as a memorial to the Northumbrian King Alcfrith. The cross, dating from the late sixth or early seventh century, is a superb example of Northumbrian art, and is artistically carved with panels depicting religious figures. The west face displays, from the top, John the Baptist, Christ in

*Bewcastle Cross*

Majesty, and a figure which may represent St John the Evangelist carrying an eagle. Or is it the representation of a hunter holding a hawk? The east face is decorated with vinescroll ornament with birds and beasts, and the other two sides include fine patterns of interlace, scrolls and chequer designs.

The Bewcastle Cross also bears a considerable number of runic markings, which have now become obscured by weathering. The main runic inscription lies below the Christ panel on the west side. The headless cross stands 14½ft (4.35m) high in the churchyard.

**Access**   Bewcastle is situated 10 miles (16km) north of Brampton, and a pleasant approach is to use the minor road passing Lanercost Priory, on the banks of the River Irthing. Cross the line of the Roman Wall, and the B6318, and proceed straight ahead for Bewcastle.

*Irton Cross*

### Irton Cross

Holmrook, Gosforth, Cumbria
OS 89, (1in 88), SD091005
A very fine cross complete with head, stands 10ft (3m) high in the churchyard of St Paul's church, Irton. The shaft includes panels of interlace, geometric patterns and petal rosettes on the front and back, and carvings of vinescrolls on the sides.

**Access**   This isolated church is approached by a narrow lane leading north off the minor road from the A595 to Santon Bridge. It lies 1½ miles (2.4km) east of the village of Holmrook.

### Sandbach Crosses (DoE)

Sandbach, Cheshire
OS 118, (1in 110), SJ758608
The two fine crosses that stand on a base in the busy market-place date from the ninth century. The taller cross is almost complete apart from the upper section of the head which is missing. All the sides of the shaft are richly decorated with scenes from the New Testament. On the east face they include the Crucifixion of Christ surrounded by signs of the four Evangelists, a Nativity scene, and Christ as one of three figures in a circle. The opposite side includes a scene of Christ before Pilate. The north face displays a dragon at the top, and below are small figure panels. There is some vinescroll

ornamentation on the south side accompanied by a panel of interlace.

The other cross is also richly carved, and displays a pattern of triangles at the base of the shaft, which is also found at the foot of the taller cross. The west side carries a number of panels containing figures, the details of which are obscure due to weathering. However, part of the central section may represent the Resurrection of Christ. The east face presents a number of scenes which may depict the coming of Christianity to Mercia. Both the east and west faces include a decorative plaited border.

**Access**  The monuments stand in the centre of the town, and can be easily reached from Junction 17 on the M6, and along the A534.

## Leek

St Edward's Church, Leek, Staffordshire Moorlands
OS 118, (1in 111), SJ983567
This cross, probably of eleventh century date, begins as a circular pillar, and then gradually tapers to a squarer shape. The shaft is divided by a raised border of interlace separating panels of chain-link and interlace above, and circular and triangular panels below. In its original state the cross was probably surmounted by a wheel-head.

A little further along the churchyard path is another cross-shaft, rather worse for wear, containing some pattern work closely resembling the county emblem, the 'Staffordshire Knot'. On the side nearest the church the shaft displays a short line of runic markings. This is an older monument, and probably dates from the early ninth century.

There are other fragments of ninth to tenth century sculptured stones to be found inside the church.

**Access**  St Edward's Church lies in the centre of the town, alongside the road to Macclesfield.

## Dearham Cross

Dearham, Maryport, Cumbria
OS 89, (1in 82), NY073364
The church of St Mungo houses a splendid tenth-century wheel-headed cross, decorated with interlace on the sides and back. The front panel is carved with a ring-chain pattern which can be compared closely with similar designs found on the Norse crosses in the Isle of Man. At the foot of the ring-chain decoration is the representation of a whale-like creature and two birds, one on either side.

A piece of a cross shaft, called the Kenneth Cross, may be found in the tower, and is decorated with scenes including St Kentigern being rescued by an eagle, and a man on horseback.

The third carved stone in Dearham church may be located in the nave resting on a window ledge. The many decorations include figures, rosettes, a bearded head, a quatrefoil and a cross. This monument is called the Adam Stone, with the name ADAM accompanied by a runic inscription.

**Access**  The village of Dearham is situated 2¾ miles (4.4km) west of Maryport, and to the north of the A594. The church is at the top end of the village overlooking the stream.

## Ruthwell Cross

Ruthwell, Annan, Dumfries and Galloway Region
OS 85, (1in 75), NY101682
The Ruthwell Cross is regarded as one of the two finest monuments of the Dark Ages in Europe, an outstanding example of the golden period of Northumbrian sculpture; the other one is at Bewcastle in Cumbria. Dating from the seventh century, it stands 18ft (5.4m) high in a special apse in the village church. It has been slightly restored after being broken in the seventeenth century, and then buried under the floor of the church. The Anglo-Saxon sculptors probably utilised ideas from the eastern Mediterranean, as the cross is ornamented with many Christian themes. These include St John with the eagle, John the Baptist, Christ in Glory, and the Flight into Egypt. The sides display rich vinescroll ornamentation with birds and beasts, and bordered with Anglian runes.

**Access**  Take the B724 west from Annan for 6½ miles (10.4km). The church lies just north of Ruthwell village, so turn right at the crossroads, and continue north for 330yd (300m) to the site.

## Eyam Cross

Eyam, Bakewell, Derbyshire
OS 119, (1in 111), SK218765
This small village at the foot of
the gritstone moors is well-
known as the place where the
Rector, William Mompesson,
persuaded the inhabitants to
remain within their village and
not to spread the Plague, which
had come to the village in a
parcel of cloth in August 1665,
to other settlements. During the
next fifteen months 260 people
perished.

In the churchyard of the
parish church of St Lawrence
stands a formidable gritstone
cross in an excellent state of
preservation. The upper part of
the shaft is missing and the
remaining section is surmounted
by a impressive Northumbrian

style head. The upper part of the
shaft, on the western side,
displays a figure holding an
object which resembles a horn.
This panel is set above circular
motifs of tight interlace, with a
similar decoration adorning the
sides of the shaft. The imposing
cross-head has a circular centrepiece flanked by figures. The
opposite side is ornamented with
spiral trumpet scrolls.

**Access**   The village is situated
in the eastern sector of the Peak
District National Park above the
Derwent valley. It lies 6 miles
(9.6km) north of Bakewell via
the A619 and the B6001 to
Calver. Turn left along the A623
via Stoney Middleton into
Middleton Dale, and then bear
right, signposted to Eyam.

*Eyam Cross*

## Other Anglo-Saxon Sculptures

### Breedon-on-the-Hill

Church of St Mary
Ashby de la Zouche,
Leicestershire
OS 129, (1in 121), SK406233
The church is situated on high
ground above the village. In
historical terms, this ancient site
has witnessed Iron Age people,
and the establishment of a

monastery in the seventh
century.

Many pieces of outstanding
Anglo-Saxon sculpture of
Mercian style have been
preserved, and are now housed
in the church. There are panels
of eighth-century frieze-work
containing vinescroll ornament,
incorporating human figures,

animals and birds. The church
tower contains a full length
sculpture of an angel. One of the
cross-shafts displays an Adam
and Eve motif, and a smaller
fragment bears a decoration of
beasts carved in the Viking
Jellinge style.

### Wirksworth, Church of St

Mary, Matlock, Derbyshire
OS 119, (1in 111), SK287539
This fine example of early
Mercian sculpture was found in
1820 upside down over a vault;

this no doubt was instrumental
in preserving its excellent
condition. It measures almost 5ft
by 3ft (1.5m by 0.9m), and dates
from about AD800. The carvings
on the panel depict scenes from

the life of Christ, including the
Crucifixion — note the slain
lamb on the Cross. The panel is
most probably incomplete, as
the Cross would have formed the
central feature of the frieze.

### Nunburnholme, St James'

Church, Pocklington,
Humberside
OS 106, (1in 98), SE848478
A very fine sculptured cross-
shaft, probably the work of two
different craftsmen, and
displaying both Anglo-Saxon

and Scandinavian elements, is
housed in the church of St
James. One side displays an
arched panel containing a
Viking warrior complete with
sword. Another panel exhibits a
representation of the Virgin and
Child, surmounted by a carving

of two winged creatures. On the
opposite side of the shaft, one
panel contains a seated figure,
and below is the carving of
another seated figure probably a
priest. This side also displays a
scene from Scandinavian
mythology.

**Dacre,** Church of St Andrew, Penrith, Cumbria
OS 90, (1in 83), NY460266
There are two interesting fragments of stone cross-shafts in the chancel. The Anglian stone of about AD800 depicts a winged beast with a human face. The other is a tenth-century shaft with beautifully carved linear figures. The four corners of the churchyard are marked by stone figures, known as the Dacre bears.

**Hexham,** The Abbey Church Northumberland
OS 87, (1in 77), NY935641
'Acca's Cross'; the shaft is superbly carved with vinescroll ornament, and dates from the eighth century.

*One of the four Dacre Bears*

*Anglian cross fragment, Dacre*

## PICTISH CROSSES AND SCULPTURES

As the first millennium BC drew to a close in Scotland, the distinction between the two principal Celtic peoples became recognised. The people inhabiting the land north of a line between the Forth and the Clyde were the Picts who spoke a variant of the Celtic language. South of this line were the Britons who spoke another version of the Celtic language. During the Roman advance into Scotland the Pictish leader Calgacus was defeated and killed at the battle of Mons Graupius on Speyside. When the Romans began to withdraw to Hadrian's Wall, the Picts harassed the legions and destroyed many garrisons and settlements. After another advance into southern Scotland and the subsequent construction of the Antonine Wall, the Romans were able to control the northern Picts more easily with the help of the native British rulers.

In the sixth century AD, groups of Irish settlers known as Scotti occupied the islands and coastlands of Dalriada, the Argyll region of western Scotland. In the beginning there was no opposition to the establishment of settlements, and they only came into conflict with the Picts when they began to extend their influence to the east.

An important event in the rise of the new kingdom was the arrival of St Columba with a band of followers from Ireland. He founded a community on the tiny island of Iona off western Mull in AD563. It was from this small beginning that Columba's Christian message was to spread throughout Scotland, even to the Northern Isles. Much of southern Scotland fell under Northumbrian control in the seventh century, and the Vikings began raiding the west coast of Scotland at the end of the eighth century. The sacking of Iona was followed by the establishment of settlements particularly in the western islands and on the east coast of Scotland.

Throughout their history the Picts fought their neighbours the Scotti, but both races were united around AD842, when the new nation of Scotland was formed under the Gaelic king

Kenneth mac Alpin. The growth and influence of Viking settlements, together with the new union of the Scots and Picts, meant that the latter became absorbed, and their separate identity simply disappeared from the Scottish scene.

The important examples of stone monuments which have survived are roughly-dressed stone pillars, or natural boulders, bearing inscriptions of abstract designs, and animals of a distinct style.

It is possible that the inspiration for the earlier Class I examples of this decorative work stemmed from Mediterranean artistic ideas through the medium of Northumbria. The symbols include, on the one hand, abstract designs of a symbolic significance, and on the other shapes of objects probably only recognisable to any viewer. Other symbols are in animal form, together with fishes and various birds. The most intriguing creature of the animal symbols is an 'elephant' design

with decorous long snout, tail and curled feet. These designs are thought to date back to the early days of Christianity in Pictland. The purpose of the symbols is unknown, but they may have been recognised as boundary markers in those times, or as a gathering point for worship and other important assemblies. The engraved stones have been attributed to the seventh, eighth and ninth centuries.

Class II stones usually take the form of heavy upstanding slabs with the figure of a cross carved in relief, accompanied by an interlace pattern, and Pictish symbols of human, abstract and animal design. Some Pictish stones have in addition to the symbols, markings in the Ogham alphabet, consisting of linear markings on a base line. The later stones or Class III monuments of the tenth century, only contain the cross and decorative work, and the old Pictish symbols are no longer present.

---

### Pictish Crosses and Sculptures
### Identifying Features

- Class I Stones: These early examples are roughly- dressed stone pillars or natural boulders bearing inscriptions of abstract symbols and animals of a distinct style.
- Class II Stones: These usually take the form of heavy upstanding slabs with the figure of a cross carved in relief, accompanied by an interlace pattern, and Pictish symbols of human, abstract

and animal design.
- Abstract symbols include V-rod, Z-rod, triple-disc, double-disc, arch, crescent, disc and rectangle, flower, comb-case, and several other minor symbols.
- Animal symbols include horse, stag, bull, wolf, boar, serpent, elephant, together with fishes and various birds.

---

### Outstanding Sites

**Maiden Stone** (DoE)
Chapel of Garioch, Inverurie,
Grampian Region
OS 38, (1 in 40), NJ704247
This beautifully executed carved stone of red granite stands alongside a by-road on higher land south of the River Urie. It is a Class II stone showing a man and representations of fish

creatures (perhaps Jonah and the whale), a decorated cross and shaft and other ornamentation. On the other side there are beasts, a centaur-like figure and other carvings of Pictish symbols. The stone is thought to be standing in its original position.

**Access**   Take the A96 north of

Inverurie for $2\frac{3}{4}$ miles (4.4km), and bear left on a by-road to Chapel of Garioch for another $1\frac{3}{4}$ miles (2.8km). Keep straight on, and the stone lies nearly a mile (1.4km) ahead. Marked as Maiden Stone on the Ordnance Survey map.

## Aberlemo

Forfar, Tayside Region
OS 54, (1in 50), NO523555
This small hamlet is noted for some fine specimens of ancient Pictish sculptured stones. First, close to the Forfar-Brechin road north of the church, are two inscribed stones set in a small enclosure. A sandstone pillar of the Class I type is inscribed with a number of symbols. At the top of one face is a serpent which is followed by Z-rod and double-disc symbols; at the bottom are mirror and comb symbols. The other stone is a wheel cross of Class II type which is decorated with angels on one face, and a hunting scene and Pictish symbols on the back.

A short distance to the south, in the churchyard, lies a finely ornamented cross-slab of the Class II type. It stands about 6ft (1.8m) high, with the cross

*Pictish stone, Aberlemno Churchyard*

*The reverse side of the Aberlemno Stone, showing a hunting scene*

engraved in a panel-like manner. On one face, the cross head and shaft is flanked with intertwining animals, and the opposite face displays Z-rod, rectangle and triple-disc symbols accompanying a hunting scene.

**Access** The roadside stones are located on the B9134 at Crosston, 5 miles (8km) north-east of Forfar. For the churchyard stone, turn right down the lane to Aberlemno, a distance of 220yd (200m).

## Trusty's Hill

Anwoth, Gatehouse of Fleet,
Dumfries & Galloway Region
OS 83, (1in 80), NX589560
On the summit of this little hill,

and with a commanding view of the valley and estuary, lie the remains of an Iron Age fort. Later on the defences were strengthened and the original

fort entrance was extended. Near this southern gateway, and incised on a rocky slab, are fascinating Pictish symbols, comprising a Z-rod, a double-

*Pictish symbols, Trusty's Hill*

*Pictish symbols, Trusty's Hill*

disc, a beast, and a circle containing a human face with curved horns. This is a Class I type of Pictish symbol stones.

**Access**  A by-road leaves the A75 1½ miles (2.4km) west of Gatehouse of Fleet. Proceed for ¾ mile (1.2km) to a crossroads and the site of an old church. A track strikes east, becoming a footpath climbing to a wooded ridge. The tree cover clears, and there is a trig point bearing right marking the summit of a hill, 276ft (84m). This is an excellent vantage point for a sight of Trusty's Hill. Strike east and descend to a little glen and climb up the other side to the ramparts of the fort. It is about 1 mile (1.6km) there and back.

### Sueno's Stone (DoE)

Forres, Grampian Region
OS 27, (1in 29), NJ046595
A Class III stone, it stands 20ft (6m) high with a wheel-headed cross and interlace on one face; on the other side there are weathered panels showing what appear to be battle scenes. There are mounted and foot soldiers, and representations of beheaded bodies. The edges of the stone display a vinescroll design.

### St Vigeans

Arbroath, Tayside Region
OS 54, (1in 50), NO638428
A cottage in the village of St Vigeans houses a collection of Pictish stones found in the vicinity of the church. The 'Drosten Stone' is particularly interesting because of its inscription in Irish lettering on a side panel. This is one of the only two Pictish inscriptions in non-Ogham script that have so far been discovered.

### Glamis

Kirriermiur, Tayside Region
OS 54, (1in 50), NO385466
Permission should be obtained to view this Class II slab which stands in the front garden of the Manse. The stone is nearly 9ft (2.6m) high, and one side is artistically decorated with an elaborate cross, a triple-disc symbol, two men with axes, a cauldron (note the pair of legs protruding), the head of a young deer and two animal-like figures. The opposite side is engraved with a fish, a serpent symbol and a mirror symbol.

**Access**  The Manse is situated in the centre of the village near to the church, and is 5 miles (8km) south of Kirriemuir via the A928.

### Fowlis Wester

Crieff, Tayside Region
OS 58, (1in 55), NN928242
A tall monument of the Class II type, the front displaying a great patterned cross, and the opposite side bearing typical Pictish symbols as well as human and animal motifs. There is also a cross-slab set into the north wall of the church.

### Dyce

Aberdeen, Grampian Region
OS 38, (1in 40), NJ877153
A Class I and a Class II stone are located at Dyce old church overlooking the gorge of Cothel. Access is via a minor road north of Aberdeen Airport, past Raiths and Kirkton, then right along a lane towards the River Don. The Class I stone is incised with Pictish Symbols, and the Class II includes a floriated cross and shaft with a double and triple-disc, a V-rod, a Z-rod and crescent symbols.

### Meigle (DoE)

Alyth, Tayside Region
OS 53, (1in 49), NO287446
Here a number of fine Pictish stones are housed in a small museum, once a school house. A visit to this outstanding collection should not be missed; they offer a splendid insight into Pictish artistic achievement. Note the huge cross-slab, labelled No 2; it has protruding bosses and is decorated with interlace. The opposite side carries human and animal figures. Stone No 3 carries the delightfully executed figure of a horseman.

**Access**  The museum is situated in the centre of the village of Meigle, on the A94 Coupar Angus to Forfar road. If closed, a notice gives the address of the custodian in the village.

### Dunfallandy

Pitlochry, Tayside Region
OS 53, (1in 49), NN947565
A Class II stone, on one side displaying a decorated cross, angels and animals, and on the other face, V-rod, 'elephant', and crescent symbols, accompanied by seated figures, a horseman and other symbols.

### Picardy Stone (DoE)

Insch, Inverurie, Grampian Region
OS 37, (1in 39), NJ609302
A Class I stone, which displays Pictish symbols, such as a Z-rod, a double-disc, a mirror and a serpent.

# CELTIC INSCRIBED STONES AND CROSSES

During the Roman period Christianity took a strong hold in Ireland, Wales and the northern part of Britain. There can be no doubt that the faith was well-established before the end of the fourth century. Although the Roman armies never invaded Ireland there is some evidence of trade, and indeed many of the benefits of Roman civilisation followed peacefully in the wake of Christianity.

By the fifth century there is evidence from tombstones that the Church in Scotland, and possibly in Wales too, was administered through dioceses, and presided over by bishops and deacons. This structure probably persisted until the seventh century, by which time monasticism was growing in popularity. Monastic organisation was better suited to the Celtic Church, as the Celts had no towns and their society was tribal.

Some inscribed stones present evidence of the period just after the Roman departure, when they were raised as monuments (not necessarily as tombstones), to a local chief or dignitary. The stones are upright pillars, usually undressed, with horizontal inscriptions in Roman capitals. They are mostly concentrated in Wales, Cornwall and lowland Scotland. In Ireland a number of the monastic settlements grew into centres of learning and artistic skill. Thanks to the monks, the native oral traditions were preserved and written down in Gaelic, and the inscription on monastic grave-slabs came to be mainly in Gaelic. Christianity in Ireland first made its mark in stone when Ogham memorials had crosses engraved upon them. First, rough simple Latin crosses are found, then Greek crosses, crosses of arcs, and crosses with wedge-shaped ends. Ogham was a simple, if lengthy, form of script, probably devised around AD300, bridging the introduction of Christianity. This strange script, based on the Roman alphabet, consisted of twenty letters formed by series of strokes above, through, or below a guideline; it was suitable for carving on wood, and was later transferred to stone. Many Ogham inscriptions are hard to read due to weathering or damage to the stone. In Ireland, Ogham continued to be used until the end of the seventh century, particularly in the south of the country.

After the first rough stones were carved with Ogham inscriptions, and later marked with simple representations of crosses, other stone monuments were erected. They can be classified into two other main groups: cross-slabs and free-standing high crosses. Cross-slabs are mainly undressed flat slabs placed on or in graves, or standing upright, decorated with a cross on one or both sides; often the design and workmanship is superb. They are frequently elaborately decorated with figures and ornamentation. They date from the seventh to the eleventh century.

The high crosses have tapering shafts of varying length and width, surmounted by a solid disc head with projecting arms, or a wheel-shaped head. They usually lead through transitional types into the Scripture Crosses depicting biblical themes, with interlacing geometrical and abstract designs arranged in panels on the shaft and cross-arms.

---

### Celtic Inscribed Stones and Crosses
### Identifying Features

**Early Monuments and Cross Slabs**

• Upright pillars of undressed stone, with horizontal inscriptions in Roman capitals.

• Some of these rough stone memorials have Ogham inscriptions on them.

• Mainly undressed flat slabs placed on the grave or standing upright, and marked with simple representations of crosses on one or on both sides.

• The slabs were often carved with some design of a cross in relief, often wheel-headed, on one or both sides. From the eighth century onwards, the style became more elaborate, and was often accompanied with figures and ornamentation.

### High Crosses
- They often have tall tapering shafts of varying length.
- The cross is surmounted either by a solid head with projecting arms, or a wheel-shaped head.
- Their designs vary in development with interlace and geometrical work, to panels depicting biblical themes.
- The designs are inscribed on the shaft and on the cross-arms.

Richly-decorated Celtic crosses are found in northern England and Scotland. Ring and wheel-headed crosses are found in Ireland, the Isle of Man and in northern Britain. There are numerous examples in south-west Wales (Dyfed) and also in Cornwall.

## Outstanding Early Monuments and Cross Slabs

### Men Scryfa
Morvah, Penwith, Cornwall
OS 203, (1in 189), SW427353
This solitary inscribed stone stands proudly in the middle of a field south of Watch Croft hill. It probably dates from the early sixth century and is inscribed RIALOBRANI CUNOVALI FILL, being the monument of Rialobran, son of Cunoval. The title Men Scryfa is Cornish for 'written stone'. The person named on this stone was probably a local chieftain between the departure of the Romans and the coming of the Saxons.

**Access**  Take the minor road from Morvah to Madron, and at a point on Bosullow Common 1¼ miles (2km) south-east of Morvah, a track leads north-east. This route also passes Men-an-Tol, the 'stone of the hole' between two upright stones, which may have once formed part of a burial chamber, but its true function is uncertain. Distance from the road is ⅝ mile (1km). Continue along the main track for another 330yd (300m), and the Men Scryfa stone is visible in the field on the left-hand side.

### Llanaelhaearn
Pwllheli, Lleyn, Gwynedd
OS 123, (1in 115), SH387448
This ancient settlement site lies at the foot of the brooding hills of Yr Eifl, and the stone ramparts of the Iron Age community of Tre'r Ceiri. In the parish churchyard are two interesting early Christian inscribed stones. They date back to the beginnings of the Celtic church, and the style of lettering indicates the late fifth or early sixth century. One stone is marked with the letters: MELITV — 'Melitus lies here'. This stone is located to the right of the churchyard path from the entrance gate. The second stone set on the northern wall of the church is inscribed with the letters: ALIORTVS ELEMETIACO (S) HIC IACET — 'Aliortus the Elmetian lies here'. This is an interesting inscription as it mentions evidence of the links between North Wales and the small northern kingdom of Elmet of South Yorkshire.

**Access**  The village is situated on the A499, 6½ miles (10.4km) north of Pwllheli. The parish church is in the centre of the village just west of the main road.

### Llangian
Abersoch, Lleyn, Gwynedd
OS 123, (1in 115), SH295289
This inscribed stone stands in the churchyard of the old church, close by the wall. This fifth-century tombstone is inscribed with the words MELI MEDICI FILI MARTINI I (A) CIT — 'The stone of Melus the Doctor, son of Martinus'. This is an interesting monument as it indicates the profession of the dead person; this type of description is not usually found in Dark Age memorials.

**Access**  The old church is situated in the centre of the village opposite a chapel. Follow the church path round to the right. The village is 1½ miles (2.4km) west-north-west of Abersoch, by minor road just north of the estuary of the Afon Soch.

## Penmachno

Betws-y-Coed, Gwynedd
OS 115, (1in 107), SH790505
The road follows the winding Afon Machno to the village of Penmachno, where the river is crossed by a five-arched bridge built in 1785. Beyond the village, the road twists and turns to follow the stream below forested hillsides, to the bare slopes of Cwm Penmachno with its extensive slate quarries. High above the western end of the valley, the line of the ancient Roman road, Sarn Helen, becomes lost midst the workings of the disused Rhiwbach Slate Quarries. Beyond the quarries the road becomes visible over the moorland and continues towards Pont Newydd and the Roman fort of Tomen-y-mur.

Penmachno was once an important early Christian centre and evidence of this is provided by three inscribed stones of the fifth/sixth centuries. The first stone, a pillar, is inscribed with the following letters: CARAVSIVS

HIC IACIT IN HOC CONGERIES LAPIDVM — 'Carausius lies here in this pile of stones'. In the late third century, the Emperor Carausius ruled Britain, and the name may have been a popular one at that time. There is a chi-rho inscription over the letters. The second pillar is inscribed with the following letters: CANTIORI (X) HIC IACIT (V)ENEDOTIS CIVE(S) FVIT (C)ONSOBRINO(S) MA (G)LI MAGISTRAT... — 'Cantiorix lies here. He was a citizen of Venedos, cousin of Maglos the Magistrate . . . .' The Roman terms in the inscription suggest that the district was still administered by a Roman-type system of government, well into the fifth century.

The inscription on the third stone reads: FILI AVITORI IN TE(M)PO(RE) IVSTI(NI) CON(SULIS). This commemorates Avitorius, and that the stone was set up in the time of the consul Justinus, whose name appears only in the

*Carausius Stone, Penmachno*

Vienne region of France, near to Lyons. Evidence records the fact that he was consul there in AD540.

**Access** The B4406 road leaves the A5, 2¼ miles (3.6km) south-east of Betws-y-Coed, and follows the Afon Machno for a similar distance to Penmachno. The inscribed stones are housed in the church in the centre of the village near to the bridge.

## Doagh Holed Stone

Doagh, Ballyclare, Co Antrim
OS Northern Ireland 14, (1in 3), J242906
This is one of a small group of monuments whose function or significance is not known. The district around Ballyclare was extensively populated during early Christian times, and this type of monument has been associated with this period. Traditions connected with them, such as fertility, childbirth, as a cure for infant sicknesses, or as trysting stones where young men and girls held hands through the hole and pledged their love, may be of a more recent date.

This splendid stone stands on top of a small rocky outcrop, and is 5 ft (1.5m) high tapering almost to a point on one side. It is perforated by a hole 4ins (10cm) in diameter, bored from both sides, and 3ft (0.9m) from the ground.

**Access** From Antrim by the B95 via Rathmore and Parkgate, then turn second left using by-roads to Newmill. Bear right for 660yd (600m), turn left and first right. The holed stone is visible on the rising ground to the right of the lane. The site is marked on the map. Distance from Antrim, 7¾ miles (12.4km).

*Doagh Holed Stone*

### Caratacus Stone

Winford Hill, Dulverton,
Somerset
OS 181, (1in 164), SS890336
On Exmoor, a fine expanse of
heather moor called Winsford
Hill commands magnificently
expansive views in all directions.
At the eastern end, near to Spire
Cross, a trackway leads to the
mysterious Caratacus Stone.
The stone is just over 5ft (1.6m)
in height and over 1ft (0.35m)
broad. After the withdrawal of
the Romans, the local tribe, the
Dumnonii, were subjected to the
infiltration of the Saxon
invaders. It is possible that some
time in the fifth century the local
chief, claiming to be the
grandson or kinsman of
Caratacus, raised the stone with
the inscription CARAACI NEPUS.
There is no evidence that the
monument was a gravestone,
and it may have been sited as a
gesture to the courage of a
British leader.

An odd-shaped shelter now
protects the stone from further
weathering.

**Access**    Take the B3223 north
from Dulverton. The road
initially follows the twisting
course of the River Barle, and
then continues alongside a
tributary, before climbing to the
breezy acres of Winsford Hill.
Just before the crossroads at
Spire Cross a trackway heads
north for a few yards to the
Caratacus Stone. Distance from
Dulverton, 4½ miles (7.2km).

### Maen Madoc

Ystradfellte, Powys
OS 160, (1in 141), SN919158
It would appear that the Welsh
church was established in the
fifth and sixth centuries. The
Christian connection is reflected
in the inscribed stones, which in
the main record the name of the
deceased. The persons
commemorated are usually local
chieftains or priests, and the
name is often accompanied with
the words *hic iacit*, 'he lies here'.
The earliest inscribed stones
were found in small family
groups alongside settlements or
ancient trackways. The
inscriptions were cut on standing
pillars of stone in the Ogham
script. Normally in Wales the
memorials have a Latin
inscription which was added
later, and this has proved to be
of great assistance in deciphering
the Ogham characters.

The Maen Madoc stone
stands in its original position
beside Sarn Helen, the Roman
road from Brecon Gaer to
Neath. This 9ft (2.7m) high
monolith has a Latin inscription
DERVAC FILIUST IVST JACIT —
'(The Stone) of Dervacus, son of
Justus. He lies here'.

**Access**    Take the minor road
north of Ystradfellte following
the Afon Llia for 2¼ miles
(3.6km), and then take the
trackway on the left-hand side
slanting away to the south-west
for another ⅝ mile (1km). The
stone stands by the trackway.

### Margam Stones Museum (DoE)

Margam Abbey, Port Talbot,
West Glamorgan
OS 170, (1in 153), SS801864,
The museum holds a fine
collection of inscribed and
sculptured stones dating from
the sixth to the eleventh century.
The earliest monument carries
the following Latin inscription
engraved in debased Roman
capitals set in horizontal lines:
BODVOC HIC IACIT FILVS
CATOTIGIRNI PRONEPVS
ETERNALI VEDOMAV — 'Here
lies Boduocus, son of
Catotigirnus, great grandson of
Eternalis Vedomavus'. Its upper
side is incised with a cross.

Another stone in the museum
displays the Irish form in
Ogham characters which was
later inscribed in Latin.

**Access**    Take the A48 from
Pyle towards Margam, and
proceed ½mile (800m) beyond
the point where the B4283 comes
in from Porthcawl. Turn right,
and continue for 550yd (500m)
to Margam Abbey. The stones
are housed in the old school to
the north of the churchyard.

### Whithorn

Wigtown, Dumfries and
Galloway Region
OS 83, (1in 80), NX444403
This famous ecclesiastical site is
associated with St Ninian, who
was born and educated under
Roman rule, and credited as the
first Christian to commence the
conversion of the Scottish
people. Whithorn is one of the
oldest Christian centres in
Britain and his mission here
traditionally began in the fourth
century. It was near here, in the
latter part of the ninth century,
that the Lindisfarne Gospel was
washed up on the shore.

Amongst the group of sculptured stones housed in the museum is the fifth-century Latinus Stone. It is one of the earliest memorial stones in Dark Age Britain, and is engraved with clear Roman letters. The inscription reads: TE DOMINU(M) LAVDAMVS LATINVS ANNORV(M) XXXV

ET FILIA SVA ANN(ORUM) IV(H) IC SI(G)NVM FECERUNT NEPVS BARROVADI — 'We praise thee Latinus, aged 35 years and his daughter of 4 years. The grandson of Barrovadus raised this up'.
**Access** The stone is one of a collection of inscribed stones,

fine interlace cross-heads and shafts now housed in a cottage museum on the road leading up to the priory. Whithorn is situated on the A746, 17 miles (27km) south of Newton Stewart, via the A714 and the B7005.

### Free-Standing Stones and High Crosses

### Cardinham
Bodmin, Cornwall
OS 200, (1in 186), SX123687
This circular headed cross, probably dating from the tenth century, stands outside the southern end of the church. Its tapering shaft displays designs of connecting spirals, ring-chain

and interlace, very similar to those carvings on the Norse crosses of the Isle of Man.
**Access** The village is situated to the east of Bodmin, and may be reached by using a by-road just beyond the important junction of the A30 and the A38. The route meanders north, then

east and north again to Cardinham. Distance from the junction SX093655, to the site, is 3½ miles (5.6km). It may also be approached from the A30 north-east of Bodmin, leaving the A30 on Cardinham Downs.

### Isle of Iona
Argyll and Bute District,
Strathclyde Region
OS 48, (1in 51), NM287245
St Columba landed here on this tiny island in AD563 in the hope of winning Scotland for Christianity. From Iona he made several difficult journeys through the Highlands and Islands. On the island his faithful band of followers built a simple monastery which was later replaced by the present abbey. This Celtic island was the cradle of the Kingdom of Scotland, and it is an excellent place to visit, to inspect the remaining signs of the early

Christian faith of Iona.
The Dark Age remains that attract attention are the sculptured high crosses; namely St Martin's, St John and St Matthew's. The former is the best example of an almost complete work. The tall granite pillar carries decorated panels on the front and the back. The designs include figures representing the Virgin and Child and Daniel. A replica of St John's Cross is visible standing in the grounds of the cathedral. Parts of the original cross, carved from blocks of slate, may be examined in the museum. The decoration includes some

splendid curved pattern work and interlace. The surviving shaft of St Matthew's Cross displays key-pattern ornamentation, interlace and figures representing Adam and Eve.
**Access** By ferry from Oban to Craignure, or Lochaline to Fishnish. Then by road across the island of Mull via Bunessan to Fionnphort. Road distance from Craignure to Fionnphort is 34¼ miles (54.8km). Iona is connected by ferry from Fionnphort. The island also possesses a hotel and a golf course, but no cars are allowed.

### Kildalton Cross
Ardbeg, Port Ellen, Isle of Islay
OS 60, (1in 57), NR458508
This magnificent wheel-headed cross, situated in an old churchyard, displays ornamentation similar to Irish

crosses. The decoration consists of abstract designs, figure patterns and interlace, and the carving on the cross arms is similar to that on St John's Cross on Iona.
**Access** By ferry from

Kennacraig, West Loch Tarbert, to Port Ellen. Take the A846 past Laphroaig to Ardbeg, and continue on the minor road for another 4 miles (6.4km). Turn right where signposted to Kildalton Chapel and Cross.

*Nevern Cross*

## Nevern Cross

Nevern, Newport, Dyfed
OS 145, (1in 139), SN083401
Nevern Church houses a fine
collection of sculptured stones.
One superb example, very
similar to the Celtic cross at
Carew, stands 12½ft (3.8m) high
in the churchyard, and is
artistically carved with
geometrical shapes, inscriptions
of interlace and Scandinavian-
type ornamentation. It is a fine
example of early Celtic culture,
although its pattern-work has
never been deciphered. Local
tradition holds to the tale that
the first cuckoo of spring is
supposed to perch on the cross,
and sing, on every seventh day of
April, St Brynach's Day.

Inside the church are two late
fifth- or early sixth-century
stones. One stone is inscribed in
Latin and reads: MAGLOCUNI
FILI CLUTORI — 'Maglocunus,
son of Clutorius! In Ogham it
reads: MAGLICUNAS MAQI
CLUTARI. The other monument
commemorates Vitalianus
Emeretos, a local Welsh
chieftain with Latin
connections. The stone is
inscribed in Latin and Ogham.
**Access**   The church is situated
on the north bank of the Afon
Nyfer, at a point where the road
makes a wide loop to cross the
river. Distances, 8 miles
(12.8km) south-west of
Cardigan, via the A487 and the
B4582, and 2 miles (3.2km)
north-east of Newport, again
using the above roads.

## Margam Stones Museum

(DoE)
Margam Abbey, Port Talbot,
West Glamorgan
OS 170, (1in 153), SS801864
A fine example of a late ninth or
early tenth-century Celtic
monument is the Cross of
Cynfelin. It is a wheel-headed
cross just under 5ft (1.48m) high
with square cross arm ends, and
decorated with interlace. The
short shaft, originally taller, is
ornamented with human figures,
and stands on a large plinth
carved with intertwining pattern
work. There is also a well carved
hunting scene, consisting of two
hounds attacking a stag followed
by two horsemen.

Amongst the other fascinating
stones is a disc-headed cross with
a wide tapered shaft, beautifully
ornamented with Celtic
interlace work. One face carries
an inscription, and the reverse
side a simple linear cross.
**Access**   Take the A48 from
Pyle towards Margam, and
proceed ½ mile (800m) beyond
the point where the B4283 comes
in from Porthcawl. Turn right,
and continue for 550 yds (500m)
to Margam Abbey. The stones
are housed in the old school to
the north of the churchyard.

## Maen Achwyfan

Whitford, Holywell, Clwyd
OS 116, (1in 108), SJ129787
This tall, 11¼ft (3.35m) high
disc-headed cross stands close by
a junction of minor roads, on
higher ground north of the
course of Offa's Dyke. This
impressive early eleventh-
century monument is
elaborately carved with an
ornamentation of Celtic designs.
**Access**   Situated 1¼ miles
(2km) west of the village of
Whitford via a narrow lane, or
some 3 miles (4.9km) west of
Holywell on the A5151. Turn
right (signposted Whitford), but
take the left fork to Gelli, and
right to the site of the
monument. It is marked on the
OS map.

## Donaghmore

Dungannon, Co Tyrone,
Northern Ireland
OS Northern Ireland 19, (1in 5),
H768655
On the B43 at the north-western
end of the village. The cross is
damaged and weathered, but
the details consist of scenes from
the Old and New Testaments
carved on the east and west
sides. The remaining faces have
a small amount of ornamentation, and carvings of strange
animals at the foot. Donaghmore is situated 2½ miles (4km)
north-west of Dungannon.

*Arboe Cross*

## Arboe Cross

Arboe, Moneymore, Co Tyrone, Northern Ireland
OS Northern Ireland 14, (1 in 5), H966756
Although nothing of significance is left of the monastic building on this Early Christian site, the sculptured cross is the best surviving example of its kind in Northern Ireland. It stands 18½ft (5.55m) high and all four sides depict scriptural scenes. Some of the figures are weathered and one arc of the cross-ring is missing. The east face includes Daniel and lions, the sacrifice of Isaac, the twelve Apostles, and Adam and Eve. The west side consists of New Testament scenes such as the

Adoration, the Last Supper, the entry into Jerusalem, the arrest and the Crucifixion. The north face also has New Testament scenes including the Baptism, and the south side includes Old Testament scenes including Cain and Abel and episodes from the life of David. The High Cross dates from about AD1000.
**Access**   Take the B18 south from the A6, and down the west shore of Lough Neagh to Ballyronan. Continue south on the B160 for 3¾ miles (6km) to Ballinderry Bridge. Bear left and proceed for 1½ miles (2.4km) to Crabtree Hill. Turn left to Cluntoe, where the Cross is signposted to Arboe.

## Donaghmore

Newry, Co Down, Northern Ireland
OS Northern Ireland 29, (1 in 9), J1035
This ring-headed cross of weathered granite, 10ft (3m)

high, includes presentations of Adam and Eve on the west side, and David with Goliath's head on a staff on the east face. The carving on the west face of the ring head seems to depict a Crucifixion scene.

The cross is situated in the churchyard of the Protestant church in Donaghmore. The site is signposted off the main A1 road, Belfast to Newry.

## Carew Cross

Carew, Pembroke, Dyfed
OS 158, (1 in 138/151), SN047037
A splendid example of a Celtic cross stands over 13ft (4m) high near the entrance to Carew Castle. The tall splayed shaft, rising to a wheelhead, is decorated with panels of carved interlacing ornament. The top panel displays a swastika

pattern, a shape which the Celts considered lucky. The whole effect is of a well executed carving of great technical merit. The wheel-headed cross is thought to be of sixth-century date, but on the back is an inscription added many centuries later which reads: MARGIT EUT REX. ETG FILIUS — 'King Margiteut, son of Etguin'. The person is thought

to be Maredudd ap Edwin the ruler of Deheubarth (south-west Wales), who was killed in battle in 1035.
**Access**   From Pembroke, follow the A4075, and the A477, and turn north just beyond Milton to Carew. The Castle is situated on the southern bank of the Carew River. Distance from Pembroke, 4½ miles (7.2km).

## MANX CELTIC AND NORSE CROSSES

The Isle of Man formed part of the area on the Celtic Church of western Britain. The earliest monuments are small slabs marked with simple

incised crosses dating from AD650 to 800. Larger rectangular slabs were erected in the ninth century, bearing in low relief representations of the Celtic ring-headed and wheel-headed crosses. The decoration consisted of characteristic close-knit interlacing patterns.

While a great diversity of Scandinavian-influenced sculpture survives in Britain, very little is pure Scandinavian in style, and is instead the outcome of Norse influence on native Celtic or Anglo-Saxon work. The finest Viking sculptures are undoubtedly those from the Isle of Man.

In the fifth century the Isle of Man was settled by the Irish, but round about AD780 the Scandinavians began to build seaworthy boats and make voyages of exploration. After reaching the Northern Isles they sailed to the Hebrides and down the western coastline of Britain to Ireland and the Isle of Man, raiding and plundering at first, but later conquering and settling. At that time, the ninth century, the Isle of Man was thoroughly Christianised, and indeed it is certain that the Norsemen did not destroy the Celtic Christianity, but gradually adopted it as their main faith.

The legacy of their stay on the Island are the wonderful tombstones and monuments engraved with pagan-religious stories. They record animal motifs, scenes from Scandinavian mythology, Odin, Thor, Loki, and events from the heroic tale of Sigurd. The cross-slabs are also decorated with bold bands of interlacing ornament and later on, the slabs often carry memorial inscriptions in the runic lettering of the Viking settlers.

These marvellous stones are to be found in the parishes of Andreas, Jurby, Malew and Maughold. There is a great thrill and sense of excitement on seeing them for the first time, so give yourself plenty of time to take in the full atmosphere and meaning of these fascinating sculptures.

---

## Isle of Man Cross-Slabs
## Identifying Features

**Celtic**
- Earliest datable cross-slabs are decorated with simple geometric patterns, such as Maltese crosses and hexafoils.
- Plain cross-slabs with protruding bosses to indicate the cross-head. The outline of the shaft, ring and base marked by incised lines.
- Wheel-headed cross-slabs decorated with tightly-spaced interlacing, sometimes accompanied by spirals and plaiting.

**Norse**
- Scandinavian art styles and motifs were added to earlier Celtic traditions.
- A characteristic design is one of interlacing ornament in broad single bands, and later in double bands.
- Many Norse crosses bear animal figures, and mythological figures, such as those from the Sigurd story from the Saga of the Norse Gods.

---

## Typical Celtic Cross-Slabs

**Maughold**
Ramsey, Isle of Man
OS 95, (1in 87), SC493916
In the churchyard of the Parish Church of St Maughold lies one of the most interesting collections of sculptured stones on the Isle of Man. Almost a third of the pre-Norse crosses are preserved here under a shelter just inside the churchyard gate. All the stones are numbered; both Celtic and Norse are registered according to the Manx Museum's official numbering system.

**Access**   The hamlet of Maughold is situated on the A15, 3 miles (4.8km) south-east of Ramsey. Nearest station on the Manx Electric Railway is Ballajora Halt, then there is a 1 mile (1.6km) walk to Maughold.

**Number 46**   An example of one of the earliest cross-slabs, from about the seventh century. It is decorated with simple geometric patterns (Maltese cross and hexafoil).

**Number 47**   Irneit's Cross-Slab. This illustrates a fine hexafoil pattern, and two clear crosses displaying thicker ends to the extended arms. There is an inscription within the circle in Roman letters recording a Celtic bishop, Irneit. The slab is dates from about the eighth century.

**Number 69**   Crux Guriat Cross-Slab. This fine slab measures 7ft (2.2m) high and almost 3ft (0.85m) wide. The upper cross-head part displays circular protruding bosses, while the ring, shaft and base are marked by incised lines. There is a simple inscription on the edge of the stone, 'Crux Guriat' —

the cross of Guriat, who probably was a British king of the Isle of Man. Early ninth century.

**Number 96**   Cross-Slab with Monks. This is a typical example

of ninth-century work, illustrating a Celtic ring-headed cross, and displaying the figures of two seated monks, one on either side of the shaft.

*Maughold Cross Slab, No 96*

*Maughold Cross Slab, No 47*

*Lonan Wheel-headed Celtic Cross*

**Lonan**
Baldrine, Isle of Man
OS 95, (1in 87), SC427793
There are several important inscribed stones of the later Celtic style displayed within the ruins of the old Church. The most impressive wheel-headed cross-slab (Number 73) is situated in the churchyard.

Dated between the ninth and tenth century, this fine monument is squat and powerful-looking. It stands 5ft (1.5m) high by over 3ft (1m) across, with a decoration of tight interlace.

**Access**   The site lies north-east of Douglas. From Onchan continue on the A2 to its

junction with the A11. Proceed for 660yd (600m) and turn right down a country lane past Ballamenaugh for ³/₄ mile (1.2km). There is a parking area just north of the site. Bus and Electric Tramway stop at Ballamenaugh.

## Typical Norse Cross Slabs

**Kirk Michael**
Isle of Man
OS 95, (1in 87), SC318909
The famous Michael cross-slabs, now safely housed in the village church, form a rich collection of skilfully worked stone monuments. They bear dramatic representations of the beliefs of the Norse settlers in the

Isle of Man, following their conversion to Christianity. The island has many attractions to offer to the visitor (its lovely coastline, rounded hills and peaceful green glens for example), but these superb sculptured stones, warrant a journey for themselves.

**Number 132**   Joalf's Cross-

Slab. This large cross-slab standing almost 7ft (2.1m) high, is splendidly decorated on both sides and along the edges. The ring-headed crosses in low relief on each face display fine interlace pattern work, and the spaces alongside the shaft carry animal and figure ornamentation. On one side of the cross-slab there can be seen spiral designs accompanying these animals and figures. The fine runic inscription up one edge is surmounted by a wonderfully clear figure of a warrior, legs astride, carrying a spear and a round shield.

**Number 101**    Gaut's Cross-Slab. This cross-slab is the most internationally famous of all the sculptured stones at Kirk Michael. It is a legacy of the generations of Norse settlers who adopted the Christian religion of the Celtic inhabitants of the Isle of Man. The Scandinavians continued the practice of erecting carved stone slabs bearing a representation of the Cross on their graves. Their cross-slabs also included Scandinavian designs and runic letters. The carving of this particular memorial has been attributed to a person called Gaut, for the end of the runic inscription reads '. . . Gaut made

**Maughold**
Ramsey, Isle of Man
OS 95, (1 in 87), SC493916
**Number 133**    A small piece of a cross-slab, probably of the late tenth century, showing the head and forelegs of a boar. Note the lines along its back which represent bristles, and the spiral engraving indicating the leg

**Andreas**
Ayre, Isle of Man
OS 95, (1 in 87), SC415993
Another famous collection of Norse sculptures is to be found safely housed in the parish church. The stones are attractively displayed at the west end of the nave, and include examples rich with carvings taken from Scandinavian mythology. The church proudly

it and all in Man'. His style of carving has been recognised in another cross at Andreas, but there are several others not bearing his name that appear to be examples of his skill.

His work is dated at about the middle of the tenth century, and is noted for its distinctive workmanship. The carvings, all executed in low relief, represent a wheel-headed cross, with bold interlace on the cross-head. On one face the shaft of the cross carries the familiar ring-chain pattern, and the long runic inscription runs down the whole length of one edge of the monument.

**Number 117**    Dragon Cross-Slab. This Norse cross-slab of the eleventh century is one of the best preserved and most complete crosses on the Island. Each face is decorated with intricate double interlacing which widens towards the foot of the cross-shaft. The monument

joining the body.

**Number 122**    This example is the broken shaft of a cross showing part of the story of Sigurd (which has been used by Wagner in the 'Ring' series of operas). At the base of the cross is the beginning of the story, and shows Loki, and Otter and the salmon. At the top of the slab is

welcomes visitors to view its treasures which are of very great archaeological value, as are the similar collections on the island.

**Number 131**    Sandulf's Cross-Slab. This outstanding memorial has flowing carvings of animals on both sides of the slab. One face includes the figures of a ram and a goat, together with hunting dogs, and a deer with a fine spread of antlers. The shaft

has a rounded top and is pierced between cross and ring. On both faces of the slab on either side of the shaft, are carvings of wide-eyed dragons with gaping jaws.

**Number 123**    The Gerth Stone. A well-carved fragment of a late tenth century cross, thought to show a scene from Norse mythology of the young woman Gerth and the tethered horse of the God Frey.

**Number 129**    Crucifixion Cross-Slab. A beautifully executed fragment of an eleventh century cross-slab, which may be a representation of the crucifixion. Above the cross-head are the figures of a cock and an angel. The cross arms display interlace with circular pellets.

**Access**    The carved stones are on display in St Michaels's Church in the village of Kirk Michael on the west coast of the island. Take the A3 north of Peel for $6\frac{3}{4}$ miles (10.8km).

the end of the story, Sigurd with his horse Grani, (head broken off), loaded with treasure. Fafnir and the wicked dwarf Rani are slain.

**Number 142**    Hedin's Cross. This is a plain slab with a runic inscription, and the depiction of a Viking ship.

on this side is decorated with a fine ring-chain pattern. The other side shows a hunting motif with a dog leaping upon a deer, and the cross-shaft carries an interlacing pattern. There is a runic inscription on the edge of the slab which when translated reads, 'Sandulf the Black erected this cross to the memory of Arinbiörg his wife'.

**Number 128**    Thorwald's

*Caernarfon Castle, Gwynedd*

*Dunluce Castle, Co Antrim*

*Abbot's Way, Dartmoor, Devon*

*Petre's Cross, Dartmoor, Devon*

Cross-Slab. The fragments of this famous tenth-century cross-slab are now set into a wooden block with the line of the cross marked on its surface. One side shows a figure carrying a book and a cross, treading on a serpent. Alongside is the carving of a fish which is an early symbol of Christianity.

The opposite side depicts a scene from Ragnarök, the last great battle which marked the end of the world in Norse mythology. Here Odin, wielding his spear and carrying a raven on his shoulder, is being eaten by the Fenris wolf. The slab illustrates the cross-roads between pagan worship and Christianity.

**Number 121**  Sigurd Cross-Slab. One side of this cross-slab fragment shows Sigurd roasting the dragon Fafnir's heart in slices on his sword. The dragon's blood runs down the sword and scalds him, and to ease the pain he sucks his fingers. (Note the head of his horse looking on.) Tasting the dragon's blood gives him the power to understand the meanings of the songs of the birds.

On the opposite side, Sigurd's foster brother Gunnar, is being bitten to death in the snake pit.
**Access**  Andreas is situated in the north of the island, about 4 miles (6.4km) north-west of Ramsey, via the A9.

*Sanduff's Cross Slab, Andreas*

## Jurby
Ballaugh, Isle of Man
OS 95, (1 in 87), SC349985
Jurby church standing alone at the end of a lane, overlooks the low lying coastline of Jurby Head in the north-west of the island. The church houses some crosses of the Norse period and also a few Celtic examples.
**Number 119**  Sigurd Slab. This eleventh-century cross-slab fragment illustrates a scene from the heroic legend of Sigurd. A serpent-dragon, Fafnir, harasses the land, and Odin suggests to Sigurd a way of killing the

dragon. Fafnir has wound her body round a vast treasure, and Sigurd digs a tunnel under her, and drives his sword up into the dragon. This cross-slab fragment shows Sigurd in the pit, killing the dragon with his sword.
**Number 127**  The Heimdall Stone. This cross-slab fragment of the tenth century displays bold interlace pattern-work, together with part of a runic inscription. The top right-hand corner of one face is believed to depict Heimdall, the keeper of Valhalla, blowing his great horn to summon the gods to the last

great battle, which was to be the end of the world in Norse mythology.
**Access**  The sculptured stones are to be found in the small side porch of the church, which is situated at the end of a lane from the crossroads at Jurby West. The church is about $3\frac{3}{4}$ miles (6km) north of Ballaugh, via the A10.

## ISLE OF MAN NORSE SHIP BURIALS

Another interesting feature of the Norse stay on the Isle of Man are the ship burials. When some of the Scandinavians settled down to become farmers and landowners, they used their famous longships for the peaceful occupation of fishing. At Balladoole, a Viking ship burial was discovered and excavated in 1945. Beneath a mound was a longship, about 35ft (10.5m) long, filled with stones and covered with sand. Although the timbers had rotted away, the outline was clearly visible by the iron marks of the bolts and nails. The chief was placed in the centre of the boat, and there were many signs to show that it was a wealthy man's funeral. Articles recovered were a decorated horse harness, leaden fishing weights, knives, flints, an earthenware bowl, a cloak pin, buckles and ornaments of a Scandinavian design. The outline of the ship at Balladoole is now marked with stones.

### Typical Sites

**Chapel Hill**
Balladoole, Castletown, Isle of Man
OS 95, (1in 87), SC246682
The site of the ship burial, overlying early Christian graves, lies on the eastern edge of the Iron Age fort on Chapel Hill, a low hill near to Balladoole Farm.
Note: Near the western end of the Iron Age ramparts lie the ruins of Keeil Vael (St Michael's Chapel), built of limestone.
**Access** One mile west of Castletown. Turn left down farm lane just beyond Ballakeighan corner. Proceed for $\frac{1}{4}$ mile (400m) where a gate on the right gives access to the site. This low hill is a splendid viewpoint across Bay ny Carrickey to Port St Mary.

*Balladoole Viking Ship Burial*

**Knock y Doonee**
Andreas, Isle of Man
OS 95, (1in 87), NX407020
The site of this Norse ship burial lies in the far north of the island overlooking Rue Point, and the sandy low-lying landscape of The Ayres. The bolts and rivets of a boat 30ft (9m) long were found in 1927 under an artifical mound that had been raised on the crest of a low hill. The burial contained weapons, domestic articles and the remains of a horse. In the field on the western side of the farm road is fairly well preserved example of a keeill. On excavation, two inscribed stones were discovered, one a simple cross-slab and the other inscribed in Roman letters and Ogham. The latter may be viewed in the Manx Museum, Douglas.
**Access** From Andreas, take the B2 minor road north to the A10. Turn right and then take the next farm lane on the left. There is access to the site, on a low hilltop 220yd (200m) in fields south-east of Knock-y-Doonee farmhouse. Distance from Andreas, $2\frac{1}{4}$ miles (3.6km).

# KEEILLS

The ruins of many early Christian chapels or keeills are found in the Isle of Man. They probably date from the time of the land division of Celtic and Norse times; some have been rebuilt as parish churches, some remain as ruins. These little churches were built on stone foundations with earth-banked walls, and were roughly faced with stone internally. They probably date from the eighth to the twelfth centuries. Originally, the walls were about 3ft to 4ft (0.9 to 1-2m) high covered with a steep thatched roof. In some cases, remains of an altar, or its foundations, can be found. Adjacent to the keeills were small cells for the priests, usually rectangular or circular single-roomed houses.

The keeill-hunting visitor should not be too disappointed on seeing the sites for the first time anywhere on the island. In some cases, the low walls seem insignificant compared with the extent of other ancient remains. However, the locations of these tiny dark-age chapels provide ample compensation in the absence of outstanding sections of masonry.

> **Identifying Features**
>
> The remains, to a greater or lesser degree, of the walls of small rectangular buildings measuring about 15ft (4.5m) long and 10ft (3m) wide internally.

## Typical Sites

**Lag ny Keeilley**
Dalby, Isle of Man
OS 95, (1in 87), SC216745,
Manx NT
This is a spectacular site in an isolated position on the west coast, above a small cliff overhanging the Irish Sea. It lies at the southern end of Manx National Trust property of Eary Cushlin. The keeill itself is a simple rectangular structure with a stone-built altar. A low circular graveyard bank with two entrances surrounds the chapel. To the north of the site lies a rectangular hermit's cell.
**Access** The keeill is accessible from the A27 at SC232767, 1½ miles (2.4km) south of Dalby. Turn right, and walk along the rough cart track for ½ mile (800m) alongside Kerroodhoo and Kella Plantation. Proceed straight ahead where the track bears sharp left and enter the Manx National Trust area. The former pack-horse track continues as a magnificent footpath, rough in places, through glorious scenery for another 1¼ miles (2km) to the site of the keeill. Total walking distance from the main road, and return, is 3½ miles (5.6km).

**Spooyt Vane**
Glen Mooar, Kirk Michael, Isle of Man
OS 95, (1in 87), SC307887
This delightful wooded glen holds the remains of a keeill situated above the west bank of the stream. The foundations of the original low walls trace out the shape of this chapel, known as Cabbal Pherick (St Patrick's Chapel). The keeill is close to the path, with signs of a rectangular priest's cell built against the south-east corner of the enclosing graveyard bank.

*Spooyt Vane Keeill*

**Access** Take the A3 south of Kirk Michael for just over 1 mile (1.7km) to Glen Mooar. As parking is restricted on the main road, take the minor road that cuts back sharp right down towards the beach, where there is ample parking space. Walk back to the main road, and cross to a gate almost directly opposite. Pass under the old railway line and follow the path alongside the stream for 550yds (500m). The keeill lies to the left of the path on the edge of a small glade. In springtime, the idyllic beauty of the little glen is heightened by the clumps of daffodils and primroses.

## Maughold

Maughold, Ramsey, Isle of Man OS 95, (1in 87), SC493916
This Celtic monastic site is one of the most interesting locations on the island. As well as its famous collection of sculptured stones, the churchyard contains the foundations of three keeills. The most distinctive remains of a keeill are to be found on the north side of the existing church. This little chapel was originally surrounded by its own graveyard.

**Access** The hamlet of Maughold is situated on Maughold Head, 3 miles (4.8km) south-east of Ramsey on the eastern side of the Island.

There is a bus service along the A15, or during the summer months, an exciting if trundling approach via the Manx Electric Railway. The nearest station to Maughold is Ballajora Halt.

*Maughold Keeill*

*Keeill Vreeshy, Eyreton*

## Eyreton (Keeill Vreeshey), St Bridget's Chapel

Crosby, Douglas, Isle of Man
SC322802
The site is situated ½ mile (800m) north of Crosby village and 4½ miles (7.2km) north-west of Douglas. The chapel is well-preserved and stands within its original oval enclosure.

## Glenlough, (Cabbal Druiaght), Druid's Chapel

Union Mills, Douglas, Isle of Man. SC342782
The keeill is located 100ft (30m) from the A1, on the left of a private lane to Glenlough farm, ¾ mile (1.2km) west of Union Mills.

# NORSE DWELLINGS, ISLE OF MAN

*Braidd Round Iron Age Hut*

*Braidd Viking Long House*

**Braidd,** Douglas, Isle of Man
OS 95, (1in 87), SC325766
The Braidd site appears to show
the remains of three successive
houses of the same farmstead,
suggesting continuity of several
centuries from the late Celtic
Iron Age into the medieval
Norse period. Adjoining the
remains, approximately 40ft
(12.2m) in diameter, of the stone
foundations of a large circular
Iron Age house, are the stone
walls of two long houses of Norse
type: one rectangular, and one
with the convex long walls of the
characteristic boat-shaped
house. The rectangular Viking
long house is about 50ft (15.2m)
long, and the boat-shaped
building is about 68ft (20.6m)
long — this is the only boat-
shaped building in the island.
**Access** The site lies on a
gentle sloping hillside offering
splendid views to the north, close
to the junction of the A24 and
A26. Leave the A24 and follow
the fence down the slope to the
site. It lies about 3½ miles
(5.6km) west of Douglas.

## Other Dwelling Sites

Other foundations of houses of
the Norse period have been
found in the island: charac-
teristically these are rectangular
aisled structures, measuring on
the average about 35ft (10.5m)
by 14ft (4.2m) internally. The
walls are composed of earth,
sometimes faced with dry-stone
walling, and on each side of the
central aisle (where the hearth is
normally found), there were
raised platforms or sleeping
benches along the long walls of
the house. Traces of such houses
are found on some of the Iron
Age promontory forts around
the Island's coast; these were, of
course, excellent defensive sites.
Examples may be seen at the
forts of:
    Cass ny Hawin, SC298692
    Cronk ny Merriu, Port
Grenaugh, SC317704
    Close ny Chollagh, Scarlett,
SC246671. House sites now filled
in, only defensive ditch and
rampart now visible.

*Cronk ny Merriu Norse House*

## ROUND TOWERS

There can be little doubt that the round towers were a protective response to the Norse raids, though they may also have been used for internal defence. They were multi-purpose structures, for use as belfries, watch-towers, places of refuge, as buildings to guard a monastery's treasure, and as symbols reaching up towards heaven. There are sixty-five round towers throughout Ireland, one attached to the church of Egilsay, one at Peel in the Isle of Man, and two in East Scotland at Brechin and Abernethy — there are none quite like them elsewhere. It is probable that they were originally attached to churches but the later examples were free-standing.

They were built of dressed stone in the traditional Irish round design, which stemmed from the small Irish building called a clochan, or beehive hut. The secret of extending this clochan shape was the use of lime-mortar, and this was not known in pre-Christian Ireland. It is likely that knowledge of this method came to Ireland with the Christian missionaries in the latter part of the fifth century, who had seen the potential of the Roman technique of lime-mortar.

The structural interest of the round towers is centred on the fact that their foundations were extremely shallow — mostly less than 4ft (1.2m) below ground. They were built in storeys, each stage narrowing internally for strength. They appear to be of standard design, as though there was one gang of builders, with a standard set of plans, moving from one monastery to the next. The sites of all the surviving towers in Ireland are known to have also been the site of a monastery of the early Celtic Church dating from the fifth to the twelfth century. In most cases doorways were several feet above ground level, and in some cases were as much as 16ft (4.8m) above ground level. The ladder could then be hauled up after the retiring monks. Some towers were filled up to the doorway with rubble or earth.

The later towers were never attached to churches, but were always built some distance away. Their defensive qualities have always been open to question, and perhaps they were built purely as prestige symbols for the monastery. There were usually five to seven wooden floors inside, linked by wooden staircases. Usually, the top floor had four windows, one pointing to each major compass point; other floors might not have windows at all. The earliest surviving examples date from the tenth century, and the best examples from the twelfth century. However, one thing remains certain, that the skill of these early builders has been proved by the number of round towers still standing today.

---

### Identifying Features

- They are always in origin free-standing, although sometimes other buildings were later constructed close to them.
- The normal height for a full tower can be estimated as between 83ft and 113ft (25m and 35m).
- They all conform to a standard design, unornamented, with a slight tapering towards the top, which gives the building its strength.
- The tower foundations are generally shallow.
- The internal space is divided into storeys with scarcement ledges for floors. Each storey has an occasional window, and there are normally four at the top.
- The tower is usually topped by a conical cap, but sometimes this was altered in the Middle Ages to low battlements.
- Most doorways are raised 5ft to 15ft (1.5m to 4.5m) from the ground.
- In all the towers, it is interesting to note how little the main dimensions vary, with the circumference at the base between 46ft and 58ft (14m and 17m).

## Round Towers Sites

### Abernethy (DoE)

Perth, Tayside Region
OS 58, (1in 55), NO190163,
Abernethy was the seat of one of
Scotland's earliest bishoprics. Its
treasure now is its eleventh-
century round tower, one of only
two that survive on the
mainland of Scotland. The
cylindrical-shaped structure is
built of well-dressed stones,
although only the lower part
seems to be the original work.
The upper section may have
been rebuilt in the eleventh or
twelfth century. Its inside
diameter is 8ft (2.4m), and its
walls are 3½ft (1.1m) thick. The
doorway arch resembles typical
Anglo-Saxon design, and inside
there are supporting ledges for
six wooden floors, lit by a small
number of narrow windows that
are Norman in character. Over
the centuries the ground level
has probably changed, for now
the door is not so high above the
existing surface.

**Access** The round tower
overlooks the market square

*Abernethy Round Tower*

from the corner of the
churchyard. Abernethy is 8
miles (12.8km) south-east of
Perth, via the A90 and the A913.
The tower stands in the centre of
the village, commanding a view
northwards to the confluence of
the River Earn and the
widening estuary of the River
Tay.

### Devenish Island

Enniskillen, Lower Lough Erne,
Co Fermanagh, Northern
Ireland
OS Northern Ireland, New
Series, Sheet 17, (1in 7),
H224469
Devenish is a monastic site on a
small island in Lower Lough
Erne, which is distinguished by
its tall Round Tower rising
majestically to a height of 81ft
(24.7m). The grey limestone
tower is one of the finest
examples in the country, and has
a carved Romanesque cornice
with a human head over each of
the four top windows. The north
facing head represents a young
boy or woman, the others are
older, bearded figures, and the
sculptures probably date from
the twelfth century. The tower
walls are very well preserved,
rising to a conical stone roof, and
it is possible to climb to the top
by means of a reconstructed
wooden staircase. Just to the
north of the tower are the
foundations of an earlier
structure, dating perhaps from
the sixth century.

**Access** Devenish Island may
be reached by taking a launch
from the waterfront in the centre
of Enniskillen. The boat is well-
appointed with good
refreshment facilities. The
journey is part of a longer cruise
around the lough, but visitors
are landed on Devenish, and
sufficient time is allowed to view
the round tower and the other
buildings of this monastic site.
Alternatively, take the ferry
(check in advance whether it is
running) to the island from a
point 4 miles (6.4km) north of
Enniskillen, via the A32 and a
narrow lane, signposted, to the
passenger ferry.

### Egilsay

Church of St Magnus, Orkney
OS 5, (1in 5), HY466304
The church was established by Bishop William round about AD1135. It consists of a nave and a chancel, the latter covered by a barrel vault which is now missing. A round tower is attached to the west end of the nave; it is very similar in design to those found near Irish churches of the eleventh century. In fact, the building is comparable with the church at Glendalough, Co Wicklow.

The Egilsay tower is some 10ft (3m) in diameter, and the only access to the tower was through a door in the west wall of the nave. Another interesting feature is that there was a room constructed under the chancel roof, with a door. Like the Irish round towers, the Egilsay structure probably served as a look-out post and a secure hiding place for the monks and their valuables in times of danger.

### Brechin (DoE)

Tayside Region
OS 44, (1in 50), NO596601, The great red sandstone tower dates from about the beginning of the eleventh century, although the spire was added in the fourteenth century. The doorway, set some way above the ground, is Irish in character with some interesting additions. Above the arch is a figure representing the Crucifixion, and below, on either side of the doorway, are figures of bishops. Note that one bishop carries a typical pastoral staff, and the other an Irish type, T-shaped crozier. At the foot of the doorway, crouching beasts lie one of each side of the door. The interior of the tower once contained seven storeys.

There are interesting sculptured stones in the cathedral, one showing Northumbrian influence, with the Virgin and Child in the centre, and another, Pictish in character, depicting David slaying a lion. In the latter example, note also the carvings of his harp, sheep and staff beside him.

**Access** The tower and the cathedral stand in the centre of the town, which may be reached by the A935, 8 miles (12.8km) west of Montrose, or 12 miles (19.2km) east of Forfar by the A94 and the A935.

### Antrim

Co Antrim, Northern Ireland
OS Northern Ireland, New Series, Sheet 14, (1in 6), J155877
This well-preserved round tower with a conical stone roof is 92ft (28m) high, the only surviving building of an ancient monastic site. The tapering doorway, 4ft (1.2m) high and 2ft (600cm) wide, is just over 7ft (2.2m) above the present ground level. There is the carving of a wheel cross above the lintel.

**Access** The round tower is situated near to a school in the townland of Steeple, ½ mile (800m) north of the town centre of Antrim.

### Armoy

Ballycastle, Northern Ireland
OS Northern Ireland, New Series, Sheet 5, (1in 1), D077333
Only the lower section of this round tower survives, some 36ft (10.9m) in height. The extremely narrow doorway is surmounted by a huge lintel which displays a curving raised panel. The structure is wreathed with ivy and stands rather forlornly close by the modern church.

**Access** The monument is situated on higher ground beyond the crossroads, nearly ¾ mile (1.1km) east-north-east of the village of Armoy via the B15 minor road. Armoy lies 6¾ miles (10.8km) south-west of Ballycastle.

### Peel

Isle of Man
OS 95, (1in 87), SC241845
The tower stands near to St Patrick's Church, the castle and the cathedral on St Patrick's Isle. It is likely that the tower was constructed in the tenth of eleventh century.

*Antrim Round Tower*

# SCANDINAVIAN HOG-BACK TOMBSTONES

Scandinavian gravestones are often of the easily recognisable 'hog-back' shape. These long ridged stones with a convex profile are thought to represent a form of protective shelter over the body of the deceased. Some examples were meant to portray a Danish house, carved with tiles or slates, and with carvings of dragon-like creatures or other animals at the ends. Some examples clearly show their architectural origins, with imitations of roofs displaying heavy curving ridges and triangular wooden roof shingles.

| Identifying Features |
| --- |
| ● Long ridged convex stones, higher in the middle than at the ends. |
| ● Some examples have carvings to represent wooden roof tiles, walls and down-curving ridges. |
| ● The ends of the 'hog-back' are sometimes carved with stylised creatures, such as dragons or bears. |

## Sites

### Heysham
St Peter's Church, Lancashire
OS 97, (1in 94), SD416617
The parish church houses a fine example of a hog-back tombstone, beautifully decorated with a frieze of men and animals. The curving roof of this memorial is represented by a moulding and a zigzag line. The carving of the hunting frieze may suggest a scene from Scandinavian mythology, with the inclusion of the deer being part of the great legend of Sigurd. The extremities of the stone are hugged by two peculiar dog/bear-like creatures.

**Access**  Take the A589 Lancaster to Morecambe road, then bear left on the B5273 to rejoin the A589. Turn left, and proceed a little way before taking a right turn to Heysham village.

### Brompton
Northallerton, North Yorkshire
OS 99, (1in 91), SE373963
The church of St Thomas houses some fine examples of hog-back tombstones. The carvings clearly represent the 'house of the dead' idea, with decorations of roof shingles, down-curving ridges and walls of wattles reproduced by interlace patternwork. At the ends of the stones are sculptured muzzled bears which support the gable ends of the houses. Note how the craftsman attempted to illustrate their furry bodies by pecking marks on the stone surface.

**Access**  St Thomas' Church stands by the green on the south side of the village, which lies nearly 1½ miles (2.3km) north from the centre of Northallerton. Take the A684, and then the minor road to Brompton.

*Brompton Hog-back Tombstones*

**Gosforth**
Egremont, Cumbria
OS 89, (1 in 88), NY072036
Inside the church of St Mary are two splendid hog-back tomb-stones; one has a crucifix at one end and representations of serpents on the side. The other stone is decorated with a battle scene, with the warriors bearing round shields facing each other.
**Access** Leave the main A595, and proceed through Gosforth bearing left towards Wellington. The church is on the eastern side of the village.

## Other Sites

*Crosscanonby Hog-back Tombstone*

**Crosscanonby**
Church of St John, Maryport, Cumbria
OS 89, (1 in 82), NY069390
An Anglo-Scandinvian hog-back tombstone may be viewed outside the church by the south wall of the chancel.

**Leek**
Church of Edward the Confessor, Staffordshire Moorlands
OS 118, (1 in 111), SJ983567
There is an Anglo-Scandinavian type of hog-back tombstone situated in the south aisle of the church.

**Burnsall-in-Wharfedale**
Church of St Wilfrid, Grassington, North Yorkshire
OS 98, (1 in 90), SE033614
The church not only contains a hog-back tombstone, but several eleventh-century crosses, and the font bearing pagan Norse symbols.

**Aspatria**
Maryport, Cumbria
OS 85, (1 in 82), NY147419
A splendid hog-back tombstone with a fine decoration of animal and interlace ornamentation.

---

## CARVED FIGURES

**Killadeas**
Enniskillen, Co Fermanagh, Northern Ireland
OS Northern Ireland, New Series, 17, (1 in 4), H206540
One of the most interesting stones in the village churchyard is the Bishop's Stone. It stands 3½ft (1.1m) high near the churchyard wall, and bears on its south side the figure of a cleric wearing pointed shoes, and carrying a bell and a crozier. The taller, narrower west side carries a crudely-carved but intriguing human face, above an interlace-patterned panel. This side carving is of similar style to the White Island and Boa Island figures.
**Access** The village of Killadeas is situated 7 miles (11.2km) north of Enniskillen via the A32 and the B82. The stone lies in the graveyard of the Protestant church on the west side of the road.

'The Bishop's Stone', Killadeas

White Island Carved Figures

### Boa Island

Lower Lough Erne, Enniskillen, Co Fermanagh, Northern Ireland
OS Northern Ireland, New Series, 17, (1in 4), H085620
Two very interesting and unusual sculptures are to be found in Caldragh graveyard on Boa Island. One stocky pillar is 2½ft (800cm) high with two figures carved on it, back to back. The figures have stunted bodies and heads with pointed chins. The arms are crossed and the figures appear to be represented as being in the squatting position. The figure on the east side has a phallus.

Close by is a similar, but smaller carved figure known as 'The Lusty Man', which came from the island of Lusty More. The head has a pointed chin with a protruding tongue, and the face has only one fully-carved eye. The arms are crossed on a stunted torso, and appear to be holding something of unknown significance.

**Access** Boa Island is situated in the northern part of the Lower Lough Erne, and the site is 330yds (300m) south of the main A47, Kesh to Belleek road, which is linked to the island by bridges. The carved stones lie in Caldragh graveyard to the east of a barn. The site is some 22 miles (35.2km) north of Enniskillen.

'The Lusty Man', Boa Island

### White Island

Lough Erne, Enniskillen, Co Fermanagh, Northern Ireland
OS Northern Ireland, New Series, Sheet 17, (1in 4), H175600
The neighbourhood of Lough Erne is noted for its collection of remarkable stone carvings.

These enigmatic carvings were once built into, or hidden in, the fabric of the church, and have now been secured to the north wall. The ruined building measures 40ft (12m) by 20ft (6m), and the eight sculptures, seven figures and one head, all date from the ninth to the twelfth century. The church's isolated position has no doubt been the main reason for the fine preservation of the figures, which measure from 2ft (0.6m) to 4½ft (1.4m) in height. Six of the figures are in three pairs: one pair representing Christ, one in soldier's dress, and the other holding a pair of griffins; the second pair show Christ with a bell and staff, represented as Christ the Saviour, and the other as the psalmist David pointing to his mouth. The third pair is difficult to explain, as they include a cross-legged Sheila-na-gig, and a seated figure holding a box. The head is wearing a bonnet and could be interpreted as a scribe — note the frowning expression.

The meaning behind these unusual and exciting sculptures has always been uncertain, and many theories have been advanced. All the full-length figures have sockets on top of their heads, which probably means that they were used as supporting pieces for other sections of internal stonework.

**Access** White Island is situated in Lough Erne and during the season a boat may be hired. The jetty at Aghinver is opposite the island, and is marked Marina on the map. Alternatively from Castle Archdale which lies 11 miles (17.6km) north of Enniskillen. Aghinver is 2 miles (3.2km) beyond Lisnarrick.

## LINEAR EARTHWORKS

After the departure of the Romans, the Marchland between the rivers Severn and Dee came into more prominence. Between AD400 and 600, Christianity had spread through the Celtic west, and part of the territory now known as Wales began to form the nucleus of a new nation, and the Welsh language began to emerge.

The Anglo-Saxons, having fought their way towards this part of Britain, began to establish their hold along the Mercian border with Wales. After the Battle of Deorham in Gloucestershire in AD577, the Saxons controlled the land to the south, and effectively isolated the Celts in the south-west, the area now covered by Devon and Cornwall. In the early seventh century, the Northumbrians won a victory at Bangor-on-Dee, and therefore, along the length of the Marches, beyond a line drawn between Gloucester and Chester, the Welsh were pushed back. The conflicts continued, with the powerful Northumbrians under King Edwin attacking North Wales and the forces of Cadwallon, Prince of Gwynedd. The Welsh leader allied with Penda, an Anglo-Saxon nobleman, and marched north to invade Northumbria, where Cadwallon was killed. Ultimately, Penda was defeated, but the Northumbrians could not push home their advantage due to increasing attacks on their territory by the Picts and Scots.

In time, the Saxons of Mercia moved westwards again, gradually driving the Welsh into the hill country where they resisted stubbornly. Consequently, in the early part of the eighth century a linear earthwork, Wat's Duke, was constructed by Aethelbald in the northern March, from Oswestry to near Holywell in present-day Clywd. After the death of Aethelbald, Offa claimed the throne, and remained as an all-powerful ruler for nearly forty years (AD757-796). In order to define the western limit if Mercian territory, he commanded a great linear earthwork to be raised along the frontier from North Wales to the Severn estuary. Today, the boundary between England and Wales roughly follows the line of Offa's great Dyke.

The immensity of the undertaking is breath-taking. It points to the supremacy of Offa's reign, a tremendous degree of organisation, and a vast labour force, all of which would be required to complete the task. Offa's Dyke effectively protected Saxon settlements from guerilla attacks, and brought about a period of comparative peace.

### Offa's Dyke

It is quite probable that Offa planned the whole work, and laid out the course and the overall alignment along the Mercian frontier. This was 150 miles (240km) long, and took a sinuous route from the Severn estuary to near Treuddyn just south of Mold. Only 80 miles (128km) of earthwork were actually constructed. No major lengths of the Dyke were raised across the Herefordshire lowlands, and from south of Mold to the Dee estuary.

In the south, the Dyke begins on the banks of the River Severn at Sedbury Cliffs, and travels across to the eastern bank of the River Wye following the line of the limestone cliffs northwards. Beyond the Devil's Pulpit, (ST543995) a ditch was cut out of the limestone rock, and even today, it is a remarkable structure, with the steep scarp of the Dyke impressively visible on the edge of the plateau. For some reason only short sections of the Dyke were built across the Herefordshire lowlands; perhaps the dense forest cover was a sufficient deterrent to any Welsh incursions.

The Dyke runs up through the central Marches taking clever advantage of the lie of the land. A particular feature of the Dyke design are the right-angled corners, to enable the boundary line to pass over the highest points of certain hills. For example, Rushock Hill (SO293595) and Cwm Sanaham Hill (SO271755).

The Dyke does not zigzag to overcome the deeply indented valleys, but pursues a straight course across high land, such as Furrow Hill (SO280665) and Llanfair Hill (SO252794). Where it does cross a deep river valley, the direct alignment is well chosen from a point high above the valley floor, thus giving a wide field of view. In places the Dyke traverses diagonally down steep-sided valleys, and crossing points are chosen where two streams meet. For example: Cwm Ffrydd, Churchtown (SO264873), and north of Edenhope Hill, River Usk, (SO263888). Beyond the Severn valley, the Dyke strikes across the deep valleys and foothills of the Berwyn Mountains west of Oswestry. The engineers skilfully selected the dominant westward slopes of hills in order to command the best views. For example, Llanymynech Hill (SJ261220) and Selattyn Hill (SJ250341).

North of the River Dee, the Dyke peters out just south of Mold, where there is the added complication of Wat's Dyke. Maybe the construction of Offa's Dyke was an act of further expansion by the Saxons pushing west from the possibly earlier frontier of Wat's Dyke.

Offa's Dyke was designed to become a barrier between the Saxons and the Welsh. Movement between the two peoples was possible only by means of a few ancient trackways that cut through the earthwork. The Dyke was also a barrier between the two languages and cultures. It is interesting to note that in certain places where colonisation had taken place before the Dyke was constructed, and in other parts where it was not built, there arose a cultural fusion of place-names. There are Old English place-names to the west of the Dyke, for example: Whitton, Kinnerton, Walton, Womaston and Harpton, and Welsh names to the east of the Dyke, such as Pentre, Trewern, Cefn Einion, Llandrinio and Llanhowell.

---

### Offa's Dyke
### Identifying Features

- It is an earthwork, usually with a ditch on the west side, and a bank on the east side.
- There are variations in the character of the Dyke to suit the physical nature and lie of the land.
- Occasionally there is an eastern ditch, as well as a western one; or the Dyke is represented by a shelf and a ditch; or in other places by a low bank and a ditch.

- In some parts the earthwork has disappeared altogether, and may only be traceable now by the line of a hedge, or by a slight bulge or hollow on the surface of the ground.
- There are still sections where the remains are impressive, with the mound standing up to 12ft (3.6m) high, accompanied by a deep ditch. Here the general overall width of the earthwork varies between 50ft to 70ft (15.2m to 21.3m).

**Offa's Dyke**
**The Most Impressive Sections**

### Knighton
Powys
OS 137, (1in 128), SO285723
The Offa's Dyke long distance footpath was officially opened in 1971, making it possible for the public to follow 60 miles (96km) of the 80 miles (128km) length of the Dyke. The complete designated walking route, from coast to coast, is 175 miles (280km), from the Severn estuary to Prestatyn.

### Offa's Dyke Path from
**Knighton**    Follow the riverside path, cross the River Teme and railway, and climb the steep hillside opposite. The route ascends steadily past Kinsley Wood, with faint traces of the Dyke slanting across Panpunton Hill, from which vantage point there are fine views of Knighton in the valley below. The path follows the Dyke across the edge of the plateau, where it now forms a field boundary line between arable land and grazing slopes. Passing clumps of fir trees, it reaches the head of Cwm Sanaham, and with only faint traces of the Dyke visible, the path climbs steeply up the scarp to Cwm Sanaham Hill, at 1,343ft (409m) above sea level. This is another noteworthy viewpoint, affording magnificent panoramas of the Teme valley and beyond. There is very little to be seen of the Dyke here on the plateau, or on the recently ploughed downhill section. The path descends steeply to Brynorgan and reaches the minor road near Selly Hall, SO266766. (For motorists, this point is 3¾miles (6km) north-west of Knighton, along the northern side of the Teme valley to Skyborry Green. Bear right, and follow the side valley to a crossroad of lanes. Turn sharp right, and descend to the Offa's Dyke path).

Cross directly over to the rocky outcrop, and follow the route over a spur of higher ground to a trackway and then a muddy section to Garbett Hall. From here the Dyke gradually and impressively climbs to the upland of Llanfair Hill, 1,408ft (429m) high. This last section shows the Dyke to its best advantage: the remarkable bank and ditch of Offa's frontier line.

Beyond Llanfair Hill, the section of the Dyke to Springhill is also very impressive, but the right of way follows along the minor road. There is no bus service at Springhill, so unless you have arranged transport, it is necessary either to walk back to Knighton, or continue past Springhill and descend to Newcastle for accommodation, or walk a further 3½ miles (5.6km) down the valley to Clun.

### Lower Spoad
Newcastle, Clun, Shropshire
OS 137, (1in 128), SO257821
From the historic town of Clun, take the B4368 west along the Clun valley to a point just short of Newcastle. From Lower Spoad Farm, the Dyke climbs steeply up the hillside in grand scale to the ridgeway along Spoad Hill. The ascent affords wide views northwards across Clun Forest, a landscape of rounded hills, deep sheltered valleys and wild moorland. From this point, Springhill Farm, the Dyke may be walked to Knighton.

From Bryndrinog Farm, the Dyke climbs out of the valley on the western slopes of Graig Hill, firstly as a tree-covered ridge and a deep western ditch, and then as a broad rounded bank on the crest of the hill. West of Mardu, the Dyke assumes a commanding position across the immediate rising ground, where it runs as a great terrace heading for the saddle between Skeltons Bank and Hergan Hill. Note the size of the earthwork near the ruined cottage of Hergan. At this point, the plan of the Dyke is confusing. It would appear that this junction was reached by two different work gangs who had difficulty in linking up. The Dyke continues gently uphill, where it is well preserved; descends to a stream, and climbs again past Middle Knuck Farm to a lane. From the ridge the impressive earthwork descends the steep hillside into Cwm Ffrydd and the hamlet of Churchtown. The distance from Bryndrinog Farm to Churchtown, following the Dyke, is some 3½ miles (5.6km). The route continues over Edenhope Hill with splendid views of Clun Forest and the Long Mynd; there is a most beautiful section down to the River Usk and on to the Plain of Montgomery, and the town of Montgomery itself. Walking distance from Newcastle-on-Clun is nearly 8 miles (12.6km).

## Wansdyke

Another major linear earthwork constructed in the Dark Ages was Wansdyke, or 'Dyke of the God Woden'. It runs intermittently across central southern England, in an east to west direction. The eastern section straddles the southern edge of the Marlborough Downs, from a point just south of Marlborough to Morgan's Hill near Devizes. The earthwork is particularly impressive as it follows the downland heights in the area of Furze Hill, Tan Hill, Easton Down and Morgan's Hill. It consists of a single bank with a ditch on the north side, and which expertly contours across the rising ground. The barrier was well-designed to give a good field of vision acros the rolling downland northwards. The central section is known to be illusory, but it may have run along the line of the Roman road from Silchester to Bath. There are traces of the western section running across the crest of the hills south of the River Avon, between Bath and Bristol.

The date of its construction is uncertain, but it was probably raised in two stages, with the eastern section built as a Wessex defence line against the advance of the Midland Angles, at the end of the sixth century. The western section may have been constructed as a barrier to halt any further expansion by Penda, King of Mercia, around the early seventh century.

Most of the eastern section of Wansdyke can be walked, on definitive rights of way. It offers a good opportunity to study the impressive bank and ditch, and to enjoy the fine expansive views.

### Access to Wansdyke

**Eastern End**
OS 173, (1in 157), SU127652
Take the minor road from Fyfield, on the A4, to Alton Barnes. Distance from the centre of Marlborough, 5½ miles (8.8km).

**Western End**
OS 173, (1in 157), SU018672
Take the minor road from Quemerford, on the A4, to Devizes. Distance from the centre of Calne, 3¼ miles (5.2km).
Total walking distance between these two points is 7½ miles (12km).

*Wansdyke*

## Other Dark Age Earthworks

### Devil's Ditch
Newmarket, Cambridgeshire
OS 154, (1 in 135), TL620605
This magnificent short defence work was part of a series of earthworks, running parallel to each other to the south-west of Newmarket. It stretches for about 7 miles (11.2km), and the massive proportions of the bank and ditch represents a tremendous feat of labour. In some respects, it is even more impressive than many parts of Offa's Dyke and Wansdyke.

All the earthworks were constructed on a sound tactical basis across a natural routeway from the Midlands to East Anglia. They cleverly made use of the natural features of woodlands, marshes and rivers as an integral part of the defensive system. Some people hold the view that they were raised by the local population to halt the incursions of the Anglo-Saxons in the fifth century. Others believe the earthworks were constructed to separate the two great power-blocs of Mercia and East Anglia.

The Devil's Ditch does not have the same scenic appeal as the undulating course of Offa's Dyke, with its backcloth of high hills and deep valleys. However, visit it in the hard, sharp light of a cold winter's day, and the experience will leave a distinct impression on the mind. A monument to fantastic endeavour centuries ago, it still stands majestically above the surrounding flat land.

**Access** The Devil's Ditch can be walked from Ditton Green to the village of Reach, a distance of 7½ miles (12km). An impressive section can be seen by taking the B1061 south of Newmarket for 2 miles (3.2km) to a point where the earthwork crosses the road. There is limited parking space, with access by footpath to the wooded section on the left, and to the higher section on the right, after passing through a thicket and over the railway line.

*Devil's Ditch*

*Wat's Dyke*

### Wat's Dyke
Ruabon, Clwyd
OS 117, (1 in 118), SJ310435
A clearly defined section of Wat's Dyke, comprising a bank and western ditch, is to be located just ½ mile (800m) east of Ruabon. Leave the A539 at the brow of the hill, and take the footpath on the left-hand side of the road. Descend to a small dip and the line of the earthwork is clearly visible on the rising ground in front. A number of fine trees now grow on the earthen mound.
Other Locations where Wat's Dyke may be seen are:
OS 126, (1 in 118), SJ296315
OS 117, (1 in 109), SJ322458
OS 117, (1 in 109), SJ290616
OS 117, (1 in 109), SJ238676

### Fleam Dyke
Fulbourn, Newmarket, Cambridgeshire
OS 154, (1 in 135), TL548541
Take the A11 south-west of Newmarket for 8 miles (12.8km). The road cuts through the ditch near to a white house on the right-hand side, and its line may be followed by footpath in either direction.

*Duddon Furnace, Cumbria*

*Packhorse way, Upper Dove Valley, crossing the
Derbyshire-Staffordshire boundary*

*Ford and packhorse bridge, Wycoller, a Lancashire weaving village*

*Lead smelting mill flues, Grassington Moor, North Yorkshire*

# CHAPTER SEVEN

# The Middle Ages

## THE BATTLE OF HASTINGS

The story behind this famous event is an intriguing one. The conflict was waged to determine who should succeed to the English throne. In AD1043, Edward the Confessor was crowned king, although England at that time was divided into areas ruled by independent and powerful earls. One of these was Earl Godwin of Wessex, who wielded a considerable influence over Edward, having helped him to secure the throne. A dispute between Godwin and Edward led to the exile of the earl and his family, including his son Harold. Prior to his accession, Edward had spent a lengthy time in exile in Normandy protected by Duke William. When he became king, he continued this friendly contact by welcoming Normans at Court, giving some Normans estates in England, and installing a Norman Archbishop in Canterbury.

The situation suddenly changed, for within a year the House of Godwin returned, and quickly re-established Saxon influence. Edward decided to retire from political life to a monastery, and it was at this point that Godwin's son, Harold, became the power behind the throne. When Harold visited Normandy, he was not allowed to return home immediately, but stayed to assist William in his campaigns in Brittany. It was at this time that Harold swore his famous oath of loyalty to William, a promise which, with its religious overtones, was not taken lightly in those days.

Harold returned to England as Edward was dying. The Saxon leaders saw Harold as the only possible successor, despite other blood claimants. On 5 January 1066, the day after Edward's death, Harold was elected and crowned king. As soon as William heard the news he began to prepare for the invasion of England, even though many of his own advisers thought that the enterprise too difficult. Meanwhile, Harold's difficulties were increasing as King Hardrada of Norway, assisted by Tostig, Harold's brother who had been skulking in Scotland, were preparing to attack York, and the Saxon defenders surrendered. Harold reacted with great speed, and reached Tadcaster with his army in six days. The following day he attacked the enemy camp at Stamford Bridge and won a complete and decisive victory. The Scandinavians needed only a handful of ships to take the survivors home.

Three days later, William landed at Pevensey without opposition, with a well-trained army of eleven thousand men, including cavalry. Harold force-marched his tired army back down to the south of England, picking up some reinforcements of peasant militia on the way to meet this threat. He had a total of six or seven thousand troops; his army contained no cavalry, and only one thousand five hundred of his original force of three thousand trained, mailed soldiers, the housecarls. The rest of his army was composed of land-owning fyrd and peasant conscripts.

Harold's bodyguard of housecarls defended the king and his standard bravely and resolutely throughout that long day, continuously repulsing attacks from archers, infantry and cavalry alike. Indeed, many of the enemy's horses were killed or maimed. Then came the crucial action of the battle, when William ordered his previously ineffective archers to shoot into the air, and not against the Saxon shield wall. It was a lucky move and the gamble paid off. Harold was struck and gravely wounded. In the ensuing confusion with the housecarls trying to protect him, the Norman knights approached and forced gaps through the shield wall. The royal guards were separated and Harold was hacked to pieces. One Norman cut off a leg, another cut off the king's head.

Norman superiority in armour and cavalry won the day, and in just one battle, William had gained a new, larger and richer kingdom.

The main effect of William the Conqueror's victory was that as king he claimed the land of England as his own, which meant that all lands was his absolute property. He took away nearly all the estates of the English lords, and gave them to his own followers, more or less in accordance with the man's importance or the size of his contribution to the invasion. In return for this land, held of the king, the lord was expected to support the king and provide and equip an army from his followers. Even the clergy held positions of the king and were therefore required to give service to the king. The tenant was expected to serve in the king's army for a period in order to discharge their obligations in guard duties or in war. England thus became a prime example of a well-organised, feudal military monarchy, where the ruler was both king and feudal lord controlling both wealth and justice.

## MOTTE AND BAILEY CASTLES

To many of the inhabitants of eleventh and twelfth century England, the castle became the most tangible proof of Norman political and military domination. The earliest castles were those associated with the conquest of southern England, but in the few years following the Battle of Hastings, castles were built at important points all over the country. It is possible to believe that it was the castle which enabled the Normans to establish their authority in England. The defensive strongholds were designed to house a strong minority against rebellions by the local population. This situation was already well-known to the Normans in their own Duchy of Normandy, whereas apart from the fortified Saxon burghs, the English themselves had had no need of castles, The scale and speed of castle building in the years immediately after the Conquest is revealed by the almost casual reference to some fifty castles in the Domesday Book. The distribution of these castles to some extent reflects the numerous uprisings against Norman rule, particularly in the south-west and the Welsh Marches. Castles were often imposed on existing settlements, in such a way that houses were destroyed and land requisitioned. The Norman answer to any unrest or potential rebellion was the construction of a visible sign of their domination. The castle was not only a means of intimidation and a symbol of domination, but a base for active operations, particularly for the armoured cavalry who could instantly respond to any emergency in the surrounding countryside.

In the early days after the Conquest, a form of castle was needed that could be erected easily and quickly, using readily available materials. A large labour force was also required, and for this purpose the local peasantry were conveniently pressed into service. This type of castle has the further advantage of being easily defended by a small number of soldiers.

There are hundreds of castles in Britain, yet of that number, only a few are comparatively well-known. The reason is that many of the early castles were simply ditch and rampart affairs, with a central wooden tower raised on a natural feature or a low man-made mound or motte. The area within the outer ditch and palisaded ramparts would house the garrison's sleeping quarters, a kitchen, stables, workshops, storerooms, perhaps a chapel, and a well. The whole of this defensive area formed the bailey. Later, a wooden tower was added to overlook the bailey, and gradually, in all these motte and bailey castles, the towers were placed on mounds of increasing height. Norman mottes vary from 10ft to 100ft (3m to 30m) in height, and measure between 100ft and 300ft (30m and 90m) in diameter at their base.

The building of an artificial mound had to be carefully prepared if it was to support a timber building, and more importantly, a stone structure. Earth from the deeply excavated ditch was thrown up to form the mound, which would be rammed down level by level and strengthened with courses of clay, stone and rubble. Access to the motte was by means of a wooden trestle bridge incorporating a drawbridge across the ditch, and a steep flight of timber supported steps to the top. The perimeter of the motte platform was defended by a wooden palisade, and a timber tower or 'keep' would be added later, perhaps as high as three storeys. The bailey was also surrounded by a timber palisade with a strongly defended gateway. The arrangement of the defences of these first castles was highly effective. The tower on the motte was a strong point, an elevated fighting platform and look-out post.

The simple motte and bailey castle came to be a common part of the British landscape. Now, these grassy mounds and ditches are scattered over the countryside, their true origin and purpose perhaps not fully recognised by people.

## Motte and Bailey Castles
### Identifying Features

- The remains of early Norman castles usually consist of an artificial mound or 'motte' surrounded by a ditch and bank. The mounds vary from 10ft (3m) to 100ft (30m) in height.

  Originally, the motte would have been defended by a wooden palisade enclosing a wooden tower.
- Adjoining the mound is a lower larger area called the 'bailey'.

  The bailey would have been defended by an earthen bank topped by a wooden stockade, and encircled by a V-Shaped ditch. Entrance to the bailey would have been through a strongly defended wooden gatehouse.
- There are a number of variations of motte and bailey castles, with one, two or even three baileys; each one may be encircled with a ditch and an earthwork.
- Other examples may include motte without baileys, and baileys with one or two mottes.
- In some cases, there are ringworks which may have enclosed a tower but no mound.

## Outstanding Sites

**Yelden**
North Bedfordshire
OS 153, (1in 134), TL013670
A considerable area of earthworks of a mid twelfth-century castle overlie the remains of an earlier settlement. The platform of a rectangular mound measuring 130ft by 90ft (39.5m by 27.5m) overlooks two large baileys and other enclosures. There are a few fragmentary masonry remains.
**Access** The motte and baileys are situated on the east side of the village beyond the River Til.

From the centre of Rushden (Northamptonshire), take the minor road east to Newton Bromswold and continue on towards Yelden. Distance 4¼ miles (6.8km).

**Berkhamsted** (DoE)
Hertfordshire
OS 165, (1in 159), SP995082
The original castle was probably built by Robert de Mortam, and its earliest defences were built of earth and timber. It is likely that all the main parts of the masonry building would have been completed by 1186. In the fourteenth century some repairs were carried out on the great tower, and the outer and curtain walls. During its lifetime, the castle was owned by many famous people, such as Katherine of Aragon, Jane Seymour and Anne Boleyn.

Although the masonry is now very ruinous, the surviving earthworks are excellently preserved. The defences include a ditch and bank encircling the motte, which stands impressively at a height of 45ft (13.7m) with a diameter at the top of 60ft (18.2m), and 180ft (54.6m) at the base. The outer defences surrounding the bailey have been much reduced and levelled, but around the exterior limits of the outer ditch, on the north and east side, is a further earthwork with a number of bastions against the bank.

The motte contains some remains of a circular keep together with a well. Originally the bailey was bounded by a curtain wall with half round towers. The main entrance to the bailey was on the south side, and access was by means of a timber bridge over the moat. This gateway was defended by a stone barbican.

**Access**  The castle is situated on the north side of the River Bulbourne, and adjacent to Berkhamsted railway station.

## Castle Acre
Kings Lynn, Norfolk
OS 132, (1 in 125), TF819151
This very interesting site lies on the higher ground on the south side of the village, and overlooks the pastoral low valley of the River Nar. Originally a Roman site, the impressive remains of an eleventh-century motte and U-shaped bailey cover 15 acres (6ha), and comprise some of the finest earthworks in England, still standing 20ft (6m) high. The line of the Roman road was retained running through the bailey from north to south. Later, the motte was encircled with a revetted shell keep 160ft (48.7m) in diameter. Within the keep was a rectangular building, 50ft by 40ft (15.25m by 12.2m). There are still substantial remains of a fifteenth-century gatehouse.

*Castle Acre*

At the other end of the village lie the substantial remains of the Cluniac Castle Acre Priory, originally founded in 1085 within the castle walls. Many of the Norman features remain, such as the fine west front of the church, with much of one western tower, three west doorways and rich interlaced arcading.

**Access**  The village of Castle Acre is situated 14 miles (22.4km) east of Kings Lynn, via the A1076 and B1145 to Gayton. Bear right along the B1153 to East Walton, and then a by-road to Castle Acre.

## Pleshey
Great Waltham, Chelmsford, Essex
OS 167, (1 in 161), TL665144
The castle covers quite a considerable area and includes a kidney-shaped bailey or dwelling area. The bailey rampart stands some 18ft (5.4m) high and is encompassed by a ditch. The motte, which is situated at the north end of the bailey, is over 60ft (18.2m) in height and is surrounded by a deep ditch. In fact, both the bailey ditch and the motte ditch still contain water.

The bailey was entered by way of a wooden bridge on the north-east side, and the motte was accessible by a causeway. The latter was replaced by a brick bridge in the fifteenth century.

In 1174, William de Mondeville obtained a licence from Henry II to build a castle but by the reign of Elizabeth I the building had become ruinous. The remains were demolished in the seventeenth century and the material reused elsewhere.

The town which grew up outside the castle was enclosed by an earthwork but the settlement never developed beyound its original plan.

**Access**  Pleshey lies on the route of the Essex Way long-distance footpath, and is situated 7 miles (11.2km) north of Chelmsford, via the A130 and a by-road.

## Tomen-y-Rhodwydd

Llandegla, Clywd
OS 116, (1in 108), SJ177516
This motte and bailey castle was well sited to guard the head of the winding Nant-y-Garth Pass leading down into the Vale of Clywd. It was built as the castle of Ial by Owain Gwynedd in 1149. The motte is situated at the western end of the bailey, and the deep ditch is still in outstanding condition. Treegirt, the bailey earthworks are also fairly well preserved. Access may be obtained through a gate on the left-hand side of the minor road to Pentre-celyn, just past the junction with B5431; or, through a gate alongside the A525.

This monument fits perfectly into its rural situation, and is regarded as a text book example of a motte and bailey fortifi-

*Tomen-y-Rhodwydd*

cation. On the one inch map it is mistakenly called Castell yr Adwy.

**Access**    The castle is situated 1 mile (1.6km) south-west of Llandegla and 11½ miles (18.4km) west of Wrexham. It stands by the side of the A525 near to its junction with the B5431.

## Clifford's Tower (DoE)

Tower Street, York, North Yorkshire
OS 105, (1in 97), SE605515
William the Conqueror visited York two years after his victory at Hastings, and built two motte and bailey castles, one in 1068 and another in 1069. The inhabitants of York rebelled against the Normans when a Danish fleet sailed up the Humber, and together they overwhelmed the garrisons. When William received news of this uprising, he sent a punitive expedition north and laid waste great areas of Yorkshire. The Danes took the opportunity to slip away quietly, leaving the local population to starve and die, for the Normans destroyed everything; food supplies, houses, crops, animals and farm implements.

One of the motte and bailey castles was rebuilt on the east bank of the river, but the other on the south bank of the Ouse has disappeared. A wooden tower was placed upon the motte, and in 1109, the Jews of York took refuge there when pursued by the mob. They were not safe because the people set

*Clifford's Tower, York*

fire to the timbers and many inside were burnt to death.

During the mid-thirteenth century work commenced on the building of a stone tower to the design of four overlapping circles, with a doorway protected by a gatehouse. The tower consisted of two storeys, both used as living quarters. In the mid-fourteenth century, the problems of erecting heavy masonry structures on top of earth mottes became apparent. The heavy stonework caused subsidence, and cracks appeared

in the walls of the tower. A considerable sum of money was spent in repairing the damage.

In the sixteenth century, Robert Redhead, the prison custodian, surreptitiously removed the inner masonry face and core of the tower, and sold the materials for profit. He was very successful, removing the turret and battlements of Clifford's Tower, as well as parts of the bailey. Clifford's Tower was so-called in the late sixteenth century, probably from the association with Sir

Robert Clifford and other Lancastrian leaders, whose bodies were hung in chains from the top of the tower in the fourteenth century. In the seventeenth century the interior of the tower was destroyed by a fire which broke out in mysterious circumstances.

When the present prominent motte was excavated, the examination showed that it was not just a raised up heap of soil, but a carefully constructed mound composed of layers of clay, stone and gravel.

## Brinklow Castle

Brinklow, Coventry, Warwickshire
OS 140, (1 in 132), SP438795
The surviving remains here consist of a motte and two bailey site, with the motte in the

eastern sector standing 40ft (12.2m) high and 60ft (18.2m) diameter at the top.
**Access** The earthworks lie at the northern end of the village to the east of the church. Take the minor road to the right beyond

the church and a footpath on the right gives access to the site. The village is situated on the A427, Coventry to Lutterworth road 6¾ miles (10.8km) from the centre of Coventry.

## Anstey Castle

Anstey, Buntingford, Hertforshire
OS 167, (1 in 148), TL404330
The earthworks consist of a splendid motte 30ft (9.2m) high and 220ft (67.0m) in diameter. A wide water-filled ditch and a narrow ditch surrounds the bailey on the north-east side.
**Access** Situated north of the church is the village of Anstey, 4½ miles (7.2km) north-east of Buntingford. Take the B1038 to Hare Street, turn left on to the B1368, and then the next right turn on a by-road to the village.

## Canfield Castle

Great Canfield, Great Dunmow, Essex.
OS 167, (1 in 148), TL595178
The site includes the remains of a fine motte, 45ft (13.7m) high and 275ft (83.8m) in diameter, and two baileys. The ditch was originally flooded from the River Roding. Great Canfield lies 4¼ miles (6.8km) southwest of Great Dunmow via the A130. After ½ mile (800m) turn right on to the B184, and then a by-road to the village. The motte and bailey castle is situated to the east of the church.

## Aslockton Castle

Aslockton, Nottingham, Nottinghamshire
OS 129, (1 in 112), SK744401
The earthworks of this twelfth-century castle consist of a motte with two rectangular baileys and accompanying ditches.
**Access** The village of Aslockton lies just north of the A52, Nottingham to Grantham road, and 3¼ miles (5.2km) east of Bingham. The remains lie on the east side of the village and may be approached by footpath.

## Some Other Sites

**Tretower Castle,** (DoE), Tretower, Crickhowell, Powys.
OS 161, (1 in 141), SO186211

**Bronllys Castle** (DoE), Talgarth, Powys
OS 161, (1 in 141), SO149347

**Longtown Castle**, Longtown, Pontrilas, Hereford and Worcester.
OS 161, (1 in 142), SO321291

**Launceston Castle**, Launceston, Cornwall
OS 201, (1 in 186), SX330846

**Mote of Urr**, Dalbeattie, Dumfries and Galloway Region
OS 84, (1 in 74), NX815646

**Duffus Castle**, Elgin, Grampian Region
OS 28, (1 in 29), NJ189673

*Tretower Castle*

*Bronllys Castle, Talgarth*

## NORMAN AND PLANTAGENET STONE CASTLES

As a result of the Conquest, the population were faced with a number of immediate changes to their way of life, as a relatively small but powerful group controlled the power and resources of the country. William had a triple task: of keeping a conquered people in subjection, of repelling foreign invasion and of asserting his authority over Norman barons. The Normans brought with them a new aristocracy, a new language, almost a new church and a new architecture. William appropriated nearly all the lands of the English lords, and distributed them to his own men who had fought for him and served him well in the campaign. In a feudal society, the king was the only person allowed to regard the land in England as his own property; everyone else became a tenant. In feudal society, lords held land of the king, and therefore owed him a duty. It was a relationship of rights and responsibilities, duties and loyalties: eg the serf had to till the lord's lands, but the lord protected the serf in his castle if necessary. Normally some form of military service would be levied by the king of his tenants. Otherwise there was another system whereby money was paid which then relieved the tenant of the duty to serve. William completed his domination by building or inviting his feudal lords to build stone castles throughout the kingdom. Within a couple of decades, these stone fortresses, symbols of Norman power, were to spring up in virtually every major settlement in the country. They followed exactly the layout of the original motte and bailey earthworks.

The stone keep was a new idea in military thinking, as it combined many of the earlier fortress features into one defensible building. A secure refuge such as this could contain many rooms, and was an obvious necessity in a hostile country. However, as the Normans found to their cost, earthen mounds take a long time to settle and many could not take the weight of heavy stonework. So in many instances the mottes were either dispensed with, or the tall square towers were built on a levelled, or a much reduced earthen mound, or elsewhere in the bailey.

Norman castles came in all sizes, and the design was affected by factors such as the site, the quality of the designer and the resources of men and money available to the lord. The internal arrangements of the keep varied, but the main facilities included the great hall, the lord's hall, kitchens, ante-rooms, stores and guardrooms. Generally, the larger rooms were divided by cross walls, and access to the other floors, varying from between two to four storeys, was by means of narrow winding stairs set within the thickness of the wall, or up spiral staircases built into the corner turrets. Other essential amenities included

*Peveril Castle*

small buttresses. The tower bases are slightly splayed to give greater stability, and the upper corners sometimes contained small towers. The lower part of the keep was usually plain without apertures; any gaps were very narrow indeed for ventilation purposes or as arrow loops. As all openings or recesses were the first targets for siege engineers who aimed to start the process of reducing the keep to a heap of stones, they were usually avoided. The main doorway was usually situated at first floor level, and was approached by a flight of steps set at right angles to the wall. This allowed the entrance to be defended more easily as attackers could not make a direct approach.

For all their outward strength, tower keeps had disadvantages which no buttresses or turrets could eliminate. Once the defenders were inside there was no chance of escape, and the attackers could patiently wait to starve them into surrender. Structurally, the corners of the tower were the weak points, and these could be attacked by mining. A tunnel was dug beneath the foundations of the tower and the stonework supported on wooden props. The cavity was then crammed with inflammable materials — straw, fat, pitch, animal carcasses — and when everything was prepared the mass was ignited. As the flames burnt through the wooden props the support for the entire weight of the masonry was removed, and the corner of the tower would collapse. To combat this weakness, square towers were replaced with rounded ones in the late twelfth or very early thirteenth century. The weaknesses were further overcome in the latter part of the twelfth century by designing and constructing polygonal and circular keeps. Other permanent improvements consisted of the addition of curtain walls around the bailey, and the provision of stone towers and a stone barbican controlling access into the bailey.

Once established, the castles asserted a tremendous influence over the people, and became a common part of the British landscape. They dominated the countryside, situated as they were in towns, on trade routes, at river crossing points, at tops of valleys and on mountain passes. They spread an aura of satisfying calm, and today, dozens of these imposing uninhabited

the chapel, and one or more wells sunk deep within the walls. The great towers were not comfortable places to live in, but gradually separate residential accommodation was added to the other facilities. Some military engineers believed in the alterative design of a shellkeep: that is replacing the timber stockade around the upper surface of the motte by masonry walls, and with buildings, timber originally, set against the inside of the wall. These interior buildings contained the kitchen, the food stores, the buttery, the chapel, the well, the workshop and a meeting hall used for eating and sleeping. In some examples, such as Restormel Castle in Cornwall, the interiors included permanent stone-built accommodation.

The great square stone towers were not exclusive to the twelfth century, and there are earlier examples than this, but the majority are of this period. Once the Normans had time to concentrate on their castle building, they expressed their skill with a magnificent sense of beauty and quality. The outer faces of the fortress were of worked stone, and behind these ashlar blocks was a core of rubble bound with mortar.

The towers follow a basic pattern; they are tall, square or rectangular, with walls strengthened by remains are beautiful monuments to the social and military life of the Middle Ages. In many parts of the country, Norman castles still look down over the centre of towns which owe some of their prosperity and growth to the sense of purpose, skill and organisation of the conquerors. Arundel Castle (TQ018073) looms over the River Arun, Rochester Castle (TQ741685) overshadows the cathedral, Richmond Castle (Yorkshire) (NZ171007) remains impregnable above the quickly flowing Swale, Caerphilly Castle (ST155871) stands majestically formidable behind its moats and Ludlow (SO508746) would just not be the same place without its castle. These facts apply to many sites up and down the land; such are the treasures we have inherited.

William's successor Rufus continued to build stone castles, and the programme was continued from the end of the eleventh century throughout the long reign of Henry I under the direction of the king. This was paid for by the Exchequer, or the cost was shared between the king and a lord, or the king and a bishop. At Rochester in Kent (TQ741685) a magnificent square stone keep was built under Henry I, and is one of the best of its kind to have survived the passage of time. It still possesses an aura of great strength and menace, rising as it does some 125ft (38m), from ground level to the top of the turrets. At Richmond in Yorkshire (NZ171007) a formidable castle was built on a commanding site overlooking the river, and guarding the approach to Swaledale. It was constructed soon after the Conquest, and the great tower was completed by Henry II. At Colchester in Essex (TL999253) the castle was built on the site of a Roman temple, and the remaining structure is the largest basically rectangular keep in Britain; it is an example of how the Normans incorporated Roman building materials.

Quite apart from determining the general features of the landscape, the geological foundation of these islands played an important role in the architectural development of castles and churches, by the use of local building materials. The Normans built in hard gritstone, grey carboniferous limestone, and were easily able to saw through the fine magnesium limestones and the warmcoloured red and sandy brown sandstones. They also used hard chalk (clunch) and square-knapped flints amongst other materials. In south-east England, they shipped over fine creamy limestone from Caen. The stonework was beautifully decorated even in some of the castles, but it is in the churches where we are still able to admire the round arches, massive cylindrical columns and the ornamentation of chevron patterns. There are also fine carvings of

*Peel Castle*

human figures, weird animals, birds and monsters in all kinds of postures and positions.

Castles and churches have mellowed with age and sun, and these fine monuments to Norman skill greatly enhance the visual character of the landscape. Nevertheless, however peaceful the castles may seem to us today, with their broken walls rising above the neatly manicured turf, let us remember that in their day they stood for war.

Henry II (1154-89) was an innovator in military architecture, and although he often employed the idea of the rectangular keep, he occasionally used the circular or polygonal keep, for example, Orford in Suffolk (TM419499). At Dover in Kent (TR326418) he included a curtain wall with square towers and two gatehouses to accompany the square keep. After the civil war of Stephen's reign (1135-54) , when hundreds of unauthorised castles were erected, he levelled many of these illegal fortresses, removed the officers in charge of those he retained, and put in his own custodians. The king enforced the right to occupy and control any castle beyond a certain size, but at the same time he allowed some private castle building, and in some instances even subsidised the cost of improvements and renovations. For example in the late 1150s, he financed a new and powerful castle at Norham in Northumberland (NT906476).

Ideas gleaned from abroad persuaded the military engineers of the day to provide the castle keep with greater protection. To this end, small projecting towers were spaced along the masonry walls surrounding the bailey. This allowed the archers to shoot at any attackers who had managed to reach the foot of the outer defences. Entrances to the bailey, which were normally points of weakness, were usually given extra protection in the form of a strong gatehouse and associated features known as the barbican. In this situation, intruders would find themselves approaching the castle in confined spaces through a passage, and at angles most difficult for fighting. There were openings in the roof known as 'murder holes', where the defenders could shoot, hurl or drop a variety of unpleasant missiles. The sides of the passage also contained apertures for bowmen to shoot through. The gatehouse tower would also be defended perhaps by a drawbridge and portcullis, as well as stout wooden doors at the inside end of the passage. The lifting machinery for the portcullis would he housed in a chamber in an upper part of the gatehouse.

The vast majority of castles were very well equipped to resist attack and very few were carried by storm. In fact, most victories came as a result of starvation or treachery. In a long siege, the success of any defending garrison would at the last count be decided by a plentiful stock of food and a good safe supply of water. Usually the castle wells were strongly defended, being sunk within the walls of tower keeps. Military architects were, naturally, continually seeking to improve the strengths of a castle's defences. At the same time, siege engineers tried to counter these measures by devising machines and equipment to scale, batter, undermine or break down the walls and towers. The art of using these siege machines became increasingly a matter for experts, usually in the form of a specialist class of soldier. There were wheeled machines carrying an iron-tipped battering ram, and the artillery included the petriaria and the mangonel. These catapult engines were able to hurl huge rocks over and against the castle walls. To combat the effects of these stone throwing machines, castles were built with thicker curtain walls and rounded towers to withstand and deflect the missiles.

The trebuchet was a much improved siege engine introduced to England in the thirteenth century. It caused great consternation amongst castle garrisons because of its higher trajectory and more accurate ranging. It was designed to hurl specially cut stones, which could be aimed to clear the curtain and burst with a shrapnel effect against the inner walls and courtyards. It is a fact that the mere sight of this terrifying engine could cause a garrison to surrender forthwith.

During the thirteenth and fourteenth centuries many castles featured greatly strengthened outer defences. Several main towers linked by strong walls were guarded by projecting towers, and the keep remained as the last strong point. In the early fourteenth century, the expertise displayed by the castle builders of Britain reached its full potential in the great concentric castles which were constructed at the beginning of Edward I's campaigns. The outer ring of massive curtain walls incorporated strong towers and a heavily fortified barbican. These defences encircled an inner ring just as strong as the first, built up the slope with its gatehouse set some distance away from the position of the outer barbican. This design allowed the inner ring to overlook and command the outer line. If any enemy penetrated the outer defences, he would be placed in a very dangerous position, in fact in a death trap between the two walls.

With such an ingenious system of defence, it is not surprising to realise that those huge and complex fortifications were often defended successfully by comparatively small garrisons. In the castles of Edward I, the permanent garrisons which manned them averaged around thirty men, which indeed was proof of the strength of these great fortifications.

Two very fine examples of concentric castles are at Caerphilly, Mid Glamorgan (ST155871), a magnificent monument with its incredible system of walls, towers, moats, dams and lakes, which is regarded as one of the grandest castles in Britain; and Beaumaris in Anglesey (SH607763), a copybook example of the concentric castle, the ultimate in defensive building.

With the increasing sophistication of castle technology, there was a greater demand for expert craftsmen in wood, metal and stone. They were highly regarded, eagerly sought after and increasingly well-paid for their work. Their prestige was such that they often received gifts of fine clothes, timber, property and land. Further,

the nobility required greater comfort in their cold, cheerless and uncomfortable castles. Henry III in particular loved comfort and had a great concern for hygiene. Glass began to appear in the windows instead of shutters, fireplaces were installed in most of the rooms, and the standard of bathroom arrangements were being improved. The lavatories (privies or garderobes) began to be placed at the end of the a passage in the thickness of the wall, behind double doors, or as far away as possible on account of the smell. In some instances they were sited over the moat or a stream, and some castles had a special garderobe tower where the privies were grouped together. Normally, the waste was discharged into deep pits and the person responsible for cleaning them out was, understandably, well paid.

Now, many of our stone castles are still the focal point in a village, town or city; not as the home of the lord of the manor imposing a powerful military presence over the local population, but as a splendidly romantic tourist attraction. However, in order to gain the most from a visit, it is necessary to understand something of their history and design, and maybe try to judge their effectiveness or limitations as a fortress. Walk the battlements and creep along the dark uneven floored passage-ways inside the curtain walls. Try to imagine your role as a defender at the top of a narrow spiral stairway. Ponder on whether a bowman could accurately direct his arrows from such narrow arrow loops. It helps to put one's thoughts and ideas into perspective.

---

### Tower Keeps
### Identifying Features

- These impressive towers are tall, square or rectangular structures with exceptionally thick walls.
- The outer walls are constructed of ashlar blocks of stone, with an interior core of rubble bound with mortar.
- The tower bases are slightly splayed to give greater stablity.
- The walls are often strengthened with shallow buttresses and projecting corners rising to small towers.

- The main entrance is usually situated at first floor level by means of external stairs. Later, this entrance was protected by a forebuilding.
- The building was usually from two to four storeys high.
- The normal layout consisted of a large hall, private apartments, a chapel, a kitchen, service rooms, defences, mural passages, straight or spiral staircases, fireplaces, a deep well and garderobes (latrines).

## Examples of Norman Castles

**Rochester Castle** (DoE)
Rochester, Kent
OS 178, (1in 172), TQ742686
This splendid example of a large square Norman keep was built in 1127 by the Archbishop of Canterbury, with the consent of Henry I. It stands close to an important crossing point of the River Medway. The outer defences encircling the keep, notably on the west side, once stood 22ft (6.8m) in height, thicker at the base and narrowing at the top. The other surviving portions of curtain wall and towers date from the time of Henry III and Edward III. The magnificent keep that dominates the site is built of Kentish ragstone, faced with creamy Caen limestone. The keep is 70ft (21.2m) square, rising to 125ft (38m) to the top of the turrets. The walls are 12ft (3.7m) thick at the base, tapering slightly towards the top. This thickness allowed the castle designer to include a number of rooms and garderobes into the walls.

Internally, the keep was divided into three storeys, in which the second floor served as the private apartments, having a gallery round it level with the windows. The third floor included a fine chapel. The interior cross-wall with central pilasters, or shallow piers, contains a well shaft which served every floor in the building. The basement contained wall chambers in the west and north angles of the tower, and the eastern angle carries a spiral stairway to all floors. On the next floor an additional spiral stair rises in the western angle to all the upper floors. The entrance to the keep, on the first floor, was reached by a flight of steps to the fore-building on the north side. The entrance from the forebuilding is decorated with a chevron pattern, and backed by a portcullis slot and bar-hole.

The castle saw action on a number of occasions. It was seized by the rebel barons in 1215, who defended it resolutely against the mercenaries of King John. During the siege, the south-east corner of the keep was mined and in due course collapsed. It was rebuilt as a round tower, and later Edward III spent large sums of money restoring the entire building. The castle is now under the protection of the Department of the Environment.
**Access** The castle is situated between the cathedral and the river, and just south of the A2, Rochester Bridge. There are parking facilities on the Esplanade near to the castle.

**Rothesay Castle** (DoE)
Rothesay, Isle of Bute, Strathclyde Region
OS 63, (1in 59), NS088646
The castle was in existence in the first part of the thirteenth century, when it was stormed and captured by the Norsemen at least on two occasions. Later, the Scots and English each took possession on various occasions, adding little bits on to the existing fabric.

The great circular curtain wall (the only existing shell-keep in Scotland) and four round towers were all built of sandstone ashlar. The entrance is on the north side, and leads through the great tower, the donjon, erected by James IV and James V. This strong structure, built of whinstone rubble, also has an attached square tower on the western side. The function of this forework was twofold, to provide a strongly fortified gatehouse and a suite of state apartments. The long vaulted entrance passage leads to the pointed arch of the older gatehouse with a slot for the portcullis. Leading off the passage there are a porter's lodge and a guard room, together with a narrow stairway to the floor above. This contains the great hall, which has been accurately and carefully restored. Above this was a second floor forming the private apartments.

The thirteenth-century curtain walls were extended using whinstone, which sealed in the original battlements. They are now some 30ft (9m) high. The walls and the north-west tower are in a good state of preservation. The interior enclosure contains a well, the roofless shell of a sixteenth-century chapel and the foundation lines of other buildings. The whole shell keep is surrounded by a deep water-moat.
**Access** By ferry (vehicle and passenger), from Wemyss Bay, crossing time, 30 minutes. The castle is situated only a short distance from Rothesay Pier.

## Richmond Castle (DoE)

Richmond, North Yorkshire
OS 92, (1in 91), NZ174006
This large and powerful castle is
dramatically situated on high
land dominating the town and
overlooking the River Swale.
The fortress was part of the early
building programme of castle
building in England, and was
built soon after the Conquest by
Alan the Red in 1071. The
earliest masonry is the curtain
wall of shale blocks on the east
and west sides. The southern
part of the west wall has a
roundheaded archway flanked
by shallow buttresses. The
eastern curtain wall formerly
had four projecting towers (one
has almost collapsed). The
original gateway was converted
into a tower keep, and a new
gateway, defended by a
portcullis, was made through the
curtain wall beside it. The keep,
attributed to Earl Conan (1146-
71), was constructed of worked
stone. The ground floor was lit
by a narrow loop in the east and
west walls, and the floor above
was supported by a central
column. Entry to the keep was
made at first floor level from the
rampart wall by two square-
headed doorways. The doorway
on the east side gave access to a
wall stair rising to the second

*Richmond Castle*

floor. Above the third floor, the
tower keep has narrow crenels
and corner turrets rising above
them.

Situated in the south-east
corner of the bailey is Scolland's
Hall, an eleventh-century
building, the main floor of which
was entered by a wooden stair
on a rubble base. The ground
floor was used for storage
purposes, and the building was
extended westwards in the
twelfth century. At this time, the
curtain wall was extended round
the cliff edge above the River
Swale.

The castle formed part of the
Honour of Richmond, which

included all the country south of
the River Tees, including the
area drained by the River Swale
and Ure to the watershed of
Rivers the Nidd and Wharfe.
The castle seemed to have a
peaceful existence, being a little
off the beaten track as far as any
serious action was concerned. Its
one claim to fame was that it
served as a royal prison for a
while, holding William the Lion,
King of Scotland.

**Access** The castle is situated
in the centre of the town at the
southern end of the market
square.

## Hedingham Castle

Castle Hedingham, Halstead,
Essex
OS 155, (1in 149), TL788359
This magnificent square
Norman keep was built about
1140, with square blocks of stone
on a natural motte. The
stonework rises to a height of
130ft (39.5m) to the top of the
towers. At the base the walls are
12ft (3.7m) thick, and the lower
sections of the wall are only

pierced by small arrow loops.
The main entrance, which has
dog-tooth decoration, is on the
first floor, and the whole
building consists of a basement
and three separate storeys.
There is another entrance on the
west side, but this access is
protected by an outside
staircase. The main entrance
was guarded by a portcullis and
a small fortified outer tower of
barbican. The four corner

turrets project slightly from the
main wall, within the thickness
of which were housed small
rooms, fireplaces and
garderobes. On the outside of
the keep a shallow buttress
supported the middle section of
each wall. It is likely that the
stables, kitchens and other
domestic buildings would have
been situated in the keep.

The great keep dominates the
village, and looks down on its

houses and Norman church as they huddle beneath the castle mound. The stronghold was once the home of the powerful De Vere family, the Earls of Oxford, who experienced varying fortunes throughout their long and sometimes turbulent association with the kings of England.

### Castle Rising (DoE)
Castle Rising, Norfolk
OS 132, (1in 124), TF666246
The keep, one of the largest in England, was built in 1150 on the site of a Roman fort. It was enclosed by massive earthworks of banks and ditches and extending for some 12 acres (4.8ha), comprising a large inner bailey and two subsidiary enclosures, one to the east and one to the west. The main enclosure is encircled by a ditch outside the earthen banks, which today still rise to a height of 60ft (18.0m) from the bottom of the ditch. The keep is faced with Barnack limestone, a noted building stone from north Cambridgeshire which was in great demand in medieval England. It is 50ft (15.2m) high, rectangular in shape, and measures 78ft (24m) by 68ft (20.4m), with three shallow buttresses on each of the long sides. The main entrance is up a splendid flight of stone steps from the south front of the forebuilding, which is attached to the east side of the keep. At one time, a doorway blocked the steps half-way; note the drawbar holes at the sides and the murderhole above. The steps lead into a small room on the first floor where the great hall, the great chamber, the chapel, kitchen and other apartments were situated. At a later date the fine entrance from this vestibule to the state rooms were blocked by the building of a fireplace. Access to the main part of the keep is by a small doorway in the corner, but because the roof and the floors of the Great Hall and Great Chamber have gone, a timber gallery has been erected at the east end for viewing purposes. Access to the upper rooms over the vestibule and chapel is by a winding staircase, and in the case of the latter, by continuing along a narrow passage in the thickness of the wall. The room over the chapel no longer has a floor, so it is only possible to look across it.

**Access**   If approaching from Hunstanton, the castle lies on the south side of the village of Castle Rising, just west of the A149. Or from the centre of King's Lynn, take the A1078 to South Woorton, turn left onto a by-road across Ling Common. The site is signposted and there are good parking facilities. Distance 4 miles (6.4km).

**Access**   The castle is situated on the north side of the village of Castle Hedingham, 4¼ miles (6.8km) north of Halstead, via the A604 and the B1058.

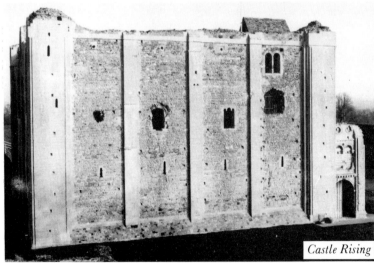
*Castle Rising*

### Restormel Castle (DoE)
Lostwithiel, Cornwall
OS 200, (1in 186), SX104614
The outstanding feature of this castle is its well-preserved shell keep wall, built of local slate and stone. The radius of the shell is almost a true circle, 110ft (33.5m) in diameter and this occupies a motte 125ft (38m) in diameter. Restormel was founded about 1100, although it probably started life earlier with a timber palisade on top of the mound. These wooden defences were strenghened by the building of a simple square gatehouse on the south-west side, followed by a wall of stone replacing the palisades. The timber buildings around the interior rim of the wall, were also replaced by fine stone apartments between 1272 and

THE MIDDLE AGES 223

1299, as well as the construction of a square tower on the eastern side. An outwork or barbican was attached to the gatehouse, and on either side steps led to the first floor rooms and on to the rampart walk. A stroll around the wall walk affords fine views across the River Fowey and the surrounding countryside. The castle apartments, which ranged round the interior wall, consisted of the great hall, state rooms, kitchen, guardroom, stables and storerooms. A well was located in the centre of the courtyard.

**Access** On approaching Lostwithiel from the east on the A390, keep on the main road as it swings in a loop to cross the River Fowey. Then take the next turn right along the minor road to Restormel. Distance from Lostwithiel, 1 mile (1.6km).

*Hermitage Castle*

*Tantallon Castle*

*Warkworth Castle*

**Some Other Castle Sites**
**Orford Castle** (DoE), Orford, Suffolk, OS 169, (1in 150), TM419499
**Dover Castle** (DoE), Dover, Kent
OS 179, (1in 173), TR326416
**Conisbrough Castle** (DoE), Conisbrough, South Yorkshire
OS 111, (1in 103), SK515989
**Kenilworth Castle** (DoE), Kenilworth, Warwickshire
OS 140, (1in 131), SP287723
**Corfe Castle,** Swanage, Dorest
OS 195, (1in 179), SY959823
**White Castle** (DoE), Near Abergavenny, Gwent
OS 161, (1in 142), SO380168
**Kidwelly Castle** (DoE), Kidwelly, Dyfed
OS 159, (1in 152), SN409071
**Chepstow Castle** (DoE), Chepstow, Gwent
OS 162, (1in 155), ST533941
**Clun Castle,** Clun, Craven Arms, Shropshire
OS 137, (1in 129), SO298809

**Warkworth Castle** (DoE), Warkworth, Amble, Northumberland
OS 81, (1in 71), NU247057
**Bodiam Castle** (NT), Bodiam, East Sussex
OS 188, (1in 184), TQ785256
**Hermitage Castle** (DoE), Newcastleton, Borders Region
OS 79, (1in 69), NY497960
**Ludlow Castle,** Ludlow, Shropshire
OS 137, (1in 129), SO508746
**Dirleton Castle** (DoE), Dirleton, North Berwick, Lothian Region
OS 66, (1in 63), NT596851
**Tantallon Castle** (DoE), North Berwick, Lothian Region
OS 67, (1in 63), NT596851
**Huntly Castle** (DoE), Huntly, Grampian Region
OS 29, (1in 30), NJ532407
**Muness Castle** (DoE), Muness, Uyeasound, Isle of Unst, Shetland Isles
OS 1, (1in 1), HP629012

## THE WELSH CASTLES OF EDWARD I

While Henry III was engaged in a civil war with his barons in 1255, the grandson of Llywelyn the Great, Llywelyn ap Gruffydd, seized the opportunity to side with the warring lords against the king. At the end of the conflict, Henry recognised Llywelyn as Prince of Wales, providing he made an annual payment to the Exchequer. In the prevailing atmosphere of mistrust, Llywelyn would not meet the king and swear allegiance to him, and eventually threatened that unless certain disputes were settled he would stop the annual payments. One of the problems was that Llywelyn's brother Dafydd, always an opportunist, had fled to England with all his supporters. In order to settle the matter the king decided in 1277 to attack Llywelyn in his mountain stronghold of Snowdonia. Edward advanced along the North Wales coast, having first established fortified bases at Flint and Rhuddlan. His strategy was to reach Conwy and blockade the Isle of Anglesey in order to prevent Llywelyn from gathering in the corn harvest. To complete a pincer movement, Edward's forces advanced from the south and established bases at Builth and Aberystwyth. Once his food supplies were cut off, and his means of escape barred, the Prince of Wales was forced to sue for peace.

Dafydd was rewarded with part of his brother's mountain kingdom in return for his help in he campaign. Even so, he was not satisfied, and changing sides once more, set out to stir up trouble by playing on the grievances of his countrymen who had suffered most at the hands of the English. In 1282, Dafydd attacked and captured the castle of Hawarden. This action placed Llywelyn in the difficult position of having to decide whether or not to heed the rallying call of his untrustworthy brother. After much deliberation, Llywelyn agreed to support the rebellion and became the recognised leader of a united cause. The Welsh soon joined battle with the English garrisons, easily captured the castle of Aberystwyth in the west, and pushed back the intruders in the surrounding area to the south.

Once more Edward sent his troops into North Wales, but on this occasion they met with much stronger opposition. In fact, the Welsh achieved a number of minor victories, including the defeat of an English force trying to cross the Menai Strait from Anglesey. In order not to be caught in a trap again, Llywelyn escaped from the encircling English forces in Snowdonia and travelled south, but was killed in a minor skirmish at Cilmeri near Builth in December 1282. His death proved a decisive factor, and without their beloved leader, who had left no heir to follow, all Welsh resistance ended. The turn-coat Dafydd was hunted down and captured, having been betrayed by his own countrymen, and subsequently tried and executed at Shrewsbury. This brought to an end to the rule of the Welsh princes.

Edward I decided to resolve the Welsh problem once and for all by dividing the principality of Gwynedd into the separate areas of Merioneth, Anglesey, Caernarfon and Flint. Each new district was to be controlled from one of the new fortresses along the coast, at Harlech, Caernarfon, Conwy and the former Welsh castle of Criccieth. The king's plan for the settlement of Wales was that every castle built would have a town borough attached to it. In time, these towns played an important part in attracting English merchants and traders to come and settle safely, protected behind their walls.

The Welsh campaigns and the construction of these magnificent fortresses proved to be a very expensive business. The strength of Edward's army depended on the normal feudal method of short-term military service and the considerable use of mercenary soldiers. Another interesting fact at this time was the size of the workforce in the castle building programme, which was a combination of paid and conscripted labour gathered in from most of the English shires.

As the construction work was financed by the Crown, a wealth of fascinating information was carefully recorded, concerning the amount of money spent on materials, when and how it was spent, the amount of wages paid out and even the names of the major engineers and craftsmen. These facts are preserved at the Public Record Office, and present a vivid picture of the life and work of Edward's castle builders. The man in charge of the design of the castles and their construction was a master mason from Savoy named Master James of St George. He was highly regarded by Edward I, who had seen examples of his work while on a visit to that part of Europe. So it is understandable that there are some examples of similar architectural details to be found in the castles of Savoy and Master James's Welsh fortresses. Look for the holes in the Watch Tower at Conwy, signifying the use of spiralled scaffolding in the raising of a round tower. Note also the decoration of the battlements at Conwy with triple stone pinnacles, and the design of the latrine shafts at Rhuddlan and Harlech. In the latter, this feature may be recognised as a small projecting buttress on the curtain wall adjoining the north-west tower.

While the work was proceeding at Harlech,

Caernarfon and Conwy, a decision was taken to build the castle of Beaumaris on the island of Anglesey. However, due to the extra expense involved in the repair of other Welsh castles, like Criccieth and Aberystwyth, there was a delay in the Beaumaris project. Later, in the autumn of 1294, circumstances warranted a revival of the idea, as the Welsh population of Arfon rebelled against compulsory military service. The town of Caernarfon was attacked, the new town wall severely damaged, and once inside the moat the rebels put to the torch everything that would burn. The rising was put down in the following year, and work quickly commenced to rebuild the shattered defences. It was then decided to build the new town and castle of Beaumaris. As well as strengthening the English hold on North Wales, the base was also well-suited to become a centre of administration and trade.

## Concentric Castles
## Identifying Features

The design of concentric castles may have been inspired by the castle at Caerphilly. Edward I's castles were based on the combination of the following elements:
• The replacement of the powerful keep by an inner rectangular or polygonal defensive wall interrupted by symmetrically-placed flanking towers.
• An outer and lower curtain wall, also

possibly with towers, making two defensive lines one inside the other.
• The above combination produced a high inner ward dominating a low outer enclosure.
• The development of a massively powerful gatehouse combining the advantages of good accommodation with all the latest defensive technology. The gatehouse was usually sited on the castle's weakest side.

## Outstanding Sites

**Beaumaris Castle** (DoE), Beaumaris, Anglesey, Gwynedd OS 115, (1in 106), SH607763 Beaumaris was the last of the series designed by Edward's master mason James of St George to control the rebellious population of North Wales. The construction work begun in 1295, continued with periods of great activity and other times with very little or no progress, over an interval of thirty-five years. Many parts of the castle,

such as the north and south gatehouses and the curtain towers, were only partially completed.

Like Harlech, Beaumaris was built on the concentric plan, the concept of which was to allow a defending force to retire from one strong point to the next, before, in extreme cases, making a final stand at the heart of the castle. At Beaumaris, the first obstacle was the moat defended by an eight-sided outer curtain

wall with twelve flanking battlemented towers. Once across the moat the attackers would encounter a barbican on the south side, defended by a shooting platform, and also find themselves in a very dangerous position in the dead ground of the outer ward. They would be overlooked by the outer and inner curtain walls and from the gatehouse towers. This would allow the defenders on both walls to combine their firepower upon the enemy. Once through the barbican, the gatehouse provided many surprises, such as portcullises, doors, spy-holes and murder holes. Finally, the inner ward was overlooked by two twin-towered gateways, and the inner curtain wall 36ft (10.8) high, with four corner towers and two mid-wall towers.

The Beaumaris gatehouses were never fully completed, although more work was done on the northern one which had some first-floor accommodation. The inner curtain walls are pierced by long mural passages at first-floor level, but can only be reached today by circular stairways from the southern corners of the inner ward. The

chapel is also sited at first-floor level in the tower on the east side of the inner ward.

Compared with other castles, this beautiful fortress must come high in the ranking of the 'top ten' castles in Britain, and is the finest of the concentric castles. Although it is dwarfed in size alongside others, regarded as being sited in a weak position by military experts, and perhaps visually less impressive than the other Edward I castles, this brilliantly designed structure is the perfect textbook example to study. Beaumaris Castle saw very little action; it never had to withstand sieges of the kind which took place at Harlech. During the English Civil War it was held for the king, but the garrison surrendered to Parliament in 1646.

**Access** The castle lies 4 miles (6.4km) north-east of Menai Bridge. Bear right along the A545 to Beaumaris, and proceed along Castle Street to the far end of the town. There are parking facilities close by.

*Beaumaris Castle, North Gatehouse*

**Harlech Castle** (DoE),
Harlech, Gwynedd
OS 124, (1in 116), SH581312
The magnificent setting of this castle, situated on a crag overlooking Tremadoc Bay, with the long line of the Lleyn peninsula and the mountains of Snowdonia to the north, has always attracted attention and will continue to do so. The castle, built between 1285 and 1291, was supervised by Edward I's master designer, James of St George. His skill was such that every wall, arrow loop, tower and gateway was sited for maximum effect, even though he

must have been fully occupied with many other castle-building projects at the time.

Throughout history Harlech Castle has featured in a number of stirring events, being besieged by Prince Madog in 1294 and attacked by Owain Glyndwr who induced the castle to surrender in 1404. Four years later, it was captured by an English army under Gilbert Talbot. In the Wars of the Roses, it was held for the Lancastrians by Dafydd ap Ieuan, who was the last commander to surrender to the Yorkists in 1468. From then on,

the castle gradually decayed, but woke from its ruinous slumbers on its resolute defence by supporters of King Charles I. An order for its demolition was given on its surrender to the Parliamentarians after a long siege, but fortunately for posterity this was never carried out.

On the landward side the castle is defended by a rock-cut ditch that surrounds the outer curtain wall on the eastern and southern sides. The other sides are protected by the precipitous nature of the land. The most imposing feature of Harlech is

*Harlech Castle*

the immensely powerful gatehouse that sits astride the eastern inner wall. The entrance passage-way was defended by portcullises, doors with draw-bars and sets of murder holes. The ground floor area served as guardrooms and storerooms, and the upper storeys of the gatehouses were used as living accommodation for the Constable and for important visitors. The inner ward of the castle has a tower in each corner, and the foundations of various buildings such as halls, kitchen, chapel, and storerooms ranged round the wall. Visitors may walk around the walls for superb views of the surrounding countryside. The castle has a water gate at the base of the crag which was reached by a defended pathway. At one time ships could probably sail close in to the sandflats, but it is doubtful if Harlech possessed a harbour. Today, the sea has retreated over $\frac{1}{2}$ mile (800m) away leaving an area of sand dunes and reclaimed land.

**Access** The centre of the village has limited parking space, but if approaching on the A496 which passes below the castle, there are parking facilities near to the swimming pool and close to the station.

## Other Castle Sites

**Conwy Castle** (DoE), Conwy, Gwynedd
OS 115, (1in 107), SH781777
**Caernarfon Castle** (DoE), Caernarfon, Gwynedd
OS 115, (1in 106), SH477626
Both Conwy and Caernarfon

Castles were different in layout from other Welsh castles, because they were built on narrow outcrops of rock whose shape dictated a linear building plan.
**Rhuddlan Castle** (DoE),

Rhuddlan , Clwyd
OS 116, (1in 108), SJ024779
**Flint Castle** (DoE), Flint, Clwyd
OS 117, (1in 108), SJ247733
Flint Castle was built to an unusual plan. There was a

*Conwy Castle*

*Rhuddlan Castle*

square arrangement with three corner towers, but the fourth tower was much larger and offset from the other corner.

**Aberystwyth Castle,**
Aberystwyth, Dyfed
OS 135, (1in 127), SN579816
Concentric castle with gatehouse but there are few and scattered remains. Destroyed by the Parliamentary forces in 1646, and its stone robbed by the local inhabitants.

**Forerunner of Edward I's Welsh Castles**
**Caerphilly Castle,** Caerphilly, Mid Glamorgan
OS 171, (1in 154), ST155871

*Caerphilly Castle*

## THE LANDSCAPE OF MEDIEVAL ENGLAND

The landscape, as we know it, of fields, farms and villages began to take shape well before the arrival of the Normans. Previously the Romans had succeeded in making improvements in farming methods with the introduction of a plough which had a much more effective performance. The implement was fitted with a vertical iron knife or coulter which cut into the turf and was capable of deeper penetration. Positioned behind the coulter was the share which sliced into the soil horizontally. Finally, the ploughed strip of earth was turned and inverted by a curved wooden mould. Improvements on this plough greatly increased the efficiency of ploughing throughout the Middle Ages, particularly on heavy clay lands. The Saxons further improved existing farming methods, and created a method of village farming which was to survive in a great number of parishes for a thousand years. The success of village farming also brought problems for the Saxons who were faced with the need to produce much more food for an increasing population. Their open-field system probably consisted of two large fields, one on each side of the village. Each field covered perhaps a small number of acres initally, but as families increased, so more woodland was cleared and added to the settlement area. Crops already cultivated in Britain included wheat, barley, oats, and rye, together with peas, beans, turnips and flax.

Apart from the well-settled eastern regions, with its numerous hamlets and open-field systems of agriculture, the land conquered by William had been slowly developed throughout the previous centuries. By 1066, the enormous task of clearing the forests for farmland was being undertaken in varying degrees in different parts of the country. However, the general appearance of the landscape in Norman England would still have been that of a heavily wooded island, marked by moorland, heathland, fenland, wide clearings and scattered settlements. The inhabitants of these tiny rural communities spent all the hours of daylight tilling their small fields and tending their flocks and herds. Their dwellings can simply be described as one-roomed shacks that provided accommodation for both humans and animals.

There is no doubt that the growing population reclaimed large tracts of land from the natural woodland cover of oak, ash and beech by the simple process of burning the trees, grubbing out the roots and clearing the undergrowth. There are place-names that suggest that an area for settlement use was reclaimed by this method, eg Brentwood in Essex (TQ597940) means 'burnt wood'. Swithland on the edge of Charnwood Forest in Leicestershire (SK550131) means 'land cleared by burning'. The pattern of narrow lanes and paths winding from one isolated farmstead to another, and the frequent patches of woodland are all characteristic of an area of countryside enclosed direct from former forest and colonised in the twelfth and thirteenth centuries. A good example of this countryside pattern today is the area of higher land between the valleys of the River Stort and River Ash on the Hertfordshire-Essex border. Here there are numerous 'Greens' and the many farms are named after medieval owners or occupiers, eg Allen's Green (TL455168). The river valleys contain long-established Saxon settlements, such as Hadham, Widford and Harlow.

Evidence from a careful study of 1:25,000 Ordnance Survey maps will show that each parish tried to incorporate a fair balance of resources, such as meadow land or marsh land by a stream or river, arable land containing the plough strips and poorer land which occupied the upper slopes and upper reaches of heathland, moorland and the tops of hills. Not all the common and waste land was entirely useless for thousands of acres were common pasture vital to the farming economy. An area like Ashdown Forest in East Sussex (TQ465305) gave common grazing rights for animals for many of the surrounding parishes, and also rights for furze cutting, bracken for litter and windfall wood. An area of moorland or heathland with a good water supply was a meeting place of several parishes. Each parish was given a share of a particularly vital drinking place for the animals in a dry, sandy area for example: Ring Mere in the Breckland of south Norfolk (TL910879).

In the South-West and in the North of England the limit of cultivation was similarly being pushed higher up the hillsides. Little pastoral farms were being established among the bracken and rocks, and their names also illustrate the description of the sites, eg Fernacre, on Bodmin Moor in Cornwall (SX151798), means 'bracken land'. On the eastern slopes of the Eden Valley in Cumbria, the church in the hamlet of Milburn (NY654293) shows examples of Norman work. A few miles to the south lies Murton (NY728216) or 'moor-tun', and close by to this settlement is the site of a single farmstead, Brackenthwaite (NY710225) or 'bracken clearing'. All these are good examples of settlements established as the result of moorland reclamation in the twelfth century.

In the heart of the Lake District the heads of the valleys were colonised, and the limit of cultivation is still clearly identifiable today. Note the typical medieval field pattern of small irregular fields and the winding access trackways in upper Wasdale (NY190088). On the uplands of the Yorkshire Dales the boundaries between the great monastic granges were marked out across the fells with mile after mile of dry-stone walling. These walls were skilfully built without any mortar; the material was readily available as a result of countless hours of back-breaking toil by the medieval farmers who cleared the stones from the moorland pastures.

In the North of England and in Scotland, the area of good plough-land was strictly limited owing to the thin, sour and waterlogged nature of the soils. Here a rundale, or infield-outfield system was practised. The infield was a carefully selected patch of relatively dry ground close to the settlement. The site of the dwelling was probably determined by the nature of the soil. The land was then maintained in more or less permanent cultivation by the manure supplied by the livestock. The plots were usually small, and were probably tilled by the use of a lighter short wooden plough. Outfield cultivation was the exploitation of heavily grazed land, often some distance from the farmstead. In time the land became too tough to plough with the type of plough available.

After the Conquest much was left unchanged; the Saxon boundaries remained, and the villages and their territories continued slowly to expand. It took many centuries for villages to reach their limits, and for the fields to attain their maximum extent, probably until about the end of the thirteenth century or the beginning of the fourteenth century. Many of the village churches that stand today were established and altered by Norman knights and clergy. Villages grew more thickly in some parts than in others; in Leicester-shire and Lincolnshire the settlements were in some cases often less than 2 miles (3.2km) apart; but in Essex, Devon and Cornwall scattered hamlets and farmsteads were linked by narrow meandering lanes, track and pathways separated by patches of woodland. The growth and prosperity of villages depended on the intensive and productive agriculture practised in the open field strip system, and backed by a high level of community co-operation.

The whole unit of an open field was made up of blocks of varying shapes and sizes, and could total several hundred strips. The strips varied in area, length and breadth, depending on the nature of the soil and the topgraphy. The ploughing of the long narrow strips roughly 220yd (200m) long, a furlong or a 'furrow long' with a particular plough shifted the soil to the middle of the strip so forming a ridge, hence the description of this type of farming as ridge and furrow. Each strip was separated from its neighbour by an unploughed grass margin. The plough was pulled by a number of oxen, and because of its length the plough team began to turn before the end of the ridge. These manoeuvres formed a ridge that was not in a straight line but had the shape of a shallow reversed 'S'.

These raised curving ridge patterns of open

*Medieval strip fields, Tissington*

field strip farming are still a common sight in the English countryside, even though many pastures were intensively ploughed during World War II. In the Midlands particularly, these ancient ridges and furrows, seemingly frozen for ever, are visible under their carpet of grass. We can also see the kind of landscape the open field system produced today at Laxton, Nottinghamshire (SK 724670). Here a patchwork strip pattern of medieval fields survives round the village — but who knows for how long? The field patterns around the village of Combe Martin, Devon (SS595465) clearly show that the settlement once had open fields laid out in strips; these plots have now been enclosed with hedges. There are also much changed forms of strip farming at Braunton in Devon, Haxey in Lincolnshire, and near to Soham in Cambridgeshire.

Even many areas which nowadays are usually regarded as being unsuitable for growing crops largely due to their altitude or harsh weather conditions once supported strip fields of vegetables or cereals to feed the villagers; for example Tissington in the Peak District, a pretty village best known for the custom of well dressing, has outstanding strip fields north of the village and west of the A515 Ashbourne to Buxton road (SK175526 and 168520).

Many of the villages prospered and grew into market towns, which played an important part in the growth of the country's economy. Much of the pattern of the open fields has been erased by ploughing and overlaid by hedging and enclosure. Despite these changes, in certain light conditions when the sun is at a low angle, these ancient plough ridges may be clearly seen. Many farmsteads now on village streets probably stand on sites first occupied before the Norman Conquest.

## THE NORMANS IN IRELAND

In 1169, the Normans invaded Ireland and secured effective control in the east, south-east and south of the island. They constructed simple motte and bailey castles with enclosures for retainers and stock, which were soon followed by stone structures. Carrickfergus Castle in County Antrim (J414873) was magnificently sited on an outcrop of dark basalt, originally protected on all sides except the north by the sea. This castle, constructed between 1180 and 1204, was an important base for the Anglo-Norman hold on Ulster. The Normans took over existing towns and founded new ones, particularly in the south-east of Ireland. As in England, the castle was a source of military strength, and the local population was oppressed not only by the Normans, but by the rivalry and subsequent operations of the Irish lords. The people enjoyed little protection against raid or reprisal from either side.

Wherever the Normans colonised they introduced the open field system of agriculture known to them in England and Normandy. The arable land was divided into several great fields with a rotational programme of crops — winter, spring and fallow. Sheep rearing was important; the animals were grazed on the commons and waste land. The open fields were divided into strips, and the land was shared out equally amongst the freeholders and tenants. An active trade was carried out between the surrounding countryside and the market in the nearby town. However, the Normans failed to make much impression on the west of Ireland, and, were unable permanently to secure all the land they had conquered. They were frequently harassed by the Irish chieftains who emerged from the forests, boglands and mountains, and were able to return to their hideouts under cover of the inevitable mists and rain.

Anglo-Norman settlement was most successful in the almost bog-free lowlands of the east and south. Although utilising open fields of some kind in the areas held by the Normans, the local population were allowed to maintain their traditional lifestyle. The local leaders, noblemen and wealthy farmers continued to live in raths, and today thousands of these farmsteads, defended by their deep dug ditches, still survive in the Irish countryside. The people not only occupied isolated dwellings, they also lived in small hamlets called clachans associated with an open field or rundale system, ie infield cultivated strips and outfield common grazing land. Today, there are still a few examples of rundale communities in some parts of Ireland.

In County Down, the landscape near Hillhall, Lagan Valley (J290642), displays irregular fields, scattered farms, winding lanes and remains of raths. Also in County Down, at Duneight (J278608), is an oval rath with a 15ft (4.6m) deep ditch and traces of a settlement or clachan that would have been occupied by the chief's farmhands.

## ROYAL FORESTS AND FOREST LAW

The Anglo-Saxon kings had had special hunting grounds, consisting of large areas of forest and open heathland. The boundaries of these preserves were defined by earthen banks, but traces of most have long since disappeared. From Saxons times, woodland had always contributed much to the local economy, as timber commanded a good price. It provided wood for fuel, house building, wattle and hurdle making, for implement handles and for basket making. It also provided acorns and beech mast for the village pigs; it was generally measured in terms of the number of pigs which it could support. After the Norman Conquest, William I and members of the ruling aristocracy ordered the creation of Royal Forests and private chases which stretched over many areas of the country. South of the Thames, the extension of Windsor Forest was recorded by entries in the Domesday Book. By the middle of the twelfth century this royal preserve covered most of Berkshire and had extended as far west as Hampshire. William even appropriated other men's lands, and the New Forest was so-called because it represented new hunting territory. North of the Thames, the area we now know as Epping Forest is a mere remnant of a tract of woodland that covered much of Essex. In the north, amongst others, there were the forests of Knaresborough, Pickering, Langstrothdale Chase and Lonsdale; in the Midlands, the forests of Delamere, Macclesfield, Sherwood, Charnwood, Cannock Chase, Arden, Rockingham and Weybridge, Huntingdon; in the south, Hatfield, Epping, Windsor, New Forest, Savernake, Cranborne Chase and the Forest of Dean. In the south-west, Dartmoor and Exmoor. In Cheshire, the forests of Delamere and Macclesfield were in the hands of earls.

The New Forest in Hampshire was created by William the Conqueror who cleared away much of the old woodland and established a royal hunting preserve in 1079. In doing so, he also destroyed the sites of a number of Saxon villages and protected the area, as others, with extremely severe forest laws. The commoners were forbidden to enclose land or to graze most animals for more than five months of the year. They were allowed to graze their pigs on green acorns, a system called pannage, only from September to November.

Throughout its long history, the New Forest has been the scene of constant disputes between kings intent on preserving hunting rights and commoners living in the forest. It was not until the nineteenth century that Parliament ended the sovereign's right to keep deer in the forest, and allowed the commoners to graze their animals throughout the year. Today, disputes are heard in the Verderers' Court in Lyndhurst (SU300080), where the documents recording the grazing rights are kept. The Verderers are the guardians of the forest, and their officers, called Agisters, patrol the area on horseback to keep an eye on the welfare of the ponies, donkeys, cattle and deer.

The Royal Forests did not always consist of woodland. The word 'forest' was originally a legal term, meaning a definite tract of land governed by special laws, and this land could consist of heathland, fenland, private woodland, ordinary farmland, villages and even towns. In addition there were mountain and moorland forests such as Dartmoor, Exmoor and a number in the northern Pennines. The special laws were upheld by assize courts whose duty it was to protect the king's deer, other animals and resources. Although the Normans were passionately fond of hunting, the Crown's interest in the forests was not limited to deer alone, even though venison was an important source of revenue and food for the Court. Animals such as wild pigs, hares and rabbits were also greatly prized. Other items considered as essential sources of revenue were timber, kindling wood, thorn thickets, brushwood and possible mineral deposits, in the form of iron and lead. Last but not least was a lucrative income in fines for poaching, and later on from the sale of licences for the privilege of assarts (a legal term, derived from the French word *essarter* meaning to grub up), ie the grubbing up of trees to make new clearings at the woodland margins.

The Royal Forests with their herds of red and roe deer (later, fallow deer were introduced from the Continent) and wild boar were strictly protected by the Normans. Severe penalties were imposed on those villagers caught poaching in the royal preserve. The taking of a deer meant death or the loss of a limb. Timber could not be cut without permission and the land within the forest boundary could not be ploughed up. Many villages lay within the limits of the forests, which meant considerable pressure on the inhabitants who dare not stray into the area to take wood, or to supplement their meagre fare with venison or pork. Even household dogs could only be kept if three claws were cut from each paw.

On Exmoor, the history of Forest Law was divided into three periods: the first edict was issued in 1184 and lasted until 1217; the second from 1217 to 1301; the third after 1301. During the first two periods, Forest Law was severely enforced, and frequent courts were held to administer it. The assize of the forest in the reign of Henry II reads:

> The King forbids that anyone offend him concerning his venison or his forests in anything. For if anyone shall offend him and be convicted thereof, he will have full justice of him . . .

In serious cases, the court's verdict could mean loss of life, blinding or other mutilation. From 1301 on Exmoor Edward I disafforested many areas and forest laws decayed. In this context, the term 'disafforested' means that the Crown sold off areas of the Royal Forest to knights, freeholders and religious houses, thus creating another important source of revenue for the royal coffers. Gradually, the penalties for trespass were relaxed, and fines appear to have been the commonest form of punishment. Another important development on Exmoor was the introduction of trial by jury, and the procedure whereby the court could uphold the rights of the subject against the warden and his foresters. Throughout the country, the Crown received enormous sums of money in releasing large stretches of land from restraints on assarting and on other forest regulations.

In the northern Pennines, the Conqueror designated vast areas of upland as Royal Forest and private chase. A form of nature conservation was applied in that deer, wild boar and other creatures were protected in order that they could be hunted. In upper Wharfedale, the village of Buckden (SD942772) was the home of the guardians of Langstrothdale Chase. Here, the Norman lords hunted the deer which gave Buckden its name. The village sits in the shadow of the 2,302ft (702m) high Buckden Pike, from whose windswept peaty slopes magnificent views can be seen in every direction. To the north beyond Kidstones Scar, the lords of Richmond and Middleham hunted Wensleydale Forest and Bishopdale Chase. Across the hills to the west lies the Forest of Bowland (pronounced locally as Bolland), a lonely tract of high rounded fells broken by gritstone outcrops. For example, Grit Fell (SD557589) is a typical Bowland landscape. When the Normans occupied the country, almost the whole of Bowland passed into the hands of a single baron, Robert de Lacy. During the next five hundred years red and fallow deer were the most important and protected inhabitants of the area.

The rocky outcrops of Charnwood Forest is reminiscent of scenery in Wales, and bracken-clad Bradgate Park (SK530105) remains much as it was during the Middle Ages, a deer inhabited parkland. In the Midlands, Henley is the picturesque town in the centre of the old Forest of Arden. Arden is a celtic word for a 'well-wooded area', and it was not a forest where under medieval laws hunting was restricted to the king. At the time of the Conquest the district consisted of patches of dense woodland and shrubland where the inhabitants cut timber and kept pigs, and was full of long-established forest settlements. Today, Henley's attractive High Street displays many old buildings such as the fifteenth-century church and ancient Guild Hall. The lane alongside the church crosses over the River Alne and leads to the ancient hamlet of Beaudesert (SP155662), its name derived from the French 'a beautiful waste land'. Here is the mound of the original Norman motte and bailey castle built by the de Montforts.

Although the process of selling-off the Royal Forests was a lengthy one, spreading over many centuries, much of the legal framework survived throughout the Middle Ages. For example, many of the laws attached to Exmoor existed until the sale of the forest in 1818.

As the Royal Forests gradually went out of favour, the creation of parks was a natural substitute. By the end of the thirteenth century, not only the Crown, but also lords, barons and bishops surrounded their strongholds and great religious houses with parks for the retention of red, roe and fallow deer. Sometimes these parks were established on moorland or woodland, and sometimes on agricultural land seized from the local population. The medieval park differed from the forest in that it was formally bounded by a bank and ditch, and sometimes a stone wall. The park served a number of purposes; it acted as a convenient larder for the palace or castle, it provided an increase of revenue, and it became a status symbol for the very wealthy and powerful. Traces of the park boundaries may still be identified attached to the castle at Devizes in Wiltshire (SU001613). At Fountains Abbey in North Yorkshire (SE274682), Benedictine monks founded the magnificent building in 1132-3 and adopted Cistercian rules. By the early sixteenth century its prosperity, due to the wool-trading skill of the monks, attracted the attention of Henry VIII and his commissioners who stripped

the walls and roofs of the abbey. Traces of the Monks Wall around the park can be clearly identified on the ground today.

The protection of forests and parks with severe laws was one of the privileges that the nobles contested at Runnymede. The charter of the forest was one of the minor points of the Magna Carta, but no less important in its impact on the landscape. The preservation of timber for the food and shelter of deer and wild pigs saved many mighty oaks and majestic beeches from the threat of the peasant's axe. The continuity of ancient woodlands and deer parks has preserved many marks made by man on the ground, such as ditches, earthen banks, tracks, pits, pounds and warrens. Often the boundaries of ancient forests and parks have survived despite the insatiable appetites of land hunters, speculators and developers in more recent times. Stretches of forgotten roads can be followed as deeply sunken lanes and narrow tracks winding their way from one settlement or isolated farm to another. The earthen 'deer-leap' banks (originally 4 to 5ft (1.2 to 1.5m) high, and topped with wooden stakes) mark the line of the ancient forest and park boundaries, with a deep ditch on the forest side and a bank sloping inwards to the fields. The bank along the south side of John of Gaunt's deerpark in King's Somborne, Hampshire (SU354304) is still 12ft (3.7m) high accompanied by a ditch on the outside.

Another landscape feature that survives, particularly in moorland areas, are earth mounds, rectangular in plan, called 'pillow mounds', raised in order to facilitate the breeding and capture of rabbits. The rabbit, a Norman introduction into England, was deliberately bred as an important source of food and revenue. Persons in charge of these artificial burrow sites were called warreners. On Dartmoor, on the side of a hill, is a group of grassy mounds once the site of a thriving rabbit farm at Huntingdon Warren (SX665671).

**Dartmoor Walk**

*Starting and Finishing Point:* Aish, South Brent, Devon, OS 202, (1 in 188), SX692607 Before 1204, for an unknown

length of time, practically the whole of Devon was royal forest and subject to the Forest Laws. A Charter was granted by King John in that year, which

disafforested all the area except for the royal hunting preserves of Dartmoor and Exmoor. Although some of the severe penalties were relaxed, a miscreant could still be heavily fined, and if unable to pay, would be cast into prison for a year and a day.

The status of Dartmoor Forest was not fully defined until the definite record of a perambulation by twelve knights around the boundary in 1240, during the reign of Henry III. Domesday does not mention the Forest of Dartmoor, but an entry states that the borough of Lydford belonged to the King, and that Dartmoor was part of the same borough. In 1239, Henry III granted to his brother Richard, the Manor of Lydford with the Forest of Dartmoor; and thus with this grant, the Forest became in law a Chase. After the death of Richard, the hunting ground passed to his son Edmund. He died in 1300, and the Forest reverted to the Crown, remaining in its possession throughout the reigns of Edward I and Edward II.

In 1337, Dartmoor Chase was granted to Black Prince, Duke of Cornwall, and since that time the royal demesne has belonged

to the Duchy of Cornwall. The boundary of the royal hunting ground lies wholly within the parish of Lydford, and no less than twenty-two parishes encircle the Chase extending from its boundary like the spokes of an elongated wheel.

The hamlet of Aish lies in the valley of the River Avon just to the north of South Brent. From Lydia Bridge walk up to the junction, turn left, and after a few strides bear right uphill. Proceed along this by-road for 1 mile (1.6km), before descending sharply to cross Glaze Brook. As the lane begins to climb out of the valley bear right at Owley. The track soon becomes a footpath which climbs steeply to Spurrell's Cross, and the disused tramway to the Red Lake china-clay workings. The 3ft (0.9m) gauge Red Lake Tramway was built in 1910, and ran for 7½ miles (12km). It was closed down and its rails were removed in 1932. The way lies to the north across the open moor, and your journey will be accompanied by a musical chorus of meadow

pipits and skylarks, soaring skywards as you approach. The route climbs gently across the eastern shoulder of Piles Hill, 1,270ft (387m). To the west, the valley of the River Erme contains many prehistoric mouments, such as stone rows, cairns, enclosures and hut circles, as well as remains of ancient tin workings. The longest stone row on Dartmoor can be seen on the west side of the valley. This magnificent wilderness is a vast open-air museum that exhibits a tremendous number of signs of man's influence on the countryside.

In good visibility, the tramway track can be left in favour of a route over the summit of Ugborough Moor at Three Barrows, 1,522ft (461m). Looking back there are fine varied views to the south, and to the north there is an aspect of miles of open moorland. You may have the company of ponies and see numbers of the hardy breeds of cattle like the Galloways and the long-horned shaggy highlands. Follow the old tramway over Quickbeam Hill, which is a safer way or a convenient escape route if the mist closes in, round a sharp semi-circular loop to the foundations of a ruined building on the left. Bear right on to the Abbot's Way footpath and cross over the Zeal Tor tramway at Crossways, near some old workings. This tramway originally carried peat by horse-drawing trucks to the peat and peat charcoal works at Shipley Bridge, along wooden rails bolted to blocks of granite. At Shipley Bridge, the rich Red Lake peat was used for the manufacture of naptha, and 'a dense cheap mineral coal' for smelting ores. It was a short-

*Red Lake Tramway*

*Clapper bridge over River Avon*

*Huntingdon Cross*

lived venture, established in 1846 and closed in 1850.

A little distance to the north-west rises the prominent conical 'Matterhorn' of waste material from the Red Lake china clay works. If there is time, the walker may continue along the Red Lake tramway track without immediately turning on to the Abbot's Way. This artificial vantage point, now mostly covered with vegetation, affords extensive all-round views across tracts of moorland.

Return along the tramway track for one mile (1.6km), and where the track bends to the right, continue straight ahead, climbing gradually to Crossways. Turn east on to the Abbot's Way footpath, which then veers to the north-east and follows a gully descending to the River Avon. Walk upstream for a short distance and cross the river by the clapper bridge. Turn right and follow the river on the path down to Huntingdon Cross.

This grey, weatherbeaten granite cross, about 4½ft (1.4m) in height, lies at the junction of the River Avon and the Western Wella Brook. The latter here forms the eastern boundary of

the Forest, and the well-formed cross, which was probably erected on the boundary of Brent Moor and the Forest in about 1557, lies just within the limits of the former royal preserve.

The hill lying between the River Avon and the Western Wella Brook is Huntingdon Warren. Like a hunting chase or forest, a warren was land set apart for the preservation of game, in fact as a breeding place

*Huntingdon Warren*

for rabbits. Where the ground was hard and stony, the raised mounds were constructed of soil and turf. Sometimes special enclosures were made, with one or two small entrances.

On the eastern slopes of Huntingdon Warren lie the tumbled remains of Warren House. There was a building, and fields here before the close of the eleventh century; today, the small walled green fields of the former intakes contrast sharply

with the duller-coloured slopes of the surrounding moor. The pillow mounds are easily located behind the house, on either side of the clear pathway as it slants diagonally up the hill slope. There is also much of interest in the immediate area: the former tin workings at the head of Western Wella Brook; the remains of a Blowing House (the only means of smelting tin ore until superseded in the eighteenth century by the reverberatory furnace) on the western side of Huntingdon Warren, close to the River Avon; enclosed hut groups and an old leat on the southern slopes of the hill. The ruins of Keble Martin's tiny church may be located in the leat just north of a wheel pit on the eastern bank of Western Wella Brook: Rev Martin became famous as a painter of British wild flowers.

From the Huntingdon Cross, return to the clapper bridge over the River Avon and ascend the hill in a south-south-west direction towards Petre's Cross, the summit of Western White-barrow, 1,575ft (480m). A bondstone on the brow of the hill marks the forest boundary line, which extends south from the River Avon to the summit cairn. In the midst of the spoiled heap of stones lies the headless shaft of Petre's Cross. It was originally erected in 1557, in the belief that this hill was the southern limit of Dartmoor Forest and the boundary with the Manor of Brent. The cross was damaged in 1850 by workmen cutting peat.

In a late autumn afternoon, the sun brings out the full rich colours of the moorland grasses, and reveals the presence of half-concealed surface water. The northern views encompass a wide expanse of moorland,

*Petre's Cross, Western White Barrow*

including Ryder's Hill, Nakers Hill, and the miry morass of Aune or Avon Head. Three-quarters of a mile (1.2km) to the east, along the ridge, stands Eastern Whitebarrow summit, 1,549ft (472m); its immense prominent cairn makes a splendid viewing platform affording magnificent glimpses of the English Channel and wide stretches of deserted moorland.

If you have walked on to Eastern Whitebarrow, head directly south to meet the Zeal Tor tramway track, if not, join it at Petre's Cross and follow it down towards Shipley Bridge.

Aish can be reached either by footpath to Didworthy Hospital, track to Lutton and road to Lydia Bridge, or by metalled lane from Shipley Bridge following the River Avon to Aish.

*Route*: Aish, Owley, Spurrell's Cross, Piles Hill, Ugborough Moor, Quickbeam Hill, Crossways, Huntingdon Cross, Petre's Cross, Shipley Bridge, Aish. Distance: 14½ miles (23.2km).

*Alternative Walk:*
Take a minor road from Buckfastleigh to Cross Furzes,

*Clapper bridge, Cross Furzes*

where there is limited parking space (SX700666). Walk to Lud Gate, cross the moor south of Pupers Hill and down to Western Wella Brook. Cross the bridge north of Warren House and follow the brook south to its junction with the River Avon,

## Exmoor Walk

*Starting and Finishing Point:*
Cheriton, Lynmouth, Devon
OS 180, (1 in 163), SS737465
Leave the centre of the small hamlet of Cheriton by the lane on the left. After a short distance take the right-hand fork to cross the steep valley of Hoar Oak Water to Stock Common, passing the univallate Iron Age fortress of Roborough Castle. Just beyond the earthwork, bear left along a track which quickly develops into a right of way across Furzehill Common. On the open moorland the route passes standing stones and hut circles. Buzzards, larks and curlews may be seen here, and in Hoar Oak Valley ravens may also be seen.

The Hoar Oak Tree on the east bank of the stream is the most famous of the ancient Royal Forest's boundary marks. The present tree is the only survivor of several planted in 1917 to replace the 'Second' Hoar Oak which lasted for 250 years; the harsh Exmoor climate makes the life of a small oak tree very difficult. The boundary of the ancient Forest is also marked at varying intervals by mear-stones, and east of the Hoar Oak Tree it is marked by John

and the site of Huntingdon Cross. Follow the River Avon westwards, and cross the clapper bridge to ascend steeply to the bondstone. Then to Petre's Cross on Western Whitebarrow. Walk east along the grassy ridge to the enormous cairn on Eastern

Knight's Forest Wall. A good stretch of the wall lies immediately east of Hoar Oak, running clearly across the heather slopes. The path continues up the valley, eventually crossing the stream, and climbs up to the peat bog at Exe Head.

From this point the route lies west for $2\frac{1}{2}$ miles (4km) across The Chains. The walker intent on finishing this short exploration of high Exmoor will rejoice in a sense of achievement as the only compensation for a difficult journey. Even in summer the land is soggy, and each foothold has to be carefully tested. In some cases, the skill of an Olympic long jumper is needed to reach the next tussock. From Exe Head take a westerly direction, veering to west-north-west, keeping a constant check on the compass bearing. The best route is along the South Chains Wall to Chains Barrow, which lies just beyond the wall to the north. The area round the trig-point is firmer, and from the barrow summit a magnificent panoramic view of the heart of Exmoor is the reward for the determined walker. The wild moorland plateau to the north is broken by several steep-sided

Whitebarrow, then descend diagonally to the clapper bridge over the River Avon. Return along the Abbot's Way via Huntingdon Cross, Dean Moor, Water Oak Corner to Cross Furzes. Distance $8\frac{1}{2}$ miles (13.6km).

valleys containing the West Lyn River, Hoaroak Water and Farley Water.

Continue along the South Chains Wall past Pinkworthy Pond and on to the line of wind-blasted beeches at Wood Barrow Gate, 1,566ft (477m). If there is time in hand and the weather is fair, there are interesting diversions a short distance to the west in the form of the Longstone Barrow and the Long Stone. The latter is a crooked pillar of slate of phallic significance, standing 9ft (2.7m) high, the most impressive standing stone on Exmoor.

From Wood Barrow follow the northern course of the forest boundary to Saddle Gate where it turns sharply eastwards. Proceed northwards descending to Shallowford, and take the footpath on the right crossing the stream and climbing over Ilkerton Ridge. The right of way leads down to the valley of the West Lyn River and to a narrow winding lane bypassing Furzehill. At a point where the lane swings sharp left, bear right by track and path over Stock Common and return to Cheriton. Distance $11\frac{1}{2}$ miles (18.4km), excluding a possible diversion to the Long Stone.

## Cannock Chase Walk

*Starting and Finishing Point:*
Great Haywood, Rugeley, Staffordshire
OS 127/128 (1 in 119/120),

SJ996226
There can surely be no pleasanter spot to start, or finish a walk, than by the Essex Bridge at the confluence of the Rivers

Trent and Sow. This superb seventeenth-century packhorse bridge, with fourteen graceful arches remaining of its original forty-three, is the longest packhorse bridge in England. Once across, the general view is one of the fine parkland, and the walk along the drive enables you to enjoy the many fine examples of horse chestnuts, oaks, sycamores and limes. Beyond the park the dark folds of the hills of Cannock Chase frame this delightful scene. Shugborough Hall, the seat of the Anson family since 1624, soon comes into view away to the right. The fifth earl, Patrick Lichfield, still occupies part of the house. The mansion, although remodelled by Stuart in the 1760s, was altered in the Regency style at the end of the eighteenth century, by Wyatt. Shugborough is under the care of the National Trust, and is managed by the Staffordshire County Council. The adjacent outbuildings house the county museum, which contains many interesting exhibits illustrating the social and industrial history of Staffordshire.

From the time of the Conquest, Cannock and its Forest belonged to the Crown. When Henry II came to the throne in 1154, the limits of Cannock Forest were considerably extended, but the Manor of Longdon was traditionally part of the See of Lichfield. It would appear that, although much of this territory was absorbed into the King's Forest of Cannock, the Bishops of Lichfield held on to a small foothold, and continued to make many assarts and other encroachments on Cannock Forest. When Henry II died in 1189, the two manors of Cannock and Rugeley remained as part of the Crown estates.

When Richard I ascended the throne, he was desperately short of cash to finance his involvement in the Crusades. He there

*Essex bridge, Great Haywood*

fore sold several royal estates, among them Cannock and Rugeley. Hugh de Novant, Bishop of Coventry and Lichfield, was the purchaser; he paid 25 marks for the estate which then became his hunting ground. The forest privileges claimed by the Bishop became a long-standing grievance and a source of annoyance to the King's Foresters. The forest rights of this area remained in dispute until 1290, when Edward I granted the land to the Bishop in return for an acknowledgement of the Crown's original right.

The 'Bishop's Chase' or Cannock Chase is but a small part of the original ancient area of Cannock Forest. The limits of the Chase were defined by streams and tracks, the names of most of which have now been lost. However, parts of this boundary run along Chad's Ditch or Dyke between Pye Green and Pottal Pool. It is about 8ft (2.4m) wide and 4ft (1.2m) deep. The excavated material, which has been thrown up on the lower side, shows that it was not intended for defence. It was probably meant as a

boundary when it was first dug, before 1290. West of Rugeley, the boundary of the Chase probably ran along Bower Lane, past Bower Farm north of Etching Hill. At the County Record Office, Stafford, the map of Cannock Chase with several commons, waste lands and encroachments in the Manors of Haywood, Rugeley, Cannock and Longdon, 1819/20/21/22 and 1824, indicates boundary stones. These are also marked on the Ordnance Survey 1:25,000 map, SK01, position SK031191.

Continue up the drive, past the Farm Museum and over the railway to reach the A513. Turn right and walk along the main road, using the pavement and then the wide grass verge, for a distance of ½ mile (800m). As the main road bends sharply in a dip, take the track on the left signposted to Mere Pool. This is marked rather ungraciously on the 1:50,000 map as 'The Hole' and on the 1:25,000 map as 'Mere Pits'. Follow the track uphill with a fence on the left, As the way descends, the track and fence veer sharply left. Ignore this turning, and go straight on to the pool. Here, a number of routes converge, but take the first of the two paths bearing left to ascend round the side of Brocton Coppice to the summit of Coppice Hill, 602ft (183m). Brocton Coppice is the remnant of the natural oak forest, and is an important habitat for fallow deer. After a few yards, bear right gradually to reach the Chase road. Turn left and continue south along the road to reach the glacial boulder on the left. The trig point is at an altitude of 637ft (194m). On a clear day, the boulder is a fine viewpoint, looking west towards the Shropshire Hills and the Welsh Borders, and north to the Staffordshire moorlands.

After many centuries as a hunting preserve, Cannock Chase was stripped of its forest cover in the sixteenth century for charcoal, and later during the development of the coalmining and iron industries. Since 1920, those transformers of the natural skyline, the Forestry Com-

mission, has blanketed many acres with a dark and featureless wall of conifers. Since 1973, the acres of public access land have been designated as Country Park by the Staffordshire County Council. Today, reduced in size as it is, Cannock Chase has been designated as an Area of Outstanding Natural Beauty.

Proceed south along the Chase Road, continuing straight on along Anson's Bank when the road swings to the right. At Springslade Lodge, join the Camp Road for ¾ mile (1.2km) to the Commonwealth and German Military Cemeteries. It is a beautiful and tranquil place, where the dead lie beneath well-tended lawns, shaded by silver birches and conifers. At SJ983154 is the site of Cank Thorn, or Cannock Thorn. Thorns were often used in olden times as boundary markers, and the Cank Thorn was on the boundary of Cannock Chase;

additionally, it was the meeting place of the three ancient manors of Cannock, Penkridge and Rugeley. A thorn bush has existed here for at least six centuries, the present one being a rooted sucker replanted in 1972 from the old stock. From the crossroads at Broadhurst Green, take the right of way south, following the ancient boundary of Chad's Dyke to Chad's Gate (SJ983142). Retrace your steps to Cank Thorn.

Leave the German Cemetery and gradually descend into the beautiful Sherwood Valley, thickly wooded with pine trees. Almost imperceptibly, the stream appears, and accompanies the path. This dry heathland with gravel and heather provides an ideal habitat for adders, so care is needed. Continue down the valley to the Stepping Stones (SJ988200), cross the stream to the track opposite and head straight on. This section is a delightful stroll through trees and green open spaces, before the A513 at Severn Springs is reached. Cross over the main road to Weetman's Bridge, which spans the River Trent, and follow the minor road to Little Haywood. Just before the second railway bridge, turn along the towpath of the Trent and Mersey Canal to the Essex Bridge for a pleasant finale to the walk.
Distance 12½ miles (20km).

**Upper Wharfedale Walk**
*Starting and Finishing Point:*
Kettlewell, Wharfedale, North Yorkshire
OS 98, (1in 90), SD968723
Outdoor Leisure Map, 'Malham and Upper Wharfedale'
Magnificent Wharfedale is set in

*Cank Thorn, Cannock Chase*

a sculptured landscape of neatly spaced villages, linked by a fretwork of green pastures and grey dry-stone walls. The pattern is completed by a succession of stout stone barns that seem to hold all these skilful man-made boundaries together. The village of Kettlewell (its name derived from the Old Norse, meaning 'bubbling stream'), is an attractive huddle of stone-built houses that cling close to Park Gill Beck. The village is extremely popular with tourists who stream up the dale, and who are content to linger and explore its nooks and crannies. It is also a favourite base for walkers, who have in upper Wharfedale one of the finest walking areas in Britain. There is ample accommodation, and the two inns close by the narrow road bridge bring to mind the old coaching and posting days. The village was an important stopping point, and travellers who had negotiated the steep gradients of Park Rash from the wild country beyond would be glad to see the comforting lights of the inns.

The two moorland heights that overlook this part of the dale are Great Whernside and Buckden Pike. These high hills are excellent view points, and from their breezy summits excellent views may be obtained of the surrounding landscape including upper Wharfedale and Langstrothdale. From Townfoot Bridge in Kettlewell, take the lane that closely follows the right-hand side of the beck. The steep hillside slopes immediately begin to close in on the two streams, Park Gill Beck and Dowber Gill Beck. Their swiftly flowing waters issuing from the flanks of Great Whernside have carved out deep gullies before joining forces above the village.

As you cross over the bridge spanning Dowber Gill Beck, there are two options for the ascent to Hag Dike. One is to continue on the track ahead; the other is to bear right on the footpath that keeps high above the northern rim of Dowber Gill. Keep to the right of the building, negotiate the limestone scar and head east-north-east across the open moorland.

The ascent from Kettlewell has been over the carboniferous limestone, and to the south-west the white rock thrusts out from the green hillsides in a series of stepped escarpments. The abrupt change of landscape is because the limestone is overlaid with gritstone and impervious clays. You enter a sombre yet still exciting world of tussock grass, pools of rich peaty-coloured water and waving tufts of cotton grass. You are likely to be startled by the sudden croaking of the grouse, followed by the softer calls of the peewits and curlews. Sheep continue to roam the fellsides as they did across the huge monastic granges of the Middle Ages. In more recent times, men have won and lost many battles in their hunt for the elusive veins of lead, and many signs of their mining activity remain in the form of shafts, adits, waste tips and ruined buildings.

After a gradual climb the gritstone outcrops appear, and then the trig-point marking the summit of Great Whernside, 2,308ft (704m). The long boulder-strewn ridge affords expansive views to the east of the Nidderdale moors, and westwards across Wharfedale to Old Cote Moor. Proceed along the ridge for another $\frac{7}{8}$ mile (1.4km) to the northern top (SD998753) and descend west-north-west to pick up a path

*Guidestone, Langstrothdale*

leading to the road between Coverdale and Wharfedale. At this point it is joined by Tor Dyke, a line of Brigantian earthworks. Follow these ancient defences in a westerly direction until you are in line with the head of Cam Gill Beck, then take the path that swings round Top Mere and ascend to Tor Mere Top. Continue on a bearing slightly west of north to reach a boundary stone on the Walden Road track. Cross over and follow the wall up to the white stone cross, which commemorates the death of five Polish airmen whose Wellington bomber crashed here during a snowstorm in January 1942. Only one survivor managed to stagger down the fellside to the hamlet of Cray. Proceed alongside the wall to reach the summit cairn and trig-point of Buckden Pike, 2,302ft (702m).

Buckden Pike commands an extensive view of upper Wharfedale, Langstrothdale Chase and the wild peaty wastes of Fleet Moss. On a clear day the three peaks of Penyghent, Ingleborough and Whernside are clearly visible amongst many other hills. The valleys and fells of Langstrothdale Chase were colonised by Anglian settlers in the seventh century; they moved up Wharfedale from the south and penetrated the region from the north, taking advantage of the Roman road from Bainbridge to Ingleton. Evidence from place-names reveal their colonisation; for example, Langstrothdale means 'long valley overgrown with brushwood', Litton means 'on the slope'. Later the Danish and Norwegian Vikings moved into the higher reaches of the chase, and their colonisation is shown by such names as Skirfare, 'bright river' and Beckermonds, 'river confluence'. At the foot of Buckden Pike, the village of Buckden is a Norman foundation established for the foresters on the edge of the chase. It became the centre of

the Langstrothdale hunting preserve. The fact that many settlements in the nearby dales were mentioned in the Domesday Book shows that the area was already well colonised by the time of the Norman Conquest. Many Norse setttelements remained as tiny isolated farms within the forest bounds, and were not allowed to expand because of the Forest Law.

The presence of these groups of vaccaries is an essential feature of the mid-Pennine forests; they are usually set in forest clearings, engaged in the breeding and rearing of cattle and some sheep. In Langstroth-dale Chase there are seven of these lodges named in 1241, with names still easily recognised today, namely: Beckermonds was Beckersmote; Cray was Crey; Deepdale was Depedale; Hubberholme was Huberham; Outershaw was Uhtredestall; Raisgill was Risegile; Yockenthwaite was Yoghamethest.

From the summit cairn descend directly to join the path at SD952791. Suddenly the

limestone appears again and with it a distinct change in the character of the vegetation. a little further along, the route is overlooked by an outcrop of Great Scar limestone. Lower down the path meets the line of an old Roman road affording a pleasant way through Rakes Wood and into Buckden village. Walk down the road to Starbotton for just over $\frac{3}{4}$ mile (1.35km). At the point where the wall following the parish boundary reaches the road, there is an old stone stoup, comprising a base and a short shaft; this marks the boundary of the ancient forest of Langstroth-dale. The boundary marker may easily be missed, for it is in the field, unobtrusively tucked away in the angle of the wall and roadside hedge; map reference SD946759. Continue down the road to Starbotton, and just beyond the village, take a signposted track on the right towards the River Wharfe. There is then an attractive riverside walk of $1\frac{3}{4}$ mile (2.8km) back to Kettlewell along the Dales Way footpath. Distance 14 miles (22.4km).

## THE MEDIEVAL VILLAGE

In the south and midlands of England, the agri-cultural routine of farmed strips in two or three open fields established by the Saxons, was continued by the Normans. The new lords, who could be knights, abbots or bishops, having been given their lands or manors by the king for services rendered, introduced no new methods of farming, but they did emphasise in a legal way the relationship between the peasant and his master. For the next few generations, the day-to-day lives of the villagers would be highly organised and regulated by the lord's officers

and officials. Their very existence would be dominated by the harsh encompassing restraints of the Norman manorial laws.

In the eleventh, twelfth and thirteenth centuries, the usual social structure of village society consisted of the lord of the manor, the priest (if the village had a church), the lord's officers (reeves and bailiffs), sokemen, villeins, cottagers (bordars and cottars). In the early days there were still some who were regarded as slaves, and so recorded in Domesday Book, who belonged life and limb to the lord of the manor. Gradually the law allowed them to make their lives easier, and they were able legally to rise to the lower ranks of the great villein class. For instance it was recorded in Domesday Book (1085-6) that the village of Knaptoft, Leicestershire (SP626895) contained a priest, two sokemen, ten villeins, six cottagers and three slaves. The Normans regarded the sokeman as a freeman, who paid cash or goods for the lands he rented. It was quite possible that the freeman owned less land than the villein or none at all. In the latter case he may have worked for wages as a craftsman, such as a miller, a potter or a blacksmith. There were no legal obstacles to prevent him leaving the manor, and if there was a dispute between himself and the lord, he could appeal to the courts of the king. He was also free from the compulsory tasks of labouring in the fields of the demesne farm. At the foot of the social ladder, the 'cottars' and 'bordars' were people who owned very little land, just one, two or three acres, and tried to make ends meet by hiring out their labour around the village. In times of bad harvests and hard winters they and their families would be the first to starve. The villein was the backbone of village life, and included most of the English farmers of the Middle Ages. The word 'villein' translated as villager, means a person who was neither a free man nor a slave, neither a sokeman or a cottar. The total of an arable holding that the villein held was a yardland, traditionally 30 acres (12ha), but in practice this amount varied considerably. During long hours spent in the fields, a benevolent lord would provide bread, cheese and ale, and would allow the villein some time to himself if the day's ploughing had been satisfactorily completed. He was then able to tend his pigs, look after his cow and feed his plough-oxen. The law allowed him to graze his animals on the common land, to collect turves and windfall wood, and cut his share of hay from the meadow for winter fodder. He kept poultry, but had to make a payment of eggs to his lord at Easter time. In return for his yardland, the villein had to work at least two-and-a-half days for the lord on his demesne land. This would entail ploughing, harrowing, harvesting, carting, thatching, ditching and many other tasks around his lord's estate.

In law, the villein was bound to the soil of his native manor, and could not leave his home to farm land elsewhere, or earn a living as a craftsman in another place. Although the villein may have been able to become a prosperous farmer, in theory, all that he earned was his lord's. He was forced to cart the corn and vegetables many miles to a market town, and the profits went into his lord's coffers. There were restrictions on his own resources, and laws which influenced the very heart of the villein's family. He had to take his corn to the lord's oven. There was an iniquitous tax called 'tallage', which could be used anytime at the will of the lord. When the daughter of a villein married he must pay the lord a 'merchet' tax, and when the villein died, death duty or 'heriot' tax was taken in the form of the man's finest beast. As a final indignity, the villein was not trusted to be responsible for his own actions. He was put together with about ten other villeins in groups called 'frankpledges', each member of which was accountable for the behaviour and work of the others. The responsibility for supervising this system, the work of the manor and the efficiency of all labour services, was held by the lord's bailiff and his assistant the reeve.

A villein could free himself from servitude if he was careful, ambitious and adventurous enough; however, he probably would need of all three, plus a good slice of luck, in order to do so. Firstly, he could try to make some money in order to buy his freedom; secondly, he could run away from the area of the manor. If the villein was successful in reaching a chartered borough, and remaining there without detection for a year and a day, then he would gain his freedom. Generally speaking, the peasant farmer's life was one of hard, unremitting toil. A good harvest meant that the peasant and his family would be assured of full stomachs whereas a hard winter could mean near starvation, illness and death. In the main, men still laboured to extract life from the earth as their ancestors had done, until they too were put to rest in it.

The Domesday Book of 1086 provides us with a picture of eleventh-century England. It gives documentary evidence of another stage in this country's evolving landscape. A great number of our existing village names are to be found in Domesday Book, but the information concerning the status of each settlement is a little misleading. The clerks engaged in the survey were referring to the taxable estates, and did not differentiate between a farmstead, a hamlet, a village or a group of villages. If each entry opposite a settlement is assumed to be for a village, then a misleading picture is given of the overall settlement pattern. Taking this aspect into consideration, it does give us a good insight about the influence of man on the eleventh-century countryside. An interesting aspect of the picture is that by this time most of the good agricultural land was under cultivation, and only marginal land, such as hillside slopes, remained. Although open-field agriculture was extensively used in the midlands and the south of England, it was not generally in operation throughout the country. People in the upland areas of Scotland, northern England, Wales, Cornwall and Ireland were occupied in pastoral farming due to the climate and the barren nature of the ground. Even so, there was limited open-field arable cultivation using an infield/outfield system, and with grazing on extensive pastures.

By 1300, the many documentary records are sufficient to give a comprehensive view of village life. In general terms throughout the midlands and the south of England, the village had its church, manor house and peasant dwellings sited close to each other. The last-mentioned would be cramped hovels, rectangular in shape, approximately 20ft by 10ft (6m by 3m). Some had stone foundations. The buildings would be nothing more than shelters, which were constructed with wattle frames daubed with clay and roofed with thatch. Once abandoned, they would simply rot away leaving little trace, except for the raised platforms or sunken areas on the ground. There may well have been an open area, or green, in the centre of the village, with trackways radiating from it. It is likely that there would have been no planning of the settlement, and in many cases side tracks diverged from the main street and headed out to the fields, some connecting with routes to neighbouring villages and settlements. However, communications at that time would be very difficult, with deeply grooved muddy holloways, occasionally passable with the addition of stones collected from the fields and dumped into the glutinous marshy sections.

Although one can only guess at the details of medieval domestic life, it would not be far from the truth to say that most of the village inhabitants lived in very squalid conditions by modern standards. One room, probably with a rough partition, made up the living and sleeping quarters on the beaten-earth floor. A layer of bracken or heather spread on the ground would provide a little comfort for sleeping. Food would at most times be frugal and monotonous, consisting or rough bread, beans and cheese, with an occasional dish of fish or meat. Honey would be the only form of sweetening, and would also be likely to be used to ferment some form of alcoholic beverage. If cooking was carried out inside the house on an open hearth, which was frequently the case, then the smoke would permeate every corner, before escaping through cracks in the walls and roof. Rubbish of all kinds would be thrown outside on the individual tofts, and what sanitary arrangements there were would likewise be made in the same place. The narrow tofts, or small parcels of land, normally lay alongside or behind each house. In hunting for the sites of abandoned homes on a suspected deserted medieval village site, thriving clumps of nettles may provide the clue. They grow well on disturbed ground which is rich in nitrogen — the result of lengthy periods of human occupation.

In cases where a manor was built in the village, the lord took the opportunity to set himself apart from the peasants, building a solid stone house, up slope, and most certainly up wind, of his subjects. In many instances, a rectangular or square-shaped moat was dug and filled with water, with a causeway access to the house. In Staffordshire alone, a county not usually noted for such features, there are today at least sixty moated medieval sites with some greater or lesser remains still visible. Close to the manor house would be the lord's fishponds and maybe the site of his watermill. The fishponds would be areas of excavated ground close to a water supply, with the earth thrown up, containing sluices to regulate the flow of the water. Fishponds vary considerably in area and shape, with perhaps one large pool, two pools or a string of interconnecting ponds.

The manor house was set in its own farming

land, and it often had a demesne farm whose lands would be worked by the peasants for the benefit of their lord. In parts of England where the nucleated village was the common form of settlement, it is difficult, if not impossible to identify the demesne farm; but in areas of scattered settlements, they often can be identified. For example, in Devon and Cornwall, there are names incorporating the word Barton, such as Tettaridge Barton, Trebartha Barton, Tredwen Barton, which signifies the demesne farm. In other areas, the largest farm in the locality usually gives a clue in its name: Church Farm, Home Farm, Town Farm, Manor Farm, Court Farm, Hall Farm, Demesne Farm.

In early medieval times, the villagers usually shared a chapel with other communities, or attended a large church that served the whole area. Most villages gained their church in the twelfth century; it was a massive and durable outward sign of the lord of the manor's power and influence over the lives of the villagers. It was the finest building in the community, built of stone, and most likely paid for by the lord. The church with its services and rituals undoubtedly was a place of mystery and awe as seen through the eyes of the ordinary people. Even though most of the service would be incomprehensible to the average villager, it would be an island of peace in a harsh world. The arrival of the priest into the lives of the villagers may well have been the chink of light in a very bleak existence. There are a number of instances recorded of a priest interceding for the villager in the manor court, as, for example, in cases of boundary disputes, and as a counsellor on behalf of a villein who wished to change his labour services on the land for rent. The villein also became free if he succeeded in a request to become a priest. The incumbent may well have spoken up for him in order to gain the lord's permission.

## DESERTED MEDIEVAL VILLAGES

There is no single cause of the disappearance of so many English villages and hamlets in the Middle Ages. Much blame has been attached to the depredations of the Black Death, but some settlements were declining well before the arrival of the plague in 1348. In some of the more remote areas, the Cistercian brotherhood pursued their policy of solitude by turning areas owned by them into great sheep walks to the extinction of number of existing villages.

By the end of the thirteenth century, the population of medieval England was rising rapidly, and this created a heavy demand for additional food supplies. As most of the good agricultural land was already in use, the landowners, both lay and ecclesiastical, attempted to make food production more efficient on this good arable land. This need to maximise food production, plus the opportunity to make high profits, led to the colonising or assarting of new land. Documentary records tell a story of countless acres of inferior marginal land being brought into cultivation. During this period of expansion, many new settlements were created, often on the sites of isolated farms on the edge of the wasteland. Many were short-lived, particularly on the dry chalklands of Lincolnshire, the Yorkshire Wolds and on the sandy soils of the Breckland in Norfolk. The thinness of the soils led to decreasing crop yeilds, which meant a gradual breakdown in the open-field system of agriculture. The clues to a village's dwindling size are the records of tax assessments in the early 1300s, which give some sort of picture of the size of its population. In 1334, the village of Pudding Norton in Norfolk had such a low tax assessment that it was hardly surprising that the village was in decline. In 1401, the fewness and poverty of the inhabitants, due to the exhausted barren soil, meant the settlement's desertion and retreat to more fertile parts. Today, the gaunt ruins of St Margaret's Church tower (TF924277) remain as a sad memorial to a community that strived long and hard to make their fields prosperous. Similarly, in the same area, the battered masonry of Egmere Church (TF896374) stands forlornly midst the humps and hollows of its deserted village.

The Black Death, or bubonic plague, was a pandemic which reached south-west Britain in about August, 1348. It was an exceptionally violent outbreak involving all three types of infection, agonising in its symptoms, devasting in its effects. Unfortunately, the unreliability of contemporary sources and the inadequacy of medieval records make any attempt at an accurate assessment of these effects extremely hazardous. The best estimate available is that approximately one-third of the people in England died; possibly a higher proportion in Wales.

Obviously such a heavy death-toll caused severe dislocation, at least temporarily: however, it is now considered probable that in many cases the Black Death did not cause the desertion of a village unless the village was already in decline. Certainly many of the documents kept by the manors record changes of tenants, and there are authentic cases concerning villages where the lord was allowed to run cattle and sheep because there were no taxpayers left. Another clue which hints at depopulation due to the plague, is the disappearance of a village name from the tax

## Deserted Medieval Villages
### Identifying Features

**Streets**
- These are to be found as holloways, which are tracks deepened in time by the passage of carts and pedestrians. Look for these signs as you cross a pasture, for the footpath you are walking on may be along the line of an ancient village street.
- Look for a simple network of holloway patterns on the ground which mark the former roads and back streets.
- The back lanes may run parallel to the main street, and be interconnecting forming a simple chequer-board pattern.
- The streets may radiate from a central open area or village green, and lead away in a random fashion. In other sites, the village may have consisted of a single main street.
- Some of the deeply-worn holloways may be etched into the ground to a depth of several feet.
- A sunken country lane or track is a good example of an ancient line of communication.

**House Sites**
- At the best sites, the remains of houses generally appear as either hollow or raised rectangular shapes, with raised edges that trace the outlines of collapsed walls, or of the stone footings.
- Look out for these rectangular units usually flanking the holloways.
- The grass-covered outlines may be very faint, or at other sites there may be no house platforms visible whatsoever.
- Although house outlines may be difficult to see, one clue is that the old floor space may still remain more level than the surrounding ground.

- In some areas the design may be that of a long house with a part for living in and a section partitioned off for the animals. Or the byre may be a separate smaller building often set at right angles to the main building.
- The peasant houses may only be represented by faint terraces on the ground.

**Tofts or Crofts**
- The long narrow or square shaped tofts of individual peasant holdings normally lie alongside or behind each dwelling.
- They are usually clearly defined with their shape outlined by the ridges of the boundary banks.
- Slight hollows around them may indicate boundary ditches.

**Ridge and Furrow Fields**
- The deserted medieval village may lie amongst signs of the ridge and furrow pattern strips of the ancient open fields. Today, this pattern may have modern field boundaries, superimposed on it.

**Churches**
- A church standing alone may signify a village that has shifted to another site, or it may be an indication that the village has shrunk leaving the present village a little distance away.
  Note that a church standing some distance from the present village nucleus may have been the result of a shift in the focus of the village due to changes in road usage, or by the creation of parks, both of which usually occurred later than medieval times.
- An isolated ruined church may point to the site of a deserted village.

rolls after 1355, although it must be stressed that the epidemic was one of the number of causes that contributed to the depopulation of villages. Its long-term effect are very difficult to assess. It may be argued that in certain areas when communities were weakened by plague, they succumbed to the intentions of the sheep-enclosure landlords a few decades later.

Another effect of the pestilence was the creation of labour problems, at least in the short term, for the lord of the manor. The surviving peasants could now press for the changing of labour services into rent, and could move away with less fear of being traced and returned. The manorial lords tried hard to retain the system of serfdom, but without success. Eventually, rising prices of goods, foodstuffs and increased wages for labour brought about more changes. Now it became the turn of the yeoman farmer, who had probably risen from villein status, to gradually enclose small strips of open-field for pasture. On the moors and hills, where the manorial system had not taken root, the sheep became kings.

### Map Clues for Possible Deserted Village Sites

Early maps can be valuable sources of information, such as Saxton's map of Norfolk, dated 1574. This revealed the former villages of Godwick, Mintlyn and Pudding Norton. Some eighteenth- and early nineteenth-century maps provide many valuable clues to hitherto unknown deserted villages. A good place to start a search for these sites is the County Record Office, especially for areas mapped before the process of Parlimentary Enclosures. The clues are descriptive field names that allude to a previous settlement, and the pattern of small hedged enclosures.

Even though the directions and relevant information to many sites are given in this book, it is advisable to familiarise oneself with the area covered by the 1:50,000 or 1in to 1 mile Ordnance Survey map. In some cases, it may be more rewarding to consult the appropriate 1:25,000 Ordnance Sheet map. A study beforehand of the area to be visited will probably save an immense amount of time and fruitless journeyings, and could make it possible for another site or sites to be visited in the locality during the same day. Look for the following clues:

● A church standing alone.

● A moated site with a fishpond, or a string of fishponds close by.

● A large empty space on the map in an area of countryside otherwise dotted with villages at regular intervals.

● Where a number of footpaths meet in an empty space for no apparent reason. It is possible that there may have been a settlement there at one time.

### Other Sources of Information

A modern edition of the Domesday Book, or a book entitled, 'Feudal Aids and Analogous Documents', 1284-1431 (Vol. 4), published by the Public Record Office; other valuable documentary evidence such as the Lay Subsidy returns, the Poll Tax returns, and the accounts of tax reliefs housed the headquarters of the Public Record Office at Kew all provide much useful information.

A visit to the vast collection of aerial photographs held by Cambridge University in Free School Lane, Cambridge, may verify or explain a particular deserted village site.

**Access** Generally, a good proportion of the sites included in this book are accessible by means of a convenient footpath, and others are in the care of the Department of the Environment, the National Trust or the County Council.

For sites where there is no right of access, it is important to seek permission to visit the site from the landowner or tenant. If there is a right of way, one should keep to the path; where it crosses a site such as a deserted medieval village, and one wishes to examine a wider area, it is also courteous to ask permission.

Responsible visitors who are genuinely interested will often be granted access to the site. However, it may be difficult during the summer months, as the sites may sometimes be surrounded by standing crops.

## Manorial Moats and Fishponds

- The location of a moated enclosure and fishponds may point to the site of a nearby deserted village. Often the moats and fishponds still have water in them.
- The rectangular or square-shaped enclosure would have been occupied by the manor house or a prosperous yeoman's house. Access was by means of a causeway across the moat.
- Today, examples may be found in many parts of the country, particularly in the English midlands.
- The site may, or may not, now be occupied by a building. If the moat is dry, often the earthworks are still visible.
- The manorial fishponds are often situated near to the site of the manor, usually with distinctive earthworks enclosing an area or areas of different shapes and sizes.
- It may be possible to detect the gaps in the banks where the original sluices were placed.
- The water supply that fed the fishponds may also have worked the lord's water-mill.

Some deserted medieval villages have excellent features, with a very good pattern of roads, and crofts with house sites visible. Some have a very good pattern of roads and crofts, but have no house sites visible. Others have surface remains that have either been considerably disturbed and are difficult to visualise, or have disappeared almost entirely.

During the summer months ground markings may be difficult to detect due to long grass and other vegetation. At other times, the village streets, house sites, tofts, and the ridge and furrow patterns of the open fields may be seen to advantage when the sun lies at a low angle and casts long shadows, preferably early morning or late afternoon.

The following sites show most of the features of deserted villages, but are only a few of the many hundreds of known sites in England.

## Deserted Medieval Village Sites

### Wharram Percy

Wharram-le-Street, Malton, Norh Yorkshire
OS 100, (1in 98), SE858642
Amid the chalklands of the Yorkshire Wolds, almost secretly tucked away in a small valley and along its gentle slopes is the deserted medieval village of Wharram Percy. Excavations begun in 1952 by the Deserted Medieval Village Research Group have continued slowly and methodically at seasonal intervals. The enthusiasts have uncovered, and are still uncovering, many fascinating insights into the world of people from the prehistoric to the Late Medieval period. There has been evidence of stone axes from the Pike o' Stickle area of the Lake District, signs of ancient plough strips beneath the hut sites, and fragments of Romano-

*Ruined church, Wharram Percy*

British pottery scattered about in the upper layers of the soil. The area around Wharram Percy and the surrounding chalk lands of the Wolds have been home to a considerable population down through the centuries.

*Wharram Percy. Deserted village site in foreground, holloway on right*

In early Saxon times a family built a hut in the valley bottom and this tiny settlement slowly expanded to that of a compact village-life community. Although the church was probably built towards the end of the Saxon period, Christianity had made its mark in this tiny settlement well before the tenth century. We can assume that the Saxon dwellings were sited on the terrace above the stream, close to the church and the mill with its dammed up pond. In the twelfth century the village expanded and moved on to the hill slope to the west. The picture is of an irregularly-sited group of houses built in rectangular paddocks or tofts. Originally the area would have been part of the open field system, as there is evidence of a boundary ditch on the edge of the slope where it levels out. The manor house was set apart from the simple dwellings with an open area or village green between them.

In the thirteenth century, the manor house site was moved to the north, and the area between it and the old site was used for new housing. This is a clear example of a lord attempting to separate himself from the peasant houses, as the population grew and the village expanded. This new housing site appears to have been planned with paddocks of a regular size and the dwellings end on to the street. The foundations of the village houses and paddock boundaries lie under the grass, but they may be seen as a regular pattern along the hillside. Sunken holloways serving the houses and fields are visible leading off the main village street. At one point, even the compressed ruts of a cart track have been discovered in the excavations, as well as the remains of a possible corn-drying kiln, still showing a smoke-blackened area. These structures were likely to have been very common, particularly in upland areas where the crops would have been difficult to dry. The kilns were in the shape of a circular oven with a long flue and a stoke hole. Within one toft or paddock were a peasant longhouse and cattle yard. Along its eastern side an entrance from the passing lane is clearly visible.

At the north end of the site the earthworks of the thirteenth-century manor house appear to cover the walls of rooms, courtyards and outbuildings. One room seems to have a raised part which was probably used as a dining area.

St Martin's Church nestles near the foot of the valley. It is now ruined and roofless, but nevertheless has a long and interesting history. Excavations have shown that it was at its largest in the thirteenth and fourteenth centuries before being reduced and narrowed. The problem was a common one; as labour became scarce, so arable farming was abandoned in favour of sheep. People without land or employment simply moved away, and the village ultimately ceased to exist about five hundred years ago.

Wharram Percy has a friendly welcoming atmosphere, where one can sit on the bankside and look at the church, or wander over the grassy ridges of the deserted village, trying to imagine the lay-out as it was, and reflecting on its succession of farming communities.

**Access** From the centre of Malton, take the Norton road. After the railway level-crossing, turn right on to the B1248 North Grimston road for 6¾ miles (10.8km) to the village of Wharram-le-Street. As the road continues to climb, take the next narrow metalled lane on the right, which then turns sharp left to Bella Farm. Just beyond the farm, a track on the right descends to the valley. There is a small parking area at this point. Walk down the track to cross the stream and the track bed of a long-dismantled railway. Bear left, and follow the way on to the site of the deserted village, which is up the slope to the right. To view the ruined church continue up the track and pass beyond the cottages. Walking distance, from the car park to the church is ⅝ mile (1km). Distance from Malton to the parking area is 7¾ miles (12.4km).

*Excavated corn-drying kiln, Wharram Percy*

### Ingarsby

Houghton-on-the-Hill,
Leicester, Leicestershire
OS 141, (1in 122), SK684055
The settlement was probably founded in the ninth or early tenth century by the Danes — the name means 'Ingwar's village'. At the time of the Domesday Book the village had a recorded population of thirty-two inhabitants. From the 1381 tax assessment, it appears that the village was much impoverished, with about a dozen poor families. Although the pestilence had taken its toll of the population, it is believed that the main cause was the exhaustion of the Liassic clay soils. The lands round about were much better suited to pastoral than to arable farming. The early settlers were ignorant of soil qualities and this pattern of events led to deserted settlements in many parts of the midlands and eastern England.

In the mid-fourteenth century the manor of Ingarsby was granted to the monks of Leicester Abbey, who eventually acquired all the land belonging to the estate. The tiny community became too small a force to continue the traditional, and now unproductive, arable farming. In 1469 the open fields were enclosed and most of the area coverted to sheep and cattle pastures. This was the end for people who had continually struggled against all the odds. They simply packed up their meagre belongings and left their hovels to rot and their fields to grass over. By 1563 the village had disappeared.

The village occupied a sloping site on the north side of a small stream to the east of the minor road from Houghton-on-the-Hill to Hungarton. The remains consist of a very good pattern of holloways and crofts or paddocks, but with no house sites visible. Two rights of way cross the site; but if one approaches from the track opposite the entrance to Ingarsby Old Hall, the village streets run down the slope towards the stream, with interconnecting lanes between them. Follow the top track to the next gate in the wooden fence, and there just beyond to the right is a solitary hawthorn tree. This holloway is much deeper than the others and is probably the main street of the village. Between the parallel streets it is possible to pick out the boundaries of the peasants' crofts. The earthworks of the old manor house moat are still visible at the north-western

*Ingarsby Deserted Village*

angle of Ingarsby Old Hall.

From the upper track there are extensive views of distant Charnwood Forest, (note the fine old railway viaduct still in situ). Looking eastwards, the rolling countryside stretches to the old county of Rutland.

**Access**  Ingarsby lies 1 mile (1.6km) north of the A47 from

Houghton-on-the-Hill, and 7m miles (11.2km) east of Leicester. In this region of Leicestershire there is a good network of rights of way, which enables the rambler to incorporate a number of deserted village sites in a circular route.

### Suggested Leicestershire Walk

OS 141 (1in. 122)

A 'figure of eight' walking route of some 16 miles (25.6km), that passes lost village sites, amid a rural landscape that includes many other points of interest.

Ingarsby, Quenby, Cold Newton, Life Hill, Billesdon, Kates Hill, Rolleston, Rolleston Wood — towards Goadby, Noseley Village, New Inn (B6047), Firsby Village, Billesdon, Green Hill, Botany Bay Fox Covert, Ingarsby.

### Sandon

Stafford, Staffordshire
OS 127, (1in 119), SJ955296
The old village was situated between the moat, around the site of Sandon Old Hall, and All Saints' Church, east of the present village. The area is now part of Sandon Park which lies on higher ground on the north-east side of the Trent Valley. In medieval times, the village lay on what is believed to have been an access route to Stone and which was conveniently sited above the marshy valley of the Trent.

An excavation in 1968-9 revealed a main street running north-east to south-west, at the foot of Black Hill. The street is now followed by the line of an old footpath which deepens into a clear holloway by the fence to the north-east. Although the evidence is indistinct on the ground, the probable house platforms and paddocks lined the main street mainly on the south-east side. Between the centre of the village site at SJ955296 and the moat cottages there appears to be depression with a central earth bank. This may well be the location of the village pond and reservoir.

Sandon, unlike other deserted medieval villages listed in this section, did not die from pestilence or sheep enclosure. Parish records show that there was still a village in existence in 1633, but its disappearance may probably be attributed to the creation of Sandon Park in the mid-eighteenth century.

Just a short distance eastwards down-slope from the church lies the manorial moat, still with water. It is well preserved, rectangular in shape, and has an outside measurement of 330ft by 312ft (102m by 94m). The inner enclosure is 160ft (49m) square, with a stone facing around much of its perimeter edge. Along the western side is a bay separated by a narrow bank from the main moat, and which may have been the original fishpond. There appears to have been some post-medieval alterations to this area of the moat. The fishponds to the north-east may be much later in origin, and probably fed by a culvert from the Stocking Brook.

The manor was acquired by the Erdeswick family in 1338, and the original Sandon Hall stood on the moated site. Sampson Erdeswick, who died in 1603, was a noted antiquary, having produced the *Survey of Staffordshire*, the first history of

*Manor house moat, Sandon*

the county.

All Saints' Church, founded in the twelfth century, has a magnificent setting in leafy Sandon Park. It is approached by a narrow deeply-worn lane from the modern village; a route

most likely used in passage from the old village site down to the valley and beyond. As the lane swings round the churchyard wall, look back to the corner where the indentations of the old holloways show on the surface of the gently-sloping pasture.

It is very well worthwhile spending some time looking at the inside of the church. The building is beautifully furnished, including much seventeenth century-work; the Erdeswick family tombs have incised tops and there is a fine monument to Sampson Erdeswick the local historian.

**Access**    The church, moat, fish ponds and the deserted village site lie in Sandon Park, $\frac{3}{8}$ mile (600m) north-east from Sandon village on the A51, Rugeley to Stone road. the lane to the park lies directly opposite the junction of the B5066 with the main road.

*Sandon Church and village holloway*

Many villages and hamlets continued to shrink in the fifteenth century, with a smaller proportion of peasants struggling to keep body and soul together. The villagers clung to their open-field strips, growing just enough food in a co-operative survival system. At the same time, the lord of the manor bought out some of the freehold tenants, increasing his own lands, and charging the more prosperous peasant tenants higher rents. It was a vicious circle. As the better-off peasants began to strengthen their holdings by gradually converting the open fields to enclosed rectangular areas, the loss of land meant hardship for the poorer peasants, and bankruptcy for the very small tenant farmers who retreated to other areas hoping for a fresh start. This left a half empty village, and the surrounding area peopled by a small number of large tenants, their labourers and owners of small holdings.

Between 1750 and 1850, practically all the open-field, meadow and common land was shared out among the big landowners and yeoman farmers as the result of Parliamentary Acts of Enclosure. The enclosure awards affected and disrupted every parish, because in most cases the largest landholder, or one or two principal farmers would draw up a scheme for enclosure and petition Parliament to introduce a Bill. This was referred to a committee after a second reading. The Bill returned to the House, passed, was submitted to the Lords, after which it would receive the Royal Assent. The names of Commissioners were recorded in the Bill, and it was their duty to be involved with the parish, to re-allocate all common holdings and to end common rights. Of course, the promoters of the petition did very well from the enclosure. The enclosures were particularly hard for the small farmer; he lost his right of grazing on the common, he lost his small parcel of land, and was forced to seek work as a hired labourer. Many of the householders were allotted small fields, which were formerly part of the old open fields or from the wasteland. These enclosures had to be fenced or walled within a certain period of time. Enclosures changed the face of the landscape in many parts of Britain to produce a chequerboard pattern of field and hedgerow, which is now so beautifully overlaid on the face of the English lowlands.

In the north of England, such as in Swaledale, the roughly rectangular fields in the valley bottoms leaves the huddle of Gunnersides'

*Edgmere ruined church*

houses to climb and measure their straight geometrical lines across the rising fellside. A true north country man would feel that a vital part of the landscape was missing without the regular pattern of these friendly grey and brown stone walls. They provide shelter for the hillside sheep,

*Gunnerside, Swaledale*

and a moment's respite for the fell walker battling against the strong wind and driving rain. They are a true part of the landscape, laboriously raised by man and so welcomed by nature that they appear to have been there since time began.

Following on from the enclosures, in many cases the lord of the manor or large landowner decided to enlarge his domain by creating a new park around the large house. As he looked out across his grounds the old village probably spoilt his view, so the settlement was either reduced or entirely demolished, except for the church, and a new village placed out of sight. In many areas this emparking has also left a legacy in the landscape, for one need only to look at the Ordnance Survey map to find an isolated church set in parkland with the manor house or hall, and the re-settled village straggling along outside the park gates. However, things are not always what they seem, for in some cases the village may have perished before the area was enlarged and landscaped.

## Some Other Deserted Village Sites

### Houghton
Fakenham, Norfolk
OS 132, (1in 125), TF793283
An example of emparking. There was a village at Houghton before Sir Robert Walpole built the great house in a landscaped parkland. All remains of the village, except the small medieval church of St Martin, had gone by 1740. Today, the church lies remote in the park, and the contemporary village of New Houghton with its houses of whitewashed brick extends up to the gates of the park.

### Hound Tor
Manaton, Bovey Tracey, Devon
OS 191, (1in 175), 'Dartmoor Tourist Map' SX748796
From the tenth century, a number of turf and wattle houses represented an early form of later medieval Dartmoor longhouse. From about 1200, these dwellings were replaced by stone structures, consisting of three small single-roomed houses and several two-roomed long-houses, the latter equipped with hearths at the living end, and drains.

### Middleton Stoney
Bicester, Oxfordshire
OS 164, (1in 145), SP532233
An example of emparking, with the mansion set in landscaped grounds, and the estate village relocated beyond the park gates. Only the church remains on the former village site.

### Towthorpe
Wetwang, Great Driffield, Humberside
OS 101, (1in 98), SE898629

### Godwick
Tittleshall, Fakenham, Norfolk
OS 132, (1in 125), TF904222

### Wormleighton
Southam, Warwickshire
OS 151, (1in 145), SP448540

### Runston
Chepstow, Gwent
OS 162, (1in 155), ST496915

**Egmere**
Little Walsingham, Norfolk
OS 132, (1in 125), TF897374
A solitary farm now stands on the site together with the tower of the ruined church, and the remains of holloways and tofts. This once flourishing village decayed in the fifteenth century, mainly due to the ravages of the plague. The church was neglected and the lead removed from the roof in the time of Henry VIII.

**Widford**
Swinbrook, Burford, Oxfordshire
OS 163, (1in 157), SP273121
A footpath leads to the isolated church on the banks of the River Windrush. The settlement was deserted due to large scale cattle rearing in Tudor times.

**Milton Abbas**
Blandford Farm, Dorset
OS 194, (1in 178), ST802020
An example of emparking. The original market town was destroyed by Joseph Damer in order to create more parkland around his new mansion. The new estate village was re-sited a little distance away to the south-east in a dry cleft in the downland. Today, the line of whitewashed thatched cottages make the perfect picture of a rural English village.

**Noseley**
Billesdon, Leicestershire
OS 141 (1in 122), SP734987
The village was enclosed and depopulated at the beginning of the sixteenth century. The ploughland was converted to pasture for sheep runs.

**Hamilton**
Scraptoft, Leicester, Leicestershire
OS 140, (1in 121), SK643073
This village suffered severely from periodic ravages of the plague. It was enclosed and converted to pasture in about 1450.

**Clopton**
Croydon, Royston, Cambridgeshire
OS 153, (1in 147), TL302488

# CHAPTER EIGHT

# Defence, Communications and Industry

## FORTIFIED DWELLINGS

Deep in the secluded valleys of the Cheviot Hills, the mist often lingers before being spirited away by the warm touch of the sun. For centuries, these sprawling slopes and secret inner recesses had echoed to the cries of men and the sounds of clashing swords. After the Battle of Flodden in 1513 there was even bloodier conflict, with small bands of raiders, the mosstroopers, making their quiet ways through the hills to terrorise the scattered farmsteads and larger houses. They came to settle old scores, to steal horses, cattle and sheep, and to burn down dwellings and crops. It was not a safe place to travel in, unless accompanied by heavily armed companions. As well as constant skirmishing across the Border, there were also inter-tribal feuds which divided the area into bitter warring camps.

In order to try and control the problem, both sides of the Border were divided into two marches — the East March and the Middle March. The responsibility for defending the Border and keeping the uneasy peace was invested in the local nobility and their followers, in the form of a royal appointment as Warden of the Marches. Their brief was to ensure justice, to settle grievances and to prevent raids across the Border from his own side. However, it was also his duty to take retaliatory measures when necessary. In a situation where it was the usual custom to attack first and ask questions afterwards, the Wardens of both sides of the Border attempted to arrange truce days. The representatives consisted of the respective Wardens with six Scots and six English, and the meetings, which were not always peaceful, usually took place at the crossing points, the 'gates' or passes through the hills.

From east to west, the locations were at Butt Roads (NT872160), approached by the Salter's Road route from the Breamish Valley or along Clennell Street from Alwinton to Cocklawfoot; Windy Gyle (NT855150) by tracks from Upper Coquet to Kelsocleuch, or by Windy Rigg to the Calroust Burn; Black Braes (NT835150) via The Street to Hownam; Gamel's Path from Redesdale along Dere Street to Black Halls (NT789105), and down to Kale Water; and from Coquet Head (NT786082) to Upper Hindhead. Today, these ancient ways make magnificent walking routes across the high watershed of the Cheviot Hills.

In areas of larger villages and greater population and along the coastal plain, the Warden of the Marches attempted to frustrate the movements of the raiding bands by organising a better system of keeping watch. Information was passed on by the watchers, the alarm was raised, and the defences manned in readiness. The isolated farmsteads who ran their flocks and herds on the grassy upland tracts were most likely to be the first targets for the mosstroopers, who entered the area through the quiet ways in the hills. As they had no hope of immediate assistance, the communities took refuge in small defensible buildings which included pele towers and bastle houses. These structures would not stop an army, but they proved quite formidable to a small band of raiders looking for easy pickings, and anxious to avoid determined resistance.

The unsettled nature of the conditions prevailing in the areas on either side of the border during the fourteenth to sixteenth centuries is reflected in the types of some of these domestic buildings. At

*Pele tower, Kentmere Hall*

this turbulent period, those who were prepared and organised survived. In Cumberland and Westmorland, lesser landowners and farmers built small strong refuges called peles (peels), into which they and their families could retreat when danger threatened. They were squat, square towers built of heavy stonework to withstand the Scottish raids. They either had a ground-floor area for farm animals and a residential part above, with the whole tower isolated from the farmstead, or a defensible tower joined to the farm building. It was interesting to note that whereas many larger fortified buildings such as castles have disappeared, their masonry carried away, many peles have survived until the present. They are quite a feature of the Border countryside, and a little pleasant detective work is necessary to discover some of these ancient domestic dwellings. Although many have been incorporated into later homes, some have been adapted to other uses, and others are scattered about the Border countryside in ruins; they symbolise the stubborn spirit of our ancestors, and their determination to survive in this rugged landscape. In Cumbria, tucked away at the head of the Kentmere Valley, beneath the slopes of Ewe Crags, lies Kentmere Hall (SD451042). The fourteenth-century pele tower has four storeys with a staircase and a vaulted cellar. The attached farm building is sixteenth-century, and replaced an earlier structure. Bernard de Gilpin, who eventually became

Archdeacon of Durham, was born here in 1517.

The Ordnance Survey maps covering the Border area will reveal the locations of a number of peles. For example, on the eastern edge of the great Kielder Forest, the scanty remains of two of them now lie hidden in clearings surrounded by seemingly endless martialled ranks of conifers. One site lies just west of Comb (NY764904).

Another slightly different type of defensible tower, is the so-called 'parson's pele' or 'vicar's pele'. These were built for the protection of the mainly Catholic priesthood. The tower of St Anne's Church at Ancroft (NU002452), was constructed as an integral part of the building.

*Ruined pele, Comb Tarset Burn*

*Ancroft Parson's Pele*

*Embleton Parson's Pele*

The stubby square tower contains a tunnel-vaulted room with a spiral staircase which leads to the upper storeys. There is another door leading into the nave. At Elsdon, a frontier village on the Northumbrian side of the Cheviots with its large central green, there is another fine example, of a fourteenth-century fortified parson's pele (NY936934). The ground floor room, 27ft by 15ft (8.2m by 4.6m) has a good lath and plaster barrel-vaulted ribbed ceiling. There are bedrooms on the first floor, and another room above them. Beside the parish church at Embleton (NU230225) the parson's pele could safely hide the priest and his household in the event of a raid. It dates back to about 1400, and contains battlements and arrow slits. There are other fine examples at Corbridge and Alnham. In all these cases, probably only a wealthy priest could afford this type of building. These towers could not withstand a prolonged assault, but they could last out for an hour or two until help came.

---

## Fortified Dwellings
### Identifying Features

**Peles**
- They were isolated square defensive towers often built of dressed blocks of stone with a random rubble core.
- In some cases the towers were an integral part of the family home or farmstead.
- Usually the ground floor was for livestock and the upper floor was residential, and could only be reached by a ladder.
- Later peles may have more than one storey, usually connected by an internal stairway, and a barrel-vaulted basement. These were similar in design to the Scottish tower houses.

- Peles were usually owned by the lesser gentry who retired to them when a raid threatened from either side of the Anglo-Scottish border.

**Parsons' Peles**
- They were defensive towers for the protection of a largely Catholic priesthood.
- The basement, usually with a vaulted ceiling, was the storeroom. There was a stairway leading to the upper storeys.
- Some parsons' peles would be attached to the church, others would be built close by.

## Outstanding Sites

### Cocklaw Pele
Chollerton, Northumberland
OS 87, (1in 77), NY940711
The tower lies just to the east of the A6079 just south of Chollerton, and on a by-road to Errington. Marked as 'Tower' on the Ordnance Survey map, this large pele is now used as a farm building. The walls, at least 6ft (1.8m) thick, are built of huge dressed blocks of stone, and rise on the east side some 35ft (10.6m) in height. The doorway on the south side has a pointed arch with holes in the jambs to take a drawbar. A stairway in the thickness of the wall originally led to the roof, but is now only intact up to the first floor. The basement is barrel-vaulted, and the vaulting that remains is a tribute to the fine craftsmanship. The first floor consists of a large well-lit room, including two mullioned windows and a very large open fireplace. There is also a wall passage leading to a garderobe. The only signs indicating a second storey are the wall corbels that supported the floor beams. This room would only have been lit by two small windows, and by the blaze from another large open fireplace. Visitors who wish to inspect the interior of the pele should enquire at the nearby farm.

### Shilbottle Pele
Shilbottle, Alnwick,
Northumberland.
OS 81, (1in 71), NU196086
The old pele tower is now part of Shilbottle vicarage, although it was not orginally so. The tower has an arched entrance on the west side leading into a vaulted room which has two narrow windows. As there is no stairway to the upper floor, access was probably by a wooden ladder which could then be drawn up for safety. The tower can also be well viewed from the nearby churchyard. On the tower wall facing this particular direction, is an inscribed stone panel with the words, 'Turris de Schilbotal'.

### Orchardton Pele (DoE)
Castle Douglas, Dumfries and Galloway Region
OS 84, (1in 81),
NX817551

### Proctor Steads Craster,
Northumberland
OS 75, (1in 71), NU248201

### Tosson Pele
Great Tosson, Rothbury,
Northumberland
OS 81, (1in 71), NU029005

### Little Swinburne Pele Little
Swinburne, Colwell, Hexham,
Northumberland
OS 87, (1in 77), NY950778

### Whittingham Pele
Whittingham, Alnwick,
Northumberland
OS 81, (1in 71), NU065118

## Bastles

Bastles or bastle-houses are defensible farmhouses of the fifteenth to sixteenth centuries, and peculiar to a very narrow strip of country close to the Anglo-Scottish Border. In many cases, bastles are confused with peles, but several features indicate differences from peles on the one hand, and more conventional buildings on the other. With a few possible exceptions, they are the only farmhouses in the British Isles which accomodated livestock on the ground floor and the farmer and his family on the upper floor. The bastles are normally of a fairly uniform plan, rectangular in shape, about 35ft by 25ft (10.6m by 7.6m) and with quite steeply-pitched gables. The walls are nearly 4ft (1.2m) thick and constructed of irregularly-shaped masonry. The ground floor has a single narrow doorway placed in one of the gable walls. The ground floor area has no windows, only thin ventilation slits. Access to the doorway to the upper floor is by means of an outside flight of steps set towards the end of one of the long walls. In the early days, the residential part was probably reached by a ladder, which could then be drawn up for safety. The doorway would be a similarly strong affair, flanked by two or three small windows.

Generally, the upper floor of a bastle had either timber beams supported on rough corbelling or carrried on a beautifully constructed stone barrel vault. The end wall away from the doorway usually contained a fireplace, and access to the lower chamber was probably by a ladder, withdrawn through a small opening in the floor. However, in some cases a stairway was installed. The bastles continued to be occupied by farmers in the Border area well into the eighteenth, and even into the nineteenth centuries.

---

### Bastles
### Identifying Features

- The typical bastle is rectangular in plan, with a ground floor and an upper floor.
- The thick walls are built of large irregular blocks of stone, or well-squared stones, rising to steeply pitched gables.
- There is a single narrow doorway at ground level set in one of the gable walls.
- The doorway to the upper floor is situated towards the end of one of the long walls, and access to it is by means of an external stone stairway.

- There are usually two small windows, one on either side of the doorway, and sometimes another in the greater length of the same wall.
- The upper floor is either carried on timber beams or on a stone barrel vault.
- Internal access between the floors is best seen in the vaulted bastles, by means of a narrow opening cut through the stonework.
- Although most bastles are now roofed with stone or slate, it is likely that the original roof was covered by thatch.

---

### Outstanding Sites

**Gatehouse Bastle North**
Greenhaugh, Bellingham, Northumberland
OS 80, (1in 77), NY787889
The hamlet of Gatehouse lies on the eastern slopes of the Tarset valley and looks out westwards to the vast coniferous blanket of Kielder Forest. What was once bleak, ill-drained hill land, has been drained and planted with Norway Spruce and Sitka Spruce on the higher slopes, Scots and Lodgepole Pine on the heather moors and Japanese Larch on the lower slopes that are favoured with deeper soil. In this area mixed planting has added much to the visual amenity.

From Lanehead, a narrow country lane heads north from the North Tyne valley, closely following the configurations of the Tarset Burn before petering out into a track on entering the forest.

The north bastle, now used as an outbuilding, is constructed of a mixture of large irregular stones with small pieces set in between. An outside stone stair-way reaches the upper storey doorway with its chamfered mouldings. The small window on the north-east side of the doorway has a blind arch cut

*Gatehouse Bastle*

into the lintel, the one to the south-west is square-shaped, and was originally divided into four lights by wooden mullions. The upper floor is supported on wooden beams set into the walls, but originally they were carried on stone corbels. The fireplace hearth at the south-west end is also supported on wall corbels, but the chimney flue appears to be of a later date. At the north-east end of the building, the original ground floor doorway has chamfered sides which

contain recesses for drawbars.

The owner who lives in the adjacent cottage is pleased to see interested visitors, and will usually give permission to view the interior of the bastle.

A few yards away on the opposite side of the road lies Gatehouse Bastle South. Much converted in the past and used as a dwelling and as a barn, the bastle now stands derelict and roofless. The walls are constructed of large irregular stones, with the gaps filled with

small pieces of rubble.

**Access**  From Bellingham (pronounced Bellinjam) follow the north bank of the River North Tyne for $3\frac{1}{4}$ miles (5.2km) to Lanehead. Turn right and proceed through Greenhaugh, then bear right again to cross the Tarret Burn, and climb gradually to a crossroads. Take the left-hand road down to Gatehouse.Distance from Bellingham: $5\frac{1}{4}$ miles (8.4km)

## Hole

Bellingham, Northumberland
OS 80, (1in 77), NY867846
This bastle now forms part of the farm buildings which stand above the River Rede on the west side of the valley. The walls are composed of rough stonework, and appear to have been heightened on the long sides. The original entrance to the ground floor was situated in the western gable end, but this is now blocked up, and another entrance made in the opposite end wall. Along the south wall an external stairway ascends to the original doorway to the upper floor. The doorway has chamfered sides and a lintel, and is accompanied by two windows of a later date. Two other smaller windows with chamfered mouldings were probably the original ones, and then they were re-positioned to light the small attic. The ground floor area is roofed with a barrel vault, which has a small ladder hole cut through for access to the upper storey. At the east end of

Hole Bastle

this floor is a small stairway to the attic, and a fireplace at the opposite end.

**Access**  From the centre of Bellingham take the minor road to West Woodburn for a

distance of $2\frac{1}{4}$ miles (3.6km). The farm buildings at Hole lie on the right-hand side of the road.

## Akeld

Wooler, Northumberland
OS 75, (1in 71), NT957296
This bastle lies at the northern

foot of the Cheviot Hills, and was probably the one referred to in the survey of 1541. It is larger than the normal bastle, being

55ft (16.7m) long internally. The doorway, which is situated in the long west wall, has chamfered jambs and a tunnel recess for a drawbar. The walls of the bastle are 4ft (1.2m) thick, and are constructed of rubble and faced with masoned blocks of stone. Note the number of large boulders at the base of the walls. Inside, the ground floor is roofed by a barrel vault, which is pierced by a small rectangular ladder opening to the upper floor. It would appear that the entire storey is of a later date. The bastle is now used for farm purposes.

**Access**   The bastle is situated in the hamlet of Akeld, some 2¾ miles (4.4km) west-north-west of Wooler. At the junction of the A697 and the B6351, take the farm track south alongside the stream for 330yd (300m). The bastle lies on the right-hand side of the track.

## Other Bastle Sites

### White House Farm
Glassonby, Penrith, Cumbria
OS 91, (1in 83), NY577389

### Ottercops Farm
Kirkwhelpington,
Northumberland
OS 80, (1in 77), NY942980
None of the bastles are open to the public, so prospective visitors should apply to the owner; for those particularly interested and tactful, permission may be granted to view the interiors.

### Holystone Grange
Hepple, Rothbury,
Northumberland
OS 81, (1in 71), NT965004
This bastle is situated near to Holystone Grange, marked as a peel on the Ordnance Survey map. The upper storey was rebuilt at the beginning of this century and modern windows installed. The ground floor area has a vaulted roof with a stone stairway leading to the upper floor. The doorway on the ground floor at the east end has recesses for two drawbars, but the original upper entrance has disappeared and been replaced by a later doorway in the west gable wall.

### Black Middens
Shipley Shiels, Greenhaugh,
Bellingham, Northumberland
OS 80, (1in 77), NY775898

## SCOTTISH TOWER HOUSES

From as early as the twelfth century, there were small fortified buildings in the Border region which were developed as a response to the historic and physical conditions in the area. Bastles and peles represented the fortified homes of yeoman farmers and small landowners on both sides of the frontier, and these were the forerunners of the residential towers or tower houses. They became the characteristic dwellings, particularly of the Scottish landed gentry, from the fourteenth to the beginning of the seventeenth century. The focus of daily life in the Border area was the need for constant vigilance against surprise attacks, and there was a great increase in the building of tower houses after the defeat at Flodden. However, this development was not only restricted to the disputed border region, but also occurred in many other parts of Scotland throughout the bloody years of the sixteenth century.

Although somewhat misleadingly called castles, tower houses were only moderately fortified, and were in effect a family stronghold, unlike the great medieval towers with their outworks, which were capable of resisting a major siege. Many of the apparently warlike features were purely ornamental, but these plain stone built rectangular structures were more than capable of resisting attacks by intruders and hostile neighbours.

The main walls were very thick, and built to take the weight of the upper three or four storeys. They were constructed of excellent quality ashlar or of roughly coursed random rubble masonry. Fire was still the main danger, and the ground floor storerooms were separated from the main quarters by a segmental barrel-vaulted ceiling. Usually there was no internal link between the ground floor store areas and the upper storeys except by a ladder through a narrow hole in the apex of the vaulting. In some cases there was access from the main stairway to the upper part, or entresol, of the two ground floors. Entrance to the centre of the main room in the tower house, the hall, and to the bedrooms, apartments and ultimately to the parapet walk, was by means of a turnpike stair set in a small projecting wing, or by means of spiral stairs within the thickness of the walls. The hall and the private rooms contained fireplaces, and were lit by small windows, which in many cases were provided with window seats. Often, small rooms and garderobes were constructed within the thickness of the walls.

---

### Tower Houses
### Identifying Features

● A plain rectangular tower constructed of ashlar or roughly coursed masonry pierced by narrow windows at an inaccessible height.

● The walls rise to a parapet which originally had battlements. The tower house often has a steeply pitched roof with typical Scottish style crow-stepped gables.

● A spiral stairway set within the thickness of the wall or contained in a small wing, links the private quarters.

● The ground floor room may have an upper section or entresol; the latter connected either from the main stairway, or by means of a ladder descending from the main hall above through a small aperture in the barrel-vaulted ceiling. Both areas would be used as storerooms, and would receive little or no natural light.

● The hall, bedrooms and other private rooms contain fireplaces, some window seats, and small rooms and garderobes within the thickness of the wall. The upper room in the roof, the garret, was reached from the parapet walk.

● The ground floor entrance to the tower house was strongly defended by a system of double doors, a heavy oak door and an inner iron door or yett.

● There may be signs of the original strong wall or barmkin that surrounded the courtyard, and which originally contained ancillary structure like the kitchen and the stable.

● In some cases, extensions to the tower house block resulted in variations or 'L' or 'Z' shaped plans, and many became disguised by later residential structures.

---

### Outstanding Sites

**Smailholm Tower (DoE)**
Sandyknowe, Smailholm, Kelso, Borders Region
OS 74, (1in 70), NT638347, This tower house is splendidly sited on the highest of a series of rocky outcrops at Smailholm between Kelso and Melrose. It is constructed of blue whinstone with dressings of alternate long and short sandstone quoins. From its elevation of 637ft (194m) above sea level, the tower commands a wide view of the surrounding countryside.

It is believed to date from the early part of the sixteenth century, and was saved from demolition in 1799 by the pleas of Sir Walter Scott, who had spent many happy boyhood hours at Sandyknowe Farm. The owner of the estate agreed providing Sir Walter wrote a ballad about the tower.

The tower is oblong in plan and measures 40ft by 32ft (12m by 9.6m). In the sixteenth century it was attacked and plundered on a number of occasions, during which times cattle and prisoners were taken. The two-door defended entrance is situated at ground level in the south wall. It opens into a small vaulted chamber with a newel stairway, and another doorway which leads to the ground floor storeroom. At one time this room was provided with an entresol or upper floor which was covered with a barrel-

*Smailholm Tower House*

vaulted ceiling. A small aperture in the vaulting allowed access by ladder to the stores.

The main hall is situated on the next floor and is reached from the main stairway. The room is lit by natural light from windows on the east, south and west walls. The windows have window seats. This pleasant room also contains a fireplace, a wall cupboard and a garderobe with a window set within the thickness of the wall. The floor above, a bedroom, also has a fireplace on the north wall, two windows on the south and west walls, and a garderobe. The stairway continues up to the top storey which has a barrel-vaulted roof and crow-stepped gables. The room has a fireplace and two windows, the larger one set within a deep opening in the wall. Two other doors lead to the north and south parapet walks.

At ground level, a barmkin wall originally extended around the edge of the rocky knoll. Now, the outstanding remains are to be seen around the entrance to the courtyard at the west end. This part contains the kitchen and other outbuildings.

**Access** The tower lies 8 miles (12.8km) to the west of Kelso, and may be approached by the A6089 and then the B6397 to Smailholm. Turn left on to a minor road in the village and almost immediately left again. The lane executes a few sharp turns before arriving at the signposted farm track to Sandyknowe. Proceed through the farmyard to a small parking area close by the rocky outcrops. The tower stands stark and impressive on higher ground.

### Scotstarvit Tower (DoE)
Cupar, Fife Region
OS 59, (1in 56), NO370113, (DoE)
The tower house stands as a notable landmark on high ground 1 mile (1.6km) west of the Hill of Tarvit. It commands a tremendous all round view, particularly across the smooth cultivated slopes of the Eden valley. The plain, strong, ashlar-faced L-shaped tower was known to have been in existence in 1579. It rises five storeys high to a parapet which was originally battlemented. The steeply pitched roof containing an attic has the typical Scottish style crow-stepped gables. The entrance door in the south wall leads into a ground floor storeroom lit by narrow slit windows. Originally this room had an upper part, an entresol, which was accessible from the main stairway. The spiral staircase lies to the right of the entrance door, in a protruding wing of the building, thus forming a connecting link to all the private rooms.

The main room of the tower house, the hall, is situated above the storerooms and is lit by three windows with accompanying window seats. The room is also supplied with a large fireplace and a garderobe. The next floor, which had a vaulted ceiling, was the lord's private apartment and bedroom. It is furnished with a fireplace and two windows with flanking stone seats. The upper part of the tower has two further rooms, a rather dark chamber, and an attic in the roof which is reached from the parapet walk. The corners of the parapet are pierced by musket-loops and the crenels indicate the arrangement of the battlements. A neat decorative pointed tower caps the small stairway wing. All traces of the barmkin have now disappeared, but originally it enclosed the kitchen and other subsidiary buildings.

**Access** The tower lies to the west of the A916, some $2\frac{3}{4}$ miles (4.4km) south of Cupar. The site is signposted along the track, which lies opposite the entrance to the neighbouring Scottish National Trust property, Hill of Tarvit. The house, renovated by Sir Robert Lorimer, is surrounded by lovely gardens.

*Scotstarvit Tower House*

**Claypotts Tower House**
(DoE)
Broughty Ferry, Dundee,
Tayside Region
OS 54, (1in 50), NO453318,
This well preserved Z-plan
tower house was built by John
Strachan. It bears two dates:
1569 on the South Tower, and
1588 on the North Tower, which
suggests that the building
remained unfinished for a
considerable time. It is a superb
building of striking aspect,
except that a modern housing
estate has been built close to one
of Scotland's finest tower houses.

The main feature of Claypotts
is the provision of circular
protective towers at diagonally
opposite corners of the central
block, which resulted in a Z-
shaped building plan. This was
to enable defenders in the towers
to fire across the face of the main
building. The tops of the
flanking towers are corbelled to
form square garrets, with added
decorations of dormer windows
and crow-stepped gables. The
entrance to the tower house is on

the ground floor along the west
wall. Here, a short passage leads
to two vaulted storerooms, as
well as access to the main
stairway and to the kitchen in
the south-west tower. The wide
arched kitchen fireplace has a
well proportioned chimney with
an oven on one side and a simple
sink on the other. There is
another stairway in the north
tower, which can be reached by
passing through the ground floor
storeroom on the northern side.

The hall, the centre of life in
the tower house, is situated on
the first floor and takes up the
whole of the central block area.
The wide fireplace has two
recesses, one on the left-hand
side to keep the salt dry and to
the right a small mural
cupboard. Opening off the hall,
the north-east tower has a
fireplace and a garderobe, and
was probably the laird's retiring
room. Close by the entrance to
the tower room is a doorway
access to the secondary or
domestic stair. Above the hall
the second floor room has a

fireplace at either end, which
suggests that there was a
partition down the centre of the
room. The chamber above on
the third floor is the garret from
which doorways lead to the
upper rooms of the towers.

The number of roomy, well-lit
and adequately heated
apartments indicate a clear
desire for comfort on the part of
the occupiers. They were also
mindful of safety, as the brilliant
design plan of the house testifies.
There are wide-mouthed shot
holes placed in strategic
positions around the only
entrance to the tower house.
Originally, the building would
have been further protected by a
barmkin which held ancillary
structures such as stabling.

**Access** The tower house
stands some 3$\frac{1}{2}$ miles (5.6km)
east of the Dundee end of the
Tay Road Bridge. Continue
along the A92 as far as the
roundabout with the B987. Turn
right towards Broughty Ferry,
and the tower house is situated
immediately on the right.

## Some Other Sites

**Jordan's Castle Tower
House** (DoE)
Ardglass, Co Down, Northern
Ireland
OS 1:50,000, Sheet 21, (1in 9),
JS561372

**Narrow Water Castle Tower
House** (DoE)
Warrenpoint, Co Down,
Northern Ireland
OS 1:50,000, Sheet 29, (1in 9),
J127193

**Glenbuchat Castle Tower
House** (DoE)
Strathdon, Alford, Grampian
Region
OS 37, (1in 39), NJ398149

**Crathes Tower House** (NT)
Crathes, Banchory, Grampian
Region
OS 45, (1in 40), NO734968

**Elcho Castle Tower House**
(DoE)
Rhynd, Perth, Tayside Region
OS 58, (1in 55), NO164211

**Huntingtower Tower House**
(DoE)
Perth, Tayside Region
OS 58, (1in 55), NO084252

**Greenknowe Tower House**
(DoE) Gordon, Kelso, Borders
Region
OS 74, (1in 63), NT639428

**Aberdour Castle Tower
House** (DoE)
Aberdour, Fife Region
OS 65, (1in 55), NT193854

**Cardoness Castle Tower
House** (DoE)
Gatehouse of Fleet, Dumfries
and Galloway Region
OS 83, (1in 73), NX591553

**Crichton Castle Tower
House** (DoE)
Pathhead, Lothian Region
OS 66, (1in 62), NT380612

## PACKHORSE ROADS AND TRACKS

The narrow winding lanes that are such a feature of so many parts of Britain are communication patterns that have existed for thousands of years. The routes of many of these ancient ways and tracks were formed long before the advent of the well-constructed Roman roads. According to Christopher Taylor in his book *Roads and Tracks in Britain* (1979), groups of Neolithic people followed the wandering tracks of migratory animals that covered a broad area without any particular plan or pattern. It is quite possible that as early as 6000BC, many parts of the British Isles were criss-crossed by countless trackways created by the movement of herds of animals, and accompanied by routes etched into the surface of the ground by the generations of men who hunted them.

Gradually nomadic life gave way to one of a settled existence. In southern England the people thinly ploughed the downland slopes, establishing fields, growing crops and keeping increasing numbers of domesticated animals. On the hilltops they constructed causewayed camps; circular earthworks with access points across the ditches where, about 2900BC, the people congregated at certain times of the year for ritual ceremonies and for the bartering and trading of goods, such as salt, stone axes and hides. The process of clearing the land for cultivation and pasture meant that farming communities required a steady supply of stone axes. Flint was the most common material used, as were other different forms of hard rock that could be chipped and polished into very efficient, highly prized axes and other cutting tools. The long unbroken chalk ridges of southern England with only light coverings of beech woodland favoured an easier passage for animals and hunters alike. For example, although no one can be certain, it is likely that the Ridgeway — an upland route along the Berkshire, Oxford and Wiltshire Downs — was developed for communication and trade. This ancient route continues to the north-east as the Icknield Way, which ran along the foot of the chalk scarp from the Thames at Goring right into Norfolk. We have a good idea how far the Neolithic tradesmen travelled with their goods because axes fashioned from rock other than flint have been found all over Britain. The Lake District's first exports were stone axes shaped from a hard volcanic tuff that outcropped in a narrow band high up around the peaks of Pike o' Stickle and Harrison Stickle in Great Langdale. There have been a number of specimens of Langdale axes found close to the line of the Icknield Way in East Anglia. Many other stone axes from Tievebulliagh in County Antrim, Graiglwyd in North Wales, Hyssington in Shropshire, and from Northumberland, Charnwood Forest and Cornwall, have been discovered in eastern England as well as in many other parts of Britain. This is sound evidence as to the volume of trade, and of the considerable movement from place to place in Neolithic times.

Today, some of these routeways make excellent walks. For example, there is a fine section on the Berkshire Ridgeway between Thurle Down (SU575814) and Fox Hill (SU233 815); along the line of Icknield Way at Deacon Hill (TL126295); and at Sty Head (NY220095) on the Axe Way from Great Langdale to the coast via Ennerdale or Wasdale. From Cardigan Bay to Wessex along the Kerry Hill Ridgeway, there is a good section from Cider House (SO110847) to Kerry Pole (SO164866).

During the Bronze Age and Iron Age (a period of about 2,300 years), the population of Britain increased greatly, and as a result, great tracts of forest cover were cleared, and much of the country was settled. Homesteads and hamlets grew into larger settlements. The settlements were not only on well-drained upland, but also in the forested valleys, on heavy clay soils and on hill slopes. Lines of communication became vital for man's survival. A settlement on the side of a hill was able to trade its produce with another community in the forested valley who made baskets and other domestic and farming implements. Gradually the local network of footpaths and tracks spread to settlements further afield as trade with other parts of Britain increased. The growth of commercial traffic really started with the establishment of a good centre with a interlinking pattern of roads, where produce and goods could be bartered and sold. Equally vital to the settlement's survival in a particular area was a steady growth in the population, and a landscape which favoured good lines of communication.

Our present road system, whatever its origin, was well-advanced by the eleventh century. The lines of the major routeways were in some cases utilised by the Romans, whose magnificently engineered roads were later used by successive invaders. From the Norman Conquest onwards, a wealth of evidence has substantiated the sites of existing and long-forgotten settlements, and of the tracks that linked them. Some of these lanes have disappeared, others still remain as footpaths or as a faint grooved indentation across a hillside slope.

In the medieval period, the growth of settlements in the right location was advanced by the creation of monasteries, and many a small collection of dwellings was transformed into an important route centre with the right to hold a weekly market and an annual fair. The network of tracks and bridle ways that served the hamlet or village became, with constant and heavy use, deeply worn into the surface of the land. In wet weather not only did they act as drainage channels, but with the passage of men, horses and herds of animals, became impassable hollows with a deep layer of treacherous glutinous mud. For instance in north Staffordshire in the early fourteenth century the track from Caverswall (SJ952430) to Dilhorne, climbed steeply out of the village to the high meadow or 'heanley'. Constant use at that time has worn a deep holloway in the soft bunter sandstone rock. Today the metalled road, still called 'The Hollows', runs downhill into the village square; a lane deeply sunk between high grassy banks, beneath a thick canopy of over-hanging trees. Travel throughout the parish appeared just as difficult in the mid-eighteenth century; after a coach journey through the area, Admiral John Leveson-Gower once remarked that he 'would rather be in the Bay of Biscay in a storm than on one of the Dilhorne roads in a carriage'. At that time, 'road' travel was still a difficult business. When the track became badly rutted another parallel route was taken, until eventually a wide swathe of ground was used by foot travellers, carts, coaches and herds of animals. This meant that the main track became obscured beneath a welter of criss-crossing secondary routes.

In the twelfth century Cistercian monks settled in Yorkshire from their native France, and brought with them their skills of animal husbandry, in particular the rearing of sheep. They established their first abbey at Rievaulx in Ryedale, followed by Fountains, Byland, Jervaulx and Salley. Elsewhere, Bolton Priory held lands in Wharfedale and around Malham, Furness Abbey around Ribblehead. The magnificent monastery of Fountains eventually became the centre of vast estates in the Yorkshire Dales, stretching westwards to Borrowdale in Lakeland. Sheep were brought down from the fells for shearing and lambing, and then driven along tracks to lowland areas and sheltered valleys for summer pasture. A network of tracks was established between an abbey and its estates, its sheep farms or granges, and between other monasteries. This network of packhorse tracks, some of which now remain as fine walking routes, were important lines of communication and trade for all manner of travellers. Strings of packhorses carried their valuable cargoes of wool to the markets and eventually to the River Ouse for shipment abroad. Alongside these roads and at important junctions, crosses were erected to protect and direct travellers.

Today, a section of one of Yorkshire's most famous packhorse trails begins as Mastiles Lane, and can be walked for a good way on an unmetalled surface. This ancient way may be followed as a green lane from Kilnsey in Wharfedale to the village of Newby at the foot of the southern slopes of Ingleborough.

The upkeep of these roads was encouraged by the Church in the fourteenth century who regarded it as a pious as well as a profitable act, and promised a number of days of remitted penance for anyone labouring to repair a road surface. After the dissolution of the monasteries, the packhorse remained the prime means of transport; teams of ponies and horses carried much of Britain's trade over a comprehensive network of routes, and indeed this method of conveyance was only ousted some five centuries later by the transport revolution of the nineteenth century.

Many of the footpaths, tracks and green roads which are found all over Britain represent a priceless national heritage. There is no better monument to man's involvement with the landscape, no better evidence of his restless energy and will to survive and succeed, than these ancient lines of communication that wander across our beautiful countryside. Due to the physical nature of the landscape, fewer routes in Britain are better preserved than those in the limestone and gritstone Pennines in Yorkshire, Lancashire, Derbyshire and Staffordshire. These tracks, some of which ran considerable distances, were part of an important network linking the large market centres, like Richmond and Halifax. The trade between the settlements, fairs and markets included grain, wool, hides, lime, salt, cloth, lead and coal. Crossing through unenclosed countryside, they took the shortest practicable route; rising from the wooded valleys, climbing over the edges, and making direct ways across the wild moorland. Evidence of former packhorse ways may be found on steep hills, where in the course of time the volume of pony traffic wore deep grooves into the surface of the ground. To ease the gradient the packhorse trains zigzagged to the crest of the hill, usually aiming for a nick or low point on the skyline. Over the centuries, continuous use and heavy rain turned the grooves into deep holloways which became filled with a deep layer of mud and water. In these circumstances an alternative way was created alongside the original route, and in many cases two, three or several holloways may be seen traversing the slopes and crests of hills. The increasing use of these trails, particularly over softer ground, led to a programme of repair and upkeep with the laying of paved causeways composed of great stone blocks, slabs or cobbles. The paved way would only be about 2ft (60cm) wide, and some parishes would only accept responsibility for the repair of a major packway.

A good example of a causeway or causey may be found at Cat Hill, near Penistone (SE248050), where a section of well preserved stone slabs formed part of the route from Gunthwaite to Cat Hill and Penistone. On Baildon Moor, at Eldwick, near Bingley, (SE134410), parts of a paved way extends from Golcar Farm towards Birch Close Lane. On the Derbyshire-Yorkshire border, the Long Causeway was a packhorse trail that followed a Roman road across the Hallam Moors. Parts of this route are paved near SK251847. Near the source of the River Dove on the Staffordshire border, a paved trackway leads from the packhorse bridge at Washgate (SK052674) into Derbyshire. There are many moorland locations where the volume of horse and pedestrian traffic has worn through the soft peaty ground down to the bedrock, giving to the casual observer the impression that the route has been paved. There is an example on Rushup Edge in Derbyshire, where the ridgeway meets the Chapel Gate route at SK099829. On the Lancashire-Yorkshire border east of Blackstone Edge, Dhoul's Pavement (SO986181), part of an old packhorse road across the Pennines, is a wide natural rock surface. The surfaces of many paved

*Paved packhorse way, Washgate*

*Hebden Bridge below Heptonstall, a Pennine weaving valley*

packhorse trails may have long since been covered by rank grasses and reeds, or simply crumbled away due to the action of frost, rain and the passage of men and animals. Today, the rambler walking along an ancient holloway should keep an eye open for any sign of the original paving through the vegetation.

During the sixteenth and seventeenth centuries in the Lancashire and Yorkshire Pennines, many smallholders lived in isolated dwellings on the fringes of the moorland linked by a network of ancient footpaths. The farms were small and poor, the waterlogged sterile soils offered only a meagre return for their labours. In order to survive, farmers kept small flocks of hardy sheep that roamed the higher parts of the moors; they provided the raw materials for the local cloth industry. Throughout the area the industry probably began with women spinning and carding the wool, and men weaving it into cloth on a primitive cottage loom. The wool trade grew rapidly, and some of the buildings in the isolated communities were adapted to include well-lit weaving rooms separate from the living accommodation. Today, many villages in the Pennine valleys around Huddersfield, Heptonstall, Meltham and Littleborough contain examples of three- or two-storeyed weavers' cottages with long rows of mullioned window lights in the upper storey. The finished cloth was taken to a main wool market, such as Halifax, and wool carried back home. As the industry grew, the cloth was collected by the packhorse wool

carriers, or 'broggers', and taken to market. These merchants or chapmen would buy and sell wool, travelling sometimes with two or three ponies or with a train of packhorses carrying other essential goods for cottage to village and from village to market. Gradually a vast network of tracks covered the valleys and across the surrounding moorland to settlements and markets on the other side of the Pennines.

A packhorse train often comprised twenty to forty ponies of the wiry strong Galloway breed or the Jaeger (hunter) pony imported from Germany, and the man in charge was often called a 'jagger'. Packhorse loads were carried in two panniers slung over a saddle, or on a wooden frame on which sacks or baskets rested. The usual load was about 2½cwt (125kg). The approach of a packhorse team sent a surge of excitement through the village. The arrival of the jaggers meant that news could be exchanged, messages taken from people in other villages and replies to be returned. The packmen took on the role of postmen, merchants and bearers of news for the surrounding isolated communities — it was a great social event for the village. The packmen knew they could get cheap beds for the night, and after the ponies were stabled and the goods safely stored, they retired to the Packhorse Inn for an evening's drinking. Other names of inns that probably were associated with packmen's routes were The Packsaddle, The Talbot and The Woolpack. There is a Packhorse Inn at Crowdecote (SK101652), just across the Staffordshire border on the Derbyshire side of the River Dove. The original inn, which was situated in an adjacent cottage, lay on the packhorse route from Leek to Longnor, and which continued up the steep hill behind the inn to Monyash and Bakewell. The route to Leek from Crowdecote left Longnor along the line of the present road, down a narrow lane past The Lane Farm to Newton, over the broad summit of Merryton Low, before descending to Thorncliffe and Leek. Merryton Low, 1603ft (489m), is the highest point of the Morridge, a long whale-backed ridge running south, and then south-east to the east of Leek. The wild uplands and windswept slopes of the Staffordshire moorlands with their steep gradients proved difficult countryside for the packhorse trains to negotiate, but there were other hazards too. On the high Morridge ridge, packmen and carriers would urge on their ponies past the reputedly haunted Blake Mere pool, an area with a bad reputation for robbery and violence.

To the north of Merryton Low, another old route from Royal Cottage to Longnor passes over to the Morridge at Bareleg Hill (a reputed camping site for Bonnie Prince Charlie's ragged highlanders). On this high and exposed section, snow stones were placed to mark the edge of this packhorse way, and they still stand by the side of the present road.

In the seventeenth and eighteenth centuries a considerable number of packhorse trains moved about the countryside. At Kendal, it was recorded that 354 pack ponies a week, in different teams, were operating from the town. Elsewhere, a network of routes carried much of Britain's trade along valley routes, across the long stretches of open moorland and over mountain passes. The journeys were not easy; there were dangers lurking behind hedges and walls as frequent gibbets testified. Crossing mountain and moorland in bad weather conditions left its toll, with records showing the deaths of packmen and their horses. John Webster and his packhorses perished in the snow between Pikehall and Hurdlow in the Peak District in 1692, while in the southern fells of the Lake District the body of a packwoman

*Abel Cross, on Heptonstall-Haworth old road*

who used to call at Langdale farms was found on the old pony route up Rossett Gill nearly two hundred years ago. Her grave lies in a secret location on the fellside close to the gill.

Before the eighteenth century, packmen and other travellers were left very much to their own devices and sense of direction when crossing difficult terrain. In misty or stormy conditions, the absence of recognisable landmarks made life extremely difficult for travellers trying to negotiate the routes of the lonely highways. In time, heaps of stones or cairns were piled up, followed by crosses which marked the bounds of the manor, or the line of the route, and also as a sign that the track has reached the top of a steep slope. For example, Edale Cross (SK077861) lies at the centre of the Peak Royal Forest and marks the boundary of land given to the Abbey of Basingwerk near Holywell, Clwyd. It also marks the summit of the packhorse way from Hayfield to the Edale valley.

In the early years of the eighteenth century, Parliament authorised justices of the peace to order the erection of guide posts or stoops at important junctions or crossing points of routes. Many were erected in the Pennine moorlands of Derbyshire and West Yorkshire during the eighteenth century. The stoops are rectangular blocks of millstone grit with lettering and often a hand on one or more faces, indicates the direction of the town or towns. On some of them markings have been obscured by the ravages of time, weather and vandals. Some of the stoops have been moved from their original positions and now serve their time as humble gateposts; others only have the base remaining. For example, on the stoop at Curbar Gap (SK260747) indicating the packhorse route directions to Tideswell, Chesterfield, Dronfield and Sheffield, the lettering can now only be made out with difficulty. The stoop on the south edge of Big Moor (SK275740), is marked Chesterfield Road on one side only. There is a three-sided stoop at Ball Cross (SK236697) which indicates the ways to Bakewell, Chesterfield and Sheffield with pointing hands. In Longshaw Park, near Grindleford, a stoop (when translated) reads: To Hathersage and to Chapel-en-le-Frith; To Sheffield; To Chesterfield.

*Hardibut Clough from the Heptonstall-Haworth old road*

North of Hebden Bridge in West Yorkshire, the twin stone pillars of Abel Cross (SD986307) are ancient way-markers on the old road from Heptonstall to Haworth. From Trawden, old roads go by New Laith and Deerstone Moor and Alder Hurst Head and Antley Gate, then across Extwistle Moor to Clough Head Stones and Heptonstall Moor to Reaps Cross (SD943303) then by Edge Lane and on to Heptonstall and Halifax.

In Calderdale, an ancient packhorse route runs from Cragg to Mankinholes, and the Te Deum stone stoop at Withens Gate (SD970231) indicates the summit of the moorland crossing; at this point the ponies were rested, the coffins lowered and prayers said for the dead. The track across the northern edge of the Cleveland Hills was once an ancient paved causeway on Urra Moor; parts of the original paving are still visible

*Packhorse bridge on Heptonstall-Haworth old road*

on this section. Alongside the track opposite the triangulation point stands the Hand Stone (NZ594015) with a rough carving of a hand and the following directions: 'This is the way, to Kirbie and This is the way to Stoxla'. A little further along is a much more ancient stone, the Face Stone (NZ597014), with the carving of a Celtic-style face. This trackway now forms excellent walking routes. Further on, the former route passes along a ridge finger called Glaisdale Rigg, where there are five stone waymarkers, erected about 1735. The stone at NZ748047 has the carving 'Whitby Road' and is set in a base which is probably older. Gradually the route descends into the valley of the River Esk where it crosses over the early seventeenth-century Beggars' Bridge (NZ784055).

*Hand Stone, Cleveland Hills*

These delightful bridges are yet further visible evidence of ancient packhorse routes. They are usually small, single-span structures, built in many cases on the site of a ford. The rugged terrain of the Pennines favoured the movement of goods on horseback and, in moorland country, several tracks would often converge on a single hump-backed bridge. For example, Three Shires Head (SK009685), the meeting point of the counties of Cheshire, Derbyshire and Staffordshire, is also the junction of four packhorse ways. The risk of losing valuable merchandise swept away by a swollen stream probably caused them to be built and determined their design. The raised span afforded greater strength, and the narrow way prevented its overloading and also made it a stronger structure, although the amount of traffic at Three Shires Head was such that the

*Three Shires Head, the junction of four packhorse ways*

*Washgate Packhorse Bridge*

bridge has had to be widened at some time. Many of the packhorse bridges date from the Middle Ages, but they continued to be built until the early nineteenth century. The original structures would be built with very low or even no protective parapets, so that the goods carried in the panniers would not be knocked and possibly damaged. A fine example of a packhorse bridge with its original low parapets is to be found over the infant River Dove at Washgate (SK063668) on the Derbyshire-Staffordshire border.

In Cumbria, a charming little bridge crosses Swindale Back close by Shap Abbey (NY535159). Near to the Pennine settlement of Marsden, the infant River Colne is crossed by an attractive packhorse bridge known as Close Gate Bridge (SE029121), with a single segmental arch and a width between parapets of 4ft (1.2m). From here an old packhorse route leads over the Pennines to Rochdale. In Lancashire, Wycoller was a medieval settlement within the Royal Forest of Trawden. This little village, tucked away at the foot of the moors, was once a seventeenth-century handloom weaving centre, and is now protected within the Wycoller Country Park. Its stream, which flows down from the moors through the charming wooded valley of Wycoller Dean, is spanned by three examples of early bridges: a clapper bridge, a clam bridge and a double arched packhorse bridge. Teams of packhorses travelled over this latter bridge (SD932393) on the route from the Pendle district ot Keighley. In Lakeland, in the upper Kentmere valley beyond the farm at Overend, a packhorse track travels alongside the River Kent for a brief interval. Here at NY459063 the river is spanned by a graceful packhorse bridge, clean-lined and without parapets. In former days it probably linked this trade route over the Nan Bield Pass with the isolated dwelling at Hartrigg, which lies opposite the bridge on the far side of the valley. The 2½in OS map shows a track coming towards the bridge, but now it stops abruptly.

Not only did packways connect settlements, villages, markets and towns, they also climbed into the hills and ended on the moorland heights. Coal was mined from shallow hillside workings or from bell pits. These depressions may be found

*Clapper bridge and packhorse bridge, Wycoller*

if one is prepared to struggle through deep heather in an area just south of the Ralph Crosses on the North York Moors. From the seventeenth and into the eighteenth century shaly coal was extracted from bell pits on Eyam Moor in Derbyshire and the tracks and pits can still be seen. South of Castleton in Derbyshire, the limestone upland is criss-crossed with tracks, often running at nearly right angles off the major roads. They run to disused lead mines, and were constructed by the eighteenth- and nineteenth-century lead miners for the transportation of the ore by packhorses. An example is at Dirtlow Rake (SK145315). The highest public house in England at Tan Hill lies on the county boundary of North Yorkshire and Durham. From the thirteenth century seams of coal have been worked from the fellside just south of the inn. It

*Packhorse way, Kentmere*

became an important junction for the roads and tracks that were used to transport the coal to the farming and mining communities in the surrounding dales. Many paths and tracks cross the extensive moorland area north of the River Swale linking up the villages, lead mines and smelting mills. From Tan Hill Inn, an old jagger road runs south-west to cross upper West Stones Dale to the ruins of Roberts Seat House, and descends to Raven Seat Farm (NY862033). The track crosses the fine packhorse bridge below the farm, and follows the line of Ney Gill to meet the present B6270. The metalled road follows the route of the jagger track over Lamps Moss to Nateby and Kirkby Stephen.

The man in charge of a packhorse train was called a 'jagger', and this name lives on in place-

*Packhorse bridge, Kentmere*

names to provide yet another clue to the existence of a former packhorse way. The following examples are in the Peak District:

Jaggers Gate:   On the old road from the Cat and Fiddle Inn and Burbage to Buxton. SK044728.

Jaggers Clough:   On the old way along the Vale of Edale. SK155873.

Jaggers Lane:   In the village of Ashover. SK348630.

Jaggerways:   Names of fields where the packmen and ponies rested. Above White House Farm. SK251534. At Carsington. SK251534.

Dent, in the Yorkshire Dales, was a place of active industry and well known as a great producer of wool, which was partly carded and manufactured for the inhabitants of the dale. However, Dent became famous as a knitting

*Packhorse way from Eyam to Bradwell*

centre producing good quality stockings and gloves, using dressed wool and worsted. At first these materials were brought in by teams of packhorses, and afterwards by little carts that were suited to the narrow and very rough Dent roads. These carts caused a terrible creaking noise called 'Jyking' caused by the wheels and axle revolving together. It is recorded that: 'The friction was partially relieved by frequent doses of tar, administered to the pegs from a ram's horn which hung behind the cart.' Coal was mined from thin seams beneath the highest of the limestone beds called the Upper Scar Limestone. Just above Dent, a green track leaves the valley of Deepdale Beck and climbs up to Great Wold. This grassy route, once known as the Old Craven Way, passes a number of swallow holes where streams disappear once the limestone beds are reached. There are signs of the bell-shaped openings of the old coal pits higher up the hillside, and beneath Greenset Crags on the eastern flanks of Whernside. This old packhorse way which carried coal, wool and other goods continues down Force Gill to Winterscales, Ivescar to Chapel le Dale. Another old way which once served the coal pits on the northern slopes of Great Coum leaves Dent via Flinter Gill, and follows the contours as a walled green track to the minor road at White Shaw Moss. Both these old packhorse ways form excellent walking routes, which afford wide ranging views of the surrounding dales and a vista of sweeping fellsides.

From medieval days, certain routes were closely associated with the traffic of particular goods. Lime was an essential ingredient in the making of mortar, and in Lancashire an old lime road ran from quarries in the Clitheroe area to Rochdale. It crosses the Nick of Pendle into the Calder valley, then uses a variety of routes over the Hameldon Hills to Dunnockshaw and Dean in the Forest of Rossendale. The Lime Way follows the high land over Todmorden Moor, through Limers Gate (SD894236), Trough Edge, Hades Hill, below Brown Wardle Hill and Man Stone Edge into Rochdale.

Another very important commodity carried by teams of packhorses was salt from the Cheshire and Worcestershire salt producing districts. As a greatly prized and essential item, salt has been transported since before Roman times. Medieval salt carriers when faced with a difficult journey across wooded and marshy land were likely to have used the ways that were there; and in the Cotswolds the use of ridges suggests that the salt carriers followed routes used by the prehistoric peoples. One route approaches the northern scarp of the Cotswolds from the direction of Droitwich to the north west, and climbs the edge via Salters Lane above the village of Hailes. The Salt Way keeps to the high ground between the valleys of Coln and the Windrush in a southerly and then a south-easterly direction towards Lechlade. Although most of this ancient route is now metalled, there are long stretches of quiet country lanes, from which there are rewarding views over this high Cotswold landscape. It is also a splendid opportunity to explore some nearby lovely villages with prosperous-looking farms, and streets lined with houses built of warm honey-coloured stone. A number of these interesting villages are situated in the folds of the countryside on either side of the Salt Way. Colm St Dennis is small and compact, its cottages closely grouped round its Norman church. From the north the way passes Salter's Hill and then the village of Salperton, which probably derives its name from 'salt-pæth', the salt path. There is also a Saltway Farm, south of the line of the old Roman road, the Fosse Way, now the A429.

A study of medieval records tells us that much

of the salt was produced from the sea by evaporation in shallow enclosures known as 'salt pans'. The Romans had worked the salt deposits around Droitwich, and later the importance of salt was such that many monastic communities were granted 'salt rights' by the king or his lords as an act of piety. Many of the place names associated with salt end in 'wich'. As this is from the latin *vicus* meaning dwelling or group of dwellings, it is not to be assumed that every place name ending in 'wich' has a connection with the production of salt. Norwich, for instance, has no reputation for salt.

A number of saltways left the Cheshire 'wiches' to cross the high moorland barrier of the southern Pennines. Many of these former salt routes are again recognisable by the occurrence of salt names. The true packhorse way has a tendency to find the shortest line to its destination. Often the salt carriers would ignore any existing track system and the natural lie of the land. This created many difficulties of gradient, particularly in the extreme south of the Pennines, where the saltways had to negotiate a succession of deep valleys and high ridges. An example of a long distance saltway is recorded in 1749 during legal proceedings against the inhabitants of the townships of Leek and Onecote in the Staffordshire moorlands. They were indicted for not repairing 'a great carriers' road that was claimed to be used by about one hundred packhorses loaded with salt each week. The carriers brought salt out of Congleton, Cheshire into Derbyshire and Nottinghamshire, and returned to Cheshire with cargoes of malt. The route from Cheshire probably passed through Ryecroft Gate to Gun Hill, where another way led directly towards Leek. From Gun Hill the saltway follows the line of the present road through Meerbrook and Middle Hulme to Blackshaw Moor. The climb up the Morridge via Stoney Cliffe to Blakemere House (now the Mermaid Inn), was so steep that forty years before, 'some of the inhabitants of Tetsworth [Tittesworth] made a stone causeway down the bank and several of the carriers contributed towards it'. According to the records of indictment, the route proceeded down to Warslow and on through Hartington and Winster in Derbyshire.

This route crossed the River Manifold near Brund Mill. The ancient packhorse bridge formerly here was rebuilt in 1891, and had been a crossing point for salt carriers from the seventeenth century onwards. The route from Cheshire in fact divided here, one route going north-east and crossing the River Dove at Pilsbury and on towards Bakewell; the other went across to Sheen, Hartington, the track to Dale End, Biggin, along the footpath from Cardle View to Newhouse Farm, down the line of the present road to Winster and on to Matlock or Chesterfield. Two other items of interest associated with the packhorse days are to be found near to Brund Mill. One is a roadside trough on the Clough (SK102614); the other is an old bargaining stone, where deals were made with hands clasped through the hole. It is now spending its days as a gate post (SK097605).

The salt industry in Staffordshire began when deposits of brine were discovered in the late seventeenth century on land belonging to Lord Ferrers in the parish of Weston-upon-Trent. The site of the works where the brine was turned into salt became known as Shirleywich, although the natural brine solution from this site was weaker than that from Cheshire. By 1700 the business was flourishing, and an advertisement was even placed in the *London Gazette* offering to supply salt to traders. The saltworks stated that they were within reach of navigable rivers for easy transportation of their product. Nevertheless, the roads in Staffordshire in the late seventeenth century were generally good, except in the northern moorland area, and the main business was probably with local customers in the surrounding district. An important landmark was the construction of the Trent and Mersey Canal in 1766-77, with the canal passing close to the works. At the beginning of the eighteenth century a branch was constructed to the works at Shirleywich. In 1834 the saltworks at Shirleywich manufactured 100 tons of salt weekly from brine raised from a saline spring into a large reservoir, from which the boiling pans were supplied. There is a brinepit bridge over the Trent and Mersey Canal at SJ978261 to the north-west of Shirleywich Farm, and there are small pools which may be relics of the old salt industry. A rival company entered the salt-making business and set up a new works in 1821 just south of Weston village, only ½ mile (800m) north of the existing factory at Shirleywich. The Weston works were producing 250 tons weekly in 1834, and together with Shirleywich seem to have supplied parts of Staffordshire by canal, but local farmers, merchants and customers in the more remote parts of the county received deliveries by cart and packhorse.

In medieval times, salt was extracted from shallow pits in the area of the appropriately-named village of Salt, some 2½ miles (4km) north-west of Shirleywich along the valley of the River Trent. Many of the shallow depressions caused by sand extraction for local needs may well indicate some of the original sites of medieval salt pits.

The routes the salt carriers took from the Trent Valley to the northern part of the county may have passed through the settlements of Milwich, Cresswell, Draycott in the Moors to

*Salter's Well, Bagnall*

Forsbrook and Caverswall, or through Hilderstone, Mossgate and down Stallington Lane towards Caverswall. However, there are traces of salt names beyond the scattered hamlet of Roughcote north of Caverswall. There is a Salters Lane which runs north-north-west towards Werrington and passes two fields on the right called Upper Salter's Hill and Lower Salter's Road. Further along on the right the lane passes Salthouse Farm (SJ940465). North of Wetley Moor, but south of the village of Bagnall, is Salter's Well (SJ929502), which probably lay on another old carriers' road to Woodhead, Birches Head and Hanley.

Many of the routes crossing over the Pennine barrier from Cheshire are well marked by salter names on their journeys to Yorkshire and Derbyshire; names such as Saltersford, Saltersbrook, Saltergate, Salter Close, Salter Sitch and Salter Croft. Along some routes are the sites of old crosses that help to establish the line of an old road. Although salt would have been the main commodity these old ways also saw the passage of jaggers, limers, broggers and badgers (a badger was a corn dealer and a seller of farm produce).

In Lancashire, an old road crosses the bleak fells of the Forest of Bowland. Salt was obviously a cargo of major importance along this trade route as the salt names testify. From the north the track follows the Roeburn valley, and as it climbs the slopes passes Lower Salter and High Salter Farms, then Higher Salter Close, and over Salter Fell before descending Croasdale and into the Hodder valley at Slaidburn. It is believed that the packhorses carried salt from Morecambe Bay to the towns of east Lancashire. A look at the map will see locations of crosses at SD587679 and SD591673.

## Packhorse Roads
## Identifying Features

• Old packhorse routes usually take direct lines across the country, but often have zigzag courses on hill slopes. Across softer sections there may be more than one track, running parallel.

• Packhorse ways may be identified by way-marks and other features, such as:

(a) guidestones
(b) stoops
(c) crosses
(d) cross-base sockets
(e) troughs and bargaining stones
(f) 'Jagger' names
(g) A paved section; causeway or causey
(h) By the position of a packhorse bridge; usually high-arched, narrow and single-spanned

structures.

• Packhorse ways may be identified by certain names that indicated the particular commodity carried, eg salt names. Old maps and records may show fields along the route named after a certain commodity.

• The clue to the line of an old packhorse route may be indicated by the names of rural inns, eg The Packhorse.

• In mountain areas, a particular track may have been a corpse road, where the dead were carried to a consecrated burying ground, eg from Wasdale to Boot, over Burnmoor, Eskdale, Cumbria. From Mardale to Shap, over Mardale Common, Haweswater, Cumbria.

## Some Recommended Packhorse Routes

### Mastiles Lane, North Yorkshire
OS 98, (1in 90)

1 A monastic way in the Yorkshire Dales from Kilnsey to Newby via Dale Head and Helwith Bridge. Distance 20¾ miles (33km).

### Walking Sections
Kilnsey to Street Gate. Distance 5 miles (8km).
Dale Head to Helwith Bridge. Distance: 2¾ miles (4½km).
Wharfe to Newby. Distance: 3¾ miles (6km).

### Motoring Sections
Street Gate to Dale Head (Junction of Silverdale Road and Pennine Way). Distance 7 miles (11km).

A good section of this ancient route begins at Kilnsey (SD975680). From the Jacobean Old Hall, and the remains of the thirteenth-century gatehouse to the old grange, the narrow lane climbs up to the summit of Kilnsey Moor. Westwards the walled green lane of variable

width meanders across typical limestone scenery. The way continues across the limestone plateau, and before it descends to cross the clapper bridge over Gordale Beck there is a glimpse of Malham Tarn and the bulk of Fountains Fell beyond. Near the crossing of the beck the stone sockets of waymarking crosses can be seen, the shafts having

disappeared long ago.

At Street Gate (SD903656) the monastic way is metalled for the next 4 miles (6.4km) to a track on the right leading to Rough Close. This was a farm belonging to Fountains Abbey, but the present green track is not a right of way, so the road must be followed for another 3 miles (4.8km) to Sannet Hall, and

*Mastiles Lane*

then bear right along the Silverdale Road to Dale Head (SD842714). This was an important staging post for the packhorse trains and later for the drovers who were coming north from Settle. Look for the base of the medieval Ulfkil Cross near to the junction of the track and road.

The old road ascends a route now taken by the Pennine Way as far as the hollow known as Churn Milk Hole. To the right rears the stepped southern end of Pen-y-ghent, and as one descends Long Lane, there is a view of the distant whale-backed height of Whernside. Beyond Helwith Bridge (SD810694) the scars of the flag and roadstone quarries are a blot on the landscape, but along the road a charming cluster of stone buildings constitutes the unspoilt hamlet of Wharfe (SD783695). Walk through the settlement and take the narrow lane that accompanies the Austwick Beck. Turn right at the minor road, then right again along Thwaite Lane into Clapham. Pass the church to cross over the beck and take the old Keighley to Kendal turnpike road towards Ingleton. Just a short distance along on the left, a guidepost

marks the route to Newby. Further on the track opens out to meet the lane leading into the village of Newby (SD727700), once a popular meeting place for drovers.

**2** An alternative route from Kilnsey to Newby via Stainforth and Feizor. Distance 17½ miles (28km).

### Walking Sections
Kilnsey to Street Gate. Distance 5 miles (8km).
Cowside Beck to Newby. Distance 13½ miles (21.6km).

### Motoring Section
Street Gate to Langcliffe Road (Cowside Beck). Distance 4 miles (6.4km).
(from Kilnsey as above).

From the road junction at SD857622, proceed down the Langcliffe road to a point just before Cowside Beck. A footpath leaves the road on the right, initially in a northerly direction, then turns westwards to pass below Gorbeck spinney. It crosses Cowside Beck and joins Goat Scar Lane near to Catrigg Force. A stile in the right gives access to this majestic fall, its double columns of water plunging into a deep gorge. Carry on down into Stainforth

village, turning right over the beck and then left past the church on the B6479. Turn right, and after a short distance take the lane on the left over the railway towards Stainforth Bridge. This elegant seventeenth-century packhorse bridge carried traffic over the River Ribble on an important route from Lancashire to Yorkshire. Now under the protection of the National Trust, it serves as a graceful memorial to the craftsmen who created it. Just below the bridge lies Stainforth Force, where the river rushes over limestone outcrops into a deep black pool. After passing through Little Stainforth, the path climbs into a grassy upland recess beneath the limestone escarpments of Smearsett Scar and Pot Scar. Follow the footpath into the hamlet of Feizor which was a monastic settlement and a staging post for the packhorse trains. The route continues along the lane westwards from Feizor, passing Wood House on the way to a junction of tracks where both lanes on the left lead to Austwick. At the north end of the village a track and footpath leads on to Thwaite Lane. Continue as route 1.

### Hayfield to Hope, Derbyshire
OS 110, (1in 111), OS 2½in Leisure Map, 'The Dark Peak' Hayfield, Tunstead Clough Farm, Harry Moor, Edale Cross, Jacob's Ladder, Upper Booth, Grindsbrook Booth,

Rowland Cote Youth Hostel. Distance Hayfield to Rowland Cote, 7½ miles (12km). Rowland Cote Youth Hostel, Jaggers Clough, Hope Cross, Hope Brink, Twitchill Farm, Hope. Distance Rowland Cote to Hope, 4½ miles (7.2km).

Return walking route recommended: Castleton, Losehill Farm, Lose Hill, Hollins Cross, Mam Tor, Lord's Seat to A625, Roych Clough, South Head, Mount Famine, Hayfield. Distance Castleton to Hayfield, 11½ miles (18.4km).

## DROVE ROADS

Over many parts of upland Britain, there are many little-used tracks which follow the valley bottoms and them climb steeply over the mountain passes, or maintain height across the ridges and crests of hills. These tracks are difficult to date; some may well be prehistoric in origin, some laid down by Roman legionaries and followed in part by medieval monks and merchants They are not easy to recognise as purely drove roads, for in mountain areas some may have been used for centuries for the purposes of driving local flocks and herds to summer pastures. This would mean a comparatively short distance, as against other routes, which with imagination and guesswork can said to run for hundreds of miles. All these form of highways, the Ridgeways, the Roman routes, the medieval packhorse tracks, the summer pasture ways, the droving roads to markets in England are intertwined. In the seventeenth and early eighteenth centuries other routes were superimposed on the existing upland network by the creation of access tracks to the bell pits for coal and to the many lead mine workings in the Pennines. These later tracks connected with industry only serve to confuse an extensive network of earlier drove and packhorse roads.

It is important to bear in mind that this complicated and confusing route pattern covered the entire British Isles but that the best preserved examples of packhorse tracks and drove roads are found as holloways, paved routes and sunken hawthorn-lined tracks in the upland areas. The continued use of some of the major routes by foot traffic, heavy lumbering carts, packhorses and herds and flocks of animals created serious surface problems in bad weather. The tracks and lanes became impassible, and so the turnpike, which originated in 1663, became a well-established method of road maintenance. In simple terms, the road users were made to pay for the privilege of using them. In the eighteenth century scores of turnpike trusts were established up and down the country, usually financed and controlled by local landowners. The turnpike

routes are usually followed by the lines of older routes, and until their demise at the end of the nineteenth century, had a considerable effect on the growth of towns and villages on trade. The coming of the railways superseded the turnpikes and the last trust terminated in 1895.

Centuries ago in Scotland, particularly in the Highlands, a man's wealth lay in the cattle he owned. Each member of a clan and his family relied on his small number of shaggy beasts to survive in a harsh environment. A herd of cattle owned by the laird formed a considerable proportion of his wealth, and became a major factor in day to day life A woman's dowry would be paid in cattle, and they would often be taken as payment of rent. The wild nature of the terrain, the countless glens and remote mountain fastnesses encouraged the thieving of cattle. Under cover of mist the reivers would sneak in, quickly drive off their prizes and simply disappear into the hills. In time, attempts were made to control this rustling, such as by branding, but to many Highlanders it was a way of life, and further attempts to control the problem met with very little success. Although the movements of stolen cattle continued, it was realised that there was the prospect of good trade over the border in the English cattle markets. Droving was a flourishing and regular occupation from the early Middle Ages, and the practice of driving herds of sheep, cattle, pigs and flocks of geese from Scotland and Wales continued up until the last century.

In Tudor and Elizabethan times, in order to combat lawlessness and thieving of cattle, laws were passed which decreed that *bona fide* drovers must have a licence to pursue their trade. For a drover to be granted a licence he had to fulfil a number of conditions: he had to be married, a householder and at least thirty years of age. The early history of the Scots droving trade has shown that cattle were being driven to England as early as the fifteenth century, with the trade growing in volume, particularly in the eighteenth century. The success of the droving trade depended on places, suitably sited, where drovers, dealers and farmers could meet for the transaction of business. A particularly strategic site was Crieff, which became an important cattle 'tryst',

Clennel Street

Welsh drovers were paid to drive the beasts to markets in southern England as a contract on behalf of the owners. These people could be wealthy farmers and part-time innkeepers. A droving scene portrays a vivid picture; a colourful and noisy procession of men, animals and dogs.

The drovers usually accompanied the flocks and herds on horseback and at the end of a day's drive would be eager for rest and refreshment at a wayside inn. The innkeeper-farmer would have sufficient notice of the impending arrival of the drovers, on hearing their warning shouts in the distance. He would have time to fasten up his own stock, otherwise his animals might become part of the oncoming herd. Many of these old drovers' inns were often farms along the route which became simple hostelries selling their own particular product of home-brewed ale, and on the journey from Wales, home-produced cider. The drovers' inns provided a grazing area for animals and farmers were also ready to offer stances for the night's stay at a modest fee. Often, some of the drovers slept alongside their charges, while the senior attendants were in the inn's sleeping quarters. The usual charge for the stance and the grazing was a halfpenny a night per beast, and old records and maps may indicate such stances or fields. For example, 'Halfpenny Fields' or 'Broad Field'. The sites of stances were sometimes indicated by the planting of a group of four or five Scots pines on a prominent knoll so that they could be seen by the drovers some distance away.

In the upland areas of Britain some of the former drovers' inns are now derelict and ruinous; others have completely disappeared. Some are still farms, others private dwellings or holiday homes, and a number are still inns. On Aberedw Hill east of Builth Wells (SO090520) is a field covered with luxuriant grass. This was Tabor Wye, the site of an old drovers' inn, whose stones have long since disappeared, and where the black Welsh cattle were pastured for the night. The stance, well manured by generations of cattle, still has the Scots pines that were planted close by. On the Hambleton Drove Road in North Yorkshire, Chequers Farm (SE475970) was once a drovers' inn, and the

a gathering point and market for the whole of Scotland. This continued until about 1770, when with the expansion of trade with England and the influx of greater numbers of buyers, a more southerly market was established at Falkirk. From here drove roads led to the Border. One popular route taken by south-bound drovers was the pass known as the Cauldstane Slap, which crosses the Pentland Hills between the East and West Cairn Hills (NT118588). A 'slap' is an opening in a dyke through which cattle or sheep can pass. The route was shown on printed maps of Peebleshire in 1775 and 1821, and is still marked as an old drove road on modern Ordnance Survey maps. At the Border, the ancient tracks over the wild Cheviots were used by the drovers, and these ways or 'gates' across the high ridges are still marked by paths that make magnificent walking routes. One example is Clennel Street that leaves the shelter of the Coquet valley at Alwinton and makes a direct route over one of the hill ridges between the valleys (NT918082).

The drives could not be undertaken without a fair amount of organisation and planning. There was much at stake, for the animals represented a considerable fortune for the drovers and the owners of cattle and sheep. In Wales, the drovers often visited isolated farms, buying the animals at a more favourable price before the large cattle fairs took place. Sometimes the surrounding stretches of turf provided an excellent grazing area for the flocks and herds. Today, it is a private dwelling. This drove road ran from Swainby (NZ477020) to Crayke (SE562705). Parts of the route are now metalled, but elsewhere there are splendid sections of moorland and forestry.

The long drives over rough country and the stony surfaces of tracks damaged the animals' hoofs, and so the cattle had to be shod. Since the animals' hoofs were cloven, each beast required eight cues or shoes of small narrow metal arcs. These either wore out quickly or were dislodged, so that the drovers required facilities for re-shoeing. These were established along the route at the inns, at other shoeing stations, or carried out by the drovers themselves during the journey. Frequently, geese were driven many miles to market, and they too had their feet protected against the hard stone tracks. One method was to prepare a mixture of tar and sand, and then drive the birds through this rather uninviting mixture. Once hardened, the coating would offer good protection over a certain distance, and then if necessary, the geese would be put through the same indignity again.

As previously mentioned, drove roads are difficult to separate from local and long distance packhorse ways, old mine access tracks and transhumance routes leading to summer pastures. Certainly many green roads were used by different forms of traffic at that time, but clues to their use as drove roads are found in records of stances and inns, shoeing stations and 'half-penny fields'. In the hills, a bright green patch of ground with a clump of Scots pines in Wales and yews in England, and signs of the former enclosure walls, are useful clues. Some old routes through hills still retain their former titles, such as Old Drove Road, Driving Road or Galloway Gate. A clue to the distribution of drove roads may be seen in the location of a fair or market, for example, Appleby, Cumbria, and at Rosley, near Wigton in Cumbria. A study of the roads leading to a particular centre may uncover visible reminders of a droving route. They can be identified as a wide road or lane usually between walls, with wide grass verges on either side of the road. Free grazing

*Hambleton Drove Road*

was an important consideration for the drovers as well as being able to keep together a large number of beasts while they were grazing. In Powys the country roads over Clyro Hill have wide verges as a reminder that the black cattle from west Wales came this way to England.

In the north of England most of the cattle passing through Cumbria were chiefly Galloways and West Highlands. These were tough hardy breeds used to living in harsh climatic conditions and on inferior pasture. They were driven on one route through Carlisle towards Penrith and rested overnight in a large open area still known as Broad Field, (NY425445). On another route south from Scotland, the approach roads in the area of Rosley, near Wigton (NY320454) still have wide grassy verges. The existing metalled roads probably lie along the routes of the old drove ways. The Galloway Gate Road (Galwaithe-gate), was a twelfth-century drove road. Two major driving routes led south from Penrith to Shap and through Lambrigg Park, Three Mile House and Old Town to Kirkby Lonsdale. There is an excellent section of this road at (SD604975), with extensive views across the Lune valley to the sweeping grassy slopes of the Howgill Fells.

In North Yorkshire, a stony track leaves the high coal road beyond Dent Station. This route from Kirkby Stephen to the Craven District was used by Scottish drovers up until the nineteenth century. The herds of cattle were grazed overnight by local farmers, who took them to richer pastures for fattening prior to sale at the southern markets. Close by is another former inn at Newby Head, which was a favourite meeting place for the butchers who attended the market at Gearstones which was once an important drovers' inn, SD779799. The road down the Mallerstang between Kirkby Stephen and the Moorcock Inn was constructed as a turnpike in 1825. Previously there were packhorse trails and a rough mountain road over the shoulder of High Abbotside. The barn at High Dyke (SD803942) was formerly the High Way Inn, and this high level route saw the passing of large numbers of Scottish cattle being driven to Hawes and the surrounding dales.

Some of the old inns along the drove routes from Wales to the English border are still providing rest and refreshment. Cattle were driven across Bryngwyn Hill to Newchurch and down to the Rhydspence Inn alongside the River Wye. Other herds straggled over Llanbedr Hill to the Maesllwch Arms at Painscastle, and thence to Rhydspence or to Clyro and its numerous hostelries. The quiet country lanes over Clyro Hill witnessed the slow passage of black cattle, occasionally grazing along the wide roadside verges. From Newtown and central Wales the cavalcade of beasts, men and dogs decended the hills bordering the Teme valley to the Red Lion Inn at Llanfair Waterdine.

*Galwaithegate Drove Road*

North of Barmouth in Gwynedd, drove routes headed from Dyffryn Adudwy to the Mawddach Estuary at Bontddu. To walk some of these, park a car at Cors-y-Gedol (SH602231) and turn down the track on the right. A short distance on the right lies the remains of a burial chamber, and the area to the east contains hut circles surrounded by a simple enclosure wall. Before crossing the Afon Ysgethin, the cottage and outbuilding on the left at Llety Loegr provided shelter and shoeing facilities. The track climbs steadily to the gap on the ridge, Bwlch y Rhiwgyr — the pass of the drovers. The drove way descends under the slopes of Llawlech, to pass an area of afforestation called Cerrig y Cledd. Cross the stream and continue beneath the rising ground of Bryn Castell on which stands the site of a hillfort. An ancient milestone which indicates the junction of tracks has the inscription Tal-y-bont 5 miles and Harlech 11 miles. From this point the drovers would have continued on to Bontddu $1\frac{1}{2}$ miles (2.4km) away. Turn sharp left and climb the long grassy ridge, curving left to attain the eastern end of the Llawlech ridge. Looking south there are impressive views of the craggy northern cliffs of Cader Idris, 2,927ft (893m). From the ridge the path sweeps down to the old stone bridge, Pont Scethin. The route continues westwards to join the long track back to Cors y Gedol. The ruined building, Tynewydd, at the foot of Moelfre, was once a drovers' inn. This circular walk is 10 miles (16km) long.

Another old droving route further north is Llanbedr, Pentre Gwynfryn, Afon Artro valley, Cwm Bychan, the Roman Steps, Ffridd Maesgwyn, Graigddu-uchaf, Adwy-dêg and on to Trawsfynydd.

From beginning to end the droving trade relied on freedom of movement, a choice of wayside grazing and no restrictions on where they could rest for the night. Gradually restrictions crept in to upset the delicate balance between prosperity and failure. One major problem experienced by the drovers was the new outlook on land ownership and management. Landowners began to object to the prospect of having herds of cattle and flocks of sheep crossing their property; wayside land was enclosed and drovers

*Dyffryn Ardudwy to Bontddu drove road. Cader Idris in the distance*

were charged for the use of it. Many of the byways that they had previously followed were now improved with better surfaces, cuttings and embankments; this restricted the roadside grazing and gave less room for the shoeing of cattle. During the eighteenth and ninteenth centuries, turnpike trusts were empowered to levy tolls on roads and bridges, which added considerably to the drovers' budget. They were also liable to a fine if convicted of an offence of nuisance on the highway, such as littering it with animal droppings. Improvements in agricultural methods meant that better grass could be grown, and root crops could be produced to feed the cattle over the winter period. This also meant that there was less incentive for cattle to be driven into England from Wales and Scotland for fattening. The final blow came with the development of steam power and the rapid growth of the railway system. The turnpike trusts lasted well into the nineteenth century and had outlived their usefulness, especially with the competition from the railways. The improvement of road surfaces, and the development of road networks under the control of local authorities had a great effect on the pattern and use of rural routes.

By the close of the nineteenth century droving had ceased, and today, it is in the hills and across the rolling uplands of this country that sections of old drove roads and packhorse tracks can still be traced. They remain as yet another important example of man's influence on the landscape, and constitute another fragment of our heritage that can be enjoyed by countryside lovers who are prepared to seek out their quiet ways.

## Drove Roads
### Identifying Features

• Drove roads are often difficult to separate from local and long distance packhorse ways, and not easy to recognise as some are now hedged and tarmaced.

• The most impressive visible drove roads are to be found in the north, in Scotland, on the borders and in Wales.

• They often keep to higher ground, crossing over the hills and through mountain passes, because of the enclosure of formerly open land, and the imposition of tolls on the eighteenth-century turnpike roads.

• Drove roads can be identified as wide roads or lanes usually between walls, with wide grass verges on either side of the road.

• Many have survived as walled unsurfaced tracks, the 'green roads' in the Pennines.

• A clue to the distribution of drove roads may be seen in the location of a fair or market centre,

eg Rosley, near Wigton, Cumbria; Appleby, Cumbria. Or in the names of old roads, such as Old Scots Road, Driving Road, Galloway Gate (Galwaithegate), Scotch Lane.

• The name of a rural inn may have an association with drovers, eg The Black Bull, Kirkby Stephen, Cumbria; The Tam o' Shanter, Brampton, Cumbria. However, this is not a reliable indication.

• In stone districts parallel lines of dry-stone walling may indicate the former line of a packhorse or drove road. The ends of a particular section may now be blocked up, but look for the old stone gate posts that may still be *in situ*.

• Old maps and records may indicate stances or fields where cattle were put to graze overnight, eg 'Halfpenny Fields', Broad Field.

## Walking Routes along Scottish Drove Roads

### 1  Little Vantage to West Linton
OS 65, (1in 62)
Just past the ruined inn at Little Vantage on the A70, Edinburgh to Carnwath road, there is a Scottish Rights of Way Society signpost which directs the walker to West

Linton by Cauldstane Slap (NT101628). The path crosses Leith Water at Gala Ford and climbs to the gap called Cauldstone Slap, 1,435ft (460m), between the East Cairn and West Cairn Hills. The route descends the sweeping heather-clad slopes to cross the

Lyne Water ¼ mile (400m) below Baddinsgill Reservoir. The old road follows the stream past Stonypath and down a tree-lined avenue to West Linton. Distance 9 miles (14½km).

### 2  Damside to Peebles
OS 72 (1in 62)
Damside lies 3 miles (4.8km) south-south-east of West Linton via the B7059 and the A701. Proceed up the track past Romanno House and over the shoulder of Drum Maw to descend to the Fingland Burn. Cross over the stream and follow the lower path round to the southern end of Green Knowe at NT188461. Look out for the forest gate, and take the

path that crosses the Flemington Burn and walk through Eddleston Water Forest to Greenside. Proceed uphill for a short distance, and where the track bifurcates, take the right-hand way. The route climbs up to a forest break and then descends to Upper Stewarton, NT217461 (not named on the 1:50,000 Second Series, Sheet 73) and on to Stewarton (Nether Stewarton on the 1in OS map). Turn

eastwards for just over ½ mile (800m), and then bear right along a narrow road to Meldon Cottage, before taking the access road left to Upper Kidston Farm. The path heads east to the far end of a narrow plantation and swings round the north end of Hamilton Hill to join a broad track past Standalane directly into Peebles. Distance 10 miles (16km).

### 3 Peebles to Dryhope and St Mary's Loch

OS 73 (1in 69)

Cross the River Tweed and walk along Springhill Road, and thence by path to the pretty Gipsy Glen. The old wide droving road, with its walls on either side to begin with, climbs up on the ridge. Follow this high level grassy way over Kailzic Hill, Kirkhope Law and Birkscairn Hill. Given the advantages of a fine day there are magnificent views over Tweeddale. Aim for the next hill to the south-west, Stake Law, 2,218ft (679m), but descend to the east of it, traversing round the head of Quair Water Glen to reach Whiteknowe Head. The direction is then south-south-east down Bright Rig to reach the track alongside the Douglas Burn and on to Blackhouse. Cross the burn and head across the lower slopes of the Hawkshaw Rigs in a south west direction to Dryhope and on to the main A708. Distance 12½ miles (20km).

An alternative droving route of approximately the same length runs south from Peebles parallel to the ridge route by following the track past Haystoun up the Glensax Burn to Glensax. Beyond, the route climbs up to the col between Birkscairn Hill and Stake Law. Then continue as previously described.

## THE BEGINNINGS OF INDUSTRY

Man has always required food, clothing, warmth and shelter to survive. Initially, he was a nomadic hunter, living a precarious existence using simple tools. He needed a hard substance for cutting and slicing which was no doubt discovered after much trial and error. Eventually flint was found to be the ideal choice; a stone that was hard and durable, and which could be chipped or knapped into tools and weapons that had remarkably sharp edges. In some areas, such as in Northern Ireland, the Lake District, Shropshire and Cornwall, other types of hard stone were discovered and brought into use. It was realised that further supplies of flint would have to be extracted from the earth as the scattered surface deposits only provided poor quality material. In Norfolk, the area around Grimes Graves was extensively exploited, and neolithic man excavated shafts up to 35ft (10.6m) in depth in order to reach the black floorstone which provided the best flint. In time the miners developed special skills and techniques using antler picks and animal shoulder blade shovels, and working in the dim smoky light given off by crude chalk lamps filled with animal fat and moss wicks. The flint was hauled to the surface in wicker baskets lined with animal skins and then knapped on the surface close by. This early industrial site became an important factor in the economic life of the surrounding district, and obviously extended its importance to areas further afield.

The majority of the early inhabitants of Britain were farmers and herdsmen, growing cereals and rearing livestock. This continued to be the case until the nineteenth century.

Before the age of steam power, man was able to construct magnificent monuments, such as Stonehenge and Avebury, using levers, rollers and muscle power. There were large numbers of labourers shifting hundreds of tons of earth and stones, to raise the huge enigmatic mound of Silbury Hill (SU100685) and the impressive Iron-Age fort on Eggardon Hill (SY541947). These massive earth-moving operations can be compared with the work of the navvies in the nineteenth century, whose picks and shovels constructed the long tunnels and massive embankments of the new railway networks.

The development of an ability to work metal, about 2,000BC, was an immense leap in technology. Metals were important to the development of the ancient world, and with the introduction of iron, iron tools and iron weapons helped to make life easier for man.

Britain was noted for its mineral wealth long before the Romans took possession of it. These conquerors were keen to exploit Britain's resources of iron, lead, tin, copper and gold. Although they left no written records to show the extent of their mining activities, many of our old mines give evidence of work done in very early times and some sites were no doubt mined by the Romans. As early as AD50 they organised the mining of lead with slave labour in the Mendip Hills. Before the coming of the Romans to Wales, the local natives had discovered deposits of gold washed down into the gravel of the River Cothi. The Romans exploited the gold-bearing pyrites by means of open-cast working, and then underground galleries at Dolaucothi, close by the present village of Pumpsaint, (SN565405). This is the only place in Britain where the Romans are definitely known to have mined gold. Evidence of Roman mines in Yorkshire, the Mendips and Derbyshire consists of pigs of smelted lead which have cast-on inscriptions. These have been found in or adjacent to mining areas where there are traces of early working. In Derbyshire, these oblong-shaped ingots of metallic lead have been found at Matlock Bank, Bradwell, Ashbourne and Tansley Moor. The first pig was found in 1777 just below the surface of the ground on Cromford Nether Moor. Now in the British Museum, the inscription reads as follows: IMP CAES HAD RIANI AVG MET LVT: or 'Property of Imperator Caesar Hadrianus Augustus, from the mines of Lutudarum'. The letters LVT are thought to represent the mines in the Matlock or Wirksworth district, or may indicate the whole Derbyshire mining field. Although a number of pigs have been found in Derbyshire, trace of these early workings cannot be identified with certainty, as there has been such extensive working and reworking of the old mining sites.

## THE IRON INDUSTRY

Iron ores were probably discovered in many parts of Britain, in outcrops or in deposits very near to the surface. The smelting of iron was either brought to Britain or was discovered by chance before the time of the Roman occupation. This was another great technological advance, for iron was a much more useful metal than gold. In time charcoal was developed as a fuel, and an iron industry grew up in areas such as the Weald of Kent and Sussex and the Forest of Dean. From early times until the end of the fifteenth century this wrought iron was produced by the bloomery hearth process. Bloomery sites are indicated by scattered heaps of cinders and slag, such as the Far Blacklands Bloomery site, East Sussex, (TQ448382). Vast amounts of fuel were needed, and coppiced wood was used to conserve timber and reduce costs. Coal was unsuitable as there were too many sulphurous impurities in it.

Towards the end of the fifteenth century the blast furnace process was introduced into England, using water-powered bellows to create a more powerful blast of air. The ore was completely melted and run into moulds as cast iron. The cast pigs of iron could then be hammered into shape at the water-powered forge. In 1700, the ironmasters were still completely dependant on charcoal and the waterwheel. Pig iron production was scattered throughout the countryside with clusters of furnaces in the Forest of Dean, the Weald of Kent and Sussex, the West Midlands, Nottinghamshire, South Yorkshire and the Furness area of Lakeland, all of which are wooded areas with ironstone ores, water and charcoal. A typical site was the charcoal blast furnace at Duddon, Broughton-in-Furnace, (SD197884).

Charcoal was easily produced in heavily forested areas, but in Britain the forests shrank quickly and the demand for iron products continued to rise. In order to meet the needs of the day an alternative fuel had to be found. Coal had been tried, but was unsuitable due to its impurities. The solution was found by Abraham Darby who realised that once the sulphur was removed, the resulting product, coke, could be used to fire the furnace. The first molten iron from a coke-fired furnace was achieved in 1709 from his furnace at Coalbrookdale in Shropshire, (SJ667047). Coke was not adopted elsewhere until the middle of the century, when its quality was improved by the use of closed brick coking-ovens. The Bedlam Furnaces at Coalbrookdale (SJ677034) were built specifically for coke smelting in 1757.

The use of iron continued to expand rapidly and it was used as an alternative constructional material to wood, brass, lead, copper and stone wherever possible. After 1750, many waterwheel frames were made of iron, and iron was increasingly used to make machinery for steam driven equipment such as the cotton spinning mule. It was used for tramways in mining districts, and eventually a steam locomotive was built to run on the iron rails. Pots, pans, kettles, fire grates, buttons, buckles, hinges and many other household and agricultural implements were manufactured from cast iron. It was used in the construction of canal aqueducts and bridges, and tons of cast iron produced at Coalbrookdale was slotted or jointed together to form the beautiful bridge across the River Severn that has given the town of Ironbridge (SJ673034) its name. It was designed by Abraham Darby III and erected in 1779, to become the world's first civil engineering work constructed entirely of iron.

To improve the quality and strength of pig iron smelted by coke, it was refined by being placed in a remelting furnace. This was the reverberatory or air-furnace developed in the early eighteenth century, in which the iron did not come into direct contact with the fuel. This produced malleable or wrought iron, in which the carbon and other impurities present in cast iron have been removed. In 1783, Henry Cort took out patents for rolling and puddling iron where the molten metal was stirred by 'puddlers' using heavy iron rakes. As the carbon was removed the melting point rose and the pure iron coagulated into a spongy mass which was then hammered to drive out the slag. The product, the wrought iron, was then ready for reheating and rolling to the required shape.

Steel is iron containing a carefully controlled amount of carbon (typically 0.5 to 1.5 per cent). The quantity produced before 1860 was relatively small and was generally of poor quality. It was made by the cementation process or by the Huntsman's crucible method before the invention of the Bessemer converter. In the cementation technique, wrought iron bars were packed in charcoal in sealed stone or earthenware vessels and then heated in a furnace for five days. The bars would be covered in blisters when removed,

hence the name given to it — blister steel. One of the few surviving stone cementation furnaces, dating from 1720, is the Derwentcote furnace near Rowlands Gill in Co Durham (NZ131565), which is being preserved by the Beamish Open-Air Museum. Another important iron working area was in South Yorkshire, with readily available iron ore and charcoal for blast furnaces, and good supplies of coal for the hearths. The villages and settlements in the Sheffield area specialised in scythes, sickles, tools and cutlery. The Phoenix Scythe Works at Ridgeway (SK403822) still uses traditional methods of production.

Fast-flowing streams from the Pennines provided power for the hammers and bellows, and turned the many grindstones made of local gritstone. Hundreds of abandoned millstones and grindstones lie either side of an old track below Millstone Edge just off the A625 Sheffield to Hathersage road (SK249799).

About 1740, Benjamin Huntsman, a Doncaster clock-maker, dissatisfied with imported steel for springs and pendulums, discovered that the product could be improved by melting the blister steel bars in closed crucibles of refractory clay. This high quality crucible steel was made at Sheffield until well into the present century. The Abbeydale Industrial Hamlet (SK326820), originally an eighteenth-century scythe works, has been completely restored with a crucible shop, hand forges, a grinding shop, tilt hammers and other water-powered machinery. The museum is open to the public and one can follow the different processes in the making of edged tools. Also in Sheffield and open to the public, is the Shepherd Wheel (SK317854) which powered an early nineteenth-century grinding shop. In the centre of the city is a complete example of a cementation furnace within the grounds of the British Iron and Steel Research Association in Hoyle Street (SK348880).

In Dr Robert Plot's *Natural History of Staffordshire* (1686) he describes the burgeoning iron industry in what was then the southern part of the county. The ore was mined from shallow pits, placed with charcoal and air blown over it by a bellows worked by a waterwheel. The pigs of iron were taken to the forges, reheated, and beaten by a

great hammer raised by the motion of a waterwheel
Lastly, the bar iron was taken to the slitting mills,
where it was rolled into sheets and then cut into
rods. It was mainly from these rods of wrought
iron that thousands of smiths, working at open
coal-fired hearths in little cottage backrooms
manufactured the small metal objects from
which they earned their living: knives, scythes,
buttons, buckles, bits, spurs, wire and nails.
There was an immense demand for rod iron, and
gradually the local supplies of charcoal became
exhausted and pig iron had to be imported up the
River Severn from the Forest of Dean. In 1766,
John Wilkinson established the first steam blown
blast furnace, and from then on, this hitherto
unknown area was to become the densely
populated and economically important region
known as the Black Country.

In the early nineteenth century, the landscape
of the Black Country was one of small agricultural
holdings with a traditional metal trade. There
was a colliery in almost every field, and often
individual enterprises combined to build furnaces
or to share the operation of a rolling mill. The
clusters of cottages grew and expanded into
separate towns; the green fields became submerged
beneath blast furnaces, engine houses, coal pits,
brick works, clay pits, coke ovens, spoil heaps
and cinder tips. The woods disappeared, and the
few fields of corn and hay struggled to survive in
an atmosphere charged with sulphur and other
noxious emissions. The separate communities
maintained their specialised manufactures: chain
making at Cradly Heath and Tipton, saddlers'
ironmongery at Walsall, springs at West Brom-
wich, screws at Smethwick, locks at Willenhall,
wire and tubes at Wednesbury, nuts and bolts at
Darlaston, hardware at Wolverhampton, and
needles and fish hooks at Redditch. Nailmaking,
which began in cottagers' hovels on the heaths,
continued in the Stour valley, and in Bromsgrove,
Rowley and Dudley.

The Avoncroft Museum of Buildings is situated
south of Bromsgrove at Stoke Heath (SO945683).
The site contains a nailer's workshop dating
from the 1860s, and a splendid reconstruction of
a chain workshop which displays the whole
chain-making process; and the Black Country
Museum at Dudley shows a picture of industrial

life in the nineteenth century.

The bloomery process was carried on in the
Weald of Kent and Sussex and in other areas,
such as the Forest of Dean and in the Lake
District, from monastic until Tudor times. In the
Weald the accessible ores were located near the
junction of Ashdown Sand and the Wadhurst
Clay formations. In Lakeland, use was made of
the rich deposits of haematite iron ores runnning
south-east from Maryport to Kirkby Lonsdale.
The Wealden ores were obtained by means of a
series of bell-pits. They would be about 6ft
(1.8m) in diameter at the top and widening
towards the bottom. They were generally shallow,
rarely more than 20ft (6m) deep. Great numbers
of these mine-pits still remain in the woods;
generally they are filled with water. For example,
Stilehouse Wood, Mayfield (TQ585302), and
Tugmore Shaw, Hartfield (TQ458372). In some
areas almost every field was investigated for ore
deposits, and many pits were only roughly filled
in creating a pattern of hummocks and hollows
in pasture fields.

Before the arrival of the blast furnace, iron was
made by the simple bloomery process using only
hand-worked domed hearths 4ft (1.2m) high
made of baked clay. The base was supported by a
ring of stones 4 to 8ft (1.2 to 2.4m) in diameter.
The process of smelting was started by bringing
pieces of charcoal to white heat, and then adding
small fragments of iron ore. Blasts of air, either
from foot or hand operated bellows, were
directed into the lower central part of the dome,
and the mixture turned plastic at about 800 $^0$C.
Alternatively, layers of charcoal and ore were
built up into a dome shape, and the heap covered
with a thick coating of clay. Once the fire had
been lit the dome was closed and the blasts of air
kept going for many hours. The purer iron
settled as a spongy mass or 'bloom' at the bottom,
and some of the slag was drawn off through a
special opening. When the smelt was complete,
the dome was broken and the bloom was taken
out, and hammered on an anvil to remove excess
slag and adhering cinder. The product was
wrought iron, sometimes of a steely nature,
which could then be used by the smith. The
bloomery sites can be recognised as heaps of
cinder usually close by small streams. As the

temperature of such hearths was so low, the slag hardly ran at all before congealing into ribbed, rounded or globular lumps. It is interesting to realise that a full year's output from a site barely exceeded 2 tons, and that would have required 40 acres (16 hectares) of woodland for fuel.

The discovery of these old bloomery sites is far from complete, although in the Weald much fieldwork has been carried out by the Wealden Iron Research Group. The locations of these sites is difficult and arduous, as many of those surviving lie hidden along stream banks, having remained protected from plough disturbance by trees and undergrowth. In west and south-west Lakeland over 300 sites have now been mapped.

---

### Identifying Features

- Sites may be recognised as areas of cinder usually along the banks or close to a stream, or washed into the bed of a stream.
- The sites may be situated in remote settings, in or near to areas of coppiced woodlands.
- There may be evidence of pieces of slag congealed into ribbed, rounded or globular lumps with a smooth blue-black surface.
- Where a former bloomery site has been ploughed, the slag and cinder may be scattered across the surface of the ground.
- The date of a site cannot definitely be determined, but evidence may be found in parish registers, recorded tithes, or map field names.

---

### Bloomery Sites

*Woodland Fell Bloomery*

**Green Moor**
Woodland Fell, Torver, Cumbria
OS 96, (1in 88), SD262898
**Access**   Take the Broughton in Furness road from Torver for 3¾ miles (6km), then turn left along a narrow lane to Woodland where there is ample parking at a triangular junction, SD248895. Take the road left, north-north-east, for a short distance, then bear right along a track through oak woods to Green Moor. Continue beyond the building, cross the stream on the simple clapper bridge, and follow the path left as it climbs the slope. Turn left at the second solitary hawthorn tree and follow an indistinct path towards the stream. The bloomery site with its bank of cinders and scattered pieces of slag lies beyond a small marshy depression above a crook in the stream. Distance from parking place 1 mile (800m).

**Iridge**
Brickhurst Wood, Hurst Green,
East Sussex
OS 188, (1in 184), TQ62/72;
752277
At a point where the Iridge
Furnace stream joins a tributary
from the south-west, slag may be
noticed under the bridge that
carries the footpath. Tap slag
lies thick in the tributary stream
for some distance above the
bridge, until the slag heap is
reached in the right bank. This
material is now being washed
out by the stream. There is
evidence of burnt clay, and the
tap slag is heavy with a high iron
content, similar to that from
Roman bloomeries.
**Access**  The site may be
approached by following the
footpath from Hurst Green past
Driftways Farm and the old
furnace pond bay, to meet the
path coming from Little Iridge
Farm. Distance: 1¾ miles
(2.8km). Or from just west of
A229 at TQ759282, by track
and then by path following the
stream. Distance just over ½
mile (800m).

**Pippingford Park**
Ashdown Forest, Newbridge,
East Sussex
OS 187, (1in 183), TQ43/53;
446314

**Waystrode**
Stony Croft, Cowden, Kent
OS 188, (1in 171), TQ44/54;
458406
Close to the ancient manor
house, there are large deposits of
cinder and slag in both banks of
the stream.

**Footlands**
Sedlescombe, East Sussex
OS 199, (1in 184),
TQ62/72;773202
Footpath from Woodman
Green, (Hancox Farm),
alongside Footland Wood
towards Cripp's Corner. The
east bank of the stream contains
pieces of furnace lining, slag and
cinder.

**Water Park**
Coniston Hall, Coniston,
Cumbria
OS 96, (1in 88), Outdoor
Leisure Map 'The English
Lakes', 1:25000, South West
Sheet
There are two bloomery sites on
the west bank of Coniston
Water, at Water Park,
SD303956, and at Springs,
SD303954.

**Oldlands Roman Bloomery**
Fairwarp, Maresfield
OS 188, (1in 183),
TQ42/52;475267

---

## FURNACES AND FORGES

In the later Middle Ages it was discovered,
probably quite by accident, that a powerful blast
of air forced through the furnace from mech-
anically operated bellows raised the temperature
sufficiently, ie to over 1200 $^{0}$C, to produce an
alloy of iron and carbon. The molten metal was
tapped from the base of the furnace and run into
a long furrow prepared in a bed of moulding
sand. This principal mould was termed the 'sow'
and the offshoots were known as 'pigs', hence the
name pig iron. The pig or cast iron, could not be
shaped by hammering because of its brittle and
strongly crystalline nature. Previously, all
ironworking techniques had been associated
with wrought iron, which is malleable. In order
to convert or refine the cast iron, it was taken
firstly to a finery forge and then to a chafery
forge. In the finery forge, it was reheated in a
small charcoal-fired hearth, and the iron subjected
to a blast of air was stirred or puddled. This action
removed much of the carbon and ultimately left a
mass of spongy iron in the hearth. The lump was
then hammered by a water powered tilt hammer
before being taken to the chafery forge. Here the
iron was simply reheated and forged into a
particular shape for sale. There is a finery forge
site in the Lake District, and it is probably the
only surviving site, albeit only partially. When it
was in operation, the forge would have included
a small building housing a finery hearth, a tilt
hammer and bellows operated by waterwheel,
anvils, ore bin and stores, and a chafery hearth.
Another building on the site possibly contained
some living accommodation as well as a charcoal
store.

## Identifying Features Today of Lakeland Finery Forge

- North of the forge lies the site of the hammer pond (now dry) and its dam.
- The leat carrying the tail race runs from the pond, past the finery hearth and into Force Beck.
- A low, squarish section of standing masonry alongside the tail race is the site of the finery hearth with the pig-hole still visible. There

would have been a waterwheel on either side, one powering the tilt hammer and the other working the bellows.
- The position of the tilt hammer anvil lies on the north side of the finery hearth. It may be recognised as a small square depression in the ground.

**Stony Hazel Finery Forge**
Rusland, Newby Bridge, Cumbria
OS 96, (1in 88), SD336897
Approaching from the south, bear left in Rusland village and proceed towards a church on higher ground. Keep to the left, and then bear right at the junction. Continue as far as a gate on the left. Follow the track until it meets a fence, pass through the small gate and along the path which cuts back to the forge site alongside the beck.

*Stoney Hazel Finery Forge*

The bloomery furnace and the later finery and chafery forges all needed water-powered forging hammers to pound, beat and shape the iron. There is a hammer head and wheel shaft on show at the Weald and Downland Museum, Singleton, Sussex, SU875130.

In the hilly core of the Sussex High Weald there is a landscape of sweeping hillsides and narrow valleys. A distant view across the Weald still conveys the impression of a wide-ranging forest, but a closer acquaintance reveals the great imprint of man over five hundred years. As with many other parts of Britain, the land can be read just like a manuscript. In the Weald, there are countless marl pits, dug in the hope that marl and clay would improve the fertility of the soil; also vast numbers of small minepits worked in the constant search of iron ore.

The most beautiful legacy of the iron industry in Sussex and Kent is the hammer pond. The blast furnaces and forges needed a good head of water to work the bellows and the hammers, and this was stored in ponds because of the irregular summer flow of the small streams. Usually, an ironworks lay just below a wide earthen dam or pond bay. Higher upstream other bays would be constructed for reserve water supplies. These reservoirs look like a string of pearls on the map. Many of the smaller ponds are now dry, the water eventually breached the bays. The enthusiastic follower of the once famous Wealden iron industry should study the various $2\frac{1}{2}$in Ordnance Survey maps of the area, and read the bulletins of the Wealden Iron Research Group for more detailed information on site investigations.

The seeking of evidence and the study of known remains is not always easy as many sites lie on private land. However, there is much to be seen using existing rights of way.

## Wealden Iron Industry
## General Identifying Features

### Furnace and Forges

● Scatters of slag and/or furnace lining in fields, or along the banks, or in the beds of streams.

● The slag from power forges usually consists of larger, rounded pieces of with a smooth blue-black surface. It could also be the product of power bloomeries.

● Blast furnace slag is like bottle glass, consisting mainly of silica. The material has a great variety of colour. It is either solid, or contains air bubbles, and therefore light and brittle.

### Hammer Ponds and Bays

● Long, thin finger-like lakes and ponds occupying narrow river valleys.

● A high earthen bank or bay holds back the water in existing hammer ponds. The flow of water is usually controlled by a sluice.

● Some furnace ponds were constructed by damming a section upstream and downstream.

● Many storage ponds are now empty of water and the bed now covered with vegetation and undergrowth.

● In many cases the earthen bays remain, now covered with vegetation, but easily recognisable. A considerable number of pond bay sites are marked on the 2½in Ordnance Survey maps.

● There are many signs of a leat feeding the pond from the stream, or evidence of a spillway on the site.

## Some Sites

### Kitchenham Forge

Kitchenham, Boreham Street,
Bexhill, East Sussex
OS 199, (1in 183),
TQ61/71;679135

According to the deeds of 1611, there were certain lands called Kitchenham, including Kitchenham Forge. Also there was land in the valley used as a pond for the forge, which appears to have ceased working in 1664.

Today, there is only slight evidence of the bay, which carries the footpath from Kitchenham Farm to Bray's Hill. The bay does not seem to span the width of the valley, but only that area close to the rising ground of Hammer Wood. The shallow ditch along the north-east boundary of the wood was the original long leat that fed the smaller pond. The hummocky ground at the south-east end of the bay indicates the forge site, and pieces of cinder may be found on, or just below the surface. At the bend of the side channel parallel to the bay, more large pieces of cinder may be discovered in the bank.

**Access**  Just east of Boreham Street take the B2204 for ¾ mile (1.2km) to Kitchenham Farm. Follow the track down to the valley of the Ash Bourne stream.

Slag and cinder, Kitchenham

Kitchenham Forge Bay

## Waldron Furnace

Horam, East Sussex
OS 199, (1in 183),
TQ41/51;566181
The site, now part of a house garden, has an ornamental pond south of the furnace bay. It is a good condition about 240ft (72m) long, and presently supports a splendid hedge which is about 400 years old, of alder, hawthorn, oak and hazel. There is a little glassy slag, particularly at the west end of the bay, where the main stream has cut a way through. The channel at the east end of the bay only continues a little distance to the south, and is probably the site of a wheel pit and a culverted leat. Fragments of Tudor roofing tile and glassy slag, have been found in molehills at the northern end of the bay.
**Access** A public footpath goes

*Pond bay, Waldron Furnace*

through the house garden from the Horam to Waldron minor road, alongside the ornamental pond and then over a stile in a gap in the pond bay. The path

bifurcates at this point, one route heads for Knabes Acre and the other proceeds towards Huggetts Farm.

## Ashburnham Furnace

Penhurst, Battle, East Sussex
OS 199, (1in 183)
TQ61/71;686171
After a sharp decline in the 1650s Ashburnham Forge and Ashburnham Furnace did not

cease production until the 1820s. These famous works situated in a beautiful wooded valley, produced fire-backs, cannon and shot. At the furnace site, the attractive-looking cottage has a small side window through

*Ashburnham Hammer Pond*

which the ironworkers' wages were paid. Opposite, the bay may be identified but the pond is dry. A little way along the track, which has pieces of iron embedded in its surface, is another pond which still contains water. There are large pieces of iron in the bed of the stream close by the track that leads to Rocks Farm. The garden of Furnace Cottage was the site of the wheelpit of the furnace.
**Access** Take the B2204 from Hazard's Green to Battle, and then left on a minor road beyond Kitchenham Farm towards Burwash. Just before the hamlet of Ponts Green, bear right on a country lane to Ashburnham Forge. Here the road rides across the pond bay of the forge. Proceed through the gate on the left and follow the bridle track up for just over ½ mile (800m), to the site of Ashburnham Furnace. There are many pieces of glassy slag on the surface of the track.

## Other Sites

### Newbridge Furnace
Newbridge, Hartfield, East Sussex
OS 188, (1in 183)
TQ43/53;455324
The main furnace was later used as a corn mill, and has now been enlarged as a private residence. One of the hammer ponds has been partially reclaimed, and the spillway still exists.

### Pounsley Furnace
Blackboys, Framfield, East Sussex
OS 199, (1in 183)
TQ42/52;529219

### Crowborough Furnace
Marden's Hill, Crowborough, East Sussex
OS 188, (1in 183)
TQ43/53;496321

### Cotchford Forge
Hartfield, Crowborough, East Sussex
OS 188 (1in 183)
TQ43/53;471338

## Charcoal Fired Blast Furnaces Sites

**Bonawe Furnace** (Scottish Development Department) Taynuilt, Connel, Strathclyde Region
OS 50, (1in 46), NN009318
The choice of Bonawe as a furnace site was governed by the extensive areas of woodland along the shores of Loch Etive and in Glen Nant. In the latter, the existing woodlands are a result of many years of felling and coppicing, but since the end of the nineteenth century the forest has been allowed to develop naturally. A constant supply of charcoal was the key factor for smelting at Bonawe. Coupled with this the site had good water-power resources, and was particularly well-placed for the transport of iron ore by boat. Charcoal was produced by burning lengths of wood in a rounded pile called a stack. Once assembled, the outside of the stack was covered with earth and turves to restrict the air supply, and the wood burnt slowly to produce charcoal. Iron ore was shipped in from the Furness district of England and from central Scotland.

The Bonawe Iron Furnace, founded in 1753, has been splendidly preserved and is open to the public. The furnace building and charging house are

in the centre of the site. Here the furnace shaft was loaded at a high level, and the molten iron trickled down the chimney to the hearth at the bottom, where it was drawn off into moulds in the casting sand. Other buildings include two elegant charcoal store sheds and an iron-ore shed. The waterwheel which provided the power for the bellows is no longer *in situ*. It is not often that a car park is interesting, but Bonawe's

parking area is among the slag heaps. There is a good opportunity to seek good specimens of slag with embedded charcoal. Close by there is a block of workers' houses, and to the northwest, a long masonry-built quay extends into Loch Etive.

**Access**    The furnace site lies to the north of Taynuilt near the shore of Loch Etive and is signposted from the main A85. Oban is 15 miles (24km) to the west.

*Bonawe Furnace*

*Duddon Bridge Furnace*

### Duddon Furnace
Duddon Bridge, Broughton-in-Furness, Cumbria
OS 96 (1in 88), SD197884
This important charcoal-fired blast furnace was built in 1736, and is the most complete surviving example in the Furness district. The furnace building makes full use of the sloping ground to ease the carriage of raw materials to the charging platform. A ½mile (800m) long leat was constructed to carry water from the River Duddon north of the ironworks in order to power the bellows.

Preservation work has been carried out on the furnace complex and the iron ore store, although the large charcoal store is roofless, and the adjacent block of workers' cottages is in a sad state of decay.

**Access**  Take the minor road running north along the west bank of the River Duddon for a few yards after leaving the main A595. A wooden gate on the left gives access to a right of way which passes between the furnace complex and the cottages. This track affords an excellent view of the whole site.

## Some Other Charcoal Furnace Sites

### Charlcotte Furnace
Cleobury North, Bridgenorth, Shropshire
OS 138, (1in 129), SO638861

### Craleckan Furnace
Furnace, Loch Fyne, Strathclyde Region
OS 55, (1in 52), NN025001

### Newland Furnace
Ulverston, Cumbria
OS 96, (1in 88), SD299798

## Coke Fired Blast Furnace Site

*Blaenavon Ironworks*

### Blaenavon Ironworks (DoE)
Blaenavon, Gwent
OS 161, (1in 154), SO251095
The ironworks was established by three Staffordshire ironmasters, Thomas Hill, Benjamin Pratt and Thomas Hopkins, in the late 1780s. By 1790, the site, consisting of three furnaces, casthouses and a steam blowing engine, was producing pig iron. Another two furnaces had come into operation by 1810. The pig iron was taken by tramway to the 'puddling' furnaces at Garnddyrys (SO260121) to be converted into wrought iron. In the 1830s the water balance lift was installed, in order to raise raw material from the furnace yard to the upper level. New furnaces were erected on the nearby Forgeside site (SO245085) in the 1850s,

and steel replaced the production of wrought iron. The production of steel at the new site led to the eventual closure of the new furnaces by 1900.

Of the original five blast furnaces built into the hillside, only one can be seen in its original state, encased with ashlar stone blocks. Stone from two of the furnaces was used to build St James' Church in Blaenavon. The water balance tower still stands and is in the process of being restored. The furnaces were lined with firebricks made from locally mined fireclay, and the arrangement and workmanship of these can be clearly seen. Workers' cottages were built around the ironworks, and a row of these is being preserved on the works site.

**Access** If approaching Blaenavon from the north, on the B4246, the site lies on the western edge of the town in North Street. At the time of writing, restoration work is still being carried out on the site, and enquiries should be made regarding access.

## LEAD MINES AND MINING

The mining of lead is almost as old as farming itself. Iron Age man discovered outcrops of this useful grey ore and they knew how to smelt it. The Romans came with skill and experience from their mines in Spain, and this technical knowledge was quickly put to good use in the Mendip Hills. As the Romans spread through the country, lead mining was organised with slave labour in Shropshire, North Wales, Derbyshire, Yorkshire and the Northern Pennines. Evidence of Roman mining activity consists of pigs of smelted lead which have a raised inscription produced by casting. These oblong ingots have been produced in a mould, and the impressed letters then stand out in relief on the pig of lead. A number of these pigs have been discovered in Yorkshire and Derbyshire and probably represent losses in transit. In Derbyshire, the mineral-rich district between Wirksworth and Matlock was known to the Romans as Lutudarum. The exact location is not known, but since the Derbyshire lead mining laws have been upheld since Saxon times in the Barmoot Courts at Wirksworth, it suggests that this area was the successor to the Roman Lutudarum.

After the Romans, the historical development of the lead mining fields was a fitful process of individual workings until the seventeenth century. Occasionally, small groups of miners formed partnerships exploiting outcrops and shallow surface deposits using primitive methods of ore dressing and smelting. Gradually, new techniques came in the form of deeper underground workings, together with improved methods of dressing and smelting. Customers required finer concentrates, and more efficient furnaces and ore hearths were developed. As the mines went deeper into the earth, water was the miners' greatest enemy. Longer levels or 'soughs' were dug for drainage and steam engines were employed for pumping. In the eighteenth and nineteenth centuries all the mechanical processes were greatly improved, with the help of water and steam power.

The three major Pennine lead mining fields consisted of Derbyshire, from the High Peak to the Ashbourne area; Yorkshire, from Swaledale to Nidderdale, and the northern Pennines from Alston Moor to Teesdale. In 1692, the London Lead Company was formed and was responsible for much of the development of lead mining and smelting in Derbyshire, North Wales and the northern Pennines. This important company began the commercial transformation of the lead-mining industry by investing first in smelting, then in mining in order to keep their smelt mills in work. The two major groups, the London Lead Company and the Beaumont Company, dominated mining operations in the northern Pennines. Their maximum productivity was in the period from 1820 to 1880. The early decades of the nineteenth century witnessed Alston Moor's heyday as a mining area, with a population rising to nearly 7,000 in 1831. At Nent Head (NY781437) just south of Alston, the company planned a new settlement near the smelt mill. Cottages were built and provided with land and gardens, and the miners-cum-smallholders could also run sheep on the upland pastures. In 1825 more cottages were built, together with a school, church, public library, chapel and bath houses.

The company showed an admirable concern for the welfare of their workpeople, also providing disablement funds and sick-relief.

Towards the end of the nineteenth century, the price of lead fell sharply due to imports of cheaper American ore. On Alston Moor, this change of fortune, together with the gradual exhaustion of local veins, led to a collapse of the industry and a decline in population. The two large companies saw little future for their industry and surrendered their leases in Alston Moor and Weardale in the 1880s. By 1891, the population of the Alston Moor area had fallen to just under 4,000, as many families left to seek work, particularly in coal mining districts.

Lead extraction had been the most important industry in the Peak District from Roman times until the end of the nineteenth century. It probably reached its peak in the 1750s when some 10,000 miners were engaged in it. The eighteenth century also saw the introduction of the steam engine for pumping out water from the lead mines, and technological advances in other forms of mine machinery to combat the immense quantities of water. In the Alport mines, hydraulic engines were placed at the bottom of shafts. A descending column of water acted on a piston which worked the pump rods. A legacy of the Derbyshire lead miner's skill are the soughs (pronounced 'suffs'). They were adits or tunnels driven specifically to drain a mine. In Lathkill Dale, the Mandale Sough was cut between 1797 and 1820. The sough tail or outlet is easily accessible, being alongside the footpath through the dale, at SK197661. As well as making use of the excessive quantities of water in the operation of hydraulic pressure pumps, some mines used boats in the flooded levels to carry out ore and waste material. The Speedwell Mine at the foot of the Winnats Pass (SK139827) is now a tourist attraction. Visitors will easily appreciate the enormity of the task of driving a level through ½ mile (800m) of solid limestone.

Mining for lead or zinc has been carried out throughout Wales. In many localities lead mining reached its peak in the third quarter of the nineteenth century, and considerable evidence of mining activity may be found today in remote parts of the country. Many investors and specu-

*Demolished church Dylife, once a lead mining village in Wales*

lators were attracted by the possibility of a high silver content in the lead; frequently their adventures were doomed to failure. Some unscrupulous promoters puffed up the most unlikely prospects. Set in the wild hills north west of Pumlumon Fawr, the mines of Esgairhir (SN735912) and Esgairfraith, (SN741912) were promoted by Sir Humphrey Mackworth and William Waller on behalf of the Company of Mine Adventurers in the late seventeenth century. They were given the title 'Welsh Potosi', an allusion to the rich silver mines of Peru. In 1854, the scene around the mines was graphically portrayed by George Borrow in his book, *Wild Wales*. The mines had an attraction that was hard to resist, and company after company lost their investments. Central Wales produced over 600,000 tons of lead and zinc ores during the mid-nineteenth century, but after the 1870s a long decline set in due to falling prices and the antics of disreputable promoters.

People interested in tracking down the many sites of the old Welsh metal mines will search through remote and beautifully wild countryside. In recent years many sites have been destroyed, particularly in forestry areas, ostensibly removing the scars of industry. In many ways, these forlorn tumbled remains possess a profound melancholy beauty, and are perhaps the most attractive of all industrial landscapes. Cwmystwyth (SN805747) is a splendid example of the area's mineral wealth. The landscape is one of sheer desolation, the destruction of a once beautiful valley. Spoil heaps litter the slopes and slide into the Afon Ystwyth; the rusty metalwork of the old mine buildings rattles and squeaks in the wind. However, the traveller who wanders alone through the ruins will experience an intense isolation, and no doubt conjure up a few ghosts of the miners under Mine Captain, James Raw, who in one year, 1858, raised 1,438 tons of lead ore. In 1872, the mine was both the richest and the oldest mine in the county of Cardiganshire. For the industrial archaeologist, the site is a paradise of waste tips, ruined buildings, adits, tramway roads, and leats. On the hillside slopes overlooking Nant yr Onnen are the striking scars of hushes radiating like the spokes of a wheel. This was a method where a strong force of water was released in order to scour away the ground surface to reveal traces of mineral veins.

For hill walkers, the mine complex lies on the route of the Cambrian Way which traverses Wales from Cardiff to Conwy.

The Welsh lead miner in the eighteenth and nineteenth centuries was often a small-scale farmer, earning a supplementary living from a patch of marginal land. Many mines, such as Nantiago SN826863, and Cwmbyr, SN786947, were located in remote hills away from village communities. Often the men travelled long distance to reach the mines, walking the lonely tracks and paths through the hills. The ways remain, unless submerged by battalions of conifers, for the benefit of hill walkers today. Often the miners stayed in barrack accommodation spending the whole working week away from home.

Before the sixteenth century the bloomery process was the usual way to smelt lead. Later ore was placed on top of a fire set in a deep hearth and constantly turned by long pokers. At the end of the seventeenth century the ore was smelted in reverberatory furnaces, the body of which was set between a powerful coal fire and a tall chimney. A cross wall at the fire end deflected or

*Surrender Smelt Mill Flue*

'reverberated' the heat down on to the ore. After 1780 long flues were constructed close to the surface of the ground in order to create a powerful draught for the furnaces, and to condense the lead fume which was highly poisonous to man and animals. A good example of a long flue is to be found running up the hillside behind the Surrender Smelt Mill, near Reeth, in Swaledale, North Yorkshire, (NY988003).

## Scordale Mine

Hilton Beck, Hilton, Nr.
Appleby, Cumbria
OS 91, (1in 84), NY762227

It is believed that the Romans mined Scordale for lead, to make lead seals and pay coffers for the soldiers. In a village census of 1787, of the inhabitants of Hilton, Murton, Dufton and Knock, thirty-seven people were employed at the mines, including women ore washers. After the establishment of the lead mining industry on Alston Moor by the London Lead Company, it opened up the Dufton, Rundale, Scordale and Lune Head mines in 1820. Hilton grew into an industrial village, changing the face of the small settlement completely. Stone buildings appeared, some cottages had an upstairs floor, and there was an overcrowding of families. The company, frequently known as the Quaker Lead Company, provided a piped water supply, bake ovens in two houses, a wash house, a school and a reading room. The village of Long Marton even had a band. Children paid a little towards their schooling, and the miners' children were educated by the company.

At the mine, there was the 'shop' which provided accommodation for eight young lads. They stayed there for the week and were looked after by the 'minder'. Miners who travelled the distance to the Lune Head workings stayed the week at the mine shop. Lune Head also had a women's shop.

Up the valley, on the slopes overlooking Hilton Beck, is the spectacular Lowfield Hush. 1811 saw the end of hushing in the Eden valley because of serious pollution problems in the River Eden. At the Scordale Mine the horse level goes in at the lowest point through a masoned arch. Mining was then carried on upwards to a flat level. Material was tipped into small trucks, and a horse pulled them along the level. Candles were placed in clay set in wall niches, and it is recorded that the horse carried an old chamber pot round its neck, with its own candle set in a lump of clay. The mixed ore, minerals and stone was sorted, and the rest beaten with flat hammers called buckers. The next dressing was to wash the material in water on a sieve so that the heavier ore sank to form a bottom layer. The ore was then crushed and placed with water in a buddle, and the resulting slurry was moved by revolving paddles. Prior to 1880, there were two overshot waterwheels working at the mine, with a water storage pond high on the fellside. The cleaned and separated ore concentrate was taken down to the smelt mill at Hilton. The lead contained a small percentage of silver which was worth extracting; even the flue was scraped to recover any minute grains.

For years, the old miners had thrown away the loose stone, the 'cawk', as having no commercial value. After 1882, barytes and fluorspar were mined at Scordale. The barytes was found in vertical seams, sometimes reaching great depths but not more than 5ft (1.5m) in width. In the early 1900s, two miners who stayed the week in very sparse accommodation at the mine, each carried a week's supplies in a pillowcase. The other twelve walked from Hilton and Murton and returned in the late afternoon. Their work started at 7.00am and finished at 5.30pm. The mined barytes came out via an iron shute with water running down. It was tipped into sulphuric acid vats, drained off, dried in kilns and ground up between granite millstones, powered at first by a waterwheel and then by a gas engine. The material was brought down to the village by horse-dray and traction engine.

In the latter years of its life before its closure in 1952, Scordale continued to mine barytes. The miner, working with a mate and a compressed air drill, drove a gently sloping tunnel from the adit for a distance of 100ft (30m). Then a 50ft (15m) rise would be cut upwards, from the top of which a further level would be begun. The barytes would be then dropped down into waiting containers.

**Access**  Scordale Mine lies 2¼ miles (3.6km) north-east of Hilton village. A right of way follows Hilton Beck to the mine, and continues beyond the head of the valley to join Swarth Beck and Maize Beck, which is on the line of the Pennine Way.

There are difficulties of access, as the mine and the right of way lie within the boundary of MoD Warcop Training Area. Notification of firing is given by the publication of a notice each month in the *Cumberland and Westmorland Herald*. Copies of the firing notice are sent not less than seven days before the day of firing.

For further information on firings, ring the Range Control Officer, Brough 661, Extension 34.

Please heed the warning notice — Keep to the footpath — at all times.

## Some Mining Terms and Identification Features

### Abandoned Mines

● Mysterious bumps and hollows in the surface of the fields.

● Indications of spoil heaps and rock debris. The tips may contain specimens of galena, zinc blende, quartz, iron pyrites, copper pyrites, calcite and fluorspar.

● Evidence of capped, partially concealed or open mine shafts.

● Remains of old mine buildings, such as a solitary chimney and former engine house.

● Indications of other pieces of ore dressing equipment such as a 'buddle', a device for concentrating ore crushed to sand size.

● The presence of an adit, a horizontal shaft driven into a hillside following a vein, or for mine access, ventilation and drainage.

● A masonry arch may indicate a sough or a level. A sough is an adit or tunnel driven specifically to drain a mine. A level is a tunnel to or along veins usually at set vertical intervals, eg 10, 20 and 30 fathom levels.

● The indications of hushes on steep hillsides, caused by the release of impounded water in order to scour away the ground surface to expose veins of ore. There are probably hundreds of these in the Pennines alone.

## Some Sites

### The Magpie Mine

Sheldon, Bakewell, Derbyshire
OS 119, (1in 111), SK172682
Former lead-mining complex of mine buildings, ruined engine house and chimney. There are many open shafts. The site is reached by footpaths from the village of Sheldon and from the minor road to Bakewell. The mine has had a fascinating history, and people who wish to look round should contact the Peak District Mines Historical Society who now hold the tenancy of the property. Members of the society use the main buildings as a field centre each weekend and often during the mid-week period. They will be pleased to help interested visitors. The address is c/o Peak District Mining Museum, The Pavilion, Matlock Bath, Derbyshire.

*Magpie Lead Mine*

*Crushing circle and wheel, Odin Mine*

### The Odin Sough

Hollowford Lane, Castleton, Derbyshire
OS 110, (1in 111), SK150832
The Odin Sough was begun in 1816 and completed in about 1845. Its tail (outfall) may be seen a few paces beyond the Peakshole Stream, with the water emerging from a low slabbed arch in the wall on the left.

## Mandale Mine

Lathkilldale, Over Haddon,
Derbyshire
OS 119, (1in 111), SK 196660
Sough entrance may be seen
below the footpath, while in
woods above are the remains of a
Cornish engine house, pumping
shaft, incline and waterwheel
pit. Downstream are the
aqueduct pillars which took
water across the river Lathkill to
power the wheel.

**Access** Park in the car park in
Over Haddon village and walk
down the steep zigzag road into
one of the Peak District's most
beautiful dales. Walk upstream
and the mine remains are almost
immediately after the path
enters the woods.

## Rutland Cavern

Heights of Abraham, Matlock
Bath, Derbyshire
OS 119, (1in 111), SK 293586
This is part of the extensive
workings in the area of Masson
Hill, originally part of the
Nestus Mine. The cavern is open
to the public. Large quantities of
ore were mined leaving huge
open chambers.

*Mandale Sough*

*Dirtlow Rake*

## The Magpie Sough

Ashford-in-the-Water, Bakewell,
Derbyshire
OS 119, (1in 111), SK 179696
Its construction was started in
1873 and completed in 1881.
**Access** It may be reached by
following the footpath on the
south bank of the River Wye for
$\frac{3}{4}$ mile (1.2km) from the foot of
Kirk Dale, or down Nettler Dale
from Sheldon. Distance $1\frac{1}{4}$ miles
(2km).

## Dirtlow Rake

Castleton, Derbyshire
OS 110, (1in 111), SK 153820
The site of a vertical fissure
which originally contained the
mineral vein.

*North Hush, Gunnerside Gill*

*Blakethwaite Lead Smelting Mill*

### The Temple Mine

Ysbyty Cynfyn, Ponterwyd,
Dyfed
OS 135, (1in 127), SN749792
This mine is sited in the Rheidol
gorge in lovely wooded
surroundings. There are the
ruins of the crusher-house,
waterwheel pits, line of the
tramway, leat, round buddles,
and adits. The Rheidol area has
much to offer, with splendid
valley, hill and forest scenery.
There is a fine choice of walks,
and, the railway from Devil's
Bridge to Aberystwyth.
**Access** A steep zigzag descent
to the Parson's Bridge over the
Rheidol, and thence by footpath
to the site. It may also be
approached by footpath from
the village of Ystumtuen.

*Waterwheel pit, Temple Wood Mine*

### Park Level Lead Mine and Killhope Lead Crushing Mill

Lanehead, Weardale, Co
Durham
OS 86, (1in 84), NY827429

This site is preserved by Durham
County Council as an ancient
monument, complete with a 33ft
(10m) diameter overshot
waterwheel. The Council hope

to open the 4ft (1.2m) wide Park
Level to the public, with the
help of members of the Earby
Mines Research Group.

*Killhope Crushing Mill*

### Blakethwaite Mine, Smelt Mill and Hushes

Gunnerside Gill, Gunnerside,
Swaledale, North Yorkshire
OS 92, (1in 90) NY937018
The beck is crossed by a huge
stone slab close by the cloister-
like ruins of the smelt mill which
has a fine arched entrance. The
flue comes down from the edge
of Gunnerside Moor from a
notch in the skyline. Note the
well preserved kiln to the right.
Follow the path south along the
eastern side of the valley to more
ruins (note the level), and as the
path slants upwards there is a
succession of hushes that have
gouged out the fellside. On the
opposite side of the valley to the
west, the remarkable north hush
can clearly be seen.

**Grassington Moor Flue and Chimney**
Grassington, North Yorkshire
OS 98, (1in 90), SE025663

**Driggith Mine**
Carrock Beck, Caldbeck,
Cumbria
OS 90, (1in 82), NY328352

**Bryntail Mine** (DoE)
Clywedog, Llanidloes, Powys
OS 136, (1in 128), SN915869

**Frongoch Mine**
Devils Bridge. Aberystwyth,
Dyfed
OS 135, (1in 127), SN723745

**Llywernog Mine Musuem**
Ponterwyd, Aberystwyth, Dyfed
OS 135, (1in 127), SN735808

*Grassington Moor Smelt Mill Chimney*

**Warning**
Old mines are extremely dangerous places. **Do Not** be tempted to enter mine levels. **Do Not** go near to the edge of a shaft — they are subject to collapse. Walk with great care on any area of old mines. **Do Not** run about, and do not permit children to run about, as real dangers lie in wait for the incautious traveller. Also, please ensure that you are not trespassing.

## WATER POWER

Water power and the waterwheel were to be major factors in technical development through the Middle Ages and into the early years of the industrial revolution. Through the centuries the waterwheel was a great aid to agriculture, and the mill and the miller were essential to the life of a rural community. From a very early date, the waterwheel was adapted to carry out a number of tasks, from turning grindstones of a corn mill to powering the hammers and bellows of a forge. In the Northern and Western Isles and in Ireland, the Norse click mill consisted of a horizontal wheel and vertical shaft driving the millstones directly without the use of gearing. This was a logical development of the hand mill or rotary quern, and one of the best surviving examples is to be found nearly 2½ miles (3.9km) north-east of Dounby on Mainland Island, Orkney (HY325228). The traditional type of water mill may be fed from mill ponds, leats cut from the main stream, in the main stream, from springs and some from tidal power; for example at Woodbridge in Suffolk (TM275488). Watermills are not always obvious; often the mill may resemble one of the local farm buildings, and the wheel may be inside. In the Weald of south-east England narrow valleys were dammed, and the resulting lakes or hammer ponds provided the power for the ironworks. In medieval Britain, the wheel powered fulling mills, where newly woven cloth was pounded under great hammers to compact the fibres together. In Northern Ireland, water power turned the machinery of scutching and beetling mills; two processes in the production of flax. It is a story of continuous development, the spinning of cotton and the weaving of wool moved from the home to the factory. These mills were erected in Pennine valleys where streams were of sufficient capacity to turn a waterwheel. Mills were constantly changing hands and being used for a variety of purposes.

The use of water power to grind flint was an essential part of the the North Staffordshire pottery industry. The district was favoured with extremely good deposits of red clays for earthenware and stoneware, and refractory clays capable of withstanding high temperatures. The area was also fortunate in having essential quantities of water and extensive supplies of good local bituminous coal. The clays, known as the Etruria Marls, lay between the sandstones and the underlying coal-bearing rocks. Although these clays had long been used for local pottery manufacture, it was not until the mid-eighteenth century that their wholesale exploitation saw the rapid growth of the six towns of Stoke-on-Trent.

From north to south, they are: Tunstall, Burslem, Hanley, Stoke, Fenton and Longton.

The local red clay contained certain iron impurities, and before 1700, many potters strove to find clays which would produce whiter pottery bodies. At first locally dug pipe clays, used for making clay tobacco pipes, were used to try and achieve the result. About 1720, large lumps of ball clay were imported from Dorset and Devon. Also at this time ground flint was introduced into the pottery body to improve its whiteness. These new materials of ball clay and flint produced a cream-coloured body, but unfortunately, the dry grinding of flint produced serious problems of silicosis in the grinding mill workers. The average working life in these conditions was three to five years. In 1726, Thomas Benson of Newcastle-under-Lyme took out a patent for grinding flint under water, a process which restricted the inhalation of silica dust.

---

## Identifying Features

- Not always obvious, as the wheel may be housed inside the mill. The building may resemble a farm building.
- Evidence of a mill pond which is used to store water until required.
- Indications of a leat or artificial channel from the main stream to the mill, and a tailrace which carries the water from the wheel back to the stream.
- Occasionally, a spring water supply may power the wheel. There are also mills where the wheel is driven by the action of the tide.
- The sight of old millstones may indicate the whereabouts of a mill.

## Types of Waterwheels

- Horizontal wheels.
- Overshot and high breast, with water falling on the top of the wheel.
- Breast, with water falling on the wheel midway.
- Undershot, water running against the foot of the wheel.
- Poncelet, an advanced type of wheel that could work with variable flows of water, flowing down a curved sluice on to curved paddles.

---

## Some Water Powered Sites

**Mostylee Mill**
Moddershall, Stone,
Staffordshire
OS 127, (1in 119), SJ917362
In North Staffordshire, the
Mostylee Mill began its life as a

fulling mill in 1716, one of possibly ten separate mills in the valley from Moddershall to Stone. The mill was converted to flint grinding in 1756. In the grinding process, the flints were

placed with water in a large wooden-lined pan of 13ft (4m) diameter 2½ft (0.75m) high, which had a central vertical shaft. Attached to it were five cast iron sweeping arms with vertical oak hanging arms, which pushed round lumps of flint in the pan lined with blocks of chert, that were bedded on alternate layers of sand and clay. The flint was calcined on the site, the fuel being charcoal from coppiced woodlands in the locality. The power source was water from the Scotch Brook stored in the mill pond. A channel from the pond fed a 17.5ft (5.25m) diameter, 7ft (2.1m) wide high breast iron-rimmed wheel which developed 88 hp. The deep long buckets on the wheel, which have been replaced, do not require a continuous flow of water. As the buckets fill, the weight of water moves the wheel, and stops momentarily until the bucket fills up again. The mill pond, which had silted and weeded up,

has now been reclaimed into an attractive stretch of water. The Scotch Brook now runs sweetly between a newly constructed and graded outfall.

Another later system of grinding on the site was by means of a cylinder lined with chert blocks. There was a removable plate on the side through which the sludge was removed.

After the grinding process, the sludge went into a settlement 'ark' where the liquid was agitated by hand. Heavy liquid and sediment sank to the bottom and the surplus water drained away by removing wooden stoppers in turn. The slop flint was pumped out on to fireclay blocks and heat dried from underfloor flues. When dried, the material was cut out with a

knife and loaded on to packhorses; later it was sent by canal from Stone to the Potteries. The mill closed in 1958.

**Access** The mill is situated alongside the A520 Stone to Leek road, 2 miles (3.2km) north of Stone. After passing two sharp bends in the narrow sandstone gorge, look for the mill access on the right opposite a building. As this is a very busy main road, great care should be taken on entering and leaving the site. NOTE At the moment the mill has been restored, but is not yet open to the general public. Interested visitors should contact the Borough Surveyor, Civic Offices, Riverside, Stafford. ST16 3AQ.

*Mostylee Mill Pond*

*Mostylee Mill*

**Beckfoot Mill**
Crook of Lune, Sedbergh, Cumbria
OS 97, (1in 89), SD619963
Davy Bank Mill no longer operates, but a visit to this lovely peaceful spot to enjoy the fine river and hill scenery is very well worthwhile. The old 13ft (4m) diameter overshot wheel, a

structure with a cast-iron frame and wooden buckets, now lies incapable of movement. The race is overgrown, the water which was tapped from a rocky dell higher up the beck no longer flows along the rock-cut leat. The wheel's power was used to grind oats and barley for domestic use and as feedstuffs for

local farms.
**Access** From Sedbergh, take the narrow road that follows the Lune valley northwards, and then left down to Beck Foot. The mill lies beyond the bridge on the left-hand side of the road. or, from the A685, Kendal to Tebay road at various points.

## Cheddleton Flint Mill

Cheddlton, Leek, Staffordshire
OS 118 (1in 110), SJ972526
The mill has been restored by a
voluntary trust and consists of
two main buildings, each with a
waterwheel. The equipment
includes: calcining kilns,
grinding pan, agitator, drying
kiln, settling ark, pumps, hoists,
plateway and waggon. There is
a wharf with a crane alongside
the mill which is served by the
Cauldon Canal. The North Mill
is powered by a 22ft (6.6m)
diameter, 5ft 9in (1.72m) wide
low-breast waterwheel. The
South Mill is the older building
and was a corn mill in the
seventeenth century. The 20ft
6in (6.15m) diameter, 5ft 6in
(1.65m) wide low-breast wheel
has larchwood floats. Many
items to do with the history of
pottery milling have been
assembled in the South Mill.
The mill is open to the public on

*Cheddleton Flint Mill*

Saturday and Sunday
afternoons throughout the year.
**Access**   Alongside the
Cauldon Canal in the valley of
the River Churnet in the village
of Cheddleton, and close by the
A520, Stone to Leek road.

## Wellbrook Beetling Mill (NT Northern Ireland)

Cookstown, Co Tyrone,
Northern Ireland
OS NI 13 (1in sheet 5), H749792
This well preserved beetling mill
lies alongside the Ballinderry
River, and visitors have the
opportunity of seeing the
waterwheel, water channel
troughs and beetling machinery.
Beetling is the final stage in the
finishing of linen, in which linen
webs were pounded for anything
from one to two days, up to a
fortnight. The pounding was
done with hammers called
beetles. This treatment
produced a sheen on the woven
bleached damask or closed the
weave in dyed or bleached ducks
and hollands, and also buckrams
for umbrella cloth, towelling,
tropical suiting, interlinings and

*Wellbrook Beetling Mill*

book-binding cloth. Originally, this work was done by a man cranking the cloth on a beam while four men on each side struck it with their mallets or beetles.

**Access**    Leave Cookstown on the Oritor road. After $2\frac{1}{2}$ miles (4km), turn left at the crossroads in Oritor village and continue for $1\frac{1}{4}$ miles (2km). Turn left down a signposted road to Wellbrook Mill.

### Ballydugan Flour Mill

Ballydugan, Downpatrick, Co Down, Northern Ireland
OS NI 21, (1in sheet 9), J462427
A ruined flour mill built in 1792. The mill contained four pairs of stones, two of them French burrs. The breast waterwheel was 20ft (6m) in diameter and 10ft (3m) wide. The mill is six storeys high, built of rubble masonry.

**Access**    The mill is situated in the village of Ballydugan $2\frac{1}{4}$ miles (3.6km) south-west of Downpatrick via the A25.

*Ballydugan Flour Mill*

### Grillagh Bridge Scutching Mill

Upperlands, Maghera, Co Londonderry, Northern Ireland
OS NI 8, (1in sheet 2), C860031
This abandoned scutching mill lies in the corner of a field close by the Grillagh River. The mill has a centrally placed waterwheel which drove a scutching shaft on one side and a vertical flax breaker on the other. At the end of the scutching shaft was a pinion to drive a later horizontal flax breaker. The building on the right is a flax store. The mill is in good condition and still houses some of its machinery and the waterwheel.

This mill is a typical scutch mill of the 1830s, which consists of a single-storeyed rectangular stone house and a breast shot waterwheel. Arranged along the horizontal shaft at intervals would be perhaps four scutching berths. In these individual recesses stood the workmen or scutchers shielded from the

*Grillagh Scutching Mill*

buffing blades, and through which they thrust flax to be scutched.

Flax must be freed from the

core of the plant by retting (that is, lying in water) for some time. When the retted flax is dried the stems can be broken and the

unwanted material beaten off by scutching.

**Access** The mill is situated just south-east of the junction of

the A29 and the B75. A track leads to the building from the south end of the road bridge over the Grillagh River.

## Helsington Laithes Snuff Mill

Kendal, Cumbria
OS 97, (1in 89), SD513903
On the site of a former corn mill is a water-powered snuff mill. Water is obtained from a weir on the River Kent which travels along a leat to the mill. The undershot paddle-type water-wheel drives the nineteenth-

century machinery, which consists mainly of grinding pans, mortars, a mixer and a riddle and shaker. The mixing and blending of various powdered tobaccos is a closely guarded secret. A comprehensive selection of various grades of snuff, packed into small attractive tins, may be seen at the mill.

**Access** On the southern outskirts of Kendal, close by the River Kent. From the centre of the town travel south on the A6 for 1 mile (1.6km) and turn left down a narrow lane $\frac{1}{4}$ mile (400m) from the intersection with the A591.

NOTE As this is a working mill, please contact the works before a visit.

## POSTSCRIPT

In gathering the material for this book, I have travelled the length and breadth of Britain, in order to give as much variety as possible in the choice of locations. The scope has been enormous and as my personal preference is for the hills and high places, I make no apologies for covering some regions more profusely than others.

It will have become obvious that man's involvement with, and impact on the landscape has left traces which go back thousands of years;

in some places, successive settlements have been built over previous ones leaving sites of great complexity. However, all the developments I have covered have left traces in the ground, and the acute and informed observer can learn much while enjoying walks in some of the world's most beautiful landscapes. I hope that I have been able to transmit some of my enthusiasm for the past and present glories of the British countryside and the remains which so profusely litter it; and if this book helps to inform readers of the significance and function of the buildings, ruins and monuments along the way, it will have served its purpose.

# Bibliography

Addison, Sir W., *The Old Roads of England* (Batsford, 1980)

Anthony, I., *Discovering Regional Archaeology: Wales* (Shire Publications, 1973)

Arnold, D.V., *Scottish Cattle Droving and the Hambleton Drove Road, Osmotherly*, (1982)

Ashbee, P., *Ancient Scilly* (David & Charles, 1974)

Atkinson, M., *Blaenafon Ironworks* (Torfaen Museum Trust, 1983)

Atkinson, R.J.C., 'Wayland's Smithy', *Antiquity*, XXXIX, (1965), 126 ff.

Atkinson, R.J.C., *Stonehenge* (Penguin, Revised Edition, 1979)

Barrow, L,. *Irish Round Towers* (Eason, 1976)

Beckensall, S., *Life and Death in Prehistoric Northumberland* (F. Graham, 1976)

Beazley, E., and Howell, P., *The Companion Guide to North Wales* (Collins, 1975)

Bell, J.H.B., Bozman, E.F., Fairfax-Blakeborough, J., *British Hills and Mountains* (Batsford, 2nd Edition, 1943- 4)

Beresford, M., and Hurst, J.G., (Editors), *Deserted Medieval Villages* (Lutterworth Press, 1971)

Bick, D.E., *The Old Metal Mines of Mid-Wales*, 5 Vols, (The Pound House, 1974-8)

Birley, A., *Life in Roman Britain* (Batsford, 1964)

Birley, E., 'The Roman Fort at Low Borrow Bridge', *Transactions of the Cumberland and Westmorland Antiquarian and Archaeological Society*, 47, (NS) (1947)

Bonser, K.J., *The Drovers* (Macmillan, 1970)

Boon, G.C., *Isca, the Roman Legionary Fortress at Caerleon* (National Museum of Wales, 1972)

Bord, J., and C., *A Guide to Ancient Sites in Britain* (Granada, 1978)

Boulton, D., *Adam Sedgwick's Dent*, (Hollett, R.F.G. and Boulton, D., 1984)

Brandon, P., *The Sussex Landscape* (Hodder and Stoughton, 1974)

Breeze, D.J., *The Antonine Wall* (HMSO, 1973)

Breeze, D.J., *The Northern Frontiers of Roman Britain* (Batsford, 1982)

Breeze, D.J., and Dobson, B., *Hadrian's Wall* (Pelican, 1978)

Brown, H., *Hamish's Groats End Walk* (Gollancz, 1981)

Brown, R.A., *The History of the King's Works, Vol 1, The Middle Ages* (HMSO, 1963)

Burl, A., *The Stone Circles of the British Isles* (Yale University Press, 1953)

Burton, S.H., *Exmoor* (Hale, 1974)

Butt, J., and Donnachie, I., *Industrial Archaeology in the British Isles* (Elek, 1979)

Campbell-Graham, D., *Portrait of Perth, Angus and Fife* (Hale, 1979)

Chadwick, N.K., *Celtic Britain* (Thames and Hudson, 1963)

Clare, T., *Archaeological Sites of Devon and Cornwall* (Moorland, 1982)

Clarke, R.R., *East Anglia* (Thames and Hudson, 1960)

Clayton, P., *Archaeological Sites of Britain* (Weidenfeld and Nicholson, 1976)

Collingwood, R.G., 'The hill-fort on Carrock Fell'; *Transactions of the Cumberland and Westmorland Antiquarian and Archaeological Society*, 38, (NS), (1938)

Collingwood, R.G., and Richmond, I., *The Archaeology of Roman Britain* (Methuen, 1969)

Colyer, R.J., *Welsh Cattle Drovers* (University of Wales Press, 1976)

Connah, G., et al, *Wiltshire Archaeological and Natural History Magazine*, IX (1965) 1ff.

Copeland, R., *A Short History of Pottery Raw Materials and the Cheddleton Flint Mill* (Cheddleton Flint Mill Heritage Trust, 1972)

Copley, G.J., *An Archaeology of South East England* (Phoenix House, 1958)

Cossons, N., *BP Book of Industrial Archaeology* (David and Charles, 1975)

Cowling, E.T., *Rombalds Way – A Prehistory of Mid-Wharfedale* (W. Walker, 1946)

Cowling, E.T., 'Cup and Ring Marks to the north of Otley', *Yorks Archaeological Journal*, Vol 33, (1937)

Crosher, G.R., *Along the Cotswold Ways* (Pan, 1976)

Crossing, W., *Crossing's Guide to Dartmoor*, New Introduction by Le Messurier, B., (David and Charles, Reprint 1981)

Cubbon, A.M., *The Art of the Manx Crosses* (Manx Museum and National Trust, 2nd Edition, 1977)

Cubbon, A.M., (Editor), *Prehistoric Sites in the Isle of Man* (Manx Museum and National Trust, 1973)

Cunliffe, B., *Iron Age Communities in Britain* (Routledge and Kegan Paul, 2nd Edition, 1978)

Curwen, J.F., *The Castles and Fortified Towers of Cumberland, Westmorland and Lancashire, North of the Sands* (J. Wilson, 1913)

Daniel, G.E., *The Prehistoric Chamber Tombs of England and Wales* (Cambridge University Press, 1950)

Darby, H.C., *Domesday England* (Cambridge University Press, 1977)

Defoe, D., *A Tour Through the Whole Island of Great Britain* (Everyman University Library, 1975)

Dodd, A.E., and E.M., *Peakland Roads and Trackways* (Moorland, 1980)

DoE Guide, *Ancient Monuments in Anglesey* (HMSO, 1977)

DoE Guide, *Burgh Castle* (HMSO, 1978)

DoE Guide, *Caerleon Roman Amphitheatre* (HMSO, 1980)

DoE Guide, *Carn Euny,* HMSO (pamphlet)

DoE Guide, *Chysauster,* HMSO (pamphlet)

DoE Guide, *Jarlshof,* (HMSO, 1953)

DoE Guide, *Pevensey Castle* (HMSO, 1978)

Drew, C.D., and Piggot, S., 'Thickthorn Long Barrows', *Proceedings of the Prehistoric Society,* ii(1936) 77ff.

Dudley-Stamp, L., *Britain's Structure and Scenery* (Collins, 1946)

Dyer, J., *Discovering Archaeology,* 4th Editon, (Shire Publications, 1976)

Dyer, J., *The Penguin Guide to Prehistoric England and Wales* (Allen Lane, 1981)

Ekwall, E., *The Concise Oxford Dictionary of English Place Names* (Oxford, 1936)

Evans, J.G., *The Environment of Early Man* (Elek, 1975)

Evans, E., *Prehistoric and Early Christian Ireland* (Batsford, 1966)

Feachem, R., *Guide to Prehistoric Scotland* (Batsford, 1977)

Fell, C., *Early Settlement in the Lake Counties* (Dalesman, 1972)

Fell, C., 'The Great Langdale Stone-Axe Factory': *Transactions of the Cumberland and Westmorland Antiquarian and Archaeological Society,* 50 (NS) 1951

*Field Guide to the Hadrian's Wall Area* (Northumberland County Council National Park and Countryside Committee, 1982)

Fojut, N., *A Guide to Prehistoric Shetland* (The Shetland Times, 1981)

Ford, T.D., and Rieuwerts, J.H., Editors, *Lead Mining in the Peak District* (Peak Park Planning Board, Peak District Mines Historical Society, 1981)

Forde-Johnston, J., *Hillforts of the Iron Age in England and Wales* (Liverpool University Press, 1976)

Fowler, P.J., *Wessex: Regional Archaeologies* (Heinemann, 1967)

Fox, A., 'Grimspound', *The Archaeological Journal,* CXIV (1957) 158.

Fox, Sir C., *Offa's Dyke – A Field Survey* Oxford University Press and the British Academy, 1955)

Garlick, T., *Romans in the Lake Counties* (Dalesman, 1976)

Gelling, M., *Signposts to the Past* (Dent, 1978)

Gill, C., (Editor), *Dartmoor: A New Study* (David and Charles, 3rd Impression, 1983)

Godwin, F., and Toulson, S., *The Drovers' Roads of Wales* (Wildwood House, 1977)

Goodburn, R., *The Roman Villa, Chedworth* National Trust booklet, 1972)

Green, E.R.R., *The Industrial Archaeology of County Down* (HMSO, 1963)

Grinsell, L.V., *The Ancient Burial Mounds of England* (Methuen, 1958)

Grinsell, L.V., *The Archaeology of Exmoor* (David and Charles, 1970)

Grinsell, L.V., *The Industrial Archaeology of County Down* (HMSO, 1963)

Hackwood, F.W., *The Chronicles of Cannock Chase* (Lichfield Mercury, 1903)

Hadingham, E., *Circles and Standing Stones* (Heinemann, 1975)

Haddingham, E., *Ancient Carvings in Britain* (Garnstone Press, 1974)

Haldane, A.R.B., *The Drove Roads of Scotland* (David and Charles, 1973)

Hamilton, J., *The Brochs of Mousa and Clickhimin* (HMSO, 1970)

Hammer, M.E., 'The Moated Sites of Staffordshire', *Staffordshire Archaeology,* No 3, 1976 Reprint

Harding, D.W., *The Iron Age in Lowland Britain* (Routledge and Kegan Paul, 1974)

Helm, P.J., *Exploring Saxon and Norman England* (Hale, 1976)

Helsby, L.F., Rushton, A.J., Legge, D.R., 'Water Mills of Moddershall Valley', 1962: Abstract by Allbutt, M., *Journal of the Staffordshire Industrial Archaeology Society,* Vol 4 (1973)

Hemery, E., *High Dartmoor* (Hale, 1983)

Henderson, I., *The Picts* (Thames and Hudson, 1967)

Hey, D., *Packmen Carriers and Packhorse Roads* (Leicester University Press, 1980)

Hindle, B.P., *Roads and Trackways of the Lake District* (Moorland, 1984)

Hogg, A.H.A., *Hill-Forts of Britain* (Hart-Davis, MacGibbon, 1975)

Hoskins, W.G., *English Landscapes* (BBC, 1973)

Hoskins, W.G., *Essays in Leicestershire History* (Liverpool University Press, 1950)

Hoskins, W.G., *Fieldwork in Local History* (Faber and Faber, 1982)

Hoskins, W.G., *The Making of the English Landscape* (Penguin, 1979)

Houghton, F.W., *Upper Wharfedale* (Dalesman, 1980)

Houlder, C., *Wales: An Archaeological Guide* (Faber and Faber, 1975)

Howell, P., and Beazley, E., *The Companion Guide to South Wales* (Collins, 1977)

Hughes, S.J.S., *The Cwmystwyth Mines* (Northern Mine Research Society, 1981)

Hugill, R., *Borderland Castles and Peels* (F. Graham, 1970)

Humphries, P.H., *Castles of Edward the First in Wales* (HMSO, 1983)

'Ingarsby': *Transactions of the Leicestershire Archaeological Society,* Vol XXXII, 1956

Jessup, R., *South East England* (Thames and Hudson, 1970)

Johnson, P., *The National Trust Book of British Castles* (Granada, 1981)

Johnson, S., *The Roman Forts of the Saxon Shore*, (Elek, 2nd Edition, 1979)

Johnstone, J.D., *Werrington, Some Notes on its History* (Reprint, 1976)

Jones, G.D.B., and Thompson, F.H., 'Excavations at Mam Tor and Brough-on-Noe' *Derbyshire Archaeological Journal*, 75 (1965)

Jones, G.D.B., and Lewis, P.R., *The Roman Gold Mines at Dolaucothi*, (Carmarthen, 1971)

Kennett, D.H., *Norfolk Villages* (Hale, 1980)

Kermode, P.M.C., *Manx Crosses* (Bemrose & Son, 1907)

Kerr, N., and M., *A Guide to Anglo-Saxon Sites* (Granada, 1982)

King, A., *Early Pennine Settlement* (Dalesman, 1970)

King, R.J., *The Forest of Dartmoor and its Borders* (J.R. Smith, 1856)

Laing, L., *Orkney and Shetland: An Archaeological Guide* (David and Charles, 1974)

Laing, L., and J., *A Guide to the Dark Age Remains in Britain* (Constable, 1979)

Laing, L., and J., *Anglo-Saxon England*, (Routledge and Kegan Paul, 1979)

Lichfield and South Staffordshire Archaeological and Historical Society *Transactions* for 1965-6, Vol VII (1967)

Lindsay, J.M., 'The Iron Industry in the Highlands; Charcoal Blast Furnaces' (Scottish Historical Review, 56, part 1, 1977)

Linehan, C.D., 'Deserted Sites and Rabbit Warrens on Dartmoor', *Medieval Archaeology*, Vol 10 (1966)

Long, B., *Castles of Northumberland* (Harold Hill, 1967)

Longworth, I., *Yorkshire: Regional Archaeology Series* (Heinemann, 1965)

Mackie, E.W., *Scotland – An Archaeological Guide* (Faber and Faber, 1975)

*Map of Ancient Britain* (Ordnance Survey, 1982)

*Map of Britain Before the Norman Conquest* (Ordnance Survey, 1973)

*Map of Britain in the Dark Ages*, 2nd Edition (Ordnance Survey, 1966)

*Map of Hadrian's Wall* (Ordnance Survey, Reprint 1975)

*Map of Roman Britain*, 4th Edition, (Ordnance Survey, 1978)

Margary, I.D., *Roman Roads in Britain*, Vols 1 and 2 (Phoenix House, 1955)

Marshall, J.D., and Davies-Shiel, M., *Industrial Archaeology of the Lake Counties* (M. Moon, 1977)

Mc Cutcheon, W.A., *The Industrial Archaeology of Northern Ireland* (HMSO, 1980)

McLaren, M., *The Shell Guide to Scotland* (Ebury Press, 1973)

Miller, R., *Orkney* (Batsford, 1976)

Millman, R., *The Making of the Scottish Landscape* (Batsford, 1975)

Millward, R., and Robinson, A., *Landscapes of North Wales* (David and Charles, 1978)

Moir, D.G., *Scottish Hill Tracks* (Bartholomew, Revised Edition, 1975)

Morton, G.R., 'The Furnace at Duddon Bridge' *Journal of the Iron and Steel Institute* (1962)

Muir, R., *The Lost Villages of Britain* (Michael Joseph, 1981)

Muir, R., *Shell Guide to Reading the Landscape* (Michael Joseph, 1981)

Mumford, C., *The Portrait of the Isles of Scilly* (Hale, Reprint, 1980)

Nicholson, J.R., *Shetland* (David and Charles, 1972)

Page, R.I., *Life in Anglo-Saxon England* (Batsford, 1970)

Pearce, S.M., *The Archaeology of South West Britain* (Collins, 1981)

Plint, R.G., 'Stone-Axe Factory Sites in the Cumbrian Fells', *Transactions of the Cumberland and Westmorland Antiquarian and Archaeological Society*, 50 (NS) 1951

Plot, R., *Natural History of Staffordshire* (Oxford, 1686)

Porter, J., *The Making of the Central Pennines* (Moorland, 1980)

Postlethwaite, J., *Mines and Mining in the English Lake District* (M. Moon, 3rd Edition Republished 1975)

Raistrick, A., *West Riding of Yorkshire* (Hodder and Stoughton, 1970)

Raistrick, A., *The Pennine Dales* (Eyre Methuen, 1968)

Raistrick, A., 'Some Dales Forests', *Dalesman Index*, Volume 7 (Dalesman, 1945-1946)

Raistrick A., and Jennings, B., *A History of Lead Mining in the Pennines* (Longmans, 1965)

Raistrick, A., *Industrial Archaeology* (Granada, 1973)

Raistrick, A., *Lead Mining in the Yorkshire Dales* (Dalesman, 1981)

Raistrick, A., *Green Roads in the Mid-Pennines* (Moorland, 1978)

Ramm, H.G., McDowall, R.W., Mercer, E., *Shielings and Bastles* (Royal Commission on Historical Monuments, England, 1970)

Rees, D.M., *The Industrial Archaeology of Wales* (David and Charles, 1975)

Renn, D.F., *Norman Castles in Britain* (John Baker, 1968)

Rieuwerts, J.H., *Lathkill Dale; Its Mines and Miners* (Moorland, 1973)

Robertson, A.S., *The Antonine Wall* (Glasgow Archaeological Society, 1972)

Rowley, T., *The Norman Heritage, 1055-1200* (Routledge and Kegan Paul, 1983)

Rowley, T., *Villages in the Landscape* (Dent, 1978)

Royal Commission on Historical Monuments, *Stonehenge and its Environs* (HMSO, 1979)

'Saltways from the Cheshire Wiches', *Transactions of the Lancashire and Cheshire Antiquarian Society*, Volume 54, 1939, pp84-142

Salway, P., *Roman Britain* (Clarendon Press, 1981)

Sherlock, R., *The Industrial Archaeology of Staffordshire* (David and Charles, 1976)

Silvester, J.W.H., *Scythe Making at Abbeydale* (Sheffield City Museums, 1972)

Smith, A.H., *English Place-Name Elements* (English Place-Name Society, XXV, XXVI, Cambridge, 1956)

Smith, P.J.F., *A Short History of Dacre Parish Church*

Sopwith, T., *An Account of the Mining Districts of Alston Moor, Weardale and Teesdale* (Alnwick, 1833)

Sorrell, A., *Roman Towns in Britain* (Batsford, 1976)

Stell, G.P., and Hay, G.D., *Bonawe Iron Furnace* (HMSO, 1984)

Stenning, E.H., *Portrait of the Isle of Man,* 4th Edition (Hale, 1978)

Stenton, D.M., *English Society in the Early Middle Ages* (Penguin, 1951)

Straker, E., *Wealden Iron* (David and Charles Reprints, 1969)

*Sussex Archaeological Collections*, Volume XLV (Sussex Archaeological Society, MCMII)

Taylor, C., *Roads and Tracks of Britain* (Dent, 1979)

Taylor, H.M. and J., *Anglo-Saxon Architecture*, 3 Volumes (Cambridge University Press, 1965-78)

Tebbutt, M., and C.F., 'Wealdon Iron', *Bulletin of the Wealden Iron Research Group*, No15, 1979, No2, 1982

*The Ancient Monuments of the Isles of Scilly*, DoE Guide (HMSO, 1974)

*The Ancient and Historic Monuments of the Isle of Man* (Manx Museum and National Trust, 1973)

Thomas, N., *A Guide to Prehistoric England* (Batsford, 1960)

Thomas-Vaughan, W., and Llewellyn, A., *The Shell Guide to Wales* (Michael Joseph, 3rd Impression, 1977)

Todd, M., (Editor), *Studies in the Romano-British Villa* (Leicester University Press, 1978)

Trinder, B., *The Making of the Industrial Landscape* (Dent, 1982)

Trueman, A.E., *Geology and Scenery in England and Wales*, New Edition, Revised by Whittow, J.B., and Hardy, J.R., (1972)

*Victoria County History: Staffordshire*, Volume 2, Editors Greenslade, M.W., and Jenkins, J.G., (Oxford University Press, 1967)

*Victoria County History: Wiltshire*, I, part i (1957), part ii (1973)

Wacher, J., *Roman Britain* (Dent, 1980)

Wainwright, A., *Pennine Way Companion* (Westmorland Gazette, 1968)

Wainwright, A., *The Outlying Fells of Lakeland* (Westmorland Gazette, 1974)

Wainwright, A., *A Pictorial Guide to the Lakeland Fells* 7 Volumes) (Westmorland Gazette, 1955-66)

Wainwright, A., *A Coast to Coast Walk* (Westmorland Gazette, 1973)

Wainwright, F.T., (ed), *The Problem of the Picts* (Nelson, 1955)

Wainwright, R., *A Guide to the Prehistoric Remains in Britain,* Volume I, South and East (Constable, 1978)

Walker, J., Revised Munn, C.W., *British Economic and Social History, 1700-1982*, 4th edition (Macdonald and Evans, 1982)

Watson, K., *North Wales; Regional Archaeologies* (Heinemann, 1965)

Weir, A., *Early Ireland, A Field Guide* (Blackstaff Press, 1980)

White, S., *The North York Moors* (Dalesman, 1979)

White, Talbot, J., *The Scottish Border and Northumberland,* (Eyre Methuen, 1973)

Whitehead, M.A., and T.D., *The Saxon Church, Escomb*

Whittow, J.B., *The Geology and Scenery of Scotland* (Penguin, 1977)

Whittow, J.B., *Geology and Scenery in Ireland* (Penguin, 1975)

Wilson, D.M., *The Anglo-Saxons* (Penguin, 1971 Revised)

Wilson, D.M., (Edited), *The Archaeology of Anglo-Saxon England* (Methuen, 1976)

Wilson, R.J.A., *A Guide to Roman Remains in Britain* (Constable, 1975)

Whybrow, C., *Antiquary's Exmoor* (The Exmoor Press, 1970)

Wood, E.S., *Archaeology in Britain* (Collins, 1979)

Wood, M., *In Search of the Dark Ages* (BBC, 1981)

Worth, R.H., *Worth's Dartmoor*, Edition by Spooner, G.M., and Russell, F.S., (David and Charles, 1971)

Wright, C.J., *A Guide to Offa's Dyke Path* (Constable, 1975)

Young, C.R., *The Royal Forests of Medieval England* (Leicester University Press, 1979)

# Index